Charles T.

M000106947

Runway Dust

Runway Dust

Airport Adventures during the Fabulous Fifties

Charles R. Furden

Time West Publishing
West Jordan, UT 84084

Runway Dust
Airport Adventures during the Fabulous Fifties
Charles R. Furden

Copyright © 2013 by Charles R. Furden

All rights reserved. No part of this book may be reproduced or transmitted in any form by any means electronic, photocopying, including information storage and retrieval systems without permission in writing from the publisher, except by a reviewer, who may quote brief passages in a review.

Drawings and photos not credited are from the author's collection
Book Design by Thayne Whiting
Salt Lake City, Utah

    Furden, Charles R.
        Runway dust : Airport adventures during the fabulous
    fifties / by Charles R. Furden.
        p. cm.
        ISBN-13: 978-0-9826716-0-3
        ISBN-10: 0-9826716-0-1
        1. Airports--Utah--Anecdotes. 2. Airports--Utah--History.
        3. Nineteen fifties--Anecdotes. 4. Furden,
        Charles R.   I. Title.

    HE9803.A35F87 2012   387.7'3'09792   QBI11-600099

Library of Congress Control Number: 2012934569

Published by Time West Publishing
P.O. Box 729
West Jordan, Utah 84084-0729
Printed in the United States of America
16 15 14 13   10 9 8 7 6 5 4 3 2

Visit our web site at www.timewestpublishing.com

Charles A. Lindbergh and Associates: ...*one individual holding one end of the banner looks somewhat out of place.*
National Air and Space Museum, Smithsonian Institution (SI 94-8819)

Dedication

I've had an old calendar picture since I can't remember when. The picture keeps popping up as one of my very favorite historical photos, not so much for what the photographer was trying to capture but of someone in the shadows.

The picture, obviously a promotional shot showing some of the more important people involved in Charles Lindbergh's New York to Paris Flight. It shows several people in various positions around the *Spirit of St. Louis*. A banner stretched across the front of the group states the manufacture of the airplane as the Ryan Company, Red Crown Aviation Gasoline as the fuel that would probably be used on the historic flight. And there, right besides the banner is Charles Lindbergh the soon to be famous pilot. Everyone in the photo looks to be professional, but one individual holding one end of the banner looks somewhat out of place. He is dressed in coveralls, is obviously a mechanic and his face is hidden in the shadows of the Ryan's wing.

I've looked at that nameless individual countless times and wondered who he was and what he was working on when he got his knees greasy. To me, he is so typical of so many of yesterday's forgotten airport workers across the country, including Utah Central, the airport of the following story.

If I were to dedicate this book to anyone, it would be to aviation's men and women standing in the shadows. Sadly most of their names will be forever lost, but nevertheless, at their time and place they were ready and did step forward to make so many dreams of flight come true.

Would it be possible that on some future date, while wandering around on distant roads I saw a small airport off in the distance? If I had a few moments, there was never an airport that I wouldn't at least drive by. I drove down a small road that ran parallel to the airport's massive chain link fence topped with several strands of barbed wire. Then out of nowhere a gate, and it was open, strange! I parked my car and wandered over.

Looking around, there was not so much as a security guard in the area. The gate was open wide enough, so that the signs listing all the Restricted and Keep Out notices could not be seen. Even the security cameras were unnoticed and pointed towards the sky. With no one around, I passed through the gate and onto the airport property.

Once on the airport's property and still a little apprehensive, I paused, looked around making sure no one in a uniform was approaching. Then with no security headed in my direction, I continued on my way.

I wandered over to the nearest hangar. There just above a small entrance door was a rather large sign, "Flight Training." That door was also open and again all of the keep out notices were out of view. I entered.

Inside there were several modern training aircraft with their flight school's logo painted on the side of each. Each aircraft was a picture of modern technology, clean, highly polished aluminum with expensive paint trimmings. All of the aircraft sported a big engine under a beautiful cowl. Along the fuselage of each aircraft there were several odd-looking antennas protruding from each. The cabin interiors were plush and very expensive looking. Up front, the panels were cluttered with strange looking instruments and lots of complicated buttons and dials, such technology for students!

I looked around at the interior of the hangar, it was immaculate, everything in its proper place. There was nothing that didn't need to be there and what was there contributed to its high tech and expensive setting. The floors looked to have been painted only hours before, no dirt, no parts, no rags and no oil spots anywhere. To me the place had more of a hospital setting than a hangar.

I could see what appeared to be a workbench over on a far wall, but it was so clean and uncluttered, maybe it was a desk? Everything seemed more on display than functional. I smiled and jokingly wondered who the very talented interior decorator was?

I then noticed a desk and a couple of nice chairs off to one side. I wandered over and sat down.

I sat there relaxing, looking and just thinking while not really noticing time. Eventually a young kid entered the hangar, and noticing me, came over in my direction. In his hand he was carrying a thick textbook on flying and in the other hand hung a brand new and very expensive looking flight case, a student pilot. We introduced ourselves and wandered into an ongoing conversation about this and that and nothing important. After a few moments, he sat down and we talked about aviation, his love for it and the fact that he was just starting his flying lessons. Young and proud, he talked about some of the aircraft sitting in the hangar and a little of his experience in them. He then asked if I had ever flown. I told him that I was a long-ago pilot but still loved to be around airplanes.

Then there were a few seconds of silence. He looked over at me, eyeing my white hair and quietly asked, "What were the old days like"? Time permitting; the following would be my answer.

Acknowledgements

It's a sobering experience to write about a happening that was a big part of your life and find so many dead ends. Often your "good" notes raise only questions, your memory leaves you hanging and all too often the people "in the know" are not available. I found out quite early that the passing of time is a continual process of door closing.

Chad Jenkins is one of the main players in the book and thankfully, he was one I was able to make contact with early in my writing. I can't count the times that I called and questioned him about people's names, what really happened, clarifications and information on engines and aircraft. Over the years he was a friend that not only was fun to talk with, but he was always willing to listen. I think that he was mildly surprised that the story of his old job would reach out like it did.

Mel Rozema, is another main player in the book. While helping me tie up some loose ends, he was telling me about some of his post Utah Central flying experiences. What a book he could write!

Earl Dedman: I met him many years after Utah Central. For the life of me, I don't know how it was possible never to have met him earlier. He spent many years at Utah Central. We can sit down and talk about the same airport happenings for hours. Thankful I am, that we did cross paths even as white haired adults. He is full of information and like me; he could never talk enough about the "good old Utah Central Days."

Danny Sorensen was the first credible aviation person not involved in the story to read the manuscript. He is just a little younger than I, and we both spent our teen years working at small airports, he at the north end of the valley and me on the west side. He is a professional stunt pilot, airplane designer and builder. I mentioned to him that I had misgivings about putting in print some of the dumb things we did back then. He encouraged me to write it like it happened, the readers would understand. Still, it wasn't an easy decision, but right or wrong, our escapades are part of the story.

Paul Swenson was the first professional to see the manuscript. I gave him a copy to look over, hoping he wouldn't throw his hands up and dump it in the garbage can. However, he somehow made it through all my errors and gave my writing some credibility. Paul was one of the first to tell me that maybe I did have something.

Thayne Whiting, who more than anyone, tolerated my learning curve in the development of the book.

Phil and Doug Dellinger are the sons of my old boss Glen. I presented them with a manuscript, wondering how they would react reading so much about their father. They not only gave me encouragement, but also offered some photos that they had found in an old family storage shed. For fifty years, I wished that I had taken some photographs like the ones they had.

Ray Haas' High Flight Productions is dedicated to Pilot Officer Gillespie Magee, Jr. and his sonnet "High Flight". Over the years, the sonnet has been printed in several different formats. Ray has dedicated himself to preserving it as it was originally written and keeping tabs on its use.

Don Christopherson: I cannot imagine what my life would have been without Utah Central. To this day, I really don't know how I got the job. He must have felt sorry for me, as I had little to offer his organization except the love of being there. Thanks Don!

I could never thank members of my extended family enough for the help and support they've provided, especially Lynn Bass and Joy Furden. Their interest, perseverance, or maybe their inquiring minds brought out some problems that were not so obvious but needed much attention.

Lastly, but certainly not the least, my family, my wife Connie and my kids, Ron and Connie who listen, edited and had more than a few valuable comments and contributions. Being shut up in my room was an all too common occurrence, but I guess they could see that this book was more than just a passing fad. Their continual encouragement will forever be appreciated.

Charles R. Furden
West Valley City, Utah
November 23, 2011

Contents

Preface

The writings in Runway Dust are a collection of happenings that occurred at the Utah Central Airport, then located some five miles southwest of Salt Lake City, Utah. My first contact with Utah Central was in the mid-fifties while in my teens. An acquaintance had invited me to help him do some work on his damaged airplane. Later, between September 1956 and December 1958, with six months off for National Guard Training, I was employed at the airport. A short period of time, but during that time the airport went from one of great activity, to one of near stagnation and then closure.

While most of my fellow workers moved on to the bigger, faster and better, I, because of some hearing problems, suddenly found myself on the wrong side of the airport fence. Left with only the memories of my once chosen occupation, the time that I had spent at Utah Central became very special. I began collecting notes and documenting the happenings at that little dirt airport. It turned out to be quite an enjoyable hobby. Later when it became obvious that aviation was changing and little airports were fast becoming a thing of the past, I began looking at my writings as a history, a book.

Through the following stories I've tried to revive some of the atmosphere that was part of our small airport. All of the stories are my personal experiences or they happened to people I knew personally. I've done my best to describe each of the happenings accurately and to the best of my memory. Some of the activities were combined and some are out of sequence. With just a couple of exceptions, the names are the names of the people who lived the experiences. I hope I don't embarrass anyone with my point of view. I have not made any effort to turn the book into a smooth flowing novel.

It's been a long time since I've talked to anyone who was even aware of Utah Central Airport's existence. But like so many other small airports around the country, it was at one time a very active airport. And it, like so many other small airports, does have a story to tell.

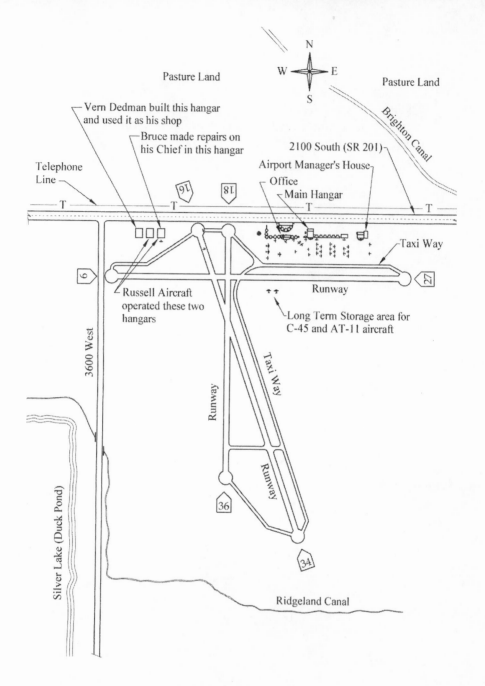

Pasture Land

Pasture Land

— Vern Dedman built this hangar
and used it as his shop

—Bruce made repairs on
his Chief in this hangar

2100 South (SR 201)

Airport Manager's House—

— Office

— Main Hangar

Brighton Canal

Telephone
Line —

T

9L

8L

T

T

T

Taxi Way

6

Russell Aircraft
operated these two
hangars

Runway

Long Term Storage area for
C-45 and AT-11 aircraft

27

3600 West

Taxi Way

Runway

Runway

Silver Lake (Duck Pond)

36

34

Ridgeland Canal

Utah Central Airport

Scale: None

Charles R. Furden

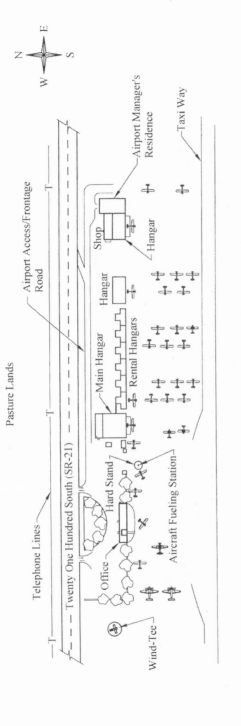

N
W — E
S

Pasture Lands

Telephone Lines

Twenty One Hundred South (SR-21)

Airport Access/Frontage Road

Airport Manager's Residence

Taxi Way

Shop

Hangar

Hangar

Main Hangar

Rental Hangars

Wind-Tee

Office

Hard Stand

Aircraft Fueling Station

East-West Runway

Long Term Storage area for broken down C-45s & AT-11 aircraft

Utah Central Airport's Buildings and Aircraft Parking

Scale: None

Charles R. Furden

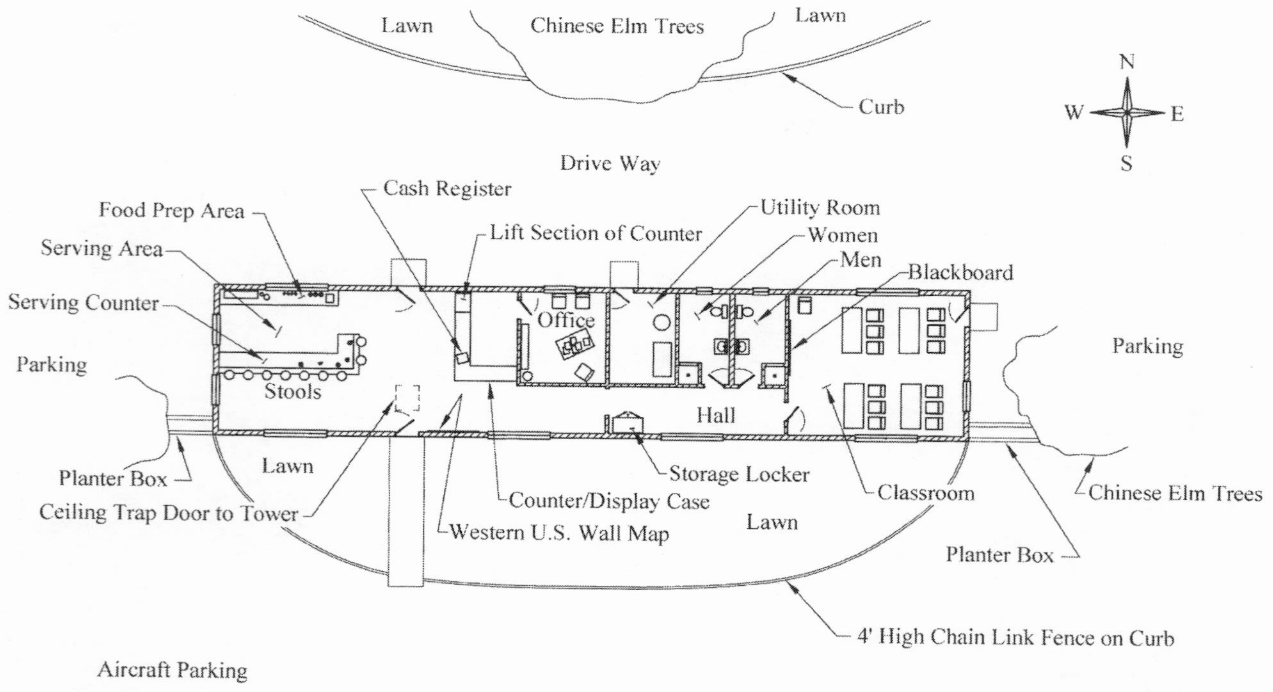

N
W   E
S

Lawn

Chinese Elm Trees

Lawn

Curb

Drive Way

Parking

Chinese Elm Trees

Cash Register

Lift Section of Counter

Utility Room

Women

Men

Blackboard

Office

Hall

Classroom

Planter Box

Food Prep Area

Serving Area

Serving Counter

Parking

Planter Box

Ceiling Trap Door to Tower

Stools

Lawn

Western U.S. Wall Map

Counter/Display Case

Storage Locker

Lawn

4' High Chain Link Fence on Curb

Aircraft Parking

Aircraft Parking

Utah CentralAirport's Office Plan

Scale: None

Charles R. Furden

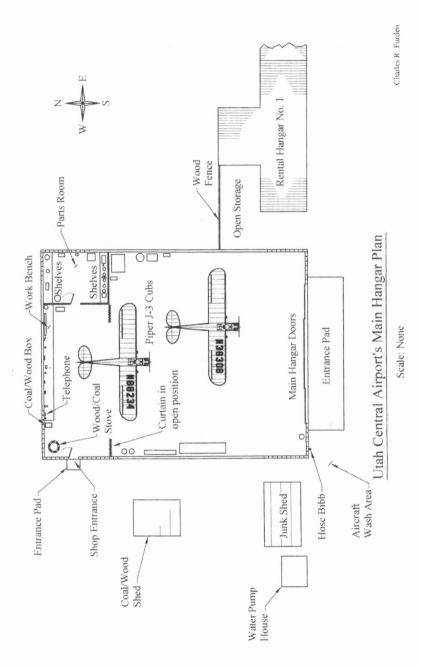

Utah Central Airport's Main Hangar Plan

Scale: None

Charles R. Furden

1

A Place for Wings

A Neighbor's Airplane

Aviation, flight and aircraft--was there anything more intriguing to a kid growing up at the end of World War II? The Salt Lake Municipal Airport was within walking distance of my house. On the north end of the airport there was an Air National Guard unit and next to it was a Naval Reserve unit. Between the two, there was a scattering of T–6s P–51s, A–26s, PV–2s, TBMs, F8Fs, C–45s and C–47s. Moreover, we, even as kids were free to wander around the aircraft, almost at will. Military personal were rather scarce, except maybe on weekends. Anyone we did run into was friendly and would often take a few moments and talk to us about their airplanes. Right after the big war security didn't seem to be a big priority. The world was at peace.

On the other end of the field, along with a good variety of civil aircraft, were the ex-military or "war surplus" aircraft as we called them. Included in that group were the Bobcats, PT–19s, PT–26s, BT–13s and Stearmans. A few were being cared for and flown, but most were totally neglected, even abandoned. It was a kid's paradise! Aviation, flight and aircraft, we were totally committed.

When I heard that there was an individual in my neighborhood who might own an airplane, I was more than a little excited. After doing some checking, I was able to come up with a name and address.

Bruce Holtby was his name, and he was about the same age as my dad. He was very friendly and in a short time we were involved in a lively conversation. The common topics discussed were aviation in general and aircraft in particular. And he did own an airplane, a little Aeronca 11AC Chief, based at Utah Central Airport. It had previously been involved in an accident, and was at that time in the shop undergoing repairs.

When Bruce mentioned "accident," it brought all kinds of pictures to mind. Mostly images that I had seen in the movies, you know, stuff like stunt pilots crashing into buildings, aircraft going down in flames and hitting the ground like a huge bomb scattering smoking debris over wide areas. I was more than a little anxious to hear all the colorful and dynamic details from the pilot who had actually been at the controls when it went down.

Bruce calmly stated that the flight began in a very normal way. He had just taken off and was climbing up to pattern altitude when his engine quit cold. The very second it quit he knew what the problem was. Fuel was not getting to the engine! The Chief has two fuel tanks. There was the main nose tank and there was also a smaller auxiliary or secondary tank located behind the baggage compartment. On his previous flight he had been using fuel from the auxiliary tank. Once on the ground he had filled up his main nose tank but not the nearly empty auxiliary tank. Then he had neglected to re-position the fuel selector valve back to the main tank. Even with a checklist, the selector valve was not repositioned.

When the engine quit, Bruce quickly put the nose down and switched the fuel selector feed valve from the auxiliary to the main tank. That done, all he could do was wait and hope that the fuel would get to the engine in time. Seconds ticked away and he was losing altitude fast. His gut feeling was soon telling him that the fuel wasn't going to reach the engine in time. His hopes began to sag. It was a textbook case of everything going wrong at the same time. He had a dead engine. He was too low to make a 180–degree turn back to the longer part of the runway. And he was too high to land on the short stretch of remaining runway. He was headed down towards the runway's overrun and beyond, lots of brush and lumpy ground. Everything that a pilot wants or needs in an emergency was unavailable. Knowing he was going down, he switched the fuel selector valve to the "Off" position and cut the ignition switch. The Chief was then a heavy glider and continued its descent towards the grass and brush.

The Aeronca, trailing soft whistling sounds, sailed over the south end of the Diagonal Runway, then over a growth of stubble weeds covering the overrun.

The gear hit hard in the softer dirt with a cloud of dust. The Aeronca rumbled and bounced into progressively lumpier ground. Suddenly, from out of nowhere, a small drainage ditch appeared running nearly right angles to the Chief's path. Seeing the ditch, Bruce, using little more than subconscious reflexes, yanked back hard on the wheel, but the lift just wasn't there. The effort took some weight off the gear but never got the wheels off the ground. The Chief flew out over the edge of the ditch and quietly settled a foot or so, allowing the gear to hit solid against the far bank. There was a hard, jarring jolt, as the tubular gear folded back against the underside of the fuselage in a hollow thumping sound. The aircraft slid a distance, leaning forward hard against the drag of the earth while trailing uplifted dirt and brush along its path. With the energy nearly spent, it slid to a stop, rocked out of it nose-down position and stabilized, almost hidden in a cloud of dust.

Almost before the little craft had come to a rest, Bruce was shoving against the door. Brush prevented its opening. He shoved again, harder. It opened a little, not enough. He pushed again. It opened more, enough for him to crawl out onto the ground.

Then working his way through the brush, he crawled out from under the wing, stood up and stumbled in the brush as he turned and backed away. Almost in tears, he stood there in silence as the cloud of dust slowly drifted away from his lifeless airplane. It was an airplane he had never seen before, low in the dirt, heavy on its belly and covered with a heavy coat of dust. Weeds and brush were piled against the lower half of the fuselage giving the Chief an abandoned look. In silence, Bruce stood there somewhat dazed, almost expecting some indication that he was dreaming. What he was seeing could not possibly be.

An odd collection of workers spread themselves around the damaged Chief. First they unbolted and removed the wings and tail feathers from the fuselage. Next they removed the cowling and then the engine. Everything was loaded on a flat bed truck and secured. Bruce stood with hands in pockets, watching; it was a sad sight indeed.

Vern Dedman, an aircraft mechanic and friend of Bruce, had a hangar over on the northwest corner of the airport where he operated a small maintenance shop. The hangar east of Vern's was at the time empty. The Aeronca Chief would be taken over to the empty hangar where repairs would be made.

The truck rumbled up to the front of the hangar and stopped. A couple of workers jumped off the truck and rolled open the large doors. Everything was taken inside and placed on a variety of surfaces-- sawhorses, cushions, tires, inner tubes, even blankets. Both wings were placed near their relative position to the fuselage. The engine was taken in and placed upside down on a tire located on the workbench. Someone thoughtfully placed a blanket over the engine to protect it from dust. Smaller parts, such as the cowling, wing struts and tail control surfaces were placed at various locations around the inside of the hangar. The airplane that Bruce had taxied out for a lazy afternoon flight, just a short time before, was now spread all over.

Once everything was in the hangar, Vern spent a few moments walking around the aircraft looking things over. He paused and looked at this, then bent over and looked at that and then wandered over to another area.

After looking at and studying every part, he went over to where Bruce was standing. They stood there in silence for a moment, and then Vern turned to Bruce and began an explanation of the damage. Together they walked, pointed and talked about parts and repairs needed. Then both pausing, Vern pulled out a piece of paper and jotted down some figures, studied them a second and then handed the paper to Bruce. Bruce looked at the figures a second and quietly nodded his approval. He knew Vern was giving him the best price possible, yet in the back of his mind he was thinking, "so much for such a small error."

Next morning, Vern was out working on the Chief. During the next week or so, he and a co-worker placed the fuselage on some elevated supports and removed the twisted gear and all the damaged fabric from the bottom of the fuselage. Damaged parts were replaced or rebuilt. A new set of landing gears was fitted onto the fuselage, and then the wings were attached. The engine was checked out and bolted to the fuselage's engine mount. At the front end of the engine, hung a new wooden propeller.

About that time, Vern found other matters starting to lean heavily on his time. Bruce also had limited resources. They put their heads together and it was agreed that Bruce would finish the fabric, under Vern's supervision. Vern then took Bruce aside and gave him some instructions on fabric work. Vern would be in the hangar next door for daily supervision and questions. The arrangement worked out for both of them. Bruce found the fabric work quite enjoyable, not to mention the money he was saving, and Vern was able to calm down some of his other customers.

It was about that time, I came into the picture. Bruce could see that I was very interested in his airplane and the work that he was doing so he invited me in as his helper. The project for me started a few days following my meeting with Bruce. The work would continue for several weekends and also a day or two during the week.

Our first day started Saturday morning, early. Bruce parked the car near the front of what I would call a fair size hangar. Then he wandered over to one of the big double doors and rolled it partially open. There he paused, looked inside for a few seconds and then came back to the car and grabbed a couple of cans of aircraft fabric paint or "dope," as it is commonly called. I quickly grabbed a box of supplies and followed him in. While Bruce finished unloading the car, I walked over to the Aeronca Chief to take a closer look. Bruce, seeing my interest, turned on the hangar lights. The entire aircraft was a patchwork of colors and texture that was making a bold statement of what was new, old and in between.

I had never seen new fabric before, and being a little curious, I walked over to an area where the fabric appeared to be in its final stages. I compared it with some of the old fabric near the patched area. The old fabric was stiff, even hard while the new was pliable and felt almost soft, a little like skin.

The cowling was standing over in one corner of the hangar and a large blanket was draped over the engine. Fairing strips that normally covered the space between the wings and fuselage were missing. All inspection openings on the wings and fuselage were without their cover plates, mere openings filled with shadows. Looking around, I could see a box of inspection plates over near a wall.

I walked over to the engine and lifted up a corner of the blanket, exposing some of the shaped steel, tubes and fins. I had never seen an uncowled engine before. Its massive complexity had me just staring and wondering. The big heavy wooden propeller was in the vertical position. A little tempted, I put my hand on the blade and tried to move it a tad. It felt to be locked in place; I let well enough alone.

Thick dust covered the windshield, and in the limited light, it was just about impossible to see anything inside. Not satisfied and wanting a better look, I worked my way around to the pilot's door. I turned the door handle; it made a clicking sound and then the door popped open an inch or two. I slowly swung the door open wide enough to look inside. It was like looking into a tomb. Shadows were deep and the dust seemed to color everything in shades of gray. The panel displayed a series of sleeping instruments that somehow looked more important than they were letting on. Stuffed into the cabin were several metal wing fairings that seem to emphasize the work at hand.

Once everything was unloaded, Bruce gave me a little tour of the aircraft and explained what had been done and the areas that still needed attention. Over in a dark corner of the hangar he showed me the old discarded landing gears. They were twisted far out of their original shape. I tried to visualize the aircraft plowing into the bank of the ditch amid all the flying dirt and dust. I remember thinking, "Boy, that must have really been something to do all that damage.

The only negative part of the job was the cold temperatures during the first couple of weeks. The hangar was constructed of cinderblock with concrete floors and a metal roof. There was no insulation and no heat of any kind. The body draws all the cold from the concrete floor, or the concrete floor draws all the heat from the body, not sure which. However, after a time, you got cold, very cold and it was impossible to get warm. Our fingers never did function properly, and heavy breathing vapor was a constant companion. On occasion, we would open up the big hangar doors trying to coax in a little warmth from the sun, but there was little benefit. No matter how sunny it looked outside there was always a cold breeze blowing. Moreover, with the breeze, there was always the possibility of dust blowing onto and contaminating the wet dope. So the doors were rarely opened.

Quite often, Bruce would stop working and explain something of interest. He explained the design and functions of airplane parts, like the propeller, why the different pitches, thickness, diameters and airfoils. He furthered explained how each propeller was custom-sized to its particular engine and airframe. The wings, the way they were twisted near the tip to overcome some of the negative effects of a stall. The function of the trim tab was explained and how it was used to reduce the flying loads on the controls. He often talked of other aircraft wings and their airfoils. Several times he referred to the Cessna's wing as a "high speed wing." He emphasized the elusive "perfect design" as a target forever shot at but never hit. One of his statements seemed to sum up aircraft design, "Every wing design, every engine, every propeller, and every airplane has its advantage and disadvantages. Nothing is perfect, just the best possible for what was wanted the most." I never dreamed that one could view an aircraft from so many different perspectives.

Occasionally we got into flying where the discussions got serious, even technical. I remember one discussion that stood out above all others. "Do you know what makes an airplane turn," he asked one day. "Sure," I said in a positive tone. "The rudder, everyone knows that!" "That's what almost everyone believes," he said in an almost apologetic tone. "If you're flying along, straight and level and push one of the rudder peddles, the inside wing will drop, the outside wing will lift, the nose will dip down and your aircraft will be skidding and headed down. The proper way to turn an aircraft is with ailerons. The ailerons tip, or bank the aircraft. With the aircraft in a bank, the lift of the wings will kind of lift the aircraft around, or turn it, if you would. However, when you tip an aircraft with the ailerons, the ailerons produce an unwanted yaw. The rudder is used to offset the yaw. You have the same problem when you are finished with your turn. You use aileron to tip your aircraft back to straight and level. Here again, the ailerons produce the unwanted yaw effect. Again, the rudder is used to offset it. Then he added, "it has been said by many experienced pilots that a turn is the one maneuver that involves most of the pilot's skills and I've never heard anyone argue that statement!

"The elevator of an aircraft, like its rudder, is often misunderstood by a good part of the general public," he continued. "Most people think that an elevator makes the airplane go up and down, kind of like the name implies. That's not really the case.

"Some people say that an airplanes' elevator is the pitch control. That is, the elevator is used to pitch the nose up or pitch the nose down. Still others say that the elevator is the airplane's speed control, that is, nose down and your aircraft will pick up speed, lots of it. Lift the nose up and the aircraft will loose airspeed. The throttle is the real elevator on an aircraft. You can make an aircraft go up temporarily by pulling back on the wheel, but to make it go up continually, you need power. Open up the throttle and you will go up, cut back on the power and there is no way it can stay in the air. Eventually you will go clear down to the ground," he finished. It all made sense. I agreed, but

I was sure glad he didn't ask me the elevator question!

The fuel system of his Aeronca Chief was also explained in detail. He again went over the mistakes that had led up to his accident and some of the feeling and impressions he experienced. As I listened to his words, I watched his hands. He, like all pilots the world over is expressionless without his hands. It's a universal and recognized sign language of recreating the behavior of an aircraft in flight. The hand language is interesting and describes events that could never be put into words.

Vern was using two of the three hangars located on the northwest corner of the airport. Except for Vern and Bruce, I never saw another individual over on that part of the airport. And there were only two aircraft on our corner of the field. Our Aeronca Chief was one and the other being a little two-place Taylorcraft that Vern had all torn apart in the other hangar.

The main part of the airport was to the east of us, just beyond the North-South runways. Over there, I could see an office building, a large hangar and a row of "T" Hangars. I could also make out about twenty or thirty small aircraft scattered around to the south of the buildings. During weekends, there was a fair amount of flying activity. I could hear engines running and see the movement of aircraft and people. Often, an aircraft would take-off or land on one of the North-South runways. I was hoping that the wind conditions might change, forcing the aircraft to use the East-West Runway, which ran just to the immediate south of Vern's hangars. It would be fun to be so close to aircraft taking off and landing, but it never happened.

Hangar-Bound No More

Late one afternoon, Bruce moved back to a position where he had an overall view of his aircraft. Then walking around to various locations, he studied the Chief from every possible angle. Occasionally, he would move in closer and run his hand over a patch or a painted area. Then moving on to several different areas, he would hold the light up against the fabric and view the other side, making sure there was enough silver on the fabric to prevent light penetration. After circling the aircraft and making numerous stops, he walked over to a far corner of the hangar and paused. Standing there in silence, he looked to be analyzing the entire project.

Then, looking over at me, he stated in a tone of voice that conveyed nothing but satisfaction, "Ron I think we've got it. We'll get Vern to sign off the logbooks and she'll be ready for flight. Next Saturday we'll take her up!" Then pausing as if he had suddenly remembered some forgotten item, he added in a somewhat somber tone, "For now, lets take her outside and see if she will still run."

We each got on one of the big double doors and began pushing them in opposite directions. Their rumbling sounds moved across the front of the hangar as the opening widened to the span of the Chief. With the doors open wide enough to let the Chief pass through, we let them coast to a stop. Bruce then wandered around picking up a few items scattered around on the floor. With the area cleared, he headed over in the direction of the left wing. I wandered over to the right wing.

At his signal, we both positioned ourselves on a main strut and began pushing. A wave of excitement crossed my body as I watched the tire begin to turn. The aircraft moved in complete silence, almost without effort. I was more than a little surprised to see how easy it was to push.

The Chief bounced over the hangar door tracks, across a concrete entrance pad and onto the gravel at the front of the hangar. There the pushing became noticeably harder. Once out in the clear, Bruce held his side and told me to swing my wing around ninety degrees.

Satisfied with its new position, Bruce walked back to the elevator and lifted the tail up. He studied the area, took a few steps and set the tail down near a tie-down rope. Bruce grabbed the end of the rope and tied it around the tail wheel spring. He brought my attention to the fact that in its present position, the aircraft's prop blast would not be directed into the open hangar.

Bruce stood in place and looked at his airplane a few seconds. Then he began an inspection of each item, almost like a pre-flight. He studied the hinges on the rudder, the elevator and the ailerons. Each control cable was inspected, along with the prop bolts and their safety wiring. I guess he was just making sure Vern wouldn't find anything embarrassing.

Opening up the engine cowling, he at first seemed satisfied just to be looking. Then he began to study hidden areas. Several times he reached his hand in and wiggled a wire, a cable, or a fitting, checking to make sure it was secure and in its proper place. He then pulled out the oil dipstick to get a reading. Not having a rag handy, he walked over to a clump of grass and wiped the black goo off.

He reinserted it and took a second reading. Satisfied, he reinserted it and gave it a reassuring push. With one hand on the hinged cowling, he studied the compartment a few seconds longer before closing and securing it.

Bruce walked around the struts and over to the cabin door, opened it, reached inside and checked the position of each of the switches. Picking up a rag from off the floor, he wiped away some of the dust that had collected on the front seat and panel. Back to the front of the aircraft, he positioned himself and turned the big propeller through a few times.

He returned to the cabin and slid onto the left seat. He sat for a few seconds looking over the controls and instruments. Satisfied with all on the inside, he began positioning the switches that would give life to the little Chief. I suddenly found myself getting excited about the upcoming start.

Shortly, Bruce leaned his head near the partially open door and yelled "Clear." Instinctively, I stepped back a few paces and off to the side. Suddenly the propeller was spinning and the sound of moving parts filled the air. It spun around several times and then flipped to an abrupt stop. Bruce seemed unconcerned that it hadn't started. He just fidgeted a bit more with whatever pilots fidget with when their engines don't start. A second time, he hollered, "Clear" and once again the propeller was spinning, but the engine acted and sounded differently. Somehow, I knew it would start.

Exhaust pipes shook and coughed. Clouds of blue smoke appeared, drifting, turning in lazy patterns. The rpm's increased and the wooden propeller became a smooth circular varnished haze. Sounds grew louder, along with a very noticeable deep uneven hum of propeller blades cutting through air. Air that only a few moments before felt almost nonexistent now seemed to be the object of a vicious attack by the whirling blades.

A little surprised with the power and noise, I stepped back a few feet as the engine continued to emerge from an almost rumbling sound to a loud and steady authoritative roar. Lingering blue clouds of exhaust smoke were pulled into the propeller and swept to the rear. A couple of small rocks jumped from the ground hitting the blade with a ping. Dust, in the shape of a miniature tornado lifted off the ground at the base of the propeller arc. It twisted and turned, leaning from side to side, almost dancing, seeming excited about the new life that it had suddenly found. Goose-bumps and pride swept across my body as I stood there in a trance, almost hypnotized by the power of the

Chief's little engine.

After a few moments, Bruce reached over and flipped a switch. Almost instantly, the engine was lifeless. The big propeller wound down and stopped, almost hard against the engine's compression. A gentle breeze blowing through the stiff winter grass seemed to emphasize the stillness.

Bruce slid out of the pilot's seat and with a little effort secured a somewhat stubborn door latch. He was obviously pleased with the performance of his engine. Looking over at me, he stated with a bit of a grin. "Can you believe it; it started right up after all that sitting. How long has it been? What an engine! Man do I love that engine!" As far as he was concerned, his Aeronca Chief was once again ready and waiting. He looked at me and with some excitement in his voice stated, "All we need is Vern's signature and we can go flying."

A couple of days later, we once again rolled the plane out into the early afternoon sun. Bruce again walked around the aircraft, but he was doing an honest-to-goodness preflight.

Satisfied that the aircraft was ready for flight, he told me to hop into the right seat. I did, almost as if I had springs on my feet. He then slid in on the left side. We each fumbled around a bit searching for the seat belt ends in the confined cabin. Then after a few seconds of mixing elbows, and somewhat in spite of each other, we were buckled in.

Bruce went over the panel and controls, touching each item and thoughtfully thinking aloud so I was able to follow what he was doing. He again pointed to the fuel selector valve showing me its various positions. The fuel selector valve was checked and then double-checked; making sure it was in the right position and feeding from the proper tank. I wondered in silence if it would ever be possible for him to take off again with the fuel selector valve in the wrong position.

The engine started right up. A short warm-up and the Chief began moving across the ground. Bruce called my attention to the location of the windsock and the runway it indicated. He then took a few seconds and explained the runways at Utah Central. Our take-off would be on Runway 34.

Near the end of runway Bruce did his final check. He turned the plane into the wind and applied brakes. Opening up the throttle, he pointed to the oil pressure and temperature gauges noting they looked good. While he was checking out the carburetor air heater, he explained about the drop in the engine rpm's. He also explained the dual ignition system or dual magnetos or "mags" as they are often called. Those being okay, he applied full throttle to verify that the engine was up to its full potential. He cut the power back and watched the engine instruments closely while the aircraft idled. For the final check, he rolled the steering wheel around and kicked the rudder pedals, making sure there was freedom of movement. He then locked the left wheel brake and applied a little power.

The aircraft swung around in a 180–degree circle. While it was circling, Bruce leaned forward to scan the sky. With no traffic, we began moving out towards the center of the runway. Brakes squeaked and moaned as Bruce turned and maneuvered the Aeronca to the starting position on the long runway. Once in position, Bruce eased the Chief to a halt with its engine resting at idle.

The cowl sat high and hid from my view most of the strip out to our front. Bruce said nothing but looked out over the cowling at the long runway. I looked at him, then at the runway and waited.

Bruce slowly eased the throttle to the full open position. The engine roared into full power, the airframe shook and we began moving. I wondered if Bruce could feel my excitement above the roar of the engine.

There was a layer of gravel on the runway. Our tires cut tracks through the cover and the engine labored heavily. To me, the gravel felt quite deep in places, and I was wondering if the plane was capable of attaining flying speed with all the drag. The Chief continued, undaunted. Gravel flew, banging and pinging against the undercarriage. Tires were pushing it aside almost with the sound of rushing water. The Chief was racing down the runway almost like an animal.

Bruce's concentration was undivided; his world was a section of runway out front where we were soon to lay tracks. Eyes seeing, mind interpreting, body responding, the movement of his feet on the rudder pedals was indeed something to behold.

Then the sound of the gravel was gone and the rumble and bumping of wheels across the uneven surface was no more. We were flying; there were only the sounds of powered flight, the engine and the wind.

The Chief settled into a path directly over the center of the runway. With each foot of altitude gained, our ground speed appeared to be bleeding off. I was finding out that the sky has a way of making the world slow down, from the takeoff, (that had been a time of intense excitement just a few seconds before), to flight, where it was almost natural to lean back, relax and take in the sights.

The highway slipped under the nose of the little Chief and continued drifting to the rear. A flock of low flying ducks headed for the lakes to the west, seeming to be traveling in a sideward motion against a backdrop of fields and fence lines. Building sizes diminished and the importance of man seemed somewhat in question. Our world was growing as horizons were being pushed back to the edge of the universe. Looking at the line where sky and earth meet, I could almost imagine the edge of the earth, where men of old once feared falling off.

Air bumps--the Aeronca took several small but sharp jolts. Then once again, the sky was smooth.

We wandered through a lazy pattern and settled in on a course to the northwest, towards the Kennecott Copper's Tailings Pond. Straight for a time, then a second turn to the southwest. I watched in awe as the details of the Oquirrh Mountain range slowly drifted towards us.

Bruce nudged me on the shoulder and pointed over to the right and high. There was a blue-with-gray-trim J–3 on a course nearly parallel ours. I watched closely as it slowly moved in towards us. It found a position at one o'clock and slightly high and held. The single individual in the back seat waved and Bruce returned the gesture.

"His name is Mel Reeves," Bruce yelled above the cabin noise. "He's just a young kid, probably still in his teens, nearly got his Commercial License. One of the best pilots that I've ever seen in my life," he added.

I watched the blue Piper hold a tight position less than fifty feet away. There was almost no relative movement between our plane and his. We flew on, side by side.

I couldn't take my eyes off the Piper Cub, an aircraft I had seen in the sky so many times, but at vast distances. Flying alongside it was something way beyond anything I could ever have imagined. Transfixed, I took in every detail, the shadow of the propeller, the exhaust stack, the floating tail, mud caked on the tires, cables, inspection plates, greasy fingerprints on the cowling, the gear hanging from the fuselage, and every movement of the pilot. Artistically

suspended, and surrounded by sky, that Cub in flight was the most fascinating thing I had ever seen in my life.

Almost forgotten-I had my camera. Without taking my eyes off the accompanying Piper, I undid the case and quickly snapped a picture. A half second
before I clicked the shutter, the Piper lifted a wing into a climbing right turn.
The move was so smooth and natural. With some space between us, he leveled out and headed west towards the Oquirrh Mountains. Alone, we turned,
took up a new heading to the south. We flew on for 30, maybe 45 minutes,
and then headed back to the airport.

On final, the thing that impressed me most about the airport was the runway, not so much its length, but its width. It looked like a narrow footpath,
even a piece of string stretched out in the middle of a big barren field. And
it didn't get all that much wider as we got closer. If I were alone, I'm not sure
that I would even recognize it as a runway.

We crossed over the dry grasslands and our shadow bounced over the little
drainage ditch where Bruce had wiped out his gear some time before. Tall
brush got shorter, then grass streaked into the gravel of the strip. Our shadow
settled on the long blurred lines of the runway's surface. Bruce held his height
a few seconds and then the Chief slowly settled, tail dropping as we neared
the runway. We made contact and Bruce once again went into the fulltime
job of direction control. The little Aeronca rumbled along the runway for a
time as our ground speed moved toward zero. The idling engine burst into
life and Bruce hurried along to the turn-off.

The airport's gas pump was located in the center of an asphalt circle. Bruce
taxied up to the edge of the blacktop, locked his brakes, revved up his engine
and cut the switches. On the far side of the blacktop were two Piper J–3
Cubs; one was Mel's. A lineman standing on a small stool was in the process
of filling up the nose tank on the second Cub.

We climbed out, Bruce walked over to the lineman and talked to him a
second about his Aeronca's fuel needs. I stood there looking around at the
airplanes in the area. There was quite a variety, but unlike the main airport,
they were mostly the older types, Cubs, Taylorcrafts, Aeroncas, Stinsons,
Ercoupes, even a Bellanca. Off in the distance, I could make out an old
yellow Beech Staggerwing.

Across the way, I could see a young man coming out of the office. As soon as I saw him, I somehow knew that it was Mel. Yet, I don't know what I was expecting, but he didn't look the part I had pictured. He had on Levis and a Levi Jacket. Every inch of him looked cowboy, his dress, his walk and his looks.

He walked over to Bruce, who was near the office, and they started up a conversation. Bruce waved me over and we were introduced. We shook hands and exchanged a few words, mostly about each other and flying. He was quite easy to talk to and I could see that he felt good about his place in life. During the conversation, Mel pointed to a Cessna 140 parked southwest of the office. It was for sale, and he told us that he had been trying to work out a deal with the owner for its purchase.

We wandered over to the side of the Cessna. As we were walking, Mel talked about some of the finer points of the little Cessna. It was all metal, had a low time airframe and engine and most of all, Mel emphasized, it was equipped for night flying. Mel stated that he needed some nighttime flying for his Commercial and Instructor's tickets. His Piper Cub was strictly a daytime bird, no electrical system, therefore no lights for after dark. The Cessna was a beautiful airplane and anyone would be proud to own it.

We three talked for a time and then Bruce excused himself and wandered into the office to pay his fuel bill. I asked Mel a few things about flying and his Piper Cub. He said that early in his life he knew that he wanted to fly for a living. Being as serious as he was, he opted to buy an airplane instead of renting. He admitted with a smile that it had been the right decision. Piper J–3s were inexpensive to buy, and cost little more than nothing to fly.

We parted, and he wandered over in the direction of his Piper. About then Bruce appeared. We talked a bit as we walked towards his aircraft. Together we pushed it back away from the gas pit and then turned it for a clear exit.

Bruce pulled up in front of the open hangar doors, locked one wheel, opened the throttle and started a quick turn. We were well into the turn when he quickly cut power. The momentum of the turning aircraft continued until the tail was pointed toward the open hangar. But Bruce had cut the throttle at such a time that there was little or no blast from the propeller blowing into the hangar. Once positioned, Bruce shut the engine down and spent a few seconds looking over the controls and instruments. We climbed out and pushed the aircraft back into the hangar and closed the big double doors.

Shortly Bruce would sell his Aeronca Chief, and that chapter in both of our lives was closed. But for me, it would forever be an interesting part of my life. For the first time, I had actually been a part of aviation. Admittedly, what I had been doing was small, but it had been a part. Dried dope on my clothing and hands, along with the smell of paint solvents was almost a status symbol to me. And flight--to feel it through the seat of my pants--was something I would never forget. I hated to see it come to an end, but unknown to me at that time, there was more coming from that little airport.

A Beginning in Question

Clark, a classmate and friend, approached me at church one Sunday. He told me that he was thinking about a job at an airport. Knowing that I had an interest in aviation, he asked me a few questions about working at an airport. I had never really worked at an airport, but I gave him a little description of what I thought it might be like. As the conversation developed, it was obvious that he wasn't all that interested in the airport as a place to work; it was just a money thing.

Being a little curious, I asked him where he got his information on the job opening. He told me that his brother had been taking flying lessons and had heard they needed help. Clark's name was suggested and an invitation was extended for him to apply. I asked him where. He casually stated Christopherson Air Service at the airport on 2100 South, Utah Central.

I was more than a little envious. I had put my application in at several airport operations, but they were all at the main airport and their response was a little less than what I had hoped. If Clark had been anyone other than a friend, I would be out at Utah Central fighting for the position. Then again, if Clark had a brother out there spending money, my chances would not be all that great. On top of that, Clark was also a very able and likeable person. Then there was transportation, Clark had a car, and I didn't. The main airport had bus service, Utah Central didn't. Even I had to admit, that, for me, getting and holding down a job at Utah Central looked to have almost more problems than benefits. Then again a job at Utah Central--I've been there. I know some of the people. It would be a little like being back home. Somehow, I could find a way.

A few days later, I ran into Clark between classes at school. I asked him about the airport job. He looked a little disappointed and said that it had "fallen through."

Then he added that part of the wages were flying lessons. He had a nice little '39 Chevie and to keep it going he needed money more than he needed flying lessons. He went into some detail on how he had tried to get more money, but everything had come to nothing. Clark was talking and I guess I appeared to be listening, but I might just as well have been in China.

The second school was out; I was out the door and headed home on the run. Twenty minutes after the close of my last class, I was on my bike peddling west, towards Utah Central.

The bike ride turned out to be something else. There was a stiff southwest wind blowing, and it fought me every inch of the way. When I finally reached the airport, I was tired. I parked my bike near the main hangar and stood in the shade for a moment trying to get some of my composure back.

Out near the front of the main hangar, I noticed a worker refueling an airplane. I took a deep breath, brushed my long hair back and headed over in his direction.

I asked him if he knew of any job openings at the airport. In a very friendly response, he told me that he had heard they did need some help on the line, but he was not the person to see about those things. He pointed over in the direction of the office and explained that the man I needed to talk to was the airport manager; his name was Don Christopherson.

I headed towards the main entrance on the north side of the office building. I cautiously opened the door and slowly walked inside. The place was quiet and appeared to be empty. To my right was a lunch counter and to my left a display case. I continued ahead a few more steps then turned left and wandered a short distant down a hall, still no one. Returning to the front door, I noticed a door behind the display case. That must be the office. I passed through an opened lift up section of the counter and slowly walked to the open door and peered inside.

A middle-aged man was bent over a pile of papers. He stopped working, looked up and with a smile asked if there was anything he could do for me. I introduced myself and stated that I was looking for Don. He smiled and acknowledged that he was Don. In the best way that I possibly could, I told him that I had heard that there might be an opening at the airport. He said there was a possibility of an upcoming opening, but a final decision had not been made. He then suggested that I try again a little later in the week. I thanked him, turned around and walked out of the office. I was jubilant! I did have a chance!

A few days later, I was once again on the same bike peddling into the same headwind, but it seemed much easier. Knowing that there might be something waiting at the end of a hard ride makes it so much more bearable. I honestly felt that the job was mine; it was just a matter of time.

When I arrived, I felt I knew my way around a bit. I crossed the parking area, entered the office and headed straight for Don's office. He was in the same chair laboring over a similar pile of papers. Confidently, I asked him about the position.

"Probably not," Don stated somewhat reluctantly. Things had apparently changed. Don went on to explain that the owner, Merrill Christopherson was selling the airport lease. Don then added that since he might be on his way out he felt he no longer had any say in the affairs of the airport. It was the beginning of nothing and the ending of everything.

Don must have sensed my disappointment, because he gave me a smile and told me not to give up and stated in a very friendly way, "Don't get discouraged, things are changing almost daily." That was all I needed. From that point on, I would stick it out until I had the job, no matter how long it took.

A week or so later, I was back full of determination. Even before he said "Nothing yet," I was planning my next trip out. The upside was the fact that the bike ride was getting easier, and I was even getting to enjoy the trip.

On the fifth trip out, I knew I had the job as soon as I looked at Don. He told me that the future ownership of the airport was still being discussed, but if I still wanted the job, it was mine. I think he even got a kick out of hiring me.

He then took a few moments to explain some of my duties and my pay. My job description could be summed up as a Line Boy and helper to anyone who needed assistance. I would get $1.50 an hour and work part time after school, five days a week. Saturdays and Sundays would each be a full workday. I could get days off as needed. There would be no discounts on flying, in the beginning anyway. When Don had completed his explanation, I stated in an excited voice, "I'll take it"! He smiled. I smiled, and we shook hands. He told me to report to work the next morning, which was a Saturday.

Unnoticed by me, one of the instructors, Ellis Dunlap or "Ellie" as I would later know him, was standing nearby. I guess he was aware of my biking. He asked me where I lived. I gave him my address and he offered me a ride saying it was right on his way. I had heard that come Saturday rain was expected, so the offer was accepted and more than appreciated.

After being hired, I couldn't think of anything except the job. What was it like working at an airport, around airplanes? It was still early, and I thought it might be fun to just wander around and get better acquainted with my new job surroundings.

I saw the worker that I had made my initial contact with near one of the rental hangars. I made my way over to where he was standing and officially introduced myself and added that I had just been hired. He stated that his name was Chad Jenkins, and he was tickled pink to see me come on board. He was the airport's mechanic and had been trying to work the line, sometimes the office and in between, squeeze in his shop work. He was covering too much and his shop work was suffering. We talked for a time about the airport and the work involved. He also explained in more detail, some of my duties and how to handle them.

I headed back towards the corner of the main hangar where I had parked my bike. Passing by the partially open shop door got me wondering what was inside. After all, I did work there and the hangar belonged to the company that I had just hired on with.

Beyond the opening, there were dark shadows. There was no way I could pass by the door and not take a quick look inside. I pushed open the door and stepped inside. Once inside, I paused while my eyes got accustomed to the light.

There was an old furnace on my left. It was one of the old types I've seen in the basements of homes. A plenum on the top had gapping openings where heat ducts might have been. I guess in its present state it could only be classified as a coal or wood stove. Just beyond the stove, to my left, a long workbench along the north wall. Tools, a spark plug cleaner, oilcans, pop bottles, rags and a variety of aircraft parts were spread over its surface. A wall-mounted telephone was just above the west end of the bench on the stuccoed cinder block wall. A small radio on a nearby shelf was softly playing a western tune.

Numerous places along the top and sides of the workbench had a variety of paint blotches where someone must have tested a spray gun before applying the paint to parts. In the northeast corner of the hangar was a small room with an open door. The single light inside revealed it to be a parts crib of sorts. I could see several cans and boxes of various sizes. On my right was a canvas curtain, in the open position. The curtains hung on a cable spanning the full width of the hangar, east to west. With the curtain closed, the hangar was divided in two sections, the north, which was the smaller area, or the workshop. The section to the south, the much larger area was for aircraft parking or storage. With the partition curtain closed, the stove would provide heat for the shop area.

The main hangar doors were on the south end of the hangar. Above and near the main doors, there was a set of uncovered wings, placed on planks, spanning between roof tresses. There were several small lights mounted on the bottom of the trusses that provided rather inadequate lighting for the aircraft parking area. Scattered around the perimeter were a few boxes, a small bench, an acetylene-welding outfit, a fifty-five gallon drum, a rudder, an uncovered aileron and a damaged propeller. On the floor, off to one side, a pile of dirt mixed with papers and a few spent aircraft nuts, washers and bolts. Nearby was a broom and dustpan.

Sitting quietly in the center of the large hangar floor were two Piper J-3 Cubs. They sat side-by-side, one ahead of the other, cabin doors and windows open, tails down, noses high, both facing the big closed hangar doors, seemingly anticipating their opening. There was something intriguing about the Cubs sitting there in the dim light. They sat in silence, somehow looking youthful, playful, and even friendly. More than that, there was a spirit of adventure that radiated from their very stillness.

The Cub nearest to where I was standing was painted the standard yellow with the number N88234 displayed across the top of the right wing and on the tail. On the far side, and parked slightly ahead, was a Cub sporting a faded tan color, with the wing and tail displaying the number N38308. Both looked as if they had been around awhile. A light film of runway dust covered the lower and aft ends of their fuselages. Each had its share of fabric patches in various sizes and locations. Most of the yellow Piper's patches were painted in mis-matched yellows or silver. The tan J–3 sported more than a few patches that had never gotten beyond the silver paint.

I circled both aircraft, walking slowly, running my hand along what ever was handy, the fuselage, wings, struts or propeller. I paused and looked at the tan J–3 and wondered how the color was ever decided upon; maybe it was the only color they had.

I then wandered over towards the open door of the yellow Cub, took a position just behind the wing struts and peered inside. I was greeted with the faint smells of oil, fabric, rubber, fuel and leather, an aroma unique to aircraft.

Unlike the Aeronca Chief, with it side-by-side seating, the J–3's had front and back seats mounted in a narrow fuselage. The Cub also sported a control stick in place of the somewhat traditional control wheel found in most civilian aircraft.

The wooden floorboards had lost a good part of their black paint in the areas of heavy foot movement. Caked dirt could be seen along the edges and beneath the seats. The seat cushions were well worn and in places were cracked and frayed, but they retained their glossy black leather appearance. A small first-aid kit was located in a small pouch on the back of the front seat. It looked like it had been there untouched, probably since the Cub had rolled off the production line.

To the rear, behind the rear seat, was a small baggage compartment with two placards mounted on the lid. One placard listed the maximum weight capacity of the baggage compartment. The second placard stating that the aircraft had been manufacture by Piper Aircraft Corp. of Lock Haven, Pa, USA. It also stated the model of the aircraft, its serial number, the engine installed at the factory and the date the Cub was manufactured.

The fuel shut-off valve and the carburetor heat controls were located on the sidewalls in recessed panels. The painted metal on the throttles, the rudder pedals, and the control columns was well worn, somewhat chipped, and in places it was polished metal.

The instrument panel was the traditional flat black. The panel displayed a compass, an airspeed indicator, an altimeter, a tachometer, and a combination oil temperature and oil pressure gauge. Just above the compass, in the center of the panel was a Compass Deviation Card, filled in with a series of faded handwritten numbers. The instrument panel had cracks radiating out

from several of the instrument mounting screws. Repairs had been made with
unpainted aluminum rivets. Centered high on panel was a little metal placard
stating, "SOLO REAR SEAT ONLY."

I leaned inside and looked out at the wings, then forward over the panel
and through the windshield. Pictures and sensations ran through my mind
as I tried to visualize what a Piper Cub would be like in flight. What does
one see, what does one feel, is it hard to fly and most of all, would I ever get
a chance?

I turned and wandered towards the door, then pausing, I looked back. I
again studied the Piper Cubs, trying to imprint every detail, every image,
hoping never to forget what I was looking at. The two aircraft sitting in the
dim light and shadows somehow represented everything that attracted me to
aircraft and flight.

I headed out to the corner of the hangar, pulled my bike away from the wall,
hopped on and headed east toward home. A gentle breeze pressed against my
back, making it one of the most enjoyable rides that I have ever had. It was
September 1956.

One Little Airport

Utah Central was located some five miles southwest of Salt Lake City and
had its beginnings shortly before the Second World War. Its creation was the
brainchild and sweat of one individual, Vern Carter. He obtained legal access
to the land, walked out into the brush, staked out the runways, and graded
off the weeds, brush and anthills. By any definition, it was a small country
airport. Nothing paved and nothing fancy in the way of buildings.

Utah Central had three runways, a North-South, an East-West and a Diagonal. The East-West was the shortest at 3,439 feet. The Diagonal was the
longest and with the prevailing winds was the most often used, its length was
4,212 feet. The North-South Runway's length was 3,476 feet. The runways
were graveled to a width of forty feet and graded to a width of about 150
feet; at least that's what the airport drawings indicated. The taxi strips and
parking areas were graveled, but at times and in places, it was a bit thin. The
native dirt was soft and it didn't take a lot of traffic for the gravel to sink out
of sight.

On the north, the airport boundary was 2100 South (SR 21). It ran east and west and was one of the main accesses to the valley from the west. Along the west side of the airport was 3600 West, running north and south. West of 3600 West was Kennecott's Duck Pond and more grasslands. To the south there were open fields and the small farming community of Granger (later named West Valley City). Not far to the west of Granger was the little farming community of Hunter. To the east of the airport, more open spaces and Decker's Lake. Beyond the lake was Redwood Road and a few businesses.

There were three isolated hangars near the northwest corner of the airport property. Vern Dedman had an aircraft repair shop in the center hangar and occasionally used the hangar to its east. Russell Aircraft Sales was a business located in the west hangar. Airport maps and drawings would list the airport operator as Russell Aircraft sales. Yet, in all the time that I was there, I never saw or met Russell.

The Salt Lake Municipal Airport, sometimes called Salt Lake Number One (now Salt Lake City International Airport) was the city's main airport. It was roughly four miles to the north of Utah Central, and in the beginning, little attention was paid to it. For a small town airport, Utah Central seemed to be in a good location and barring unseen circumstances it would be there for a long time.

Vern Carter was not what you would call a high-powered businessman. He just kind of did his own thing, and he did know aviation. He not only made a fair living, but his doings seem to be what the pilots in the area wanted. For that, he was highly respected, and over time he developed his own group of dedicated followers. The clientele at the airport were all about the same grade of airplane lovers and airport bums.

When Utah Central was first laid out, the standard passenger aircraft using the main Salt Lake Municipal Airport was the Douglas DC–3. The Douglas was a smaller, twin-engine aircraft and it flew a rather tight pattern around the airport. A few years later, newer and larger aircraft began appearing, aircraft like the four engine DC–4s and Constellations. They required a bigger pattern that put them right over the top of Utah Central. It soon became apparent to Vern that these aircraft were using much longer approaches going into the Salt Lake Municipal Airport. Being a man of vision, he could see that not too far in the future, these, and probably yet bigger aircraft would be flying approaches right over his little airport. Big aircraft flying low over his airport was something he wanted no part of. The more he thought about it, the more he felt that it might be best if he moved on. Utah Central was put up for sale.

Merrill Christopherson was involved in the operation of the Provo Airport, located on the eastern shore of Utah Lake. When he heard Vern Carter wanted out of Utah Central, he was very interested. He contacted Vern and arrangements were made, putting Utah Central under his control. Merrill hired his nephew, Don Christopherson as manager of the new Christopherson Air Service based at Utah Central.

One of the first things Don did was to finish the main hangar. Vern Carter had built the walls, and then for whatever reason the construction had come to a halt. Don purchased trusses, lumber and roofing that gave the hangar its final shape. Then there was the floor. Vern Dedman was interested in a Continental C-85 engine that Don had for sale. Don, knew that Vern was good with concrete flatwork, so he told Vern the engine was his if he would put the floor in the hangar. Don would supply the concrete and Vern would do the work. Vern accepted and shortly the hangar had a new floor and Vern had a new engine.

After Vern Carter sold Utah Central, he went over to the east side of the Salt Lake Valley, near Draper, Utah. There, Vern found a remote parcel of land not far from some beautiful mountains. He built his new airport and put it into operation. Everything was perfect. It was just what he wanted.

But soon other people were looking at the vast emptiness around the perimeter of his airport. They bought property, built homes and settled the area. Then some of the residents got wondering why so many noisy airplanes were flying over their nice quiet neighborhood. People complained and had meetings. They said, in a nice way, that they did not want an airport in the area. Vern Carter was asked politely to leave. Before he had his bags packed, developers were surveying the airport property for housing developments. I guess it was a win, win situation for nearly everyone, the residents got the airplanes out of their skies, the developers made some money, many people were able to purchase some very nice dream homes near some beautiful mountains, and Vern, well, he was once again headed for what he preferred, less populated areas.

After Vern moved out of Draper, he went south a short distance and picked out a spot two miles northeast of Lehi, Utah. There he built another airport. For whatever reason, the Lehi Airport was built small and stayed small. Many people in the area never knew it was there. Apparently, Vern Carter was satisfied. As far as I know, he spent the rest of his working days there.

A Day at the Beginning

The night before I started, sleep was out of the question. I was excited about my new job and that was all that I could think about. What kind of work would I be doing? What would it be like to work at an airport, around airplanes, lots of airplanes?

Somehow, I managed to doze off, but I was awake and up long before the alarm went off. I dressed and forced a bit of food down. That finished, I still had time to kill. I waited around the house for a time. Still a little too anxious to sit in one place, I wandered up 1400 South to West Temple where I would meet Ellie.

Still a little early, I leaned up against a telephone pole and waited some more. My attention wandered up to the gray and almost dark sky. The papers had predicted rain and it looked like that's what it was going to be. Yet I was hoping that the gray was a morning thing and not rain clouds. Would there be work for a Line Boy when no one was flying?

Seeing my ride pull up to the curb was an encouraging sign. If a flight instructor was going to work, there would probably be something for me to do. In a roundabout way, I asked Ellie what everyone would be doing if it did rain. He stated that it was a little hard to say, but there was always plenty going on at the airport. I relaxed, leaned back and found myself in a lively conversation with him concerning airplanes, flying and Utah Central.

Once at the airport, I was surprised to see so much activity going on at such an early hour, especially after the gloomy weather reports. Apparently, pilots knew a little more about weather than I did. One plane was in the pattern and a second one was taxiing out. Down on the line several people were walking around, maybe they would also be going up.

I checked in at the office to get my very first assignment. Don looked over at an individual sitting at the lunch counter and stated that his plane was at the pump, waiting for gas.

While walking towards the fueling area, I remember studying the little tricycle gear Ercoupe and the area around the gas pit. It was my first official duty, and although it was a simple task, I still wanted to make sure that there would be no problems.

I opened up the heavy steel pump house door, entered and turned on the master switch that was located just above the pump. Don had casually mentioned that the gas pump would occasionally display an ornery streak and refuses to start. However, he assured me that a good whack with my foot would get it going every time.

There was a recessed gas pit about fifty feet southeast of the pump house. The pit had a heavy metal swing lid or cover. With the lid closed, it covered the pit opening and was nearly flush with the ground. The lid was of heavy gauge steel and I guess while closed, a car could cross over it without causing damage. Nearby was a little three-step stand that stood about thirty inches high.

I swung open the pit lid just past the vertical; there a chain held it in a nearly upright position. The pit was about three foot square by two foot deep and contained a recording meter and a rolled up fueling hose. There was also a clipboard inside with paper forms for recording sales. An On/Off switch was mounted on the sidewall of the pit. I cautiously flipped it with my foot. Not knowing what to expect, I felt some satisfaction when I heard the pump start up. The owner's instructions were to "top the tanks off." Probably being over cautious, I peered into the cockpit and checked the electrical switches.

One by one, I unscrewed the filler caps of the two-wing and single nose tanks and put in what fuel I could. My first sale was a few cents short of a dollar. After replacing the caps, I pushed the Ercoupe back away from the pit. With that simple little task, I experienced my first unanticipated problem; nose wheel aircraft behave a little funny when pushed from the front end.

Over near the front of the main hangar, Ellie and Roy Mower were trying to hand prop the companies' Piper PA–12 Super Cruiser. Apparently, the battery had run down during the night and the engine was being a little stubborn. Roy, the chief flight instructor, senior in both age and experience, was doing the propping. After a few tries, he waved it off as a hopeless cause. Somewhat out of breath, he went over and sat down on a nearby patch of grass. Half smiling and half laughing at his unsuccessful efforts he jokingly remarked, "It'll never start, it has way too much compression."

Ellie took his turn at swinging the prop but soon he, being a middle age individual, was also exhausted. Next thing I knew they were calling Chad over to give it a try, "Hey Chad, come here a minute and show us old timers how to get this ornery cuss started!" Being what appeared to me as a little modest, he at first declined saying, "Don't give up so fast, it'll start!" However, with a little coaxing, he was soon standing at the front end of the big red Piper.

Chad did most of the aircraft mechanical work around the airport and even though he didn't have his A & E license, (Airframe and Engine); he was one of the most respected mechanics around.

Chad's real ace in the hole was his youth and strength. He stood near the prop and instructed the individual in the Piper to open up the throttle. He then followed with the statement, "Switch off, brakes on." With verbal verification, he grabbed the blade of the prop and turned it backwards a few times. It looked a little like the engine was being unwound. Then he again stood clear and stated, "Switch on, throttle closed, brakes on." The individual in the PA-12 leaned out the window and repeated the instructions. Chad pushed on the hub to verify that the brakes were on. Then positioning himself, he gave the blade a hefty pull, it spun around aimlessly. He tried again, still nothing. He tried again; it caught, ran a bit rough and then smoothed out. Soon it was purring like there had never been a problem.

The rest of the day was on the job training. I received instruction on the do's and don'ts of moving aircraft. "Always remember to be aware of props and wings, on both parked and moving aircraft," seemed to be the watchwords of the day. Someone casually mentioned that nearly everyone has walked into a wing tip or stationary prop at one time or another. Cleaning dirt off soft plexiglas windshields and windows was another subject. Making sure fuel tanks are really topped off was also mentioned. No one wants to get halfway to his destination only to find out that he is just a little "too" short on fuel. "Believe me it's a real public relation problem," someone added. Then there were the different types of oil and the pump house. Cleaning the office was also part of my duties. Lastly, at day's end, I was to do a line check making sure all aircraft are properly tied down for the night. The final comment, "When home in bed and you hear the wind blowing, you don't want to be wondering if some airplane was left untied.

During that first day, Chad took me over to one of the Cubs and showed me the basics of hand propping. It's simple enough, but I guess you've got to do it a few times to feel comfortable.

I also found out that a working day at Utah Central was anything but eight to five. I had arrived at 7:00 A.M. and was still up to my elbows in work at 8:00 P.M. That day and all the following days were long in hours but short in time. Lots of interesting duties and just being around airplanes made the hours go by fast. All in all I was sure glad I got the job.

A Teen's Mount

With the job came the need for transportation. It was frustrating because I didn't have a lot of time to look and even less money to spend. Then one of my family members mentioned that Charles Jensen, a neighbor a few houses to the north, had a car for sale, a 1940 Oldsmobile 4-door Sedan. Years earlier, he had been my scoutmaster and as neighbors go I knew him quite well. I went over to take a look.

The car was sitting out in his back yard surrounded with weeds. Apparently, it hadn't been driven for some time. Through all the dust you could see that the body and interior were flawless, looking almost as if it had just come in from Detroit. It was black in color and with a little wash and wax it would really look great.

My initial hang-up was the fact that it wasn't a two door, hot rod Ford or Chevy. Most of the cars in my high school parking lot were lean, trim, mean and fast looking. But that Olds was anything but. It would probably feel more at home parked out in front of a mortuary. Moreover, it had one of those automatic transmissions. Hydra-Matic Drive they called it. All my friends had "stick shifts." Automatic transmissions were for old people who were not very good at shifting gears.

Other than what it was not, the thing that was hard to adjust to was its size. It was big, four big doors big, front-to-back big, side-to-side big and top-to-bottom big! To me, it looked bigger than a Fleetwood Cadillac.

Not being an expert on buying cars, I had brought my dad along to get his opinion. He, like everyone of his generation grew up on Model A's and T's and was quite a good mechanic.

Charles slid into the driver's seat, put the key in the ignition and started it up. Dad, listened, walked around and looked underneath the car in several different areas. He went up to the front end, lifted up the hood and looked at the engine. He then reached in and fidgeted with some wires and other parts. He sat down in the driver's seat, revved the engine up a couple of times and let it idle. Seeming satisfied with the engine, he turned on the radio and moved the dial across a couple of stations. He also turned on the heater, defroster and checked out the windshield wipers.

It was obvious that he was quite impressed with its mechanical, interior and exterior condition. I personally think that he would have been happy with any car that was not "one of those wild souped-up jalopies." Sadly, I would have been most happy with one of those souped-up jalopies!

My dad let me do most of the talking, as he trusted Charles and I guess he figured it was time I learned the ways of the "real world." After quite a lengthy discussion, I found out that I was not quite the cool negotiator that I hoped I might be. Maybe scoutmasters know their kids better than kids know their scoutmasters. The price started at one hundred dollars. After pleading poverty and every other sad story that I could think of, I had him down to a rock bottom price of ninety-eight bucks, which to me was a small fortune. I was however able to work out some very favorable terms on the payments. He let me have the car with no money down, and the payments would be spread out over several months, with no interest being charged.

After everything was said and done, I drove home in my new Olds feeling good; I had my own "wheels" and no longer had to depend on others for rides. I had no doubt that among all my friends, my car was the best running and most comfortable. Besides, the two bucks I saved on its price was enough for a hamburger, a movie and gas enough for an evening dragging Main Street, at least on paper. Things were looking pretty good.

However, in the circle of my "buddies," the back seat of the Olds was often referred to as "Ron's Dance Floor." Another cute little comment was, "If one was in the back seat of Ron's Olds and wanted to talk to someone up front he had to take ten steps forward to be heard." A teen's car it was not, but it was good transportation and I was glad to have it.

One With a Legend

As soon as things settled down, I got myself lined up for some flying lessons. Without a lot of inner debate I chose Roy Mower as my instructor. Roy was older, walked a little slower and because of his gray hair he stood out in just about any group on the field. Chad had once told me that Roy had been in aviation almost since its beginnings and most of that time he has been an instructor. I guess just being around him made me feel a part of where he had been.

Prior to my first flying lesson, I got wondering what it would be like going up with him. The day before the flight, I asked Chad what I could expect from him as an instructor. He smiled and said, "Roy is the most laid back instructor you will probably ever have the chance to fly with. He never gets excited; he takes his time and he's always there to give a student whatever help he needs."

He paused and added, "As an example of how laid back he is, well, once, I was up with him and we were on Final. There was an old barbed wire fence stretching across our approach to the runway, quite a ways back. I was clear of it by a mile! But I could see Roy sitting up front, leaning forward, and I knew what he was looking at, the fence. He watched it for a few seconds and then in his drawn out voice said, "C-h-a-d, t-h-a-t f-e-n-c-e, I t-h-i-n-k y-o-u-'r g-o-i-n-g t-o h-i-t nope! Ya missed it"

Chad continued half laughing, "I guess that was Roy's style of humor, but after all this time I still get a kick out of the way he said it."

The big day finally arrived, October 6, 1956, my first day to fly the Piper Cub. On that first flight the Cub of choice was 88234. I guess I was a little partial to the traditional yellow.

My flight was scheduled for late afternoon, but for me, my preparation for it was an all day process. At every opportunity, I was over with "my Cub." I checked the oil, topped off the tank and did several thorough preflights. About midday, I pushed it over to the wash area and gave it a good scrubbing with plenty of soap and water. After cleaning it up on the outside, I grabbed the glass cleaner and shined all the windows, insides and out. Then with a pan of soapy water, I went through the cockpit. The seats, floorboards, cabin walls, instrument panel, even under the seats. I doubt if it had been that clean in years.

Whenever the Cub completed a flight, I serviced it and then pushed it over to a convenient spot and tied it down. Then every time I walked by I gave it a good look, sometimes to admire, other times just making sure it was ready. To say I was excited about taking lessons would be a gross understatement!

I can still remember walking out across the ramp towards the Cub and my first flying lesson with Roy. He was at my side explaining things about the Cub and the flight. I listened intently to his instructions while admiring the J–3 that we were approaching.

The bright yellow Cub was a strong contrast to its setting. Fall grass in its golden shades spread around in thick and thin patches at the edge of the Cub's heavily worn tie-down spot. Ropes hanging from the wings looked almost to be ribbons on a Christmas present waiting to be untied. Behind and above the Cub, a crisp blue sky made more exciting by an occasional dense white cloud. What more could a kid possibly ask for?

"With proper pre-flight, good weather and paying attention to your surroundings, you should never have any problems," Roy stated as we began untying the ropes.

Together we walked around the J–3 as Roy listed all the items that needed checked. I listened and asked an occasional question. He also gave me a rundown on all the good and bad points of the Cub. His bottom line was "There's nothing better to learn to fly in." It's slow enough to give the student time to think, strong enough to get him through his inexperience and very forgiving to all but the most severe mistakes."

With the walk-around and pre flight complete, Roy told me to climb in. I climbed into the back seat, and he took a position outside, near the front seat. While I was doing up my belt, he went over everything in the cabin. He talked about each instrument and control describing its operation and function. He also discussed the areas of limited visibility of the Cub and the need to continually check out the blind spots, both on the ground and in the air. Taxiing, airport patterns and traffic were also discussed.

He then went over the start-up procedures, along with some of the obvious do's and don'ts for hand propping. I've often wondered if it were possible for a person doing a hand-start to receive serious injuries due to a miscue. I must have shown a little concern as he quickly assured me that there would be no problem. He added that he was always very cautious, whether there was a student or a seasoned veteran in the cockpit.

He turned the six-foot prop over a couple of times while the engine gave off a variety of clicking, sucking, blowing and wheezing sounds. Roy then gave it a little push near the hub to ensure the brakes were on and holding. Then with everything ready, he stepped up more squarely to the propeller, positioned himself, placed both hands on the face of the blade and pulled down with a good healthy pull. The engine was instantly alive and the little Piper airframe shook in a friendly way. A steady breeze blew by the open door and windows, bringing in the faint aroma of burning fuel.

Roy stood there for a few seconds with his eyes on the little Continental. Satisfied with all that he was seeing, he then wandered over to the Cub's door in a rather wide path around the turning propeller. Once at the door he lifted himself up and sat on the edge of the opening. He was in a somewhat awkward position, but with little effort he somehow swung his tall lean frame into the front seat.

While settling down, he scanned the panel, fumbled for his belts and then subconsciously clicked the ends together and adjusted it to his waist. His attention settled in on the instrument that was a combination Oil Pressure and Temperature Gauge. After a few seconds, he tapped the face of the instrument a couple of times with his finger. Pausing, he studied the readings. Satisfied, his attention drifted elsewhere. I've seen actors portraying pilots in old time movies tap their instruments like that. I guess to make sure they were not somehow hung up. I thought it was kind of neat.

He motioned to start taxiing. I checked the windsock; it indicated Runway 34. I eased the throttle forward and after a bit of resistance, the Cub was moving freely across the ramp. We were on our way.

As we made our way down to the south end of the strip, I made a series of "S" clearing turns, some of which were large and others not so large. I had intended to make them all of uniform size and was hoping Roy had not noticed the variety, but I'm sure he did. We finally came to the Run-Up area and I felt a little relief in the fact that my inability to execute proper "S"-turns would no longer be displayed.

Roy talked me through the throttle settings, the mag check, the carb (carburetor) heat check and finally the trim setting. Everything checked out, and the Piper was ready for flight. I cleared for traffic, moved out onto the runway and lined the Cub up on the center of the strip.

Slowly, I opened the throttle creating the unforgettable sounds of a Continental engine under full power. Faster and faster the Cub raced towards my first flight, sounds never before heard, feelings never before felt, and sights never before seen. The plane wandered off center and Roy habitually took over long enough to get it corrected. The wheels were spinning, bouncing over and through the gravel. As we gained speed, I could feel Roy make an occasional correction on the rudder. A solid bounce and we struggled into the air, and then slowly settled back to the surface. Another short ground run and we lifted off into a solid climb.

The Cub drifted to the left and I somehow over-corrected to the right. By the time we were over the highway, the runway was more than just a little to my left. I had the uneasy feeling that if I had let the plane go where it wanted we would have centered over the runway. I skidded, slipped, lurched and wobbled around the turns and then made my last rather clumsy turn exiting the pattern. Roy pointed me in a northwest direction, over towards the Kennecott Tailings Pond.

Once over the tailings, things got a little busy. We did stalls, turns, climbs and glides and then we did them all over again. The world became one of light and shadows, of distant landscape rolling, sliding, drifting and tilting out in front of the windshield. Roy talked and showed and then I tried to duplicate. He commented, made corrections and we went through them again.

"Nose dropping, get it up, not too much, watch the horizon, you're climbing," the voice echoed somewhere between the body being pressed into the seat and then being lifted up against the belts. "Rudder, you're using a little too much, ease up a bit, more aileron, you're skidding, that's it, you've got it, see, can you see it, can you feel it?"

Words are heard, a second of pride and then the words "more rudder." The words shatter the success. The mind is willing, the desire is there, but the arms and legs do everything wrong. How much rudder is too much, not enough? I can't feel it.

Is that right, no it can't be? The bank is getting too steep, way too much back pressure. More instructions. "Don't concentrate on one area, watch the entire picture." Conflicting movements mixed with instructions, "Why does the airplane do that, that wasn't my intent. Boy I bet that impressed him."

Instructions given, student hears, executes, right rudder, left rudder, up elevator, down elevator, too much elevator, not enough aileron, it's skidding again, even I can feel it. "I did it again, stupid!" The Cub progressively pays more attention and obeys to a higher degree. Success comes, then again failure. It comes again, slowly but it comes; more and more the student and the Cub see eye to eye.

Desire endures beyond the frustration, a thought flashes through my mind, "I think I'm getting it!"

When Roy finally turned around and told me to head for home, my right arm was numb from rolling the stick around. My back ached, my body was tense, and my mind exhausted.

Rudder and aileron applied, the Cub gently rolls over into a bank. Out beyond the windshield the world slowly drifts by. A direction comes into view and I again apply rudder and aileron. The wings gently roll back to level and the Cub is on a southeast course.

The tension and frustrations of trying to do the unfamiliar with perfection were behind. I relaxed and my mind wandered into areas of the pleasant aspects of flight. For no real reason, I felt like a veteran. The satisfaction was enormous.

In reality, I'd learned a very small part of what I needed to know, but I felt good about where I had been and what I had learned. The Cub and I were coming to an understanding. We were becoming friends. It would never treat me as a complete stranger again.

There were two things of interest that Roy showed me, one particular to the Cub with the swing-down door. He dropped the lower door and went into a series of stalls. He pointed out the fact that the open door would begin to "float" just about the time the J–3 was ready to break into a stall. That little bit of knowledge is not required but something of interest. The second was doing a 360–degree turn or full circle. If done properly, you would fly right back into your own turbulence, giving your aircraft a little rocking motion at the point you started.

Clear of traffic, we made our entrance into the pattern. Roy gave me the stick and said that he would work the rudder. While we were coming down, Roy kept feeding me instructions, "A little less power, drop your nose a bit, wings level, watch your airspeed, level out, start the flair, that's it, keep it off the ground, stick back, hold it back, back, back." I was just a foot or so off the ground when it started to break into a stall. Roy quickly pulled the stick back the last inch or so and the Cub settled onto the surface like a feather. He made everything look so easy.

We continued rolling down the runway and soon came to a near stop. I gave the Piper a little power and continued for a time and then I turned off the runway and onto the taxi strip.

Roy turned around and asked me how I liked the Cub. I smiled and told him I loved it. I'm sure he knew what my answer would be long before he heard the words. I looked around the cockpit and then out at the struts and wings spread out to the sides. The brush and grass were drifting slowly to the rear, and somewhere in the background the sounds of gravel under balloon tires, soft wind moving over the wings and the little Continental running quietly. Who in their right mind would not love the Piper Cub and even more, who would not love its world?

We taxied over to the gas pump, shut down the engine and climbed out. I was a little stiff and Roy smiled as I stretched my limbs. We talked about the flight and Roy filled me in on why we did some of the maneuvers. Like so many good teachers, he took a great interest in my desire to fly and me in general. He had patience with my inexperience and always talked and treated me as the pilot I had always wanted to be. With his enthusiasm and confidence, I had little doubt that someday I would be that pilot.

Roy headed over in the direction of the office and disappeared between the parked aircraft. I pushed the Cub a little closer to the gas pit and grabbed the stand and hose. Climbing up the stool, I removed the gas cap and inserted the nozzle into the tank. The fuel made a hollow splashing sound in the partiality empty tank with fumes slowly rising in a twisting motion from the nozzle opening.

While the tank was filling, I studied the aircraft that I was becoming more and more acquainted with. The broad wings then looked rather heavy with their thick airfoil. At my side, the cooling Continental engine that somehow seemed almost alive and personal with its warmth and ticking sounds. The curved windshield reflecting a blue sky, clouds and a somewhat distorted me staring back at myself. Beyond the glare, a cabin filled with shadows, empty seats, a control stick leaning off to one side, the throttles in the closed position and the doors in the open position. Everything seemed poised, ready, waiting for another flight, another adventure. I hoped the dream would never end.

2

The New Crew

Friends Reshuffled

When I applied for the job at the airport, Don had mentioned that their lease might not be renewed. Discussions were on-going and decisions were in the making that may or may not affect us employees. Days, weeks passed, the lease renewal date drew nearer. All conversations centered on the date, what would happen and how each of us would fit into someone else's plans. It seemed with each passing day the rumors pointed more and more towards new owners and probably a new crew. We were all hoping they were rumors only, but none of us really knew.

With the prospects of a job disruption, I was rather surprised one day to hear Roy and Ellie laughing and joking about a possible layoff and the ensuing stampede over to the main airport and hopefully new jobs.

"You haven't got a chance; I'll be hired on long before you get there!" Ellie stated with a big grin. "I've been secretly putting together a hot rod jalopy; the thing is hotter than a firecracker. It has a super big veee-eight motor, with twin four-barrel carburetors, a polished duel exhaust system and it burns nothing but that scientific blended, Indy race car formulated, high-test, high-octane racing fuel. You'll be a day behind me in that worn out junk heap you drive, if you can even get it started! But I'll try to put in a good word for you."

Roy smiled while listening to Ellie and his hot rod tale. Then with a smile and in a rather boastful way said, "Hold on there Ellie and don't count yr chickens before there're hatched. I've got a little project of my own. Bought one of them there war surplus B–29 engines, you know, the big one, the Wright radial something or other with more than 2,000 horses, with a big four blade controllable pitch propeller; multi-stage turbo supercharged and its got to have at least a dozen barrels in its toilet size carburetor. I mounted the whole package on a J–3 Cub airframe.

The engine is so big and powerful that I had to put lead in the struts and fill all the tubing with horse glue to keep it from flying apart. All I've got to do is walk by the thing and it starts jumping up and down. Why that power plant is so blooming powerful that it's airborne and at altitude before the starter gets the engine up and running. Hate to tell you this Ol Buddy, but your hot rod car won't even be coughing when I get my first paycheck. But if I get a moment, and IF I think about it, I'll put in TWO good words for you!"

Then they both laughed and playfully slapped each other a couple of times.

Chad had no idea what he would do or where he would go. He was a good mechanic but he didn't have his license. But with his experience and reputation, he would have little trouble finding employment.

Then there was me, I was the one carrying around the short stick. My employment at the airport was measured in days. Days that were productive to me, but to a prospective employer they probably represented little more than an introduction. Both Kemp and Kelsey and Thompson Flying Service over at the Salt Lake Municipal Airport, were small outfits. And sadly, they were the only ones in the immediate area. I had made applications to both and neither would even take the time to tell me "No." Entry jobs, like what I would be seeking were definitely limited.

After what seemed a lifetime of rumors and speculations, I happened to notice Don approaching Chad and me early one afternoon. Looking at and studying the solemn expression on his face, I knew that the decision to keep or sell the lease had finally been made. He gave no indication as to what had been decided. That had to be a bad sign. I held my breath, too scared to even hope.

Then, about four feet away, Don broke into a grin. I could never put into words the joy I felt at that moment! The lease had indeed changed hands. The airport would be under new management. Chad and I would stay! Then the downside, all flight instructors had received their termination notices. It was a bittersweet pill. I was of course ecstatic that I would be staying, but watch-

ing Don, Ellie and Roy packing their few belongings and driving off into the
sunset was not an easy thing to do. That one flying lesson with Roy was the
first and last time I would ever go up with him.

Christopherson Air Service had been sold out to a fixed base operator by
the name of Roy Theurer. Roy had a successful flight school, charter, and aircraft tire recapping business located at the Logan Cache County Airport, just
northwest of Logan, Utah. He had been trying to expand for years, and when
Utah Central came along, he grabbed it. Our new company's name would be
Valley Airmotive.

Our new manager would be Glen F. Dellinger. He had been in aviation
since he was a kid. Not counting what had been lost, I felt good about the
way things turned out.

I never did hear what happened to Ellie and Don, but Roy Mower found
employment over at Kemp and Kelsey's Flying Service. There he had the job
of flying "Power Line Patrol" under a subcontract with the Utah Power and
Light Company.

A short time later, we got word that Roy was in the hospital with cancer.
Then almost overnight, we heard that he had passed away. It was a shock to all
of us. How could it have happen so fast? His death just didn't seem fair.

Shortly after his passing, there was a benefit program held in his behalf over
at the Salt Lake Municipal Airport. During World War Two, the Salt Lake
Airport was a major base for the assignment of crews to heavy bombers before
being sent over seas. Roy's benefit was held in one of the old military buildings left over from the war.

With These Men

Glen Dellinger, our new airport manager grew up in Lander, Wyoming.
Even as a lad he knew he wanted to fly. As soon as he was old enough to
ride a bike, he was spending most of his free time at the Hunt Field located
just outside of Lander. Not a big airport, but he became friends with some
very early pilots, not to mentions being around some historical aircraft with
classical names such as Alexander Eagle Rocks, Jennies, Great Lakes Trainers,
Lincoln Standards, American Eagles, Fleet Biplanes, Waco Travel Airs, Ryans
and Curtiss Robins.

Airport definitions were a little hazy back in the early days of aviation. As one old-timer I talked to said, "Back then most airports around this part of the country were runways with unwanted livestock or rangeland with un-wanted aircraft and which definition was in use depended on whom you were having the conversation with."

Airport managers, if there was one, were always dreaming of fences around the airport's perimeter to keep out grazing livestock, but ranchers wouldn't even discuss the idea. They felt that good grazing land, even bad grazing land for that matter, is too valuable to waste on them "flying machines. They use way too much land and have no real value to humans."

Early aircraft were mostly fabric. And back then fabric was painted with a Cellulose dope, and for some unknown reason cattle loved its flavor. Some have suggested that the fabric's oxidizing surface tasted a little like salt, and cattle love salt.

Hunt Field, at just about any given time, had a mixture of cows and air-craft in the same proximity. Cows are always hungry, and it was only a mat-ter of time until some cow began sniffing at and nibbling on the aircraft's fabric. It was often love at first munch. And once they started nibbling they found it hard to resist. They would lick, rummage and chomp trying to get more of whatever it was they loved. Glen said a cow could pretty well strip an aircraft during a single night. And I guess because of bad table manners, wooden aircraft parts such as ribs and stringers also suffered extensively during the feast.

There is not a lot of middle ground between a rancher, who has a stream of tears running down his cheeks, while standing over a very expensive cow, its belly full of airplane fabric and has obviously gone on to greener pastures. And the pilot, with tears in his eyes and a lump in his throat, who is the owner of a much loved and expensive aircraft, whose broken, striped and somewhat consumed airframe was a cow's final meal.

"That airplane you're looking at is very expensive, and I would like to know who is going to pay for the damages? Why didn't your dumb cow eat grass like other cows"?

"What! To heck with your crummy airplane, look, look what your stu-pid airplane did to my daughter's favorite pet and prize-winning cow! What is your airplane doing parked here in the middle of my pasture anyway?"

"What do you mean your pasture? This is an official airport!" Needless to say, not a lot of lasting friendships came out of those encounters!

Glen would, on occasion be hired as a cattle guard to spend the night sleeping beneath a wing of an aircraft. During bad weather he would often curl up in a cockpit with a canvas draped over the opening. Always sleeping with one eye open, he was ready to scatter any approaching cows back to more neutral feeding grounds.

He went up with, and took flying lessons from anyone who was willing to give them. In the mid thirties, when he was a very youthful 13 years old he soloed in an old Eagle Rock bi-wing.

Glen later went through the Army's Glider Training Program, got his Pilot's Wings and a Commission in the Army Air Corps.

After the war, he stayed on in aviation as a charter pilot, flight instructor, spray pilot, and anything else that would keep him in the air and put food on the table. He also spent time working for the State of Utah as a consultant. There he was instrumental in developing the use of aircraft for patrol work with the Utah Highway Patrol.

While he was doing charter work for an FBO (Fixed Base Operator) at the Ogden Airport, (now Ogden-Hinckley Municipal Airport near Ogden, Utah), he got word that Roy Theurer was looking for an airport manager. Glen immediately applied for the job. He and Roy discussed the upcoming position and Glen felt he had a good chance at landing the job. At the end of the interview, Roy said he would get back to him. However, Glen didn't hear from Roy for what he thought was the longest time and had just about given up on the job. Then one morning, at four thirty, Glen heard a knock on his door. It was Roy, telling him to pack his bags. He had the job.

On the east end of the hangars was the living quarters that had once been Vern Carter's, the builder of Utah Central Airport. Glen, his wife Doris, and their family would take up residence there. When Glen was hired, his living quarters were still being remodeled. With his residence not ready, his family would spend a few more days in Ogden, and Glen would spend a few uncomfortable nights sleeping on the floor of the then unused classroom of the office building.

On a very dark afternoon, Glen flew his family into Utah Central aboard the companies' Cessna 182. Kay Andersen, one of Roy's pilots at the Logan Airport was there to meet them. After getting their few things out of the Cessna, they all drove over to the Wing Inn. It was a little roadside café located on 2100 South, just east of the airport property. There, Glen, his family and Kay had an evening meal. Kay, not a long-time employee himself, gave Glen a little run-down on the business as he knew it.

Glen was a stocky individual about medium height, who sported his premature gray hair in a crew cut. He always wore the standard flying boots and was never without his aviation sunglasses. He was friendly, easy to get along with and I never saw him excited about anything. His opinions were always by the book, firm and fair.

Melvin Darnell, or Happ as we knew him, was one of the first flight instructors hired under the new management. I can't remember where he came from, but he did have time in the Navy. He was always talking about his experiences in the military and the stories were always interesting and mostly humorous. To me, it seemed he had been everywhere and done everything. He was outgoing, always open to opportunities, full of energy and a great pilot. During my early flight training, he was my instructor.

Max Green, another flight instructor was hired shortly after the company was organized, but for the life of me I can't remember his first day. One day he was just there. He was lean, very tall, six-foot-three or even four, and like Glen, always wore his premature gray hair in a crew cut. Some kind of chemist by trade, but he could not get flying out of his blood. Max was not a great lover of the Piper Cub, mostly because he was just too tall. It was both hard and awkward for Max to get into its front seat, once there, it was very uncomfortable, and it was almost painful for him to exit. For him, a cross-country flight in a Piper J–3 Cub was not something he enjoyed.

Dick Thomason, another Flight Instructor was also hired early. He was a native of, or recently came from Grand Junction, Colorado. Rather tall and a little on the lean side, he never seemed to be in a hurry for anything. Very quiet, unless he saw something that was not quite right. Earlier, he had spent some time as a charter pilot, and I guess he had seen more than a few people who were a little nervous about flying. Occasionally, with some added humor, he would pass on a few of his experiences about the fears that some people have in airplanes. More than once, it had occurred to me that he would make a great stand up comedian talking about the humor of our profession.

Mel Rozema, a native of Bennion, a suburb of Salt Lake City, hired on towards the end of the first group. Mel and I were both high school teenagers and we both had the same job title. We both loved to fly and we were both taking lessons as soon as our work schedule permitted. Probably a tad younger than I, he looked a tad younger than his age. During his early flight training, humorous stories (and they were probably a bit exaggerated), were circulated among the airport staff concerning some of his experiences. It seemed, as the stories go, that whenever he landed at a strange airport, because of his youthful looks, a platoon of authorities would rush out demanding documented proof of his age and experience. I'm sure that he was more than just a little tired of people telling him he looked too young to be flying. For some reason, its still very easy for me to picture him walking out to the flight line with his bundle of maps, manuals and plotter in hand.

Smitty Dent, also a flight instructor, hired on a little later. I'm not sure, but I believe he was from Bountiful, a little community north of Salt Lake City. To me, he was a cross between a college kid and a young businessman. Smitty was a serious individual; very professional, well educated, likable and well dressed. He was also a very good pilot.

Chad Jenkins was from Hunter, just a few miles southwest of Utah Central. He had worked at the airport for several years, and I guess with that he was often referred to as an old hand. Chad served his aircraft apprenticeship with Vern Dedman, who had a maintenance shop on the northwest corner of the airport. Vern also taught Chad how to fly in Vern's old Interstate Cadet. Chad and Vern were both true-blue Cadet fans.

Was Chad mechanically minded? Well, sort of. He ate, slept, dreamed and lived mechanics. Aside from his airport duties, he was always tearing down, fixing or rebuilding cars and car engines. The old Ford Flat Head V–8 was the most available engine back then and I guess Chad could probably tell its designers a thing or two about its workings.

Chad owned a 1952 Mercury two-door hardtop. Everything about it represented the "spirit of the fifties." To give it that extra sleek look, everything hanging on the body was removed, and the scars were covered over or "leaded in" as Chad called it. No door handles, no trunk lid emblem, no keyholes. Everything on the car was smooth, nothing to mar its sleek looks.

To enter, you had to leave a window ajar to access the inside door handle. To access the trunk, there was a cable with a handle located near the driver's seat that you pulled to pop open the trunk lid. The removable headlight rims were also leaded in smooth. To replace the headlight, one had to go in the wheel-well to remove and replace the headlamp from the rear. The car's rear end was lowered (much lowered) via means of "shackles" mounted on the rear springs.

With the rear end lowered as it was, it had a sleek, fast, and ready-to-take-off look. The car was finished off in a beautiful metallic blue. You really had to see it to believe it. Teens were doing everything they could think of with their cars back then. In the mid-fifties, there was a special bond between teenagers and their cars that you rarely see today.

To break the boredom of the lunch hour, Chad would often work on cars and engines. During one lunch hour, I saw him put a LaSalle engine into a '39 Ford, never saw such a tight fit in my life. Jokingly I told him that I could probably throw a bucket of water on the top of the engine and not a drop of it would ever find its way to the ground. There is more truth to that than smiles.

Chad, along with several of our part-time mechanics were also involved with Model A hot rods. You could buy an over-the-hill Ford Model A Coupe for thirty or forty bucks. The old engine would be yanked out and replaced with a bigger more powerful engine, usually a Ford Flat Head. With the new engine, the Model A would really go. After dark, with the airport close, (we had no lights for after dark operations) there would be races up and down the East-West Runway. They were exciting, fun, and often quite humorous.

Kay Andersen, I'm not sure when he was hired, but it must have been before Roy took over Utah Central. He initially worked out of Roy's Logan airport but would occasionally spend some time at our field. After things settled down at Logan, Kay spent time at our field on a semi-permanent bases. His first day at our field is a story in itself. Kay was a transplant from Mesa, Arizona.

That was Valley Airmotive's beginning crew at Utah Central. There were other people who would come later, some for a time and others who were just passing through.

A Cut Above

Like many parts of the country, the Salt Lake Valley has a mosquito problem. There are literally hundreds of acres of stagnant water along the shores of area lakes and rivers where mosquitoes thrive. To keep this pending problem in check, the counties had Mosquito Abatement Districts set up. It was their responsibility to control the mosquito population (everyone agrees that elimination was out of the question). During the mosquito season, these districts would hire out spray planes and pilots from operators like Valley Airmotive. For those who could handle the spraying, it was a moneymaking opportunity.

Both Glen and Roy could see the advantages of being involved in the program. As soon as Utah Central was operational, Glen started scanning Trade-a-Plane (A Classified Paper listing aircraft and parts) and making numerous telephone calls trying to locate a suitable spray plane.

He found a Piper PA–18 Super Cub in Bismarck, North Dakota. The airframe and engine information looked good, and it was set up with the type of spraying equipment Glen was looking for. After a little dickering, the aircraft seller declared that, if after inspection, Glen still wanted the aircraft, it was his at the agreed upon price of $3,500.00. Next day Glen was in Bismarck to sign papers and take delivery.

The seller had removed the spray booms and had them wired to the port side of the fuselage for the flight to Salt Lake. Other than that, the aircraft was rigged and ready for spraying. Satisfied, Glen accepted the aircraft and the sale was final.

Glen made a couple of wide trips around the pattern, making sure there were no problems with the aircraft. Once satisfied, he pointed the nose in the direction of Utah. He made a fuel stop at Casper, and then a little detour over to Lander, where he spent the night with relatives. Early the next morning Glen was again in the sky and headed for Utah Central.

A preliminary contract with the Davis County Mosquito Abatement District was already agreed upon and signatures were just waiting for the purchase of a spray aircraft.

With a spray plane on line, the contract was signed. After that, Glen spent a good part of his time out spraying. Almost as soon as the spraying started, Glen and Roy were looking for a second spray plane and pilot.

Shortly, a second spray plane was located up near Ketchum, Idaho. It was also a Piper PA–18 Super Cub. Unlike Glen's spray plane, the second one would be leased. Things were a little busy at the time so Glen hired a pilot to ferry it back.

When the pilot arrived at the Idaho airport early in the afternoon, he expected to give the Piper a pre-flight and fly away. Like many schedules it was something shot at but not quite hit. He spent a good part of the afternoon sitting around the office reading magazines. Then with the Piper still not ready, he tried to read them all again.

It was early evening when Glen called the airport staff together and told us about the incoming spray plane. The aircraft was not equipped with a radio and its scheduled arrival was shortly after dark. A little concerned with Utah Central not having runway lights, Glen wanted to take precautions to ensure its safe arrival.

At sundown, we were to assemble our cars just southwest of the office building. If the pilot needed runway lights, our cars would provide them. Glen also gave us some guidelines as to where he wanted the cars parked.

He smiled; and with a little humor, mentioned a past experience concerning car headlights being used as runway lighting. It seems that one of the cars had parked at the end of the runway, in line with the aircraft's landing path. It was a very efficient location with the headlights pointed right down the middle of the runway. Trouble was, the pilot approaching from the car's backside, was unable to see the car clearly, and the airplane's tires creased the top of the car as it settled down towards the strip. Luckily, the aircraft landed safely, but it could have been a major disaster. He emphasized parking off to the side of the runway, with the headlights shining down the strip at a thirty to forty-five degree angle.

Just after sundown, as instructed, we all headed for the assembly area. With everyone out of the cars we talked and joked while scanning the sky. There was not a lot of small aircraft flying around so we could pretty much assume that about any small aircraft would be the one we were waiting for.

With twilight fading into darkness and no sign of our aircraft, we headed out to our assigned parking places along Runway 16. Half of the cars headed for the east side of the runway and the other half headed for the west side. Each car was parked in a somewhat staggered position from the car on the opposite side. With our cars in position, a few individuals climbed out and stood around while others just leaned back and relaxed.

Shortly, we saw what we assumed was the Super Cub's lights off in the distance. We followed them for a time to verify that the aircraft was headed in our direction, and then we turned our headlights on.

With its landing light on the Super Cub buzzed the runway once, probably for the pilot to verify his location. He then climbed into a normal pattern.

The Piper drifted over the highway in a perfect glide path, passed over the end of the runway and made a beautiful three-point landing. It continued its roll beyond the reach of our lights and out into the darkness. He then taxied over to the taxi strip and headed towards the ramp.

Our job complete, we headed for the parking area, parked our cars and then wandered out to the ramp to greet the pilot and check out our new spray plane.

Both spray planes were Piper PA–18 Super Cubs. The Super Cubs were very similar to our J–3 trainers, except for heavier construction and the cowling around a bigger engine. Unlike the J–3's nose tank, the Super Cub's fuel tanks were located in the wings, which shifted the weight around enough to force (some people would say "allow") the pilot to fly from the front seat. The PA–18s were also equipped with some nice big wing flaps. Glen's aircraft had a radio and one would shortly be installed in the second aircraft.

The spray equipment on both aircraft was similar with the exception of the spray holding tanks. Each tank had a different design and each was mounted in different locations. Glen's holding tank filled in the spot vacated by the rear seat. The second spray plane had a somewhat streamlined tank mounted on the bottom of the fuselage, just below the cabin area.

The spray distribution systems were identical on both aircraft. Five or six spray nozzles were located on a pipe or boom, mounted and hung from the main wing strut of each wing. A single wind driven insecticide pump was mounted on each aircraft, near the root of the left landing gear strut. If I remember right, the capacity of each holding tank was about thirty gallons, and it took about forty-five minutes to drop a load.

Glen hired a new pilot to fly the second spray plane, a very experienced woman. Her name was Norma; but for the life of me, I cannot recall her last name, or even where she came from. Kansas or the Dakotas comes to mind, but I'm not sure.

When she was in her teens, she, like most young people needed a job for a little extra spending money. The only thing available in her small town was a newspaper route, which suited her fine. Being out in some wide-open farm and ranch country, the distance between houses was often measured in miles, which made bike riding and hand delivery out of the question. Understandably, she decided it would be more to her liking to deliver her papers in a somewhat unconventional method, by airplane. Somewhere along the line, she, at a very early age had gotten her pilot's license and had access to a Cessna 120.

The paper was not a daily news type but more of a weekly newspaper. With the distances involved, the air deliveries worked out better than any one would have guessed. It even made the farmers and ranchers feel a little special knowing they were getting their personal copy delivered by airplane. Besides, Norma was in love with airplanes and flying. So it was a win/win situation for everyone involved. Later, she jokingly told me that she would have delivered the papers for nothing if she could do it with her airplane.

Like most things, often referred to as being simple, there was a learning curve. However, she was young, a natural pilot and had the desire. First thing she did was to establish safety rules and flying procedures. There were all kinds of variables, the surface winds, the speeds of the aircraft and obstructions.

At times, because of the location of trees or buildings she had some rather odd approaches or departures. Each drop was approached with caution and more than a little planning. Still no matter how much planning went into the delivery, her papers, would on occasion end up "on the top of the house or up in some tree." If she caught the error she would make a second, more precise approach, making adjustments as required. Most times, the second copy would land in a more accessible location. However, if the paper landed in some tree and she didn't see it, "Well there are probably some people out there still trying to figure out how to get their paper down," she stated with a grin.

Both of our spray aircraft were based at Utah Central but they rarely made spray runs from our field. Each morning, sometimes together, sometimes separately, they would fly to a predetermined site near where the day's spraying would be conducted. The sites, often referred to as "loading sites," were simply handy fields, big enough for aircraft operation. Preferably clear of large rocks, mud, weeds and brush. Interestingly, on one occasion Glen made a statement concerning their so-called "loading sites." "Some sites fell a little short of the published guidelines," he stated with a smile.

At the loading site, Davis County had a crew, along with a supply of the spray solution and the equipment needed to load it aboard the aircraft. After dropping a load, the aircraft would return to the site for more spray solution. The cycle would repeat itself many times over.

On one of their assignments, the two sprays planes were to spray an area near Farmington Bay. The bay itself was crossed with a series of man-made dikes. Each dyke had a narrow access road built along its top. Without any handy landing sites, it was decided to use the dyke roads for landing and take-off strips. By any standards, the dike roads were not runways of choice. Understandably, the dikes' one-lane dirt roads were a little on the narrow side and in most cases had very little maintenance. On each side of the road, there was a very narrow shoulder. With little more width than the road, the dikes abruptly dropped off to the water, three feet or so below. I guess a person can get used to about anything and after several landing and take offs, both Glen and Norma felt somewhat comfortable operating from the dikes.

On one particular run, I don't know if it was during a take-off or landing, but one of Norma's spray booms caught some brush on the dike. It didn't cause an accident or even do any damage, but it scared the daylights out of her. The boom is nothing more than a pipe hanging from the main wing strut. With the supports somewhat limited, you could grab the outer end and flip it, much like the brush did, and it would cause a lot of racket and vibrations as it whipped and twanged back and forth. Between the loud twanging and the narrow road they were flying from, it just about did Norma in. She never did feel comfortable spraying after that. Glen took her out of the spray plane, but kept her on as a flight instructor and charter pilot.

Late one afternoon, I was in the process of fueling aircraft. At the time, there were four or five aircraft parked around the hard stand waiting for my attention. As I topped one off, it got pushed to the rear a few feet, and then another one was pushed up for its fuel. When things were busy, as they were at that time, it was normal for me to refuel all the aircraft around the gas pit and then I would push each over to its tie down spot.

A young man, a few years older than I had been standing over near the fuel pump house watching the activities. After a few moments, he wandered over and asked if he could give me a hand. He was built like a football player, probably in his early-to-mid twenties. I had never seen him before and his offer surprised me a little. To be honest, I was a little behind schedule, maybe even feeling some pressure, but in fact there was little anyone could do to help me catch up. But not sure what was going on, I gave him the benefit of a doubt and invited him over.

Together we positioned ourselves on the tail of a Cub and pushed it clear of the pit. With that done, we then moved the next aircraft up into its place. As we worked to clear the congestion, we got into a conversation and it didn't take long to see that he was quite a likeable guy.

As our conversation progressed, he brought up the fact that he had just been hired and was actually a fellow employee. He was a flight instructor who had learned to fly over at Kemp and Kelsey's. He expressed hopes that there were plenty of students around so he could build up his flight time. There was also the possibility that he might be assigned a spray plane if things worked out. Apparently, or at least maybe, he was the new pilot who would take over Norma's spray plane. His name was Sam Buttars, and he was raised up north in Trenton, Utah.

Even though the planes were spraying mosquito larva, there were often thick clouds of adult mosquitoes in the area. Every time the sprayers flew through one of these swarms, often many times during a working day, the aircraft became a collecting surface for mosquitoes without numbers. Every leading edge from front to back, and from wing tip to wing tip was covered with mosquitoes. They appeared similar to a build-up of ice, dark, black ice on the frontal areas of the aircraft. Often the layer was nearly an eighth of an inch thick and often the windshield took on its own little furry texture.

The initial and casual instructions from Glen were, "Ron, the spray planes are a mess. Could you get 'em cleaned up a bit?" A mess they were, and what to do to get them cleaned up to even a near normal appearance made my head spin. I honestly didn't know if I was to use a putty knife, a broom or simply take them out behind the hangar and repaint the aircraft with mosquitoes in place.

Water was the answer. I pushed one of the aircraft over to the wash rack and hosed it down a section at a time. That helped, and I could see that I was headed in the right direction. I worked out a system of hosing the mosquitoes down, waiting a soaking period, and then, before everything had dried out, I hosed the aircraft down again. Next, with a bucket of soapy water, a rough sponge and lots of scrubbing, I would have my nice looking airplane back. The process worked well, but the stink of countless mosquitoes soaking, well let's just say the clean-up best not be done just before dinner.

The engine compartment was another problem. Engine cooling air brought mosquitoes in by the hordes, some went on through and out the discharge opening, most it seems were flattened against the cooling fins and baffle plates. Moreover, as long as there was heat in the engine compartment, the mosquitoes were cooking. The "out-of-sight, out-of-mind" factor didn't apply because of the ever-present aroma. Several times, I removed the cowling and really cleaned everything up the best I could, but it was hard, dirty and without any long-term benefits. The engine compartment cleaning gradually evolved into something a bit more superficial.

During the spraying, flying ducks were occasionally hit. Usually causing very little damage to the aircraft. However, if a duck hits the leading edge of a Piper's aircraft's wing, it can cause a dent, sometimes a rather pronounced dent. The Super Cub's wing had a light aluminum skin wrapped around its leading edge, just under the fabric. One of the main benefits of the skin is to minimize damage caused from bird impacts and the likes. But, I have a feeling the Piper engineers were thinking mostly of stuff like mosquitoes and humming birds. A duck, being somewhat larger, could and sometimes did make a noticeable dent. To give some credit to the designer, none of the duck impacts compromised the safety of our aircraft.

As far as the pilot's safety, I guess you could say that the propeller protected the windshield and ultimately the pilot from the full impact of a flying object the size of a duck. That is not always the case though. While spraying the wetlands west of Bountiful, Glen did have an experience with one unlucky duck. He was right on the deck making a run when the duck winged into his path. Glen could see that it was headed right for him, but his subconscious reflexes had only enough time to flinch and tilt his head a couple of inches.

The duck somehow made it through the propeller arc and continued on towards the windshield. It hit high and a tad to the left, with a loud pop that was near the loudness of an explosion. Immediately, duck and shattered plexiglas were flying everywhere inside the cabin. The hapless bird hit the left side of Glen's helmet. It was a glancing blow, and other then putting some temporary stars into Glen's vision it had little effect. After the bird bounced off Glen, its twisted body then continued back into the cabin, banging into the spray-holding tank and then with another loud thud it wedged itself into the space between the top of the tank and the cabin's headliner. Glen was experienced enough to shrug off all the distractions and hold course through the noise, flying glass and duck.

About forty percent of the windshield was gone and immediately there was a loss of control. The elevator was extremely touchy and unpredictable. Apparently, the hole in the windshield was causing a disruption of airflow over the elevators and rudder, rendering them somewhat ineffective. After fighting for control with the sick, rudder and throttle, Glen found that his most effective, though limited control was a combination of throttle and ailerons. He gave the engine a little power and managed to climb to about a hundred feet. He then began thinking about getting the Piper back on the ground, in one piece. The nearest place to land, with people who could help, was the loading site. He jockeyed the Super Cub around in a direction towards the Mosquito Abatement crew.

Lining up on the make-shift strip, Glen fought his way through a precarious approach. When the little clearing drifted into a suitable position, he eased back on the power and jockeyed the Super Cub down to a somewhat awkward landing.

Glen shut the engine down, took a deep breath and tried to relax. It was then that he noticed how weak and shaky his arms and legs were. He gingerly climbed out of his Piper, walked around to the front of his aircraft and studied the damage.

One by one, members of the ground crew appeared and soon everyone was standing at Glen's side staring at the shattered windshield. No one could believe what they were looking at; nothing that serious had ever happened before. By any standard, Glen had to be either very lucky or a very good pilot, or a lot of both.

They had no way of making permanent repairs at the loading site. The ground crew found some tape in one of the trucks. Then, using the larger pieces of broken plexiglas and some cardboard they plug up the hole in the damaged windshield. It was temporary at best and a little more than humorous. One of the workers stated with a grin that the Piper looked "like one of them old-time movie pirates with a patch over one eye."

A little blind to the left with his patched-up windshield, Glen bounced down the dusty strip and into the sky. Once airborne, good control was confirmed and Glen felt confident that the patch job would hold. He eased the Cub around and took up a heading towards Utah Central.

I hope the reader can appreciate the drama in Glen's story. I talked to him several times to get it in its fullness. Not being a big thing to him, the experience didn't seem worth talking about. His answers were never in paragraphs but rather in short sentences, phrases or simply a word here or there. Every statement was without emotion, to the point, concise, and very business-like, nothing beyond the question asked, "No that wasn't a problem.

"… No nothing like that.

"…The duck went through the windshield, hit my helmet and ended up in back.

"…The elevators didn't work like they should, so I had to use throttle and ailerons for control." The most complete and dramatic sentence he gave me was, "When the stick was moved, you just didn't know what was going to happen."

I loved the Super Cub sprayers and at times felt a little sadness in the type of work they were doing. Who in their right mind would take a good looking Piper through dark clouds of swarming insects, building up insect scum on engine cooling fins, plugging carburetor air filters and defacing paint and plexiglas? Yet with all the image problems the spray aircraft were confronted with there was another side. After cleaning them up at day's end, I would on occasion, stand back and study them in their silence. You couldn't look at them through the same eyes as you would other aircraft. They were different. Like a worker with the tools of his trade hanging from their belt, the spray planes did command a certain amount of attention. One could almost sense they were a cut above by the way they stood out in a crowd. Somehow, they were special.

Spray pilots, they too are a different breed. They fly by different rules. They work at altitudes where only the very best trod. Flying on the very edge of all the established physics that give aircraft the right of flight they faithfully do their job. Aircraft do not fly well in hot weather, unlike cold air that is thick and heavy; the hot summer air of the mosquito season is thin and light. Propellers lose their efficiency, wings loose some of their lift, balking at carrying even normal loads, and engines that are fed a near-starvation diet of thin hot air just can't deliver their full rated horsepower.

Working in a hostile environment, loaded to the max, the spray pilots fly their aircraft at the very bottom of their world, measured almost in inches off the ground. Spray pilots and their aircraft do command a certain amount of awe and respect.

On one occasion, Glen and Sam were flying back to Utah Central after a day's spraying when Glen noticed Sam's aircraft behaving erratically, kind of bouncing back and forth. Glen jumped on the radio and asked Sam what the problem was.

Sam replied in an upbeat voice "Hey there's a neat song on the radio." Sam was flying to the beat of some teen-age music on one of the area's popular radio stations. Glen was a little older than Sam and didn't get into that stuff quite as much.

So on they flew, the gray airplane with the fatherly figure flying solid and straight as an arrow, almost trying to distance himself from the young kid in the brown and yellow Piper, whose airplane was flopping around in the sky in ways that only young people could understand.

Occasionally, during my duties, I got to taxi them around some, which to me was a little special. I was hoping that someday I would get to fly one or both of them, but the opportunity was never in the cards.

One scene that brings back the best of the atmosphere and memories of Utah Central's activities was that of Glen and Sam sitting in their randomly-parked spray aircraft getting ready for an early morning run. Engines just kind of lopping at idle with the cowering grass bent over in the prop wash. There was the ever-present, but faint smell of burned aviation fuel drifting around their aircraft. An early morning breeze playing with shirtsleeves, cooling and even chilling bodies. Squawking seagulls in loose formations headed out to whom knows where. Soft colors, selected by someone who knows best about those things displayed in a delicate summer sunrises. Wings covered with morning dew, reflecting the full sky, giving each aircraft an almost exalted glow.

Glen and Sam sitting in their aircraft watching instruments and making final adjustments to belts and helmets; Chad standing silently under a wing--one arm resting on a main strut, a soiled rag hanging from one of his pockets, a wrench from the other, listening, studying each aircraft for something amiss. It was a scene so typical, so common; pilots, mechanics and aircraft--each a small part of something that, together, made a lasting impression.

Tall Wings

A few weeks after starting, I checked in at the office early one afternoon. Spread around the room were six young men, all decked out in dusty flying boots, faded Levis and an array of expensive leather flight jackets. Two had laid claim to the lunch counter; one of them had his hair draped over a partially empty coffee cup. Another had found a lounge chair to his liking; one was sitting on the floor slouched awkwardly against the wall. The others were sprawled on the floor. None looked comfortable, but apparently each had found some contentment in their positions. My entrance apparently had not caused the slightest distraction to their sleeping forms. I stood at the door a few seconds, studying their limp bodies while wondering who they were.

Then I noticed Glen over behind the counter and walked over in his direction. Once at his side, he quietly explained that the individuals were "Ag Pilots." Pilots, who with their aircraft followed the growing season around the country, dusting crops. Apparently, with their work done in one location they were in transit to "greener pastures." Maybe, with it being fall, they were done spraying for the season; Glen had not bothered to ask. Their six airplanes were sitting out by the gas pump; three had been refueled, three still needed fuel.

As I turned and headed for the door Glen added, "Take your time, these guys need a little shut eye."

My approach to their aircraft was a memorable experience to say the least. There were six big fabric bi-wing aircraft scattered around the gas pit. Boeing PT–17 Stearman Kaydets, leftover trainers from the Second World War. Just walking through their shadows put one in a different time and place.

It was obvious that none of the aircraft were for show. All were what I would call workhorses and they looked like they had been out in the field for some time. I had no doubt that they were well taken care of, mechanically at least. Their physical appearance-- well that was something else. Someone had spilled a fair amount of oil on one of the boot cowls; handprints and rag smears seemed to indicate a halfhearted attempt to minimize the mess. Multiple handprints in smeared dust and oil were signs of maintenance activity on most of the aircraft. Each had more than its fair share of exhaust stains, dust and patterns of dried mud caked along their fuselages, wings and tails. Obviously, like our spray planes, their strips of operations were fields, country roads and cow pastures.

Modified for dusting, the front cockpits had huge hoppers built into the area once reserved for the flight instructor. An aluminum sheet covered the hopper and streamlined the fuselage. The covering gave the aircraft a long sleek look with the single rear cockpit opening appearing to be much further back than necessary. Big dust discharge funnels hung on the bottom of the fuselage just below the hopper.

Apparently, at the beginning of the season, the six aircraft were painted in a dark navy blue. They must have been a very handsome and impressing group in one uniform color. But that was then, the aircraft I was then looking at had seen some hard use. One sprayer had a different colored rudder, yellow; two had odd colored ailerons, one was a bright red and the other silver. The hopper cover on one was painted with a mismatched blue. There were more than a few off-colored fabric patches on the aircraft in various locations. Judging from the location of most of the patches, the damage had probably been caused by brush. I've heard that the Stearmans were a tough breed. Maybe the crews felt any field was adequate, regardless of conditions.

Then there were the engines; they were huge, different from anything I had ever seen on any Stearman. The first thing that got my attention was the massive circular wall of jugs, big, impressive all covered with cooling fins. Then there was the huge exhaust collecting system leading to a gigantic discharge pipe. A mammoth two-blade propeller, looking to be plated in chrome, hung on the front of each aircraft. In a word, everything related to the power plant was "bigger," much bigger. Each engine stood out in front like some kind of muscle ad, proud and boasting, looking almost proportionally too big, overly developed for the somewhat antique airplane they were mounted on. No one walked by one of those power plants without being impressed-guaranteed!

The fuel tank was located in the center section of the top wing. There were several built-in steps and handholds that led up to a little strip of non-slip surface placed on the top of the fuselage, just behind the engine.

I had never refueled a Stearman before and taking note of where all the steps and handholds were located was kind of fun. And climbing up with the hose, I felt akin to a firefighter climbing a ladder. Once standing in position, I was about ten, twelve feet in the air, a unique experience for a gas boy at Utah Central. Never had I been able to look down on any airplane quite like I was looking down on Stearmans that day.

After topping off the three aircraft and checking their oil, I got looking at the windshields. It was customary to clean the windshields after an aircraft had been refueled. And those windshields needed cleaning. I used to think our Piper sprayers had some dirty windshields but compared to those Stearmans; the word dirty was almost a sanitizing statement. One of the windshields looked as if the pilot had made an effort to clear some of the dirt off, but what a job. He must have spit on the glass and then smeared it around with the elbow of his jacket. I chuckled and jokingly wondered if the pilots had to stand up in their seats to see where they were going. Maybe they were all religious and used revelation for guidance.

I collected a handful of clean rags and the windshield cleaner from the pump house. As I was cleaning up the windshields, I got looking into the cockpit and couldn't help but notice the thick layer of dust covering everything. I thought it might be fun just to clean up the insides a little. Everything I could reach I cleaned, even some of the structural tubing.

After I had done all that I could do, I grabbed the tally sheet and headed for the office. Once inside I gave the clipboard to Glen.

With my appearance, the pilots somehow sensed that their rest time had come to an end. They rolled around, yawning and stretching, sometimes displaying signs of not being too steady. I wondered if any of them could even remember the feel of a real bed.

Debts settled, the pilots wandered out to their aircraft in a somewhat staggered group. As they approached their airplanes, one commented on the clean windshields. I appreciated the comment; many times your work goes unnoticed.

The aircraft had been parked in a manner that best accommodated refueling. The pilots ganged up on each individual aircraft, pushed it away from the pit and into a position where it was clear to taxi. Each pilot then wandered around his aircraft doing its preflight, a few made stops at their baggage compartments to stow or retrieve items. As each pilot finished his preflight, he crawled up into his cockpit.

There were the sounds of cockpit activity, control sticks being shoved off to one side, movement sounds as each pilot tried to find sitting positions that agreed with their bodies, straps slapping the cockpit's interior, and the clicking of belts being snapped in position. Flight helmets were donned and somewhat forced into position with two hands, then straps securely buckled.

A few casual words were exchanged, a personal dig here, a smart remark there and some one-liners that I thought were pretty clever, but others in the group never so much as acknowledged the words spoken. Joking aside, heads then bowed and focused on interior gauges, controls and switches. One or two final bodily adjustments, a quick look around to verify aircraft was clear of obstacles and all pilots were ready. Someone yelled, "Clear" and the others followed suit, then one or two more seconds of silence.

The starter on one of the big Pratt and Whitney's engines engaged and filled the air with its high-pitched whine, then another and then more. Mighty two-blade propellers turned with great effort and then caught and spun into a haze, engines coughed, caught, missed, caught again and kind of loped along in a rough, almost unsteady rhythm. Huge exhaust stacks twisted and belched deep hollow unearthly sounds. Engines shook and twisted on their mounts. Blue smoke drifted freely at every quarter, twisting and turning, some being drawn into huge propeller arcs and swept away into obscurity. Each pilot sat with little movement, seemly unaware of all the man-made thunder. Their heads hung low while watching instrument needles gain life and slowly move into their proper positions. Big engines doing little more than resting but presenting themselves as something best stayed clear of, if not feared.

Through the struts and flying wires of one of the aircraft, I could see one of the pilots wave me over. I cautiously walked over into the propeller blast and smell of exhaust smoke. I stopped and stood braced with legs spread at the side of the fuselage, pants, shirt and hair whipping, fluttering and streaming in the stiff wind. He handed me a fifty-cent piece and yelled a "Thank you" that was hardly discernible in all the wind and noise. I hesitated, but he said it was OK and shoved the coin further in my direction. Then smiling, he stated that he really appreciated my services. I took the coin, stepped back beyond his wing tip and once again took my place as a spectator.

Pilots' heads lifted, turned and observed their wingspread. Throttles eased forward, propellers raced faster. The barbaric rough sounds disappeared and the mighty engines roared into a smooth, yet solid chorus of thunder, power and authority. Grass, dust, dirt and gravel lifted and became clutter in a man-made windstorm. I stumbled back a step, half-frightened, half-wondering if the mammoth engines would self-destruct in a white cloud, taking with it all forms of life within a thousand feet. How could mere steel, bolts and nuts possibly contain that mass of energy? Their thunder dominated all that was, everywhere, through every cell of the body they manifested their power. The very earth shuddered, even trembled as throttles moved their power up to greater levels. Big aircraft tires began to turn, depressing new ground as they eased forward. Their journey was beginning.

I had never really understood until that moment, the thrill men experience watching and being around big powerful aircraft engines. How could steel and fire have such a dominating effect on humans? As I stood there listening, watching and feeling, the effects would be impossible to overstate.

Proud, tall, almost-boastful, they passed by. I wondered if they sensed my envy and were actually flaunting, making the most of all they were.

I watched them taxi away, turning tails towards me, moving out in a staggered line, doing their "S" clearing turns. Together, they took form, like a huge prehistoric serpent, weaving side to side, moving across the earth, unchallenged.

Nearing Runway 16's run-up area, they each swung wide and drifted into position for their final check. Wheels locked, controls moved, engines roared creating dust storms beneath their tails that covered 2100 South. Then one by one throttles were cut back to idle and they sat in silence a few seconds.

Aircraft engines again roared, creating more turmoil as the aircraft moved out towards the runway. Still on the roll, the aircraft spread out into their final take-off positions.

They moved forward into progressively higher speeds. Then slowly the fleet of Stearmans lifted from the surface of the earth, almost as a unit. Like mystical gods of thunder they climbed into the heavens and heading south to some unknown destination beyond the horizon. Recognizable forms became moving dots against the sky. Noise, the hallmark of their power and authority steadily waning but continued its echo across the sky; deceptively, it never seemed to come from the diminishing specks, but from the full expanse of the heavens. Then the Stearmans were gone, hidden in the distance. Man, did I feel left behind.

I turned and headed for the office in the much-noticed stillness. In my hand I still clenched the fifty-cent tip. The presence of the coin gave me mixed feelings. Extra money was always welcomed, but I had been paid extra for doing something I really enjoyed. Any time of the day or week, I'd gladly give him that much and more if he would let me climb on his Stearman.

Beginner's Luck

Glen called me over one day and introduced me to our newest flight instructor, Kay Andersen. I had heard his name and had even seen him around a couple of times, but there had never been any official introductions. Apparently he was one of the first hired by Roy, but had been busy up north. Kay had also been working behind the scenes helping Glen get our Salt Lake operation set up. With most of that work completed, Kay was being reassigned to help out on our flight line.

He had a stocky, if not muscular frame, was rather dark complexioned and had a full head of thick curly black hair. Friendly and very quiet, he rarely spoke unless he was asked a question or if there was a problem.

The three of us stood there while Glen spent a few moments explaining the student flight program to Kay. True to unwritten policy, Kay was also informed that if he needed any help with whatever, anytime, day or night, "we'll be there to help." Then looking over at me, he added with a grin, "Won't you, Ron?"

Kay was a former Naval Aviator who had at one time flown Grumman Wildcats and was also part of the Naval Reserve squadron over at the Salt Lake Airport. So as far as experience, he had been around. As far as Piper Cub flying time, maybe it had all been in the past. I really hadn't heard.

At any rate, Glen suggested that he take a short familiarization flight in one of our Cubs. It was also suggested that Kay get the feel of the instructor's seat, which was the front. Glen looked at me and stated with a smile that I would fill in as "ballast." The Cub was designed in such a way that there was a weight and balance problem with only one person up front. I guess you could call me dead weight or simply a warm body. But I didn't have a problem with that; any reason for going up was a good reason.

I untied the tan J–3 while Kay looked it over. Once the ropes were off, I took my place in the rear seat. Kay finished with the preflight and wandered over to the front of the Cub.

Shortly the engine was up and running. He stood there for a second and then headed for the cabin, climbed in and buckled up.

Kay put the Cub through every basic maneuver that I knew and a couple that were beyond anything that I had ever seen before. I tried to follow what he was doing with my eyes dancing back and forth between the stick, the controls and the horizon. I guess when you're fairly new at flying; just about everything is a major learning experience.

I was really enjoying the flight when right in the middle of a maneuver he abruptly broke off, put the Piper into a steep dive and headed back towards the airport. I was a little surprised as we had only been up for about twenty minutes, and he seemed to be in too much of a hurry.

He completely ignored the normal landing pattern while rocking his wings back and forth looking for traffic. The Cub rolled sharply onto Final as soon as Kay could negotiate the turn. About then, I definitely knew something was wrong. But what? I leaned forward hoping for some indication of what was going on. A portion of the front floorboard caught my eye. It looked shiny and wet.

He made a hot wheels landing, rode the brakes heavily while fighting a light tail. Then turning off the runway, he raced through some grass, bounced over some lumpy ground, tore through some weeds, plowed into some soft dirt and came to an abrupt stop. During the last few feet of travel, he cut the mag switch and shut off the fuel supply.

The little Cub was still rocking back and forth when Kay yelled, "Get out"! I unsnapped my belt, hit the door handle, pushed the lower door, letting it bang into the side of the fuselage. Then swinging the window up I tried to hook it on the bottom of the wing. It banged into the hook but failed to catch. Dropping down, it walloped me a good one on my arm. Half holding the window up and grabbing the overhead structural members, I started swinging my feet out the door. Everything seemed tangled up and in the wrong place--my legs, my feet, the stick, the front seat, even the cabin's side-walls. I was banging, pulling, bending and bouncing off everything trying to clear my extremities.

Somehow, I got my feet on the outside of the cabin. Then I found my legs swinging around in space looking for some kind of contact, a strut, a step; anything that would aid in my decent to the ground. Frustrated, I finally pushed clear, half sliding and half dropping down to the ground. Then with the window banging and dragging against my upper body, I backed away from the Cub, turned and broke into a run.

Behind me I could hear Kay doing his share of bumping and banging as he maneuvered for a hurried exit. With all the commotion I glanced back, almost wondering if he was going to make it. I could see that his right foot was hung up on the front edge of the door opening. With more than a little effort, he jerked it clear and headed for the ground, not entirely feet first. Somehow, he halfway caught himself before he made a full prone landing. Then stumbling and running, almost on his hands and feet, he fought his way to an upright position. Regaining his balance, he broke into a run just a few steps behind me. We ran a short distance then Kay stopped, turned around and looked back.

Sensing that he had stopped, I followed suit. I turned and then cautiously took a step or two back to his side. We stood in silence studying the aban-doned Cub sitting in middle of a drifting cloud of dust. Kay was looking and probably seeing something and I was looking but not seeing anything.

Then I caught sight of a few drops of sparkling liquid dripping along the bottom of the fuselage, gas! That's why the front floorboards looked wet! Somehow, somewhere, we had developed a fair size leak near the fuel tank while doing maneuvers. You'd think with that much fuel on the front floor-boards I could have smelled it, but the J–3 had a fair amount of air moving through the cabin.

The Cub's fuel tank was mounted in the upper fuselage, sandwiched be-tween the instrument panel and the firewall. The fuel line, with a shut off valve was mounted on the bottom of the tank. The line then ran forward, just above the legs of the front seat occupant, penetrating the firewall and then it runs out to the carburetor mounted on the bottom of the engine. Any fuel leaking aft of the firewall would end up on the floor of the Cub or even on the legs of the front seat occupant.

Kay stated, in his typical, never excited voice that he had been a little reluctant to tell me about the leak because he didn't know what my reaction would be. With the hot engine exhaust discharging just to the front and below the flammable liquid, there was probably reason for him to be concerned. It must have been a memorable first day for Kay.

Kay was somewhat of a wild card around Utah Central. We didn't see a lot of him as he was often out of the office on company business. Occasionally, even after his "permanent" assignment to Utah Central, he spent time at the Logan Cache Airport. Whenever we had charter work, Kay would probably be the pilot, if he were available. Wherever he was needed, that was where he was. In between, he was a flight instructor. During the early part of my training, he was my instructor on several occasions.

If I could somehow, and probably unfairly, classify most Utah Central flight instructors in one or two categories, I would put most under the heading of "adventurous" or maybe "determined." That is, they appeared to me as young men who would be willing to live out of a suitcase and bed down in almost any corner of any hangar while building up experience in the field they loved. Monetary accumulations could never be classified as their immediate goal. I do believe however, that each instructor could picture himself quite easily at some not-too-future date sitting in the very front left seat of a Boeing 707 with a big bulge in his wallet. Utah Central was a means to that end. While building up flight time and experience was a sacrifice, they still seemed to enjoy the ride.

To me Kay was just off to the side of that profile. I'm not even sure why I felt that way. He never talked much, so it was a little hard to put a handle on what he was really looking for. But doing what he was doing, one had to assume the airlines were somewhere on his horizons. With all that, it was somehow easier for me to picture Kay sitting in front of a fireplace, surrounded by family and reading the afternoon newspaper.

Days of the Week

One of my early off-line duties was runway maintenance. Runways, especially the dirt and gravel type require lots of upkeep. Aircraft traffic has a tendency to cut ruts, move gravel, laying bare some areas and loading up others.

The turns along the taxi strips and the touchdown areas of the runways were especially troublesome. Weeds could also be a problem.

Part of the airport's inventory was an old red, X-Army, three quarter ton Dodge truck that had been around for who knows how long. Someone had made a twelve-foot long by six-foot wide drag out of some heavy steel channels. As you pulled the drag up and down the runways, the gravel would be spread out nice and even and weed growth would be discouraged. Looking at the big picture, it worked pretty well. But pulling the drag did have its moments. One problem encountered while dragging was the gravel would occasionally build up at the front of the drag. If enough gravel piled up, the load often became more than the old Dodge could pull and everything would come to a grunting halt. The only way to get it moving again was to clear away some of the excess gravel with a shovel. It was not all that hard to do, but it sometimes took a little time.

Occasionally if the wind was just right, a thick cloud of dust would form and drift along at the same speed as the truck. With both the truck and the dust moving along together, there was a lot of coughing and an occasional cute word or two.

Mel Rozema had an interesting experience while dragging the runways early in his employment. He was working the East-West Runway on one particular hot and dry day. Aside from the heat, things were going pretty good. The truck was running smooth and there had not been any trouble with the drag. He was relaxed and even enjoying his carefree duties. Not paying a lot of attention to what was going on behind, he happily pulled the drag down the edge of the runway. After he had finished dragging the full length of the runway, he started his turn for a return pass. At that point, he happened to look back in the direction from which he had just come.

Panic shot through his body. Along the path where he had just passed were flickering flames, along with clouds of heavy gray smoke. It was the beginnings of a healthy grass fire. Obviously, sparks from the metal drag had set the dry grass stubble afire. Newly hired, young and wondering if the airport just might burn down with all fingers pointing at him, he got a little excited. Having a history of starting airport fires is not a good beginning in one's chosen career!

In a cloud of dust, he headed back towards the fires with the drag bouncing wildly behind. He skidded to a stop, grabbed a shovel and headed for the fire. Shovel after shovel of dirt and gravel was thrown at the flame. His effort was without effect, the flame continued to spread. He tried beating the flame with the backside of the shovel, that had little effect, so he frantically did a little of both. Lucky, other airport workers noticed the problem and in short time the full crew was at Mel's side throwing dirt and beating flames.

After a few moments, the fire was contained and then died a beaten death. When the fires were finally out, there were some tuckered out people standing around. Fighting grass fires is not an easy job!

My first and foremost responsibility was the line. Normally after every flight, our school aircraft were parked near the gas pit where I would service them. Once the aircraft were serviced, I would move (usually push) the aircraft to the parking area and tie them down.

Customers would also park their aircraft at the pit when they needed service. If I caught them as they pulled up, I'd get a rundown on what was needed. Sometimes they would just hop out and head for the office. If that were the case, I would wander over and get the information. After servicing the aircraft, I took the information over to the office where the staff took care of the billing. If an owner needed help moving his aircraft or if he needed a prop, I was usually there to assist him.

One of my duties was the pump house. Inside, on the left was the gas pump and on the right there were several shelves against the wall. Part of the shelving was stocked with cans of oil, both the detergent and non-detergent. On one shelf there was a small drainage pan covered with a screen.

The Continental engine air filters that were in use back then were the metal mesh type coated with a light film of oil. We always had three or four spare air filters on hand. After use, the dirty air filters were cleaned in solvent, air-dried and then taken to the pump house and placed on the drainage pan. There was always a little residue oil remaining in oilcans after the contents had been dumped into aircraft engines. We placed a drained oilcan, in the upside down position on top of the filter. After the residue oil had drained out and coated the air filter, the oilcan was removed and the filter was allowed to drain off all the excess oil. The filter was then placed aside ready for use.

We had a wash rack (an area near the hose bibb) where we could wash aircraft. During the wet and muddy seasons, this was an ongoing duty.

Exhaust stains, oil and dirt on the aircraft's undersides were also one of my responsibilities. Once I felt the need or at Glen's suggestion, I would grab a can of solvent, a couple of rags, crawl under an aircraft and clean away. I really didn't mind doing it, but for a teenager such as myself, it was something that was a little harder to stay on top of. With an aircraft sitting on the ground, the dirt on the underside didn't show up that much. I guess you could call it an out-of-sight, out-of-mind thing.

Near day's end, I would check with Glen to identify aircraft scheduled out early the next morning. During inclement weather, we kept the aircraft hangared whenever possible. If one was scheduled out early in the morning, be it one of our spray planes, one of the school's aircraft or a transit aircraft, I made sure it was parked in an accessible spot. I've heard of cases where an early morning pilot had to move six or seven aircraft before he could get to his. That was something we tried to stay away from.

I was also responsible for keeping the main hangar clean. The main door of the hangar faced the prevailing southern winds, and often the doors were open. With that, it could be said that I could sweep it out just about anytime I wanted. It was there that I got an appreciation of Bruce and the way he swung his aircraft around, keeping the prop blast clear of the hangar's interior.

It wasn't a common thing, but occasionally, some individual would pull up to an open hangar and point the aircrafts' tail towards the door opening with their engine revved up. At the very least, the blast of air could pretty much undo a clean hangar. I've never seen it happen, but I've heard that a good prop blast directed into an open hangar could move and even damage hangar-parked aircraft.

The office cleaning was mostly emptying garbage cans, sweeping, rest rooms and occasionally mopping the floor. During the wet season, with all the mud and foot traffic, the "occasional mopping" of the floor took on major proportions.

Chad was in charge of the maintenance department, and he was responsible for everything that came through the shop. We also had a part time mechanic by the name of Dorwain Wahlquist, or Wally, as we called him. He was by profession, a full-time line mechanic with Western Airlines. At Utah Central he worked at our side making sure the shop was on top of the work. He also signed off the logbooks.

One of my duties was to give Chad a hand whenever possible. And enjoying the shop work like I did, I was over in the hangar at every opportunity. Many times, I found myself involved with some interesting project and a customer would pull up to the gas pit. Reluctantly, I'd drop everything, and head out and attend to his needs. I could see why Chad was so anxious to see someone hired for the outside work. It must have been near impossible for him to run the shop while doing line duties.

I guess Sam could see that I had an interest in aircraft, so he talked to Glen and got me the official title of "Mechanic's Helper." With that title, it was official! I was no longer just a "Line Boy." I was officially part of the shop. My duties didn't change, nor did I get an increase in pay. Officially, I was shop first and line second, unofficially I was line first and shop second, same as before. However, with my new title, I felt a part of the shop. That was my place, and my line duties, well, they were part-time no matter how much time they took.

About the time of my "promotion," a poster appeared on the shop wall, near the entrance. Obviously, it was a little humor to celebrate my new job title. I bet there were a few smiles as it was being hung. I know it brought a smile every time I passed by. It was quite a large poster and sported a picture of a backwoods, pathetic, non-educated type of individual. He was dressed in a pair of filthy, worn out, over sized coveralls with a soiled rag hanging from his back pocket.

Resting on his long, uncombed hair was a dirty, beat-up baseball cap with a twisted visor. In one hand he held a monkey wrench and a large hammer in the other. His posture was sloppy with his body twisted in a sagging sort of way. His face radiated some contentment and a lot of bewilderment that was somewhat offset with a "Wow, would you look at me" smile.

Sadly, the smile also indicated the need for some major dental work. I suspect the income from the above work could keep the graduating dental class of 1955 in Cadillacs throughout their working careers.

At the bottom of the poster the caption read, "Gall lee, yestaday I couldn't evin spel meckanik, but tooday, I are one!"

I started out on some rather basic shop work and as I got more involved I was able to take on more complex tasks. My early duties were cleaning engines, spark plugs, changing oil, greasing wheel bearings and the likes. As time went on, I was able to get into a little airframe work, which mostly involved replacing worn out parts and painting structural tubing. I also got involved with some metal repairs and more than a little fabric work.

Like many things at Utah Central, fabric-covered aircraft were on their way out. Metal aircraft, by any standard was the new name of the game. Metal is stronger, has more of a modern look and is practically maintenance free. Yet fabric is unique; it will always be in a class by itself. Somehow, it's a bridge across time to the hands that pioneered the very first aircraft.

Like many things of the past, it's more personal than its "modern" and "better" counterpart. The hands that cover an aircraft with fabric have a very close relationship with their work. You don't bolt or rivet fabric in place; you work and develop it through many stages. The worker puts part of himself into the job and some say the fabric leaves a little something with the worker.

To me, tearing a fabric-covered aircraft down for recovering was like taking the wrappings off a Christmas present. It was the most interesting thing in the world a guy could do. At times, it was dirty work but looking into or even exploring the inners of an aircraft offset that very slight inconvenience.

To a degree, most aircraft on the field looked as if they came off the same drawing board. Specifically though, the details of each are vastly different from another. A Piper was different from a Taylorcraft and an Aeronca was different from a Stinson. Each manufacture had its own unique way of designing. Some used an abundance of wood, others like the Cub, unless it had wood wings, had very little. There were elaborate control systems in some, and then a few were so simple a kid out of grade school might have designed them. It was interesting to see the different approaches that aircraft designers used.

Fabric-covered aircraft are a lot like the model airplanes we built as kids. Both the model and its full-size counterpart have spars, ribs, bulkheads and stringers. And uncovered airplanes, whether they be models or the real thing, are impressive and there was some sadness, on my part at least, to cover up all that hand-crafted beauty.

Fabric is placed over the airframe's surfaces and secured with dope. Then several coats of clear dope are brushed on. In between, the fabric is sanded, to smooth out the rough texture. With each coat, the fabric took on a smoother, glass-like feel.

After the wing had received a few coats, we did the rib stitching to secure the fabric to the wing. To position the wing for stitching, a series of pads or cushions were placed on the floor and then the wing was placed on the pads, leading edge down. We had some very long needles laced with some very durable twine. With Chad on one side of the wing and me on the other, we poked the needle back and forth.

On each side of the wing, the twine was tied in a special knot before the needle was reinserted and pushed back through the wing to the other side. The stitching had special requirements as far as the knot and their spacing. A bit of experience was handy to place the knots so they were not so apparent on the finished wing. A tape-like fabric is then placed over the knots along the ribs to protect and secure the stitching.

After a number of clear coats were applied, we changed over to silver dope. The silver pigment in the dope prevents the harmful ultraviolet rays of the sun from penetrating the fabric, which could and would eventually damage the underlining fabric, twine, varnish and wood.

With enough silver dope in place to stop all sunlight penetration, we were technically through with the doping. Most aircraft fabric was finished off with a color, but not all. A case in point was our Cessna 120, it had fabric wings and they never went beyond silver dope. With a metal fuselage and the fabric wings being finished off in silver, it gave Cessna an all metal-like-appearance.

There were two types of dope then in use at Utah Central. One was an enamel dope that gave the finish a metal, glossy, almost-wet look. It had a beautiful hard shell finish that was a sight to behold. However, if it ever needed patching or repaired, as school ships sometimes do, it was almost impossible to blend the patched area in with the original fabric finish. To make repairs, you actually had to scrape off areas of the hard enamel shell. Then with part of the surface dope scarred, it was nearly impossible to blend everything into a final smooth finish.

The second type of dope and the type most often used by us was butyrate dope. It didn't have that nice glossy finish; but repairs were much simpler and easier to blend in. In the beginning, our yellow Cub was finished in enamel and the tan Cub was finished in butyrate. Working with and patching fabric on the two aircraft over the months was a constant reminder of the vast differences between the two finishes.

In the middle of the shop we would have a wing or maybe a fuselage. With a can of dope in one hand, a brush in the other, Chad and I would be slapping dope on a section of fabric. In the background, the radio would be blaring out teenage music. Half singing, half talking, our conversations would bounce back and forth between the coming events of the evening, to cars, probably airplanes, sometimes girls, occasionally marriage and maybe even politics.

During the summer, we would have the shop curtain pulled back and every door in the hangar would be wide open trying to coax in a little air. On a cold day we would have the curtain drawn, most of the doors shut and the furnace stoked up to the limit. Fumes from the dope would build up and were often a problem. Somewhere along the line, one of us would notice that we were getting a little goofy. Comments would be made concerning the problem and the need to clear the air a bit.

Brushes and dope would be laid aside; it was break time. More often than not, we would wander over to the office, grab a soda and sit down at the lunch counter. During the warmer months, we usually ended up under a tree or beneath a wing of some airplane; our conversation would hardly skip a beat. After about a half hour, the shop air would improve and we headed back. Why we never had a fire or succumb to the fumes, I'll never know.

Once an airplane had been recovered in our shop, it in many respects was almost remanufactured. Nearly every bolt and nut was inspected, every rib, stringer and spar had been cleaned and probably refinished, and every inch of tubing had been gone over, inspected and refinished. When the work was completed and the aircraft was being rolled out of the shop, it was hard not to view the aircraft as something you created. The pride one experiences while being so totally involved with that type of work is enormous.

The single grade of fuel sold at the airport was 80/87 octane. We had a 6,000 gallon underground storage tank located a short distance northeast of the fuel pump house. During the years that I was working there, the going price of fuel was 38 cents a gallon. Sadly, it will probably be a while before any of us see that price again.

The discharge of the fuel pump was slow by any standard, and the nozzle did not have an automatic fuel shut-off. For the smaller aircraft like the Cubs and Taylorcrafts the slow discharge rate and lack of automatic shut off was not a problem. However, filling a Stinson or a Beech Staggerwing with dry tanks, well that was a horse of a different color. Those guys had big tanks and in most cases, it took almost forever to fill em up. I've wondered on more than one occasion if my feet would sprout roots before the tanks were topped off.

On a cold day, the fuel from the cold underground storage tank made the nozzle feel like it had been packed in dry ice. Gloves helped, but they only slowed down the inevitable, they didn't stop it.

On hot days, fuel expansion could be a problem. Relative cool fuel from the underground storage tank pumped into the tank of an aircraft that had been sitting out in the hot sun is a perfect setup for fuel expansion. The expanding fuel would work its way out of the filler neck, run over the surface of the wing and down onto the ground.

Early in my employment, I stood there dumbfounded, wondering if the expansion and resulting overflow would ever stop. How does one turn off a problem like that? With people standing around watching, it was embarrassing to say the least. I tried to judge the room needed for expansion, but that was a little tricky. If time permitted, I would allow for expansion, wait and judge the results, often adding a bit more fuel. Like all endeavors, experience helps and I slowly developed a feel for topping tanks in hot weather.

Most times, we had an ample supply of fuel on hand. Occasionally, we would sell an abnormal amount to transient aircraft, or flying activity was unpredictably heavy, or maybe the fuel truck didn't show up like it should have. For whatever reason, a couple of times our underground storage tank ran dry. In order to keep our school ships in the air; Glen would organize a flight over to the Salt Lake Municipal Airport. All of the company aircraft in need of fuel would assemble with pilots. In the aircraft grouping, there would be one aircraft equipped with a radio for control tower communication, usually one of the spray planes.

Once assembled, we would all take off like a big flock of geese headed north for the four or five mile flight. The spray plane would clear us and we would land as a group. Once on the ground, we would head over to one of the fixed base operators, Thompson or Kemp and Kelsey for a fill-up. It was usually enough to get us by until we could get the fuel truck out.

Nearly all of the aircraft based at Utah Central were small two seaters covered with fabric and dragging around tail wheels. Almost without exception, the owners were everyday working people. They loved aviation in any form, whether it is flying, fixing, polishing, watching or simply talking about it.

Many of the airport regulars were older people with a little time on their hands. Most had been in or around aviation most of their lives and had watched its development from an almost buggy stage to that of supersonic jets. They were in a sense, an eyewitness to the history of powered flight. They stood tall, knowing their generation had experienced what no other generation would ever experience. And, being in their retirement years, they all enjoyed an occasional get-together with their own kind for a little reminiscing. They, as a group, were often classified as "Airport Bums." Being rightfully proud of their unique heritage, their chests puffed out an inch or so every time they heard their title mentioned.

One individual would be sitting at the lunch counter or out in one of the hangars. A second or third--maybe more--would join. Grown men, most with gray or white hair would be sitting around in a circle, talking about all the great feats of all the great pilots. Aircraft and engines--they seemed to know more about every model of every aircraft and engine ever built than the designing engineer could ever hope to know. Aircraft design was analyzed and suggestions or praise would be made. Difficult mechanical and aeronautical problems were discussed and solutions would be developed and stated.

Even though much of their talk was down-to-earth, often, like fishermen, humorous tales often had a flavor of exaggeration about them. During a story, the speaker would minutely duplicate moments of flight with their hands while describing the event in vivid and colorful words. Faces would study the movements and listen intently. Somewhere the hands and words would come to a climax and expressions of laughter, astonishment, disbelief, and sadness and sometimes even booing with items being thrown around the area. Grown men doing what every little kid loves to do, an enviable role.

Occasionally, I would sit in on the edge of their circle and steal a few of their memories, but it was their circle and I could only listen. There was something special about the twinkle in their eyes, the manner of their speech, the years of their experience and the depth of their knowledge. I could BS, tell stories and I even had a few things to brag about, but my experience could never reach into the past with theirs. I don't know if any upcoming indi-

vidual would or could ever be part of their world. They, for the most part, ignored the beyond, but the past they wouldn't or couldn't let go. It was part of
their being.

Somehow, without forethought, I knew that the old timers would always be
there, and I would always be allowed the pleasure of their stories. They had
been around forever, hadn't they? They were like the mountains, indestruc-
tible! Yet, somehow, the simple passing of a few years and I would find only
empty chairs.

On just about any good weekend, with good weather, business was quite
brisk. The Korean War had ended (an agreed-upon stalemate) and the G.I.
Bill was in full swing. On more than a few summer weekends, it took some
fancy footwork to keep the aircraft fueled so as not to disrupt schedules. On
one occasion, one of the instructors remarked that he had been in the air for
nearly thirteen hours. That was not a typical day, but it was fun to be involved
in so much flying activity.

Part of the requirements for Private Pilot Flight Training was the attendance
and completion of an authorized flying school. To accommodate students
and provide them with the most complete program possible, the company set
up an FAA Authorized Private Pilot Ground School.

We cleaned out the classroom in the east end of the office building. Some
tables and fold-up chairs were brought in. Kay, who was a member of the
Naval Reserve over at the Salt Lake Municipal Airport, brought over some
old Navy Safety Posters to hang on the walls. They were interesting because
all the posters were humorous and illustrated World War Two-type aircraft.
After everything was in place, we had a very comfortable classroom environment. Glen and the flight instructors set up the educational curriculum based
on FAA guidelines.

For ground schools to be FAA certified, the company had to demonstrate
adequate material content and the ability of our instructors to teach the required material. One day, a couple of FAA staff members were over to give
their go/no-go decision for our school. They checked out the qualifications
of our instructors and reviewed the textbooks. The school was also required
to have a classroom instructor lecture on a subject chosen at random. Kay,
Glen and Happ and a part time teacher by the name of Jerry Higgs were the
instructors. Kay was selected as the one to present the demonstration class

to the delegation.

He stood up in front of the class and answered a book of questions about himself, the staff and the school's program. Satisfied with the answers, the officials then asked Kay if he would give the school's standard lesson on FAA Rules and Regulations. Kay started in on the subject as if it were a regular classroom session. The officials listened for quite some time and then cut Kay short, saying they had heard enough and were quite satisfied.

I sat through the entire presentation and was quite impressed with the way everything was put together. I especially thought Kay did a super job and admired his ability to stay cool while under such scrutiny.

I couldn't sign up fast enough and was one of the students going through the first class. If I remember right, there were about seven or eight of us.

We had weekly classes that covered all the required subjects. The program also included a tour through the old Salt Lake Municipal Airport's control tower. And to our good fortune, some new and first time radar equipment had just been installed. For the Salt Lake tower, it was the beginning of the new high tech age. We had heard rumors about the new radar and even a few wild stories about what it could and could not do. Needless to say, we were anxious for some on site observations. Much to our delight, the tower personnel were as anxious to show us their "new toys" as we were to see them.

The entire class stood there in awe, with mouths hanging open as we all looked at and studied all the electronic boxes and the scopes displaying all their little fascinating "blips." The radar was even picking up automobile traffic on North Temple. The technology in that control tower made us all feel like we were standing on the flight deck of a Buck Roger's space ship. To say we were impressed would be an understatement. And questions? We had a ton of em. Some of which were a little off the wall, and I guess the tower personnel got quite a kick out of more than a couple of them.

Our front office had a small display case under the counter. It contained a few items that were for sale, mostly instruments (one altimeter), navigational supplies and a few books. One day, I entered the office and noticed Glen unpacking a pair of boots to place in the displace case. They had the height of cowboy boots hitting just above the ankles and were very stylish. Sam and Happ were there and seemed especially interested and were really giving them the once over. Turning them over and around they studied the leather and every seam inside and out. As they looked the boots over, Sam and Happ were making all kinds of comments. Occasionally they asked Glen related questions, "How much? What sizes do they come in? How long to get a pair?" They both were sold on the boots and placed an order on the spot.

A couple of weeks later their boots came in. Glen later told me that Sam and Happ were two very excited guys when the boots finally arrived. They tore open the boxes like a couple of kids on Christmas morning, throwing the packing paper in all directions. Then sitting down on what ever was handy, they yanked off their old shoes and slipped into their new "Flying Boots." Almost transformed, they discussed and modeled the boots for each other. Their style and beauty was discussed with pride. They walked around the room then paused, stomped one foot, then the other, looked, almost studied, then walked some more. "The pant leg, pull it up, no hang in on top of the boot, no not both, just one, Yah that's the way, that's it, hey that looks great! You gotta have one pant leg hung up on the boot, yah that's the perfect causal look!" one of them stated. The boots and their looks were fully approved.

True to the fact, just about every time I saw them after that one pant leg was hung up on the top of a boot. I had to admit that it did look neat, but I often wondered what does a guy do in the morning to keep his pant leg hung up all day. Then one day I noticed Happ and Sam walking across the ramp. Suddenly, Sam stopped and looked down at his pant legs. Happ also came to a quick stop and together they were studying Sam's boots. About then, I noticed that both cuffs on Sam's pants were hanging at full length. Sam bent over and very carefully tucked one pant leg into the top of his boot, for that natural and casual look. Then without any fanfare or further discussion, they both continued on their way.

"That's how they do it," I remember mumbling to myself. Then thinking of how neat their boots looked, I glanced down at my cuffs. I wonder? Bending over, I tucked one pant leg of my Levis inside the top of my work shoe. Having laced shoes and not open top boots made for a tight fit, but I finally got the end of the pant leg tucked in. Standing up straight, I looked down. The cuff, well it was not naturally puffed out and artistic-looking like Happ's and Sam's. It looked more extruded in a very abnormal and almost painful sort of way. And my shoes, they were scuffed around the toes, and the oil smudges added nothing to their looks. Somehow, no way, did they have the look of

"Flying Boots!" I yanked at my pant leg, pulling it out of the shoe. In a cloud of dust I stomped my foot against the ground until my pant leg settled down to full length. I continued on my way a little disappointed. I guess Professional Pilots are in a class all by themselves!

The Passing of History

Chad learned to fly in an old Interstate Cadet. His instructor and owner of the aircraft was a mechanic and good friend by the name of Vern Dedman, the same Vern that had made repairs on Bruce's Aeronca Chief.

Both Vern and Chad preferred the Interstate Cadet to the Piper Cub. And a little to my dismay, Vern never passed up an opportunity to semi-bash the J–3 while comparing it to his beloved Interstate. Chad, while not really downing the Cub, stated that the Interstate did have some good points over the J–3. "It has a high-speed wing, making it a little faster. If you compare wings, you'll notice that the Interstate has an airfoil on both the top and bottom and its a bit more streamlined. The Cub's airfoil is thick and flat on the bottom. Also, you fly the Interstate from the front seat, which is a little roomier with better visibility. And it sits a little higher off the ground, giving you a little more clearance," he once stated during one of our casual tech talks. However, at my request, and with some reluctance, Chad would also admit that the Interstate did have some negative points when stacked up against the Cub. "The Interstate's stalls are a little more unpredictable and it is definitely a little less forgiving." He also stated, "The J–3 can probably get into the air quicker."

He then moved into neutral territory by saying, "The airplane a person learned to fly in would always be a little special to a pilot." And I guess to paraphrase something that Bruce had said while we were working on his Chief, "...an airplane is like a balance sheet, each and every aircraft has a negative and plus column. The perfect airplane exists only in the eyes of its pilot and his use of it."

And me, not having time in the Interstate, I was a little reluctant to judge the pros and cons of the two aircraft. Yet, and I'm trying not to be partial, but I personally felt the lines of the Piper Cub are a little more graceful than the Interstate's. Obliviously, I would never boast even that little statement to Chad or Vern, especially Vern!

Occasionally, Vern would have business on our end of the field and would sometimes take a few moments off and drop in for a cup of coffee and a cigarette. One day, things were a little slow so I grabbed a soda pop and went over to the counter and sat down on the stool next to him. Vern smiled his approval, lit up a cigarette, took a deep puff and blew the smoke off to one side. Pausing a second, he dropped the still-smoking match into a nearby ashtray. Then with a few awkward movements, he transferred his coffee cup from the counter to his hand, crossing his lanky legs and leaned back with one elbow on the counter.

For years, he had been telling his "old time stories" to anyone who would listen and with me being the new kid on the block, I guess I was about the only one who had not heard them. Actually, I had heard of his story-telling and was looking forward to the opportunity of hearing a little of what he had to say. Vern, I'm sure, could sense my interest and viewed me a little as a captive audience, and that was fine with me.

He rambled on about little things and then settled in on flying and the way it was in the old days. "Back in those days," was the phrase that he always used to start any new topic. "Getting a Pilot's license was a little different than it is now. Some instructors would simply teach the student the basics of taking off and landing. When he felt his student could get the airplane up and down safely, he soloed him. After his solo, he then taught his student some of the finer points of flying, like stalls and all that kind of stuff. They didn't have any rules or guidelines back then so you learned to fly the way your instructor wanted to teach you."

"Back in those days, when you flew cross country you did it a little differently. Aircraft engines were new, they were still being developed and most had bugs that hadn't been worked out. You know, they could quit anytime, anywhere. You had to be prepared. When in the air, you always had your ears tuned to the sounds of the engine, one eye on your engine instruments, the other eye somewhere out front looking for indications of the wind direction and a good emergency landing spot.

"Before a tentative emergency field was behind you, you were looking around for another site a little further out. At any given time, you always had your eye on the best landing spot available for a possible emergency. Open water and mountains were the things you had to be careful with. In the old days, when you flew over water or mountains, you held your breath a lot.

"Unscheduled landings were not that uncommon. But usually, they were not that big of a deal; good pastures and fields were everywhere. Them old airplanes could land on just about any field, or even on any old dirt road. Not like them new airplane they have today, them ones with nose wheels. Why anyone would want to buy an airplane with a nose-wheel I'll never know. Nose-wheel struts bend too easy, you could never land them on even a good pasture. In an emergency, the nose wheel would be half your problem."

Vern paused, then brushed his long uncombed hair back and continued. "Back then, we didn't have aviation maps. Road maps were more available and that's what a lot of us pilots used. Road maps showed the roads and that's what you followed. All roads lead to towns. If your engine quit and you had to land on a road, even if there wasn't any town nearby there was always someone around to give you a ride. Even if you had to walk a distance, it was still better to be on a road.

"When you flew over a town and you weren't sure of its name, you just looked around a bit. Back in the old days, most all towns had their names painted in big letters on a barn or water tank or somewhere on a building for pilots to see. And if you couldn't see a sign on a building or a tank you could buzz the roads. Sometimes you could find a road sign and you could usually fly low enough to read it. If you couldn't see a sign, you could always land and ask a farmer for directions.

"Back then, there weren't many radios in airplanes, so you couldn't talk to anybody if you needed help, everything was up to the pilot. Even if you had a radio, it probably didn't work very well or even at all.

"Back in those days," he continued, when you reached your destination, more often than not there would be no official airport like they have now days. Most landing fields were no more than cow pastures, sometimes with ground swells, gullies and even livestock.

"And even if it was a so-called real airport, it was wise to buzz it. That was the only way to be sure there weren't no cattle or farming equipment where you wanted to land. Farmers don't care where their cattle graze and most weren't too particular where they park their equipment.

"Airplanes had no brakes and no steerable tail wheels back in those days. Main wheels were just wheels bolted on an axle, like a little toy wagon. Tailskids were just what the name implies, a stick mounted on the tail of the airplane to keep the tail out of the dirt. I've even seen one mechanic use an old ax handle for a tailskid; didn't last quite as long, but it worked.

"A tailskid helped the aircraft run straight on takeoffs and landings, so there it was a plus. Remember you had no brakes or steerable tail wheel for directional control. So if you wanted to turn while taxiing, well the tailskid made it harder.

"If someone was around, it was more or less their duty to come over and help. People like that were called 'Wing Walkers.' While you were taxiing, they would walk along holding your wingtip. They helped the aircraft turn and kept the wingtips out of the dirt. Occasionally you would get some kid that didn't know what he was doing, like some farm boy who was just trying to get out of his chores. They would push that way when you wanted to go this way or pull this way when you wanted to go that way. On those occasions, the pilot did a lot of yelling trying to make the walker understand. Sometimes the wing walker understood, sometimes he didn't and sometimes he just didn't care. Thankfully most wing walkers spent a fair amount of time around airplanes, so they had a pretty good idea of what was needed.

"Another thing you had to careful with was dinging wingtips. Most early airplanes had very narrow landing gears. The wings of early airplanes were not strong enough for mounting landing gears, so they were mounted on the fuselage. Fuselages were relatively narrow and that was what the landing gear track would be, narrow. And them old narrow-track airplanes had a tendency to ground-loop, dropping a wing tip into the dirt whenever you turned even a little fast. You had to be thinking and planning every second.

"Ever wonder why the main wheels on them early airplanes, like the World War One's Spads and Fokkers were mounted so far forward? It was to put lots of weight on the tailskid. With no brakes, dragging a heavy tailskid in the dirt was the best way to slow an airplane down. On the other hand, during takeoffs, you wanted to get the tailskid out of the dirt as soon as possible. Once you got the tail in the air, getting your airspeed up for rudder control and flight was much easier.

"Like I said, most of the early airports were just big open fields, most times just pastures. And you were not required to use the runways, because most times there weren't any. You could take off or land into the wind in about any direction, if there weren't any cows. As airports got busier, runways were laid out. Early on they were simply graded, sometime they spread oil on em to hold down the dust and a few had gravel spread around to help keep you out of the mud. Still there were soft spots, mud holes, hidden drainage ditches, and even gopher holes. With all the bumps and holes, it was pretty easy to bust a prop. A lot of pilots used to carry an extra prop on the side of their airplane for just such an emergency. A few even carried a spare tire strapped to their airplane. You never knew when you were going to ding a prop or blow a tire. Later, they began to develop better runways, concrete and asphalt. That caused tailskid problems. Tailskids don't last long on them hard surfaces, that's when tail wheels and brakes came into being. Airplanes with wheel brakes and tail wheels were a lot easier to taxi."

He then hesitated, and then with a bit of reminiscence and maybe even a little sadness he continued, "We had a lot of different engines back in the old days. Most of them, like the old Kinner, Wright-Hispano, Ranger, Wasp, LeRhone, Continental and Lycoming Radials you don't see or hear about any more. I guess they are pretty much all gone now.

"The one I remember best was the old OX–5; at one time they were everywhere. It was a wonderful engine! Maybe a bit on the heavy side, occasionally a little temperamental and sometimes a bit unpredictable, but it was a good engine and it was easy to work on. With a couple of wrenches, a screwdriver and some baling wire you could fix just about anything.

"Good engine, wonderful engine, watered-cooled you know! Water-cooled, had a radiator same as a car, same thing exactly. There was a funny thing about them water-cooled engines. You could be flying along at a certain altitude, go up a few feet and the engine's cooling water would boil. Steam would start hissing and blowing out from underneath the radiator cap right back into your face, just like in them old Model A and Model T cars. Then you could go down a few feet and it would stop boiling. Go back up, and it would boil again. It has something to do with the air pressure in the atmosphere or something like that.

"You could do that all day long...as long as your water held out. Some people didn't like steam from the radiator blowing back in their faces. A few airplanes, like the Travel Air 2000 were designed with the radiators mounded on the bottom of the aircraft. That helped a little, but them old radiator systems were always a problem.

"Back in the old days, if you had a girl in town and you wanted to impress her, you could buzz her house. There weren't no law against it. Fly right down the middle of main street, tree top level if you wanted. Everyone would look up, grin and wave. Most people thought it was really something to see an airplane flying that close, unless maybe you woke up a baby or something. Moms with sleeping kids usually got mad. Sometimes your girlfriend's father would get mad if he knew it was you. But on the whole, most people really enjoyed watching airplanes fly that low."

Then pausing his looks became a bit more serious, almost as if he remembered something. He then added, "Its probably best they don't let pilots do that no more."

About then, I think we were both feeling a little guilty sitting around discussing the good old days. He had things he needed to be doing and I'm sure I could find something to do. Without any real ending, the stories just came to an end. Vern paused, leaned over and smothered his cigarette in the ashtray. Then he took one last sip of coffee and placed the cup on the counter. Turning slowly around on the stool, he leaned forward, stood up and paused to stretch his long body frame. Showing signs of being a little stiff from sitting, he wandered over towards the door.

I sat there a few seconds and watched him open the door, walk out onto the ramp, pass under the wing and through the shadow of our shinning new Cessna 172, the one with the nose wheel.

3

Days Remembered

Command Undecided

Early in my training, I was with Happ practicing takeoffs and landings on Runway 9. Visibility was above minimums, barely. Clouds hung heavy, dark and low. Signs of a pending snowstorm were everywhere. The dampness and cold of the day seemed to penetrate every fiber of the body. It was one of those days where you just sat in the cabin and shivered.

We were on our third takeoff and everything seemed normal. The Cub was climbing out nicely and the end of the runway was just drifting to the rear. It had not been a real bad landing, but it certainly needed some improvements. Sometimes it's hard for a student to see things as they really are, and it's really quite easy to blame problems on a nonexistent crosswind or even an untimely puff of air! At any rate, I was trying to figure out why I had bounced around like I did and what I needed to do to get it right. With the turn to the Cross-Wind Leg coming up, I put the landing out of my mind and began looking around for possible traffic.

About then, I began having a gut feeling that we weren't climbing like we should. I subconsciously pushed the throttle forward. It was already against the stops. I hadn't been watching the engine instruments during our climb out, and I spent a second wondering if it was my imagination or if there was a real problem. A quick glance at the rpm gauge verified that the engine was indeed a little short.

With things the way they were, I promptly forgot about the turn. Happ, up in the front seat just sat there and seemed totally unconcerned. He must be aware of the low rpms, but maybe he didn't see it as a problem. The Piper Cub, with its tail down, was no longer climbing but struggling to hold its own.

I went through the basic checks. First I checked the main fuel valve; it was in the full open position. Looking up to the wing root area, I checked the mag switch; the indicator was pointing to BOTH. I turned it against the BOTH position to make sure that it was really there. It was in position. I know I had plenty of fuel, because I had visually checked it. "Ice, Carburetor Ice, that's all it could be," I remember mumbling to myself.

I had used Carb Heat on landing; but before starting the take off run, I had pushed it to the OFF position. Is it possible for ice to build up like that in such a short time? I quickly reached down and pulled the Carb Heat knob out to the ON position. The engine shuttered and shook as the rpm's dropped off even more. I expected a drop but not quite so much and with a little less fanfare. With the engine already sluggish, the additional drop put the rpms way below the normal range.

The rough-running engine was verification of carburetor ice. I knew that in time the carb heat would clear out the ice and all would be okay. Knowing that was of little comfort, as I couldn't help but notice that the plane was beginning to settle and we were already much too low.

Not wanting to be near stall conditions, I eased the nose down. The air speed drifted into more respectable numbers. With the rough running engine, the dropping of the nose and the low altitude, I was beginning to feel a little uneasy. I held my breath while waiting for the heat to clear the ice. Seconds passed, seconds that seemed an eternity, and the engine continued to rumble at less than full power. What's taking it so long?

With my preoccupation, I had still not made the pattern turn and wouldn't have dared with the problem up front. Wondering where we were, I quickly glanced around. Everything looked strange. Never had I been so low that far out from the end of the runway. I looked to my left, towards 2100 South. It had never been so high on the Cub's side window. The carburetor heat was still fighting ice, the engine wasn't putting out, and we continued to settle.

Suddenly, it became a real concern to me. We were going down! I glanced up at the rear view mirror; Happ wasn't even looking in my direction nor did he appear concerned. Gee, the engine isn't running right; we're losing altitude, surely he must be aware of what's going on! That guy knows Continental Engines like the palm of his hand. I bet he could tell you how many bugs were spread-eagled on the air filter by the way it was running. Why doesn't he help, say something or even turn around and smile?

The Wing Inn slowly drifted by, real close. It wouldn't be long until we would be looking up at buildings if things didn't improve and quick! Out of the corner of my eye I could see the prop flickering. I think I could have visually counted the blade revolutions.

I shook the control column trying to get Happ's attention, no response. With his hand not on the stick, he probably didn't feel it's shaking. Still he must have noticed the rocking of the aircraft. "Come on Happ, do something, we've got a problem here," I mumbled to myself. I grabbed his shoulder and shook it. He turned around and I yelled in a very concerned voice, "We've got carb ice!" He turned to the front and hesitated for what seemed the longest time then calmly put his hand on the throttle and took the controls.

You wouldn't believe the load that was lifted from my shoulders. No matter what happened after that I knew everything would be all right.

We had already crossed over the only set of power lines, so that was something we needn't worry about. Out front stretched open flat lands with scattered brush. Everything was covered with about four inches of snow. The snow undoubtedly made the ground look smoother than it really was, but still, I couldn't see a problem. If we did go down, the Cub might bounce around in the brush a bit, probably without sustaining any damage. Still a dead stick landing with icy water dripping out of the carburetor, who needs it!

With Happ at the controls, I was able to settle back, even relax while watching the drama being played out before us. With the Cub still settling, Happ, almost as if he were sitting in a classroom, started jockeying the throttle. The engine sputtered, rebelling against the throttle movements. It caught, there was some life for a second and then it sputtered and dropped off. He kept jockeying the throttle. The engine gave me the impression that it wanted to quit and get it over with. But Happ just wouldn't let it.

Gradually the engine started picking up and running progressively smoother. When it finally had the power to hold its own, there was only about six feet of daylight between our tires and the ground.

Shortly, we had full power and the little Cub was gaining altitude like there had never been a problem. Happ reached down and pushed the Carb Heat back to the OFF position.

He shook the stick indicating that the controls were once again mine. My faith in Happ had been raised to a new level. I turned off our eastern heading, got back into the pattern and continued with the lesson.

I made a few more practice landings and then taxied the Cub up to the gas pit and shut the engine down.

No sooner had the propeller flipped to a stop when Happ turned around and lit into me like a Pit Bull would tear into a rubber duck. He let me know in very positive and certain terms that I was in the pilot's seat, no matter where it was located, left side, front side or back. "If you sit in that seat, you are in command" he stated. And then added, "The aircraft is your responsibility, not the passenger, not the instructor, not the mechanic, not even your mother. I don't care if the Pope is in the airplane and you grew up together. Ron you gave up too soon, you dropped your responsibility on someone else; you turned your back on your problem, never, never give up! Keep trying every avenue possible; do everything, anything you can think of. Don't ever walk away until you've exhausted every source, every option and every idea, good or bad. If nothing works, reach out and grab, do something different, anything! Get help if its available, ask questions, but you're still responsible and still in charge. Quitting is never an option! Do you understand"?
"Yes"
"Any questions"?
"No"
"It's been a good lesson and hopefully you've learned. Come on, I'll buy you a pop."

Wind, Rain and Mud

It had been yet another miserable day with periods of thick angry gray clouds rolling and twisting across the sky. Here and there were fall-outs of long gray misty curtains that drifted down to the earth in light and heavy bursts of rain, so delicate and artistic from afar but so harsh and cold in reality. A cold wind played in the trees, racing through, around and out, teasing and stripping off the few remaining leaves. Standing water was everywhere, with ripples that huddled and shivered against the downwind shore. Heavy wind prints raced across vast stretches of the grasslands while tormenting the taller brush. Student flying had been non-existent and pleasure flying, by its own definition was out of the question. Even hangar flying by the old timers had been put off until better days.

The instructors had found more reasons to head home than to stay. Glen had a meeting and had also left early. Chad was in the hangar trying to get a job out. I had worked the office most of the day, but early evening and the lack of activity had given me reason to lock up and head out to the shop.

The wind beat against the hangar doors and occasionally you could feel it playing with the roof. But inside it was almost cozy with the old coal stove stoked up, some good music and no one around to bother us. There's something almost homely about being in a warm hangar while just outside Mother Nature throws a tantrum.

Off in the distance, an engine; we paused, looked up and listened. At first, it sounded more like a heavy truck moving down the highway, but after a few seconds we both knew it was an aircraft. Question was, where was it headed, The Salt Lake Municipal Airport or Utah Central? Then it thundered right over the top of our hangar. It was so low that its passing felt like the decking was being lifted off the roof.

I quickly walked over to the entrance and peered out through the glass in the door. Headed west and noticeably low was a big maroon Stinson 108. With the heavy wind, his flight path was right over 2100 South and he was crabbed into the wind. No question about it, he was headed for the Diagonal. Watching the aircraft banking onto final, I silently hoped he would bypass refueling and head for a nice tie down. Tomorrow would be a much better day for refueling. However, I knew it was standard procedure for aircraft to top off at the end of a flight. No matter, wherever he was headed, he would probably need some assistance. I grabbed my coat and hat and headed out.

I stood at the gas pit with the wind and rain in my face while following the Stinson through his landing. With the wind like it was, I found myself wondering if he would even be able to taxi. I felt a little apprehension with only Chad and I on the field. If he needed help, he would need lots of it. However, the Stinson was a relatively big airplane, maybe it was heavy enough to hold its own. I watched closely for any indication of trouble.

Almost hidden in the mist, the Stinson raced down the taxi strip. It rocked back and forth, as the wind played with its long wings. Occasionally the wheels of the undercarriage dropped into water and mud filled depressions. As the tires invaded the relative peaceful mire, brown water reacted angrily and was instantly vaporized and blown to the rear by the prop blast. Occasionally, a thin web-like curtain of brownish water could be seen sliding down the underside of the fuselage.

It was obvious from his weaving back and forth that the heavy winds presented the pilot with an almost insurmountable challenge. Even the most seasoned pilot would have his hands full under such conditions.

I watched with some anxiety as the aircraft splashed and rocked through puddles, wondering if the water was getting to his brakes, making them somewhat ineffective and adding to his problems. If he ever felt that he was about to lose it, I hoped that he would have the sense to shut it down and let Chad and I give him a hand. The big maroon Stinson continued.

In some ways, I had to admire the guy. Most people I know wouldn't be caught dead out in that wind. I don't know who he was, but a lack of skill and self-confidence definitely were not two of his shortcomings.

I found myself wishing I had the ability to do what he was doing, and then smiling to myself I mumbled, "but maybe with a little more common sense." Yet I realized that without really knowing what his circumstances were, I had no right to pass judgment as to why he was out in such a mess. He kept on coming.

As he neared the hardstand, I found myself backing away. The roaring sounds of the huge whirling propeller sent wild vibrations that pounded against my body. Angry turbulence mixed with visible humidity somehow seemed trapped, confused, unable to escape but continued its fight for freedom. Heavy moaning brakes, hot and steaming from being over-worked, locked and the wheels froze. The big aircraft leaned forward trying to overcome the resistance then settled back. Still at high rpm's, the mighty engine continued snarling, beating the air with its huge blades, seemingly boasting to the world that it was still in command. Then the switches were cut. The big propeller wound down and stopped, leaving the aircraft rocking and creaking uncomfortably in the gusty wind. Only then could I hear the uneven pattern of rain against the aircraft's metal and fabric skin.

The pilot was obviously relieved, but unlike his big engine he seemed to take a little more time to unwind. He sat there staring, almost as if he couldn't believe he had actually made it. Then sensing my presence, he somewhat snapped out of his trance and looked over at me with eyes that were semi-unfocused.

Without expression, he opened up the side window. Then greeted with the cold wind he leaned back and closed it a bit. Cautiously leaning forward again, he put his face closer to the opening and shouted, "Top off the tanks." Seeing I had gotten the message, he promptly closed the window.

I moved my stool to a position under the leading edge of the wing and pulled the hose out of the pit. Fuel was soon flowing into the Stinson's tank.

In windy conditions, there are good ways to park an aircraft and then there are ways that are not quite so good. Parked like it was, the wind was playing directly on one wingtip, putting the Stinson in a somewhat heavy rocking mode. Then again, with the wind gusting like it was, there was probably no good way to park.

I cupped my hand around the filler neck opening trying to keep the rainwater from entering the tank. With the fuel discharging, I had little to do except wait and think about the wind, the rain and the cold. I tried turning my body in such a way that the rain wouldn't hit my face, but I was only partially successful. Each drop that hit my exposed skin was frigid and felt like a bee sting. "Didn't my grandmother once tell me that rain is soft water?

With the wind rocking the plane and the settling darkness, it was impossible to tell how empty the tanks were. I was hoping they were more full than empty or I would be one frozen kid by the time they were topped off. On that point, good fortune would smile somewhat in my direction. The tanks were not all that empty.

As the tanks were nearing full, another little problem developed. The wind was rocking the aircraft enough, so that the fuel inside the tanks was sloshed around from side to side. Occasionally, it would splash up and out of the filler neck opening. It eventually got to the point where everything I was putting in was splashing back out. About then, I figured it was time to call it quits. I replaced the fuel caps, climbed down and began coiling up the hose in the pit.

The pilot had remained in the cabin during the fueling, filling out his logbook, collecting and looking at papers, packing a few of his personal belongings and just waiting. About the time I was winding up the hose, I think he realized that it was time to get out and finish up his business.

Fighting the wind, he pushed the door open and slid out and down onto the ground. Without pausing, he ducked under the wing strut and stood at my side long enough to suggest that we go over to the office.

There I made up a bill indicating the amount he owed. Pulling out his wallet from his back pocket, he handed me some currency. Then the billfold went back into his pocket and he pulled out a handful of coins from his front pocket. He carefully counted out the correct change and placed the silver in my hand. After a few seconds of serious thought, he counted out an extra fifty cents and placed it in my hand saying, "Would you check the oil, I'm sure it won't need any, and if not you can keep the change." Another short pause, and then he added, "When you're done, just push it off to the nearest tie-down; anywhere will be fine. I sure would appreciate it"! With those words spoken, he was out the door.

Aircraft cowlings on smaller aircraft are made out of some pretty light gauge metal, and in the wind it was something else trying to keep it from going airborne. Then in the darkness, I couldn't make out the reading on the dipstick. I finally admitted that I needed a flashlight, so I closed up the cowling and headed over to the pump house. I found a flashlight, but I couldn't get it to work. I pulled my coat up a bit tighter and headed over to the hangar. After a bit of searching, I found one that worked, after a fashion. The Stinson needed oil!

After adding a quart of oil, I buttoned up the cowling, moved the stool clear of the aircraft and walked over to the main wing strut. Finding a good position near the fuselage, I pushed the aircraft to the rear. The heavy Stinson slowly moved across the hard stand, which had a slight downward decline. Then the main wheels hit the spongy wet soil and settled into their own self-made depressions. The aircraft refused to move another inch. Walking to the rear of the aircraft, I positioning my self against the side of the fuselage, near the tail. I pushed it to the side. There was movement, and then the tail wheel rotated one-quarter turn, dug into the soil and refused to move another inch. I returned to the front end and tried pushing again, first from one strut, then the other, again no progress. "A Stinson definitely ain't no Piper Cub," I remembered grumbling. Wrapping my arms around one of the wet front tires, I tried rotating it, anything to get movement, no luck. I then repeated the task on the other tire, still no movement. With the weather like it was and at the late hour, there was no way I could leave it out overnight and untied. It was about then that I wished that the pilot had left a key--wishful thinking.

Frustrated, I walked around the Stinson, looking, thinking and hoping for inspiration. For me, inspiration, even during the best of times, comes sporadically and often in broken bits and pieces, and at that moment it never came at all. The big maroon aircraft just sat there in the wind, rocking at the pleasure of each gust. Its appearance gave me the feeling that it was alive with a full personality, staring straight ahead, unconcerned, snobbish, stuck-up, self-centered and not really caring if I froze to death or not. I wanted to kick it where it really hurt, wherever that was!

As a last resort, I headed for the hangar and told Chad of my dilemma. He offered to come out and give me a hand. I knew he would, but it made me feel a little guilty taking him away from his work. Yet I also felt the two of us could muscle it over to a tie down spot in just a moment or two.

Wrong! The wheels moved across the spongy ground only with great effort. The tail was like a great sail gathering in all of the angry wind. At times, we were both pushing on one side, trying to keep it moving in a direction with varying degrees of success.

When we finally made a tie down spot, the shallow ruts and depression from previous aircraft parking were major obstacles. We fought the ruts, the wind and the soft earth for every inch. When we finally said "enough is enough" the aircraft's position was near marginal, but the ropes did reach and we were able to get the knots secured. When finished, we both admitted that no matter what major calamities were headed our way, things were definitely on the up-swing!

Bent Pride

Cecil Francis was an older guy, about eighty, I think. Back then I used to think all people with gray hair as being about eighty. Admittedly, most of the time I was wrong. I do know that along with the gray hair he was retired and walked rather slowly.

Cecil was always well dressed in the finest western clothing, right from his white cowboy hat down to his western style cowboy boots. The only thing he lacked was a set of jingling silver spurs and maybe a Colt revolver strapped to his waist. Because of his western dress, I always assumed that he was a retired rancher of sorts, but I never knew for sure. He was very interesting to be around and well liked by all. Whenever I saw him out on the field, I always made an effort to go over and say a few words.

He loved to fly and during good weather you could count on him being out at least once a week. And even with all of his fine western clothing, he could only be classified as an "airport bum." If there were even a couple of old timers on the field, Cecil would be in their midst, discussing aviation and the old days.

Cecil had a little single engine airplane called an Ercoupe. It was a rather sleek looking, two-place, side-by-side, twin-tail, low wing airplane with a nose gear. It sported a Continental 85 hp engine under the cowling and if I remember right, it had a cruising speed of about ninety-five miles per hour. The J–3 cruises around seventy-five, with about the same engine.

An individual by the name of Fred E. Weick had designed the Ercoupe and by all accounts that I've heard, it was a masterpiece of engineering. He came up with an ingenious system of linking all the controls together, the rudders, the ailerons and the elevator into the steering wheel, thus eliminating the standard rudder pedals. The steering wheel also turned the nose wheel for ground handling. There was a single pedal mounted in the middle of the floor. It operated, simultaneously, both wheel brakes on the main gear. The Ercoupe was advertised as easy to fly, spin proof, and one of the world's safest airplanes, statements that were never contested.

Sadly and without merit, a handful of people classified the Ercoupe as something less than a "real airplane" because it didn't have rudder pedals as part of its controls. And a few individuals pushed it to the extreme saying that "Ercoupe Pilots" were not "real pilots" because they flew Ercoupes that were not "real airplanes."

The most frequent technical example given about the so-called shortcomings of the aircraft was the fact that to lose altitude (many aircraft, including the Ercoupe didn't have flaps back then) you had to cross control, or put the aircraft into a "slip." "All macho pilots" slip their airplanes, but you needed rudder pedals to cross control or slip real airplanes. And I guess that led to the final insult, that if you didn't have rudder pedals you must not know how to use them. A statement that in Cecil's, and most other cases was simply not true.

On that particular day, Cecil had flown earlier. While his Ercoupe was being refueled, he had wandered over to the office and joined some of the guys in a bull session. Later, I was there to help him reposition his airplane so he was clear to taxi over to his tie down. I then followed him over to his tie down spot to help him with the ropes.

While I was lacing the tie down ropes through the rings on the wings, he secured the rope to the tail ring. Normally, he was quite talkative, but on that particular day he was real quiet. I could see that something was bothering him but didn't try to pry.

Once the airplane was tied down, he stood near the tail without expression, just looking. I walked over to his side. Then he opened up. It seemed some of the guys had been playing down his beloved Ercoupe. I can't imagine them saying too much as they were all very friendly people. But whatever they had said, the remarks, however unintended had hit Cecil in a very tender spot. He loved his Ercoupe and anything said against it he took very personally.

Sounding like a defense lawyer, he began talking about the technical qualities of his Ercoupe. I was all ears, as I've never heard the good and bad points of an aircraft discussed like that before. He talked and talked, hitting and emphasizing each good point.

"Its ability to sit on the ground, not tied down in a fair amount of wind is unsurpassed," he stated in a trembling voice. "Park a high wing aircraft and an Ercoupe, side by side in a high wind, with no tie downs and the high wing aircraft would be on its back in a minute, but not the Ercoupe. It would just sit there, unaffected by the wind," he stated in a boastful way.

"And as far as losing altitude on final," he continued in a matter of fact tone, "Well if I had to, I can make a series of short "S"-turns, loses altitude just fine, no need to slip it." Then pausing a second he smiled and added, "If them guys were good pilots, they wouldn't need to slip their airplanes."

Then sounding even a bit more boastful, he stated with a little devilish grin on his face, "And them so called pilots. I don't know how many so called good pilots I've seen skid their aircraft through one turn, then rock it through another and mush it into another with tail wagging like a dog with bad rudder and aileron coordination. Half the time they do a lousy job doing what their bragging about, and yet they've got the gall to come over and brag about their great flying ability while looking down at me, baloney! If you want a little extra work to do, get a plane with the fancy little rudder pedals, if you want to sit back and enjoy the sky, get an Ercoupe."

He kept on talking, mostly variations of what had been said, and the more he talked the better he felt. He finally ran out of good things to say about his Ercoupe, he paused, thanked me for listening, hopped into his car and drove off. He knew he had a good airplane.

Working the Wonderland

My car tracks were the first to be laid out in the deep white blanket of snow. The annoying rumble of tires disturbing gravel was noticeably absent. Headlights reflected and sparkled abnormally bright off white snowfields in ways that could never be described. Snow covered trees, draped over the office parking area, created feelings of indoor confinement. I rolled to a stop amid the sounds of squeaking snow, silenced the engine and studied my surroundings for signs of yesterday's familiar world.

Everything was covered in a heavy blanket. It was quiet, deathly quiet, sounds from both man and nature were non-existent. It was a scene without time; the world was waiting for its birth. The color, the stillness, the beauty, is it real? How could such beauty be possible?

The storm had dropped the heavy dense blanket and the wind had blown it around, giving everything strange new shapes. To identify a couple of the aircraft, you had to study the deformed shapes, their patterns, bits of exposed color, a serial number or even a single exposed part.

A nearby Cessna 172, upended with its load of snow, had its tail sitting heavy on the ground. Its nose pointed towards the still dark skies, leaving the nose wheel hanging high in the air. Somehow it looked to be the victim of some kind of huge and unknown predator that had pinned it to the ground where it remained frozen, screaming silently in its agony.

Not far away, I could make out our little Piper Cubs. They looked to be loaded almost beyond their structural limits, pleading in silence for relief from the terrible fate that had befallen them. In the subdued morning light, I tried to visualize the same aircraft in flight, soaring from one corner of the sky to another, sun flashing warm on their out stretched wings as they roamed freely, playing in their environment. Somehow those warm, blue skies seemed more dream than real.

Dragging my feet through the heavy snow, I passed through some of the parked aircraft, mostly just looking. Then something prompted me to look out to the south, across the wide empty expanses of the airport's flatlands. Then my eyes were drawn up towards the reshaping clouds. My tracks came to a stop; I paused, leaned against the handle of my shovel and took a deep conscious look at the dissipating storm clouds. I don't think I had ever stood in place and studied the heavens like that before. The early morning sun was still below the mountaintops, but there was light, an eerie light that seemed to be everywhere and yet coming from nowhere. In every direction, slow rolling masses of gray misty clouds were expanding, contracting, churning and twisting, changing in form and color almost before my eyes. Shades of dark and light mixed freely with tones of purple and orange. Here and there, stringy, delicate clouds hanging like long sheer curtains. Against the horizon, majestic mountains, bold and beautiful were emerging from behind gray clouds, presenting themselves as the next main attraction.

Then there was the silence, the stillness and peace, impressive beyond all earthly description. It was almost as if all the mighty guns of all the great wars, and all of the mighty thunder from all of the great storms of all time had suddenly, in the space of a fraction of a second, come to an abrupt end. The silence was overwhelming, making more of an impression than the clap of thunder. Not a void, but something that could be sensed and felt, something that penetrated not only the body, but every corner of the spiritual being.

I wished that somehow, whatever was out there would remain, if only for a short time. Any change, no matter how slight would only take away. After a moment of admiration, I turned to face the task of snow removal. But I was compelled to turn back and take one final look. Was I feeling more than I was seeing? What makes it so hard to turn away?

I cleared the heavy snow away from the north entrance of the office. There was also a short walk on the south side. Each shovel full was an effort, and I silently tried to compare the work completed against the magnitude of work left. I had a hard time visualizing normal airport activities anytime soon.

The snow around the fuel pump house door had to be cleared away before the door could be opened. A short distance away, the gas pit was buried under heavy mounds of drifted snow. I walked around, dragging my feet and poking my shovel into the heavy white mass. Once the lid was located, I cleared the snow away from the pit area. Then looking around at the piles of snow that I had just created, I wondered how they would fit into the movement of aircraft, what to do with so much snow?

I grabbed a push broom and headed for the Cubs. Pushing and pulling at the heavy white, the snow fell to the ground in heavy, muffled "woomph" sounds. Each stroke of the broom brought relief, and I could almost see the Cubs rise from their depressions. Once cleared, they stood proud, as always, looking to be ready for students.

A car drove in, then another and another. Soon the full crew was on site. Each individual procured a shovel or a broom, each doing a little section of what needed done. Clearing a footpath here and another there was hard enough, but when we started working on even small areas for aircraft movement, we knew we were facing a monumental task. But being persistent and working together, we did make a little progress. About noon, we had cleared the immediate areas around the main hangar, the office and the gas pit.

Glen had hired out some snow removal outfit to clear the snow from the airport's roads, runways and parking areas. They had some heavy road plows and a front-end loader, but even with that they had their hands full. Our aircraft ramps and parking areas were relatively large and with the depth of the snow like it was, the stacks of white piled up fast. The piles were huge and they were everywhere. They lined the ramp, the parking areas and both sides of the runways. We even had a few located in the middle of the ramp. The mounds of snow changed the landscape in monumental ways, we hardly knew our way around our own airport.

After the snow removal crew had finished up their work, a few of us wandered over to the intersection of the East-West and Diagonal Runways. The full length of each strip had been cleared to a width of about seventy feet. You couldn't see over the snow piles at the sides of the runways. It was a feeling of standing in the bottom of intersection ditches. We all stood there, feeling a little uneasy, while discussing how everything would play out when flying activity resumed.

Taking off or lifting out from the "ditch," as they were later called added a whole new dimension to flying. It was out of the ditch, above the snow piles and into the sky. Landings had their own sensations. The impression was almost of settling below the ground (snow piles). We used to hear about people in "Link Trainers" landing below the ground elevation, but in a symbolic way we were actually doing it. To add to the humor, a few jokes began circulating as to what you set your altimeter to, the runways or the snow.

On one occasion, an aircraft went over on its nose on the Diagonal Runway. He busted a prop, but other than that, no harm done. From the ramp, one had to climb up on a snow pile to see the upended aircraft. Then all you could see was what appeared to be a red tail sticking out of the snow.

A few weeks later, with spring approaching, Glen and I were standing out on a mound of snow near the south side of the ramp. Glen mentioned that he was thankful that the snow season was nearly over. He stated that it had been a bad winter and it had been very expensive to hire out all the snow removal equipment. He paused, then looking over in my direction he asked if I knew how many props had been lost on the airport during the winter, both school and private? I thought for a moment and then stated that I wasn't sure. He looked serious, even a little sad and said, "eleven." I couldn't believe it, but together we counted 'em up. Sure enough there were eleven.

Our office, like most small airport offices was a hub for people coming and going. During the summer months, it had quite a friendly environment and did not require a lot of time or effort to keep it clean. But then there were the periods of mud following the rainstorms or melting snow. Keeping it out of the office with all the people going in and out was impossible.

The office was the last item on my list of daily things to do, partly because it wasn't all that fun and partly because it was easier after everyone had left for the day. During the wet seasons, there were times when I just stood at the door and wondered if it was even worth trying. In places, the mud was so thick that a broom did little more than smooth out the goo. One pass moping was out of the question and frequent changes of mop water were the norm. But it did get cleaned, sometimes with a lot more effort than this teenager really wanted to expend.

With muddy feet climbing in and out of aircraft all day, it doesn't take long to get the interiors dirty. Windshields were also a problem. You just couldn't wipe them clean. Plexiglas scratches easier than anyone would ever think possible. It took a lot of water or cleaner and some very tender and thoughtful wiping with soft rags to clean them properly.

The wet and rainy seasons were sometime long and often hard, but thankfully, there were always better days just around the corner.

Big Foot

Not being a big fan of galoshes, or boots as I call them, I at first tried to stay clear of any mud that might be around. But working on a dirt field with lots of moisture and traffic, well it just couldn't be done. Like 'em or not, boots were needed.

So one night after I got home, I spent a few moments rummaging through several closets looking for something that would keep my feet dry. Luckily, I was able to find an old pair of boots. They were the heavy "buckle up" type and sadly much too large for even my big feet. But not wanting to spend good money on such things, I decided over-sized or not, they would be okay.

Next day I had my boots on and found some pleasure in the fact that I need not be quite so concerned with the muddy areas. And having dry shoes after working in and around mud all day was rather nice too. Oversized boots however do have their down side, as I was always accompanied by the muffled sounds of boots that were a little out of step with the feet.

While working at the airport, my flight training was often scheduled and then adjusted per workload. But much to my satisfaction, there was an ongoing effort by everyone to make sure I got up somewhere around the time that I was scheduled.

One day, a couple of hours before a scheduled flight, Max informed me we were going up. I could tell that he was in a hurry as he was untying the Piper as he spoke. Normally I had a few moments to get ready, but on that particular day I knew that if I wasn't ready right then, my lesson would probably be delayed or abbreviated, something I'd rather not see happen. I ran over to the hangar, grabbed my heavier coat and headed back to the J–3. Normally I took my boots off in an effort to keep some of the mud out of the cabin, but on that day I never gave them a thought.

The rudder pedals for the student/pilot in the rear seat are located at the sides of the front seat, which meant one had to slide his feet in a channel like passage between the front seat and the sidewalls of the cabin. I remember it being a bit snug with my boots, but the snugness must not have impressed me enough to give me any concern. I could move the rudder pedals, and I guess that was the bottom line.

I was still a very low time student and Max was showing me some of the basic maneuvers. He was up front doing this and that, and I in the back seat trying to follow and then duplicate what he had just shown me.

All of a sudden he started kicking the rudder pedals back and forth. I was caught off guard and a little bewildered with his movements. Then he said in a much louder than his normal booming voice, "A good pilot does not freeze up on the controls, relax a little!" A little perplexed at his remarks I answered, "I am relaxed"! Then things were okay for a moment or two. But soon, Max was again kicking the rudder pedals and again telling me to relax. In normal conversation, Cub occupants are required to talk rather loud to be heard above the noises, but at that moment we were both on the verge of yelling trying to clarify a problem that may or may not have existed. But somehow, neither of us never really understood what the other was talking about. "Relax!" he was yelling, while kicking and jerking the rudder pedals back and forth. "I can't relax any more or I'd be asleep," I quickly replied. "Something is wrong--the rudder controls, they're dragging," Max yelled. Then it hit me like a truck, I could then feel the problem. It was my boots! I leaned forward and I told him about my boots in my best, "Gee I didn't know" tone of voice!

Without another word, Max rolled the Cub over into a very steep descending turn and headed back towards the field. We plowed through the air losing altitude like a rock. Rolling this way and then that, he entered and winged his way through the pattern. It was cut way down in size and before I knew it we were on Final. He made a very short landing and then rode the brakes till the Cub was clear of the runway. The Cub slid to a stop amid a fine display of flying snow and mud.

Then turning around, he stated in very positive terms, "You've got fifteen seconds to get out, get the boots off and get your fanny back into the airplane." He is normally a pretty mellow guy, but sometimes, Wow!

Trying to hurry, I tumbled out of the Cub almost like I had been dumped out. With my somewhat uncontrolled exit, I hit the ground almost unprepared, setting up some humorous movements with my two left feet. Luckily, I somehow caught myself before I was fully spread out flat in the snow and mud. I was very thankful that I didn't go all the way down, as the snow was rather wet and I could only imagine what Max would have said or even how I would have felt.

Standing on one foot in the snow and trying to remove my boots was out of the question, sooner or later I would be flat on my back and that was something I did not want right then. I sat on the main wing strut cluster near the fuselage. As fate would have it, the struts were covered with some very wet snow and mud. My hands were also wet and cold. Ignoring the discomfort, I continued tugging and pulling. But sitting on the struts and trying to get one boot off left me with only one foot on the slippery snow, and it kept slipping out from under me. Precarious as I was, I spent a second or two trying to re-position my body into a more secure position. That little movement brought on a few more penetrating remarks from Max about how I was wasting "his valuable time." Not a lot of words were spoken, but he had me convinced that having a wet cold bottom, losing my footing and going down on my hind end was not something I needed to worry about. I frantically kicked, tugged and pulled my boots in every way possible.

The wind from the propeller was frigid, and the cold wet slush soaking my hind end felt almost to be burning. The boots seemed to be much harder to get off than they had ever been before. Everything that could possibly go wrong was going wrong; I had even missed undoing a buckle. And all the while, Max was leaning out of the cabin and yelling in my ear. One second he was giving me instructions on how to do what I knew how to do and the next second he was giving me graphic description of everything I was doing wrong (like I didn't know I was having problems!) At the end of each comment, he insisted that I correct my procedure, and quick! Was I frustrated, yah, I think so!

With the boots finally off, I stood up and looked around wondering what to do with them. They were too wet and muddy to put into the Cub's baggage compartment and there was only an expanse of snow and brush spread out before me. "Well... are we going to spend the rest of the day looking at the scenery?" Max stated in a long drawn out and rather impatient voice. Without really looking for a destination, I sent the boots sailing into the sky. I think I was in and belted up before they landed. And where they landed, only God knows.

The second half of the flying lesson was much more successful.

Gremlins, Alive and Well

It had been raining most of the day. Everywhere there were puddles reflecting cold gray skies along with patterns of falling rain. Most pilots were reluctant to even think about flying. Yet, like the end of so many stormy days, the dark afternoon skies cleared giving way to broken clouds and warm sunshine.

One pilot driving by was caught up by the beauty of the early evening skies and decided that he wanted to go flying. I watched with mixed feelings as he started up the wet, but clean PA–12 and taxied it out through the mud and standing water towards Runway 27.

Because of the activity going on in the hangar, the school aircraft had been outside most of the day. About the time the Cruiser was taking off, I began the job of getting everything back into the hangar.

Putting our aircraft into the main hangar was about as much art as work. We normally loaded about six aircraft into a hangar that was designed to hold a somewhat smaller number. Some of the aircraft were rolled straight in, tail first; others were headed in towards the corner of the main door and then swung around and entered tail first.

With everything inside it was crowded, wings crossed over the tops of cowlings, tails were tucked in under wings, and building corners were filled with tails, wing tips and so forth. If one airplane was out of position, something going in later wouldn't fit. With everything in, it was tight, and I mean tight.

I had space in the front of the hangar reserved for the PA–12 that was still out shooting take-offs and landings. Between the muddy conditions of the runway and the fact that it was getting rather late, I had been expecting the pilot to call it quits. But the late hour and mud didn't seem to be a problem with the Cruiser pilot.

With the hangar loaded with everything except the Cruiser, I decided to go outside and wait. Maybe my presence would hurry him up a bit. I wandered out to the gas pit, pulled up the stool, sat down and waited.

I sat there watching the pilot do one landing after another. After a time, I was beginning to wonder if he would ever call it quits.

Tired of sitting or maybe a little anxious, I wandered out a short distance near the east-west taxi strip, leaned against a parked aircraft and watched him do yet more take-offs and landings. I guess it was a little selfish, but out near the strip I was sure that he would see me and get the hint. But he either didn't see me, or he didn't get the hint or maybe he thought I was impressed with what he was doing and I just wanted to watch. At any rate, he just kept on shooting take-offs and landings.

I had to admit watching the Cruiser doing its landings and take-offs was something to behold. The aircraft did a lot of bouncing and rocking amid lots of splashing mud and water. And I couldn't help but notice that his windshield was getting, or was in fact, already quite dirty, muddy-dirty. With the windshield like it was and the fact that he was landing into the setting sun, well I guess that would account for some of his rather hard landings. He probably couldn't see the runway! With things like they were, I was more than a little anxious to see him call it a day.

He finally pulled up to the hardstand with his engine screaming with heavy rpms. Looking at the windshield splattered with mud, I cautiously positioned myself off to one side, making sure I was clear of his path. For the sake of common sense, I was hoping he could see out a little better than I was seeing in!

As the pilot was shutting down, I looked over the aircraft with its unique patterns of mud. Most of the brown red silt was on the fuselage in patterns spreading out from the main gear back across the fuselage. The spinning tires had also loaded up the bottom of the wings just above the wheels. What was a little difficult to understand was how so much of the gritty goo was on top of the wings, cowl and windshield. What is an airplane doing to get mud out in front and above like that? I made a quick glance over in the direction of the wash rack making sure it was clear of aircraft.

After servicing the Cruiser, I pushed it the short distant over to the wash rack. It was rather dark, but there was enough light from the pole light for me to give it a much needed wash job.

I uncoiled the hose, turned the water on and waved the sparkling stream across the muddy Cruiser. With lots of water and more than a little rubbing, it began to emerge from under its patterns of mud.

With the washing completed, I coiled up the hose, stepped back and took a look at the Piper half hidden in the evening dusk. With the pole light and the standing water reflecting the sparkling wet PA–12, it looked like a million bucks. I couldn't help thinking that what I was seeing would make a terrific Piper Advertisement in some fancy flying magazine. I wish I could have taken a photo and captured all the feelings and sights of that moment, but I knew it would be impossible.

I taxied the dripping Cruiser over to the entrance of the hangar, swung it around and pushed it in tail first. Like everything that had gone in before, it was a tight fit.

With some rumbling that sounded overly loud in the stillness of the evening, I closed the big hangar doors. With that, my world was one of soft lights, aircraft and a familiar space found only between the four hangar walls.

Moving around the aircraft was a testimony of the compacted parking. To travel more than a few feet in about any direction, took a little planning. To move a short distance in one direction, it might be easier to take a detour around the perimeter of the hangar. In yet another direction, it took a little squeezing, and in another direction it might take some fancy bending under or leaning over. Some areas were just too tight, and if you didn't want to walk way over there and then back to somewhere else, you could always get down on your back and wiggle under a fuselage.

The only human sounds were the sound of my feet on the concrete floor and airplane compartments doors being opened and closed as I did a final interior and oil check. I was never in a hurry; I had my duties and I could do them at my own speed and pleasure. Looking back, I've got to admit that I quite enjoyed those moments of checking out the hangared aircraft at day's end.

With my work finished, I was headed towards the light switch near the main doors, when I heard a loud sharp pop, almost an explosive sound followed by the unmistakable sound of metal skidding across concrete. Simultaneously, there was the heavy hollow sound of airplanes banging together.

Then it was deathly quiet. I had never heard anything like it. Cautiously I looked around with more than a little apprehension. Then I noticed the PA–12, leaning a bit heavy on one wing. I moved around to get a little better view of the red Piper.

Its left wing was resting on the cowling of the Cessna 120. Moving over to yet a different position, I could see the left tire of the PA–12 was all puffed up like a huge donut. The tube was bulging out along the outside edge of the very deformed tire. The freed inner tube was about three times bigger in diameter and nearly twice its width. My mind was spinning trying to make sense out of what I was seeing and what had happened. Then looking around, I saw a metal object on the far side of the hangar. It was part of the Cruiser's tire rim.

The PA–12 had split rims and apparently the rim bolts had failed and the pressure of the tire had blown the outer half of the rim across the floor. With-out the containment of the rim, the tire and tube puffed out in all directions. It looked like something you'd see in a comic strip.

The PA–12 had been making some very hard landings that evening. Why all of the rim bolts had sheared off while sitting quietly in the hangar, I'll never know.

A Man and His Airplane

Al Andersen was a quiet sort of a guy, and a frequent visitor to the airport. He was always friendly but never one to go out of his way to say much of anything to anyone. If you could see someone sitting in the background, or doing his thing off in the distance it was probably Al.

A while back, before my days at the airport, Al had heard of a Stinson up in Idaho that was for sale. It seems the owner had landed it on a friend's farm field. Then after a nice visit, he hopped into his airplane and tried to take off. But he found out that it was a little easier to land on a short field than it was taking off. He tried several times but he just couldn't get off. Hoping the cooler air might make a difference, he tried again early the next morning, still no take off. Discouraged, he parked the Stinson behind some chicken coops and walked away. The farmer was a friend, so there was no problem leaving the aircraft for even an extended period of time. Weeks became months. Then loosing interest and realizing that his neglected Stinson would soon be junk if left outside any longer, the owner decided that he had better sell it while it could still be called an airplane. He placed an ad in the classified section of Trade-A-Plane.

Al had been looking for a "Fix-'Er-Upper." When he saw the ad he knew it might just be what he was looking for. With his limited budget, he could do most of the rebuilding himself and have a fine flying machine at minimum cost.

He contacted the owner and the condition and price of the aircraft were discussed. After a little dickering, a tentative deal was made. It looked like Al was the proud owner of a somewhat weathered aircraft.

Al got hold of his close friend and aircraft mechanic, Vern Dedman. A short time later, Al, Vern and Vern's son, Earl were on their way to Idaho in an old flatbed truck.

They contacted the farmer and together they all headed out through some tall grass towards the abandoned airplane. The farmer, while trying to be cautious so as not to discourage the sale of his friend's "aeroplane," stated in a roundabout way that he couldn't understand why anyone would pay good money for a flying machine, or anything for that matter, in such poor condition.

When the group rounded the corner of the chicken coop and saw the airplane for the first time, Al, Vern and Earl came to an abrupt halt and stood there in silence looking at the derelict Stinson. They knew its condition was bad but it even looked worse. The fabric was faded and breaking up. Bird's nests could be seen in the engine air intakes and several places along the decaying wings. The wings, cowling and windshield were covered with so many bird dropping that the surface appeared to be almost whitewashed. Both tires were flat and the weeds were up to the aircraft's belly and above, giving the aircraft a frightened, dejected and sinking-out-of-sight look. Dozens of the feathered creatures were circulating overhead, protesting their being disturbed. Seeing and hearing all the chirping birds the three individuals were seriously wondering if they would soon be targets.

Vern, a man who often expressed his thoughts out loud was the first to speak, "If you've got a pilot and more than five gallons of gas in that thing, you'll never get it off the ground, at any airport." Al looked over at Vern trying to decipher the meaning of the statement. Still not sure what Vern meant, he glanced back at his airplane. Somehow, it did look a bit heavy. But still, Al was thinking Vern was referring to an aircraft's diminished performance at the higher Idaho elevations.

The aircraft was an early 1940's Stinson, Model 10A. It was a three-place airplane with the third person sitting in the rear, sideways. Up front was an old Franklin 4AC–99 engine, rated at ninety-horse power.

The three of them inspected the Stinson, looking it over while discussing its needs and the probable restoration costs. What it needed, in a word, was everything. But with the low selling price and lots of work on Al's part, everyone felt it would still be a super deal. Al was a proud owner of a Stinson.

After all the talk and curiosity had been satisfied, they unloaded their tool-boxes and started its disassembly for the trip to Salt Lake.

Once in Salt Lake, the old fabric was stripped off and everything was examined. As expected, the harsh Idaho weather, birds and rodents had done their thing to the Stinson. There were areas where the wood was rotten and other areas where it had been chewed up. The wood in the elevators was especially bad. In many areas, metal was rusted way beyond the clean-up stage.

After all the wooden parts had been cleaned up or replaced, everything was varnished.

Damaged or rusted steel tubing was cut out and replaced with new steel. The metal tubular airframe was sandblasted to remove all rust, bad paint and stains. Then the sand blasted airframe was degreased and painted. Sheets of new white fabric were draped over the wings and fuselage. It was trimmed, secured and doped through the silver stage.

About the time the last few coats of silver dope were being applied on the fabric, Al drove up in his truck with a drum of orange colored aircraft dope. He had gotten it at some kind of surplus sale, at a very good price. Vern told him to take it back, stating that it was probably too old. Al said he couldn't take it back and insisted that it would be okay. Vern mumbled something about it being his airplane and walked away. So Al painted the Stinson in a very orange with a black stripe down the side. And whether it was the spray gun, the paint mixture, the age, or whatever, the dope finish was a little less than perfect. It looked good going on, but once it had dried there were thousands of little pinholes that had developed in its surface. If one looked closely, the finish resembled the surface of an orange peel, and true to its looks, the defect is commonly referred to as "Orange Peel." Although it did not compromise the safety of the fabric, it was disappointing to say the least. It made Al feel a little better that the pinholes could be seen only when one stood quite close. From the distance, the old Stinson looked great. Bottom line, Al had a set of wings and to him that's all that mattered.

Both Al and Vern knew the aircraft was a little underpowered for Utah Central's elevation. They both agreed that a bigger engine would solve the power problem. They needed permission from the FAA to install a higher-rated power plant, but their application was turned down. So it was back to the original Franklin. Vern did a complete overhaul to maximize its power.

Al was proud of his Stinson and he flew it regularly. Seeing it taxiing by as it headed for a runway was almost an expected sight on just about any weekend.

On one occasion, Al had what I would call a minor mishap with his Stinson. It was not serious, but it could have been. I had noticed Al shooting landings on Runway 16. Then a short time later, I could see his Stinson sitting on the ground near the north end of the runway with its engine shut down. Al was standing near the front of the aircraft and appeared to be working around the propeller hub. Knowing there must be a problem of some kind, I hopped into my car and drove out.

Apparently he had made his last approach a little low and had hit one of the telephone lines that ran along the north side of the highway. One end of the wire was wound around the crankshaft, between the cowling and propeller, and the rest, about twenty feet of it, was strung out behind his aircraft. The front of his cowling sported a newly created crease where the wire had made contact.

Al was in the process of trying to unwind the wire, but without tools he was not having a lot of success. I had some wire cutters in the car. They helped, but it was still slow going. Al, like always, was laid back, not excited, nor even a little nervous about what I would call a very close call.

After both of us had spent a fair amount of time cutting, pulling and unwinding, we finally had the wire cleared out. He thanked me, hopped into his Stinson and started the engine. Then after listening and watching the gauges a few seconds he taxied back to the parking area.

Al loved his Stinson. You could almost say they were inseparable. Jokingly, I used to wonder who belonged to who, the Stinson to Al or Al to the Stinson. They were an active part of the Utah Central and together they gave it part of its personality.

4

Living the Adventure

Alone at Last

Take-offs and landings, then more take-offs and landings, I felt I had them mastered them to a degree anyway. Just how much practice does a guy need anyway?

I had just made a landing that I thought was somewhere between excellent and perfect when Happ motioned me to pull over to the side of the runway. Whenever an instructor pulls you over like that its probably going to be a lengthy lecture. It's never a period of extended praise. A little bewildered and not really knowing what to expect, I put in a little right rudder and wandered over through some stubble grass and made a gentle turn to nearly parallel the runway. Then cutting the power back to idle, I eased in on the brakes, drifted to a stop and waited for whatever was coming.

Happ turned around and started going over all the basics. Plan ahead, think, watch traffic, watch your airspeed, watch altitude, keep proper alignment, watch for carb ice, commit only when ready, check traffic, stay alert, and so on and so on. Here I was just about ready to solo, or at least I had aspirations. And in my own humble opinion I was competent enough to get the plane up and down in one piece. And to be honest, I was getting a little anxious to try.

He finally finished, paused and waiting for my acknowledgement. I caught the clue and answered positively, "Got it!" Then except for the distant loping of an idling engine there was no sound for a second or two.

Then, like he just remembered where we were and what we were doing he added, "Now let's try it again and this time I want it letter-perfect." I applied a little power and the Piper had moved about a foot. He quickly turned and yelled, "Don't you think we ought to check traffic so we don't get killed." I was somewhat surprised by his statement as we were aways off the edge of the strip. And I did have full intentions of swinging around and checking the traffic. Sounding a little irritated, he told me to stay put while he got out and checked. I sat there somewhat puzzled. He undid his belt, swung open the window and dropped the door. Then with a little repositioning, he swung his feet out through the opening and slid down to the ground. Grabbing a strut, he swung around to the outside and headed for the tail. Once there, he cupped one hand over his eye's for shade and peered into the direction of possible traffic.

After a few second, he returned and said it was clear. Then without further words spoken, he started to tie up the front seat belts. I watched a bit dumb-founded while thinking along the lines of what the heck is going on here? Then with a very serious expression on his face he stated, "Let's see if you can take this thing up three times, and land it three times without making me regret that I ever knew you." With my mouth hanging open, he unhooked the window from the bottom of the wing, lifted up the door and positioned them for closing. Without another word, he smiled, stepped back, turned and walked away.

Then it hit me. He was turning me loose! I was to take the Cub up by my-self three times and land it by myself; three times, solo. Somehow I always thought the solo process was a little more official, more exact, with some pre-planning, explanations and full anticipation, you know, "Tomorrow you are going to solo at exactly three o-clock, be there!" It was a day I had been anticipating forever. Yet, watching him walk away and then looking up at the empty front seat, well I guess my subconscious was telling me that it might be a good time to feel some anxiety.

Trying to look positive while re-channeling my thinking to the task at hand, I finished latching the door and window. Still a little unsettled, I re-adjusted my seat belt, even though it was fine and then doubled-checked the already secured door and window. With nothing more that I could do, I took a deep breath and glanced around at the controls and instruments.

I knew I could do it and was even very much looking forward to taking an airplane up alone. But still, I was a little nervous. I looked over at Happ. He was standing back near the edge of the taller brush, head cocked to one side, hands in his back pockets, one leg stretched out a bit and sporting a look of curiosity.

I looked up and down the strip the best I could and not seeing any traffic I applied power. It took a little extra power to get the Piper moving in the softer dirt and grass. Traffic; don't forget to check for traffic! I lowered my head trying to see under the wing while I held left brake and rudder. The tail swung around bouncing on the uneven surface in the direction of Happ. Without thinking and before I could catch myself, I had turned the propwash right into his face and blasted him good with some of Mother Nature's finest. "Oh Man"! I took a quick glance back in his direction. He had his head ducked and his back was turned towards me with a storm of dust and weeds flying past his crouched body. Damage done, I tried to put the blunder in the background and continued to swing the tail around.

Traffic clear, I bounced over the shoulder and onto the runway. Then swinging around, I positioned myself on the center of Runway 16 and made a few minor adjustments for alignment. Trying to think like Happ would want me to think, I began wondering if I should go to the end of the runway, but decided that there was still plenty of strip left. Then I sat there for a second trying to think of anything that I might have forgotten.

I found myself mumbling, "You've done this plenty of times before, what are you worried about?" Even if on occasions I had bounced around a bit, all my landings had been fair landings, at least for the last four or five hours of flight time. With that thought, I was able to relax a little.

I opened the throttle a short distance and held, I listened and felt the engine climb in numbers and power. I suddenly found new sensations going through my body: stomach flutters, anxieties, nervousness, electricity, enthusiasm, excitement, adventure and even chills. Everything came together as nothing less than the thrill of a lifetime. I knew I was right where I wanted to be!

The throttle was pushed through its final phase of travel, the engine was at full power. The J–3 immediately jumped forward. The abrupt movement was unexpected. The Cub is small and somewhat underpowered by most accounts. By the book, Happ was about half its payload and with his absence there was a huge difference. It was almost startling the way the half-empty Piper dashed out from its starting position. While still trying to get my thinking out in front, the tail lifted off the ground. I was in the middle of saying "Wow" when the main wheels popped free. A wing dropped and I picked it up. Then I noticed that I had wandered off the runway's center a few feet. I quickly made corrections, while wondering if Happ had noticed all of my little errors.

I held the Cub in a level flight attitude, but I could feel its desire to climb. With plenty of airspeed, I pulled the nose up to trade off some speed for altitude. The yellow wings grabbed the solid air and eagerly began to climb. It was behaving like a kid, who for the first time in a month was free to go out and play!

With my body heavy in the seat, I began to think about what I was doing and where I was. I was flying "Solo," in a plane that seemed hotter than I ever thought possible. It was almost alive, like it wanted to swing and dance as we sailed along. The sky, the earth below, the clouds above and the aircraft itself, everything familiar seemed to be different in new and exciting ways. The front seat was empty and I could see the panel and windshield unobstructed. The circular propeller haze out front roared with power. The wind trailing from the aircraft whistled and hummed as the Cub slid through the air, lifting ever higher.

For the first time, I alone held all power to command, to make decisions on where the aircraft and I would go, up or down, here or there. There just wasn't anyone else around to contest. I rolled the stick and could feel its lively response. My body felt like it was going to explode. Goose pimples swept over me in waves, a chill ran up my back. I wanted to yell, to tell the whole world what I was doing and how exciting it was to be alone in the sky and in control of an aircraft.

Suddenly, it occurred to me that no flight is a success until pilot and airplane are back safely on the ground. I had to get back into the pilot's seat and pay attention to what I was doing.

I made adjustment to throttle and trim, and then I dropped down a little, to a more proper pattern altitude. Glancing over at the runway, there was some pride in seeing that its position was perfect.

I pulled Carb Heat and was about ready to ease the nose down. The normal drop in engine rpm's from the carb heat made my stomach jump a bit. I paused a second and listened. The drop was normal, but I still spent a few anxious seconds wondering if there was a problem behind what I knew to be normal. Forcing myself to relax, I cut back on the power, putting the Cub into a glide.

When I had position I eased onto Base Leg. As the turn progressed, I leaned forward enough to keep the runway in view. Then dropping my right wing to level, I cleared the engine and checked the runway for traffic.

I rolled into the final turn that would line me up with the runway, again leaning forward for a bigger picture of the strip. The runway slid into perfect alignment. I crossed over the highway and it passed silently to the rear.

Too fast, the approach was a little hot. But I ignored the speed deciding to let it bleed off in a long float. Then I got thinking about the light aircraft. I misjudged and started to settle prematurely. While working through the corrections, the Cub broke into a stall. Even before I hit, I knew everything was all wrong. The landing ended up being one of the worst I've made in a long time. The bounces were high and seemed to last forever, one right after another. I hoped Happ was too far away to see all the bouncing, but I knew he could see everything just fine.

I let the Piper drift to a near stop before attempting the next take off. Off in the distance, I got a glimpse of Happ standing at the side of the runway. But then, he was standing erect with arms folded and appearing to be watching me intently. I wondered if he was a little nervous, maybe even with some regrets. Probably. Gee, I hope not!

I applied throttle and again was pleasantly surprised to feel the way the J–3 responded. It seemed that the lack of an instructor had put a little twang in the old Cub.

The second landing was better, mostly because I was comparing it to the first one. I had one more chance to do a landing that I could feel good about. One more chance to show Happ that he had not soloed someone who had no idea how to land a Piper Cub, the easiest airplane in the world to fly.

I went through great pains to make my last landing textbook perfect. I started with a longer downwind, went through Base and then onto Final. The rollout put me in a perfect path and I took great pains to keep it there. I continued to make even minute adjustments in both power and position. Nearing the ground, I started easing back on the stick. I continued to lift the nose and when it stalled out, the drop was near non-existent. The tail wheel gently touched the dirt and then the main gear settled softly and bounced once, about one half inch. I could hardly feel the wheels skidding across the gravel.

A perfect landing at the end of my solo flight, I could live on that satisfaction for at least a month and probably a lifetime.

The date was November 23rd, 1956; the aircraft a Piper J-3 Cub, tail No N88234.

Cubs on Line

I don't think I've ever walked by or up to a Piper J–3 Cub without admiring its looks. With "jugs" or cylinders sticking out of the cowling, somehow resembling big dark eyes, a propeller spinner that looked very much like a button nose and a carburetor air intake opening just below the propeller hub that looked nothing short of a puckered up mouth, I could very easily see a friendly face. I've heard several people refer to the Cub as "cute." And the name "Cub" would probably indicate cute, but I know several individuals who think the Cub is "beautiful." It does have the looks that everyone could and most did love. And for the people who flew and worked on her, well don't try and tell them she doesn't have an adorable personality. The exception to that statement might be the green students who were having a bad day. The Cub has perfected the art of student teasing to a very high degree.

Sitting and waiting patiently at a tie-down with her tail low, nose high, door and window open, maybe a seat belt hanging over the side, the J–3 was a perfect advertisement for fun. And unlike most advertisements, the Cub lives up to its promise. Not to brag, but back when Cubs and Cub pilots were a dime a dozen, I felt a sense of pride in the fact that I flew Cubs and was indeed a certified "Piper J–3 Cub pilot."

Each type of aircraft has its own standard preflight inspection. In the case of the Cub, it's pretty basic, a walk around the exterior looking for damage, loose hinges, pins, wires, bolts or missing this or that. It was also tradition to kick a tire and shake the prop. There was seldom a problem and I think the Cub's simplicity gave a lot of pilots a false sense of security. There were a couple of pilots that did little more than look at the knots in the tie-down ropes that they were undoing. But we did stress the preflight, and most students and pilots did comply.

The Cub's fuel tank is mounted between the instrument panel and the fire-wall, with the gas cap located just a few inches in front of the windshield. Piper's standard fuel gauge consists of a floating cork on the bottom of a long indicating wire that pokes up through the gas cap. As the fuel level varies, the floating level of the cork exposes different lengths of indicating wire. The longer the length of wire exposed above the cap the more fuel there is in the tank. When the top of the wire is bouncing around on the top of the gas cap, or nearly hidden, it's a good time to start wishing you were sitting on the ground somewhere, preferably at an airport. Two of our Cubs had "modern" fuel cap gauges that reminded me of the type found on the old Model A cars. They were circular gauges mounted in a housing. As the fuel level dropped, the gauge turned, giving different readings.

Checking the Cub's fuel was part of the preflight. It was policy never to assume the fuel level solely by the gauge (or exposed wire). The best, and pre-ferred way to check the fuel level was to get the refueling stand, climb up and visually check the fuel level. Most pilots would never take the time to round up the stand and carry it over to their Cub for the gas check. Taller individu-als could stand on the Cub's tire, remove the fuel cap; and with a little stretch-ing, some good daylight and a nearly full tank, the fuel level could be visually verified. Sadly, most weren't blessed with that much height. I've seen some pilots stand on the tire and insert their finger into the tank opening. If the tank was full, a wet finger was a good verification. If the tank was just a tad low, or just below a dangling short finger, creating some aircraft movement by jumping up and down on the tire would usually create enough sloshing of the fuel to wet the finger. If none of the above worked, you had to assume you had less than a full tank. With that, the Cub was usually pushed over to the gas pit and topped off. Normally though, after each flight, it was standard procedure to pull the Cub up to the gas pit where it would be refueled.

The Cub's engine oil level is checked via an oil cap mounted dipstick lo-cated on the starboard side of the engine. The cowling had a circular open-ing around the protruding engine cylinders (jugs are their common generic names) and there is ample room in the opening to reach into the engine com-partment and pull the dipstick. But in doing so, you need to fish your arm down between a rear cylinder and a portion of the exhaust pipe. With a cold engine there is no problem. However, if the engine is hot, it behooves you to pay a little attention to what you are doing. It is quite easy to get a bit of a burn from one or the other or even both. Most people who have spent time around Cubs have experienced at least some redness on their arm.

The preferred time for setting the altimeter was just before the pilot climbed into the Cub. Occasionally we would see some pilot all belted in and ready to go, and then suddenly take off his belt, lean way forward and set his altimeter. On at least one occasion, I had one buckled-up pilot ask me to set it for him. The instrument panel was just a hair too far forward for most people to reach while belted in.

Back then, whenever a group of pilots assembled to discuss some of the more interesting or humorous aspects of aircraft, someone would, without fail, bring up the entrance or exit procedures for the J–3. As soon as the topic is mentioned, some would smile, others would grin and a few would outright laugh.

The smiles are not without foundation, and jokingly, the sometimes rather humorous procedure does in fact exist, at least in the minds of the people who have entered the doors of the Piper Cub.

The procedure requires a few properly sequenced steps, hand placement, leg bending, ducking and positioning. Sadly the back seat was the easier of the two to mount. The front was higher, had fewer available steps for foot placement and more obstructions. A missed movement could turn the slightly awkward entry into a bit of an extended or humorous endeavor. On the other hand, veterans such as our instructors could swing up into the front seat with the grace of a ballet dancer. Max Green, with his towering height and size might be the exception to that statement.

Most of us younger, low-time pilots did all of our flying from the rear seat, as we didn't feel all that comfortable up in the front. And I guess to be honest; it was a good way to reserve the best seat in the house for the chief pilot. So invited passengers invariably ended up in the front seat, the somewhat less desirable spot.

For guys wanting to take their girls up in a Cub, it was sometimes approached with a bit of apprehension. Explaining or demonstrating all the movements of established front seat entry procedure to a girl impressed them little. You could almost see some of them questioning the logic of such a door. A friend stated that his girl made him turn his head while she went through the ceremony. I'm sure some girls wondered if it was proper for young women to climb around like that. Yet without fail, there were always a few gymnastics type who could slip in like it was a slipper.

The rear seat was definitely the roomier of the two. Its rudder peddles were proportionally further out so that even a fairly tall person could stretch a bit. Actually, I thought the rear seat was quite comfortable, if you didn't sit there too long. Space didn't permit a lot of body adjustments.

The Cub doesn't have an electrical system, no wires, no battery, no radio, no lights, no electric panels, no buttons and sadly no starter. Every time a J–3 is started, it is done manually, by hand. All of us at the airport tried to make ourselves available for anyone needing a prop. Most times it was not a problem, as there was usually someone around somewhere. But there were times however, when one wanted to go up and, for whatever reason help was just not available. It was especially frustrating for new students. Feeling a little lost, they would stand around mumbling whatever students mumble when they wanted to go flying but couldn't.

The proper hand-starting or propping of a Piper J–3 Cub is simple, but it does require two people, at least, to do it properly. There's the pilot sitting inside at the controls, and a second person standing out in front of the aircraft. The person out front would call to the pilot "Switch off." The pilot would double-check the switch making sure it was off and would call back, "Switch off." Then he would apply the brakes to lock the wheel breaks. The individuals out front would always assume the switch was "hot," no matter what the pilot had said. The out-front man would push on the aircraft near the hub of the propeller to ensure the brakes were on and holding. Then if need be, he would position the propeller so that a blade was in the ten o-clock position. In that position it would be up against an engine compression point. That's where he could get the most leverage and flipping it through the compression would give it a little extra kick. The propeller was installed in that position so that it was right up against a compression point. With everything ready, the outside man would yell, "Switch On." The pilot would turn the mag switch to the "BOTH" position and call back, "Switch On." The man at the prop would then position himself, grab the blade a short distance from the hub and give it a snappy pull-down. Most times it would catch and start on the first pull.

Occasionally, the engine might run rough for a few seconds. As soon as the engine was up and running the oil pressure gauge was monitored to make sure the pressure was moving up indicating that oil was doing its thing. The outside man usually stood off to the side for a moment or two watching the engine and pilot, sometimes out of curiosity; and I guess to provide help if any was needed.

The old Stromberg Carburetors on the Cub's Continental engine didn't have an accelerator pump so the primer was often essential for starting the engines. If the engine hadn't been run for a time we gave it a shot or two of primer. If it was a cold day, we might give it a couple of extra shots. After priming, the blade might be pulled through a couple of turns to distribute the fuel. Often, you could hear the fuel in the carburetor and cylinders. Some described the sound as a "sucking" sound, others called it a "squishing" sound.

In every profession in the world procedurals shortcuts are developed. And Cub pilots did have ways of propping their own without the aid of a second person. One procedure was for the pilot to tie down the tail of his aircraft (The J–3 has no parking brake). With everything ready, he would turn the mag switch ON and crack the throttle. Then returning to the front of the air-craft, he would give the propeller a good flip. With the engine running at idle and everything under control, the pilot would then untie the tail, cautiously walk around to the cockpit, hop in and fly away.

At times, Chad and I would self-prop the engine, without the tail rope. Probably not the brightest thing in the world to do, but nevertheless, we on occasion did do it.

With the mag switch and throttle at their proper settings, we would stand outside in front of the right landing gear with one foot in front of the tire acting as a "tire chock," if you would. Our reach was long enough, so that we could reach the throttle with one hand and the back of the propeller blade with the other hand (nearly). In that position we could, if needed, cut the throttle in a millisecond and in theory our "chalk foot" would prevent any movement of the aircraft, at least long enough to get things under control. With everything ready (that is, the controls and the propeller positioned), we could pull or flip the propeller blade down from its backside. Once the en-gine was running and everything was under control, we would swing around the strut, climb in, buckle up and be off.

I used to think this method was our unique way to prop a J–3 and was known by only "we special few." But I happened to mention it to a pilot friend many years later, thinking it might be something new to him. He casually stated as a matter of fact, "Yah we did that all the time."

Like most tail-wheel aircraft, visibility is not the best from the back seat of a Cub. With the tail sitting on the ground, the nose blocks out a good part of the view directly ahead. While taxing, we made slow "S"-turns to keep clear of problems.

A stiff crosswind can be a problem while taxiing. With a hard wind hitting the nearly full side of the rudder, a Cub's tail wheel has a tendency to swivel, letting the J–3 head off in unwanted directions. Once the wind is in control, and the Cub starts to swing around, re-establishing control can be difficult if not impossible. When the winds were too high we stayed home.

We had a Run-Up Area near each of the runway's take off positions. There we put the aircraft and engine through a series of final checks. Oil pressure and temperature were checked to make sure their readings were up where they should be. We also tested the "Carb Heat." Carburetor ice was something that we had to be constantly on guard against. The magnetos, or the dual ignition system, was also checked. We also had a trim tab that we checked; making sure it was set in the take-off position. The adjustment handle looks and operates much like the window handle in a car. At least some of the time, in some of the Cubs, the friction in the system was so great that the cables would slip over the pulleys, either at the adjustment handle in the cabin or at the jackscrew in the tail, or both. With the cable slipping, there was just a lot of handle turning without trim adjustments being made. However, even with the trim system's malfunction and a bad trim setting, it was not a serious problem. The extra muscle needed to overcome an out-of-trim Cub with the control column is not that great. We also did a full power check to ensure the engine could deliver its full power. If everything wasn't in the prescribed limits, we headed back to the hangar.

Before moving out onto the runway, we always made a 360-degree clearing turn to check for pattern traffic. This was especially helpful, even essential in the J–3 as the visibility from the rear seat was not the best in some directions. With each wheel having its own separate brake, it was quite easy to spin the aircraft around while scanning the sky for traffic. Some even thought it was kind of fun.

There were no radios at Utah Central, so if the pilot was satisfied with his aircraft and the traffic; he taxied the aircraft out to the take-off position.

Once on the runway, I would always roll my controls around one last time to make sure they were all moving freely. Then easing the throttle forward, I would usually start the take-off run with a fast taxi until the plane was tracking on center and under full control. Satisfied with alignment, full power was applied and we were on our way.

Because of the relatively high nose, reference to the strip is off to the front quarter sides of the cowling. Once the speed builds up, a little forward pressure on the stick would bring the tail up. With the Cub running in a level attitude, the visibility over the nose is vastly improved. Just before reaching flying speed a little back pressure on the stick would put the Piper in a bit of a nose high attitude and it would lift off as soon as it was ready, a blistering thirty-nine mph indicated, if I remember correctly. (The Piper Cub's airspeed instrument was calibrated in miles per hour; knots would come later.)

Taking off was one of my favorite parts of flying. As little as the Cub's engine was, it created lots of excitement. There is nothing that signaled the beginning of an adventure like a Continental engine screaming in at full power. The propeller whirled at breathtaking speeds, windows rattled, and fabric drummed as the aircraft started moving over the ground. It moved slowly at first, but the ground soon came rushing in faster and faster. Balloon tires moved in and out of ruts, bouncing over high spots and riding through depressions. Then, the ground rumbling would cease and you found yourself in flight.

The performance figures of a Cub were more interesting than spectacular. With twelve gallons of fuel in the tank and the engine burning something like 4.5 gallons per hour, the Cub could fly some 200 miles without refueling. In the confines of the J–3's cabin, that was about as far as most pilots wanted to fly without a break. Not having a rate-of-climb instrument and a rather short memory, the rate-of-climb numbers are a bit vague. I did read somewhere, that with a 65 hp engine, the Cub climbed in the neighborhood of 400 to 500 feet per minute. With an 85 hp engine, you could probably add a couple of hundred feet per minute to the above figures. If our Cubs had a 75 hp engine, I suspect its rate of climb would be in between those numbers, which, when compared to most other light aircraft is a little on the slow side. Probably best put by Max, one of our instructors, "If it can't out-climb a Cub, it probably needs a new set of plugs." The Cub boasted a cruising speed right around 75 mph, shuttered at airspeeds above 120 mph, and lost all interest in flight just below 40 mph.

The Cub with all of its ill-fitting doors and windows was anything but draft free. There was an ongoing effort to reduce or even keep out the cold winter air, but we could only do so much. Weather-stripping, once in place, was often short lived because of all the people climbing in and out. On one winter flight, I happened to notice my right pant leg, the one near the closed door. My pants were fluttering in the breeze. Apparently, the weather-stripping along the bottom edge of the door was missing.

The Cubs did have a heater, a little muffler heater. However, with all the ill-fitting doors and windows, the lack of insulation, the proportionately large glass area, thin fabric and the rather cold temperatures of the Mountain West they were not up to the job.

With the cold temperatures, dressing for the occasion was a must. And a few of the outfits that came through were boarding on humorous. I had to smile when I noticed one heavily bundled-up student headed for his Cub. Not wanting to stare, I continued on my way, but I have always wondered how he fared, climbing into and then sitting down in the narrow cabin all dressed up like he was.

Visibility in the J–3 was both excellent and bad. Off to the sides and down, the view was ten points above perfect. But the wings were pretty effective in blocking out the upward view. A window was located in the cabin's ceiling, but it was small and it seemed never pointed at what you wanted to see. Most people didn't pay much attention to it, and I guess some didn't even know it was there. The view looking forward was fair, but as one individual stated, "sitting in the rear seat of a Cub is a little like being in a tunnel." I thought that description was a bit of an over-statement. But with an empty front seat and the narrow cabin, I can see how he got that impression. To me, the restricted visibility of the Cub was most noticeable when turning onto Base or Final. The lowered wing in the turn blocked out much of what the person in the rear seat wanted to see. To keep the runway in view, one really had to lean forward.

With a passenger on board, the pilot in the rear seat was sometimes required to do a bit of neck stretching and bobbing back and forth to see forward, especially the panel. Most veteran front seat passengers, like our instructors, knew what the rear seat occupant needed to see and made it a point to be out of that alignment, at least as much as possible. It was only after I was taking up passengers did I come to appreciate the way they were able to minimize their presence.

With every flight there comes a landing. When circumstances permitted, I loved doing a long, straight-in approach for that final event. Even as far out as five or ten miles. My instructors used to say, "Every good landing has a good approach." I guess with the long approach, perfection was easiest to obtain. Yet there was more to it than a perfect landing, the long approach is relaxing with its laid-back adjustments and simple corrections. The set-up seemed to develop almost without effort.

The Cub has no wing flaps. A non-flying friend once asked, "How do you slow it down?" Does one ever need to slow a Cub down? Losing altitude is really what wing flaps are best at. If an approach was a little high and some altitude needed lost, flaps are probably best, but without them, slips are next best. And I've heard from several people that the Cub is one of the best slipping airplanes ever built. Slipping or cross controlling the J–3 could get it gliding almost sideways and losing lots of altitude fast. Once you were down to the desired altitude, you could release the controls and the Cub would immediately flip into its normal glide attitude.

We did two types of landings in the Cub. One is commonly known as a "wheels landing." In a wheels landing, you simply fly the Cub's main gear onto the runway, with the aircraft in a near-level attitude. When the main tires hit the surface, you push the stick forward a tad to hold the aircraft down. Then you would let the tail settle as the air speed bleeds off. As far as landings go, the wheels landing is a little on the "hot" side. But it is popular and used by many of the pilots at the airport. However, for most pilots flying the school Cubs, the "three-point," or "full-stall" landing was most often used. And I guess the most important reason the three-point landing was emphasized was because if you fly tail wheel aircraft, you should know how to put the tail wheel down and keep it back there.

In the three-point landing, you'd glide the airplane down to within a few feet of the runway and level off. As the aircraft settles with the loss of air speed, you apply continuous back-pressure on the stick to keep the airplane in the air as long as possible. When it has absolutely no flying ability left, hopefully the nose will be high, the tail will be low, the stick will be all the way back and the Cub will be just inches off the runway. Then it will stall out and settle the last few inches to the ground. If everything is done properly, the tail wheel will make contact first and then the main gear will softly follow. And if it is super right you can hardly feel the runway dirt move at touchdown. As one Cub pilot put it, "It's like landing on a field of clover."

True to the real world, not all things came together as planned. That is, occasionally, the aircraft would stall out before you were ready. Which probably means the tail wheel is high or the aircraft is just a tad high or both, and then "KAWUMPH." The main wheels would hit first and bounce. Then the tail wheel would drop down and smack the ground and bounce, then back and forth between the main gear and the tail wheel until all momentum was lost. It was very embarrassing, and probably felt a lot more ridiculous than it really looked. There's a cute little name for the back-and-forth bouncing, "porpoising." (No disrespect intended towards the marine mammal, the nickname is simple an illustration of its swimming pattern, not its ability.)

If you bounced hard enough, you could do damage to the aircraft, but I don't recall anything really serious happening to any of our Cubs. There were however, several tail draggers based on the field that displayed signs of wrinkles in the fabric along the bottom of their rudder, an indication that a hard bounce had pushed the tail wheel up into the bottom of the rudder frame.

The almost slow motion of a Cub's three-point landing makes life real easy on the J–3 airframe. All kidding aside, three-point or stall landings in a Cub are really quite simple. There's good reason for the famous saying, "Lands as easy as a Cub."

Easy or not, for most (me included) there is a learning curve. And my learning experience includes a landing or two that was somewhat less than perfect, maybe even real bad. But sometimes even the bad ones are fondly remembered. I remember on one occasion, I had wandered over into the rough at the sides of our narrow runways. It was extremely embarrassing, and I felt like a complete idiot as the Cub bounced wildly around on the lumpy grass and anthills. I, in a near state of panic, happened to get a glimpse of Max's face in the rear view mirror and he was looking at me. His complexion was red, his eyes were filled with tears and he was laughing.

If one learned to fly on the old "tail draggers," switching over to nose wheel aircraft was a piece of cake. However, if one learned to fly a nose wheel aircraft first, switching over to tail wheel aircraft could, at times, be a little frustrating. We had one high time pilot come through that wanted to log some tail wheel time. He had never had any tail wheel time, or at least his tail wheel experiences were way back in his past. It took him a couple of interesting landings to get his tail wheel to behave. Our chests stuck out a mile as we followed his learning curve.

Because of my love for the Cub, or preference, or maybe because I was wearing blinders, I had always viewed tail-wheel aircraft as somewhat superior to nose-wheel aircraft. Then one day a good friend took me aside and gave me the real lowdown on nose-wheel aircraft.

"Nose wheel aircraft are better in just about every way, better visibility, easier to take off, easier to land and much easier to taxi in a stiff wind," he stated as a matter of fact. I think he could see that he had really burst my bubble because after a short pause he quickly added, "Of course in the areas of rough field operations and just plain having fun, tail wheel aircraft are unsurpassed."

Four of us were in a Cessna 182 waiting for take-off clearance on the old 34 Runway at the Salt Lake City Municipal Airport. We were next to go as soon as an approaching Douglas C–54 landed and cleared the runway. Seeing we had a moment or two to kill, everyone got involved in some light conversation.

Then someone happened to notice the approaching Douglas. He casually stopped talking and began to stare. One by one, each individual in the Cessna followed suit, all conversation ceased, all heads turned with all eyes glued on the big military transport. It was obvious that he was doing something just a little different from the typical long, flat, by-the-book, airline approach and landing.

The approaching C–54 aircraft was a beautiful picture to study. Four big engines, at or near idle, huge wing flaps dragging in the air, landing gear reaching out, tail hanging low and nose high and lifting. Even with the looping of our Cessna's engine, you could have heard a pin drop. The Douglas transport drifted over the fence, looking almost like the tail skid would take a strand or two of wires off the top. The pilot was making a short-field, or maybe a full-stall landing, as much as was possible in the big nose wheel transport. Touch down. Big tires shuttered as they hit solid on the runway. Clouds of blue smoke erupted, swirling, looking almost to be trapped between the wings, flaps and ground. Tailskid low, near concrete, and the nose held high with its nose gear hanging in space, almost looking like unneeded baggage.

The instant the tires made contact our cabin was filled with cheering, clapping and a lot of "Wow, Man-Oh-Man, is that guy good or what!" None of our cheering was follow the leader; it was spontaneous. His landing was nothing short of beautiful. Tail wheel, nose wheel, any good landing is something to behold.

The Cub is very simple in design and construction. The entire aircraft is fabricated of metal tubing, wood or aluminum spars and ribs with sheet metal strategically located here or there along the fuselage. All this wood and tubing was then streamlined with fabric. Even the interior headliner (top, sides and back) was fabric. A mechanic once told me that, aside from the engine, the simple wheel brake assembly was the most complex part of a Cub. The engine is also very simple in construction. It's a basic four-cylinder, air-cooled power plant. Any ten-year-old kid could tear it down with a couple of wrenches. It did however take a little more expertise to put it back together again, at least for it to run properly for any length of time.

As far as flying, the Cub is the minimum needed to get you up, give you some experience and/or fun and get you back down safely, no more no less. It was inexpensive, slow, simple, and not a lot could go wrong. A student pilot could bang it around some, without the mechanics pulling out their hair and screaming words no one had ever heard before.

However, the Cub's simple and basic design has a down side. Smooth and streamlined it was not. We often referred to the J–3 as a "pretty dirty airplane." That is, it has a lot of struts, ill-fitting parts, gaps, exposed wires and a relatively thick, high lift airfoil, all of which creates a fair amount of drag. High speeds in a Cub are elusive to say the least. Someone once said that no matter what you put on the front end, you just couldn't get much more in the airspeed department. It might make a lot more noise, feel more powerful and climb better, but it just wouldn't fly that much faster. It seems for every unit in higher airspeed, you pick up a whole bunch more units of drag. High speeds were never a priority in the Cub's design.

For most of its production life, the Cubs came with wooden propellers. For a time, both our Cubs had wooden propellers. Then the prop on 308 was damaged and replaced with a new metal propeller. After the change-over, Max couldn't brag enough about the new propeller, "It's the perfect prop for that J–3. There is nothing you could put on the front to make it perform better," he stated boldly on several occasions. Yet for me, with my limited experience, I just couldn't see that much difference, if any. And to be honest, I envied Max for his feel and experience in the Cubs.

Both the metal and the wooden propellers that we used carried the Sensenich brand name. The metal prop was thin, sleek and much more efficient. The wooden prop was thick with its many layers of beautiful laminated wood all varnished up to a shining gloss. One was modern and neat looking; the other was old, classical and (somewhat) a work of art. To me they both had their place, and I was always a little hung up on which one I would buy if the decision were mine.

It was a standard safety procedure, if one were flying solo, to tie up the front seat belts to ensure that the loose belt ends would not flop down onto and get tangled up in the rear rudder pedals. The pedals were located just to the sides of the front seat.

During periods of high or gusty winds, aircraft controls surfaces have a tendency to bang back and forth. Modern aircraft have built in control locks. It's a locking device or means, usually mounted in the cockpit, for holding the rudder, elevator and ailerons in a fixed and locked position. Over at the Salt Lake Municipal Airport I've seen linemen slip in temporary external "gust locks" on the older DC–3's to secure the control surfaces and prevent them from banging around in the wind. Our Cubs had no gust locks of any kind. I don't know if the wind would cause any damage to smaller aircraft like the J–3, but the banging is certainly unnerving. At quitting time, or during windy conditions, we would fasten and cinch up the rear seat belts around the rear control column or "stick." With the belt securing the stick, there was little or no movement in the ailerons and elevators. There were some springs mounted on the lower end of the rudder that tied into the tail wheel. Those springs had a tendency to dampen the effects of the wind banging the rudder back and forth. And with no "quick fix" to further secure the rudder, it was left to fare on its own. We never tied the front stick up with the seat belt as we always had the nagging feeling that somehow, someone might forget to untie, or even check the free movement of the controls before their flight. Stranger things have happened!

For a production aircraft, the J–3, along with most of the other fabric two-place aircraft of the period, is near the bottom of the weight charts. The book gives the empty weight of the Piper Cub at a little over 700 lbs and a maximum gross weight of around 1200 lbs.

A couple of us low-time teenage Piper Cub pilots would on occasion brag a little, trying to impress people with our great feats in aviation. We never achieved a fisherman's story-telling status, but we did stretch, or maybe over-emphasize the truth a little. And I guess to be truthful, we didn't have an abundance of bragging material with the J–3, but we did the best we could. Often when discussing the great aircraft we flew with non-flying people, we would casually mention that we were flying aircraft that weighed nearly half a ton. For some reason, many non-aviation people, especially girls, just can't visualize something hitting the scale stated in tons (or fractions thereof) as being able to get into the sky. Of course, we couldn't elaborate too much or they would catch on.

As far as bad things happening to Cubs, well it just didn't happen that often. Of all the Piper Cubs flying in our area, I personally know of only three serious accidents. One was our Pegleg that had valve trouble. It was a non-injury accident with minor damage. On another occasion, a pilot was chasing horses up near the Oquirrh Mountains and flew his Cub into some power lines. He was thrown clear and survived. His Cub, actually a PA–11, a variant of the J–3 was totaled. The third accident was a young couple using a Cub to scare up pheasants for a hunting party on the ground. They went into a high-speed stall and hit flat and hard. The aircraft was totaled and it was fatal for both occupants. I guess that for a few, maybe the plane was so safe that some thought it was impossible to have a serious accident, which of course is just not true.

We did have two minor incidents at Utah Central, one even being a bit humorous. The first one happened to 308 while Max was up with a student. I was out on the line when I happened to hear a whistling sound. I looked up and saw a J–3 winging through the skies with only the sound of the wind trailing it. The propeller blade, normally invisible, was fixed in a near vertical position. The Cub was right over the airport, had plenty of altitude and was obviously being maneuvered into position for a dead stick landing. Glen was nearby and headed for the office. I turned to get his attention, but his eyes were already on the little tan airplane. We both knew Max was up there with a student. Glen studied the aircraft for a few seconds, then stated something along the lines that there would be no problem and continued on his journey towards the office. To me, Glen's actions were a show of confidence in Max's ability as a pilot. I also had no doubt about the outcome, but at the same time, I wouldn't have missed it for the world.

Sure enough, with only the sound of the wind to accompany the Cub, Max winged through a variety of turns. Then he rolled out of a final turn and put the little Cub into a glide. His positioning was perfect for the runway. The Piper continued its glide a few seconds, leveled out and touched down in a light cloud of dust. While still rolling, Max pulled off the runway and drifted to a stop. There it sat for a few seconds. Then the door flipped open and the window was lifted up and locked in the open position. Soon you could see the backside of Max sitting on the edge of the door opening. With some effort, he wrangled his tall body around, swung his feet over to the ground and walked up to the front of the Cub. He put one hand on the blade, moved it into a more desirable position and then stood there a second while apparently talking to the student. He then gave it a flip. It caught. He stood back, paused, and studied the running Continental for a few seconds. Then with a little effort, he was back inside. The plane spun around clearing for traffic and was soon in the air again. It was obviously carb ice.

Sometime later, while out fueling, I heard the oddest sound, almost like a steam engine. I turned around and there was a Cub taxiing across the ramp with hissing, zapping and exhaust sounds all mixed together. I studied the aircraft, trying to figure out where all the racket was coming from. After a few seconds, I noticed that the top spark plug on the front starboard cylinder had worked itself out. The spark plug, still attached to the ignition wire was grounded against the exhaust pipe. A blue spark would periodically zap the metal exhaust stack, and the piston of the still running engine was pumping air out through the vacant spark plug hole with lots of hissing sounds. There were two individuals in the Cub and they both could probably see the problem. I did notice though the front seat passenger had a somewhat irritated look on his face. I'd say he found little amusement in the zapping and hissing steam engine sound.

An airport acquaintance grabbed me by the arm one day and told me the following story. It seems that four Idaho high school kids had pooled their money together and came up with a $400.00 Piper J–3 Cub. It had a high-time engine and the fabric was faded and full of cracks. But it was flyable, and that's what the kids were after. None of them had a license, or for that matter had so much as soloed, but to their credit, each had a couple of hours of dual flight instruction.

The Piper Cub was famous as the airplane that "anyone could fly." The opinion of the teenagers must have been, "If anyone could fly it, they certainty could!" They borrowed some "how to fly books" and studied them till they felt they knew what they needed to know. Then one by one, each hopped into the Piper and taxied it around to get a feel of its handling characteristics. They verbally shared experiences on the finer points of taxiing and the prospects of manned flight. Shortly, each took his turn and soloed successfully, with some flights being a little more humorous than others. They all flew for some time after soloing without any serious or even minor mishaps.

Then one day, one of the youngsters decided to go flying. There was a stiff breeze blowing, but he was young and had lots of confidence. He jumped into the little Cub and headed for the runway, which was a section of pasture temporarily cleared of livestock.

Once in position, he opened up the throttle and away he went. Unnoticed though, he had a rather brisk tail wind. He had either forgotten what he had read, or he had somehow missed that chapter all together, or simply hadn't noticed the direction the wind was blowing. At any rate, he was taking off with the wind and with that he had some problems. A tail wind requires extra ground speed and a longer take-off run. My storytelling friend was grinning from ear to ear while speculating on what the youngster must have been thinking when he was "flying across the pasture doing about sixty, splashing in and out of cow pies but just couldn't get his Cub into the air." My friend was actually having trouble getting the story out through his sobs, tears and laughter. More and more, I was wondering what was best, the story or the storyteller. I just stood there smiling, watching and hanging on each word, hoping that another humorous statement might somehow follow.

Through all the hysteria, somehow the story continued. It seems that the hapless youth and his Cub finally ran out of pasture and then in the mist of flying brush, fence posts, barbed wire and dirt, the Cub skidded, slid, banged, bounced, crunched, and finally, making all kinds of funny noises came to a much-anticipated stop. The youngster jumped out, took a few steps back and looked at the J–3 in total disbelief. Nothing on the Cub was in its proper place; the parts were all mixed up. It was a total loss! The youth did not sustain any injuries from the accident. However, he did sustain substantial and prolonged verbal abuse from other members of the club.

If our Cubs were to be left outside over night or during bad weather, it was policy to close their doors and windows, which is a little more involved than just banging them shut.

The door of the Cub is located on the starboard side, and it was a combination window that swung up and a door that swung down. Together they pretty well opened up the full side of the cabin. The lower door, hinged along the bottom, had a set of locking pins in the upper forward and upper aft ends to secure it to the fuselage frame. The door side window, hinged along the top, had a channel edge along its bottom. With the door and window closed, the window channel fits over the top edge of the door. They both needed to be closed at the same time for the channel to fit properly over the door so the pins could engage the airframe. With the window channel in position over the door, the locked door held the two in place.

To close up a Cub at day's end, you would stand on the door side, reach through the open door, unscrew the friction screw lock on the port side window and slide the window down. Then stepping back, you partially closed the entry door and window on the starboard side. It was just kind of "wedged" or propped in a semi-closed position. Then assured it would stay in the "propped up" position, at least momentarily, you would walk around the Cub to the port side, reach through the open window and across the cabin, twist the inside door handle, and pull the window and door shut.

Next, release the handle to set the door pins in the locked position. Pulling your arms clear of the cabin, the port window was then raised to a nearly-closed position. The friction screw lock for the port window is on the inside, but there was usually enough drag on the metal window frame to hold the window up in place. The sliding window was left open enough so that one could slide it down from the top edge. Then first thing in the morning, the reverse procedure was done to open up the Cub.

During working hours, at least in good weather, the Cub doors were always left open. With everything open, the Cub looks to be making a "lets go flying" statement. A Cub with its doors closed is like an ice cream store with a "Closed" sign in the window.

There was not a lot of security built into the Piper J–3 Cub. There were no locks on the exterior door or window. The magneto switch (the switch that turned the ignition on or off) was also non-keyed. It was located in the cabin, up near the root of the left wing. And starting the Cub was simple, first turn the fuel shut-off valve to the ON position (if it was even off), set the throttle, turn the mag switch ON, and flip the prop. With no locks, anyone could start the engine, climb in and fly away. But back then, at least at Utah Central, theft was never a problem.

If space was available, we always tried to get the Cubs in the hangar at night. However, often, because of maintenance activity, hangared transit aircraft or customers with early morning flights, hangar space was not always available for the Cubs. Understandably, our Cessna 172 and 182, being as expensive as they were and a bit of a showpiece for our company, were first in. It was almost an unwritten rule that when there was not hangar space for all, out went the Cubs. When they did get in for the night they were usually unloaded early the next morning and left outside for the day. I spent a lot of time sweeping snow and ice off their tender wings. Heavy rain was also part of their environment. But what I hated most were the high temperatures of the mid summer's sun. You could almost see it burning the fabric up.

Pushing a Cub around was really quite easy, even for a single individual. Probably the handiest way, when pushing it to the rear, was to push it by the leading edge of the horizontal stabilizer. There is also a handhold on the starboard side of the lower fuselage, near the tail. With the handhold, you could lift the tail and move the Cub in about any direction. I saw one individual lift the tail of his Cub up and rest it on his shoulder as he walked over to a new location. The Cub's tail is light and putting it on one shoulder is easy enough. However, if he ever stumbled and fell, it could be a little noisy if not down right embarrassing. Pushing the Cub from the nose is also quite easy, but directional control can be a little awkward.

Cubs, because of their openness, have an ability to let a pilot experience a special relationship with Mother Nature. When flying in warm weather, one could open up the right side and slide down the window on the left. I guess you could almost say that the pilot became part of the sky, and to a degree; it was possible to forget you were in an airplane. Over time, you got used to the noise of the engine, or at least its hammering mechanics had a way of moving to the background. I remember spending hours flying low over the vast wheat fields in the southwest part of the valley with the door and windows open. On occasions, I would be able to follow the patterns or depressions in the grain, created by some mystical force called the wind. The depressions looked to be almost an invisible hand stroking, caressing and soothing in gentle whispers. As the wind moved along (not that much slower than the Cub), you could sometimes follow a single pattern or depression across miles of grain fields. I would drift above the waving grain in suspension, and unnoticed I would watch, wonder, and marvel at nature's little secrets and hidden beauty. Why Mother Nature permitted me to have such a personal relationship, I'll never know.

Looking back, you had to say the Cubs were fun to fly, but more than that, flying back then was carefree. Everything was simple, the aircraft, the airports and the skies. Moreover, anyone who really wanted to fly could.

If a person had any desire to own an aircraft, there were plenty of inexpensive models to choose from. And gas at thirty-eight cents a gallon--does it, or could it get any better? Sadly, back then, none of us could really appreciate what we had until it was gone.

While waiting for a departure on a Delta Airlines flight in the mid nineties, I happened to notice an airline pilot standing nearby. With a little time to kill, I struck up a conversation with the Captain about his job and some of the aircraft that he had flown. He was polite and friendly. Yet he was an airline pilot and his position and responsibility was apparent. He, almost mechanically, rambled through a list of some very impressive aircraft that he had listed in his logbook. Then hoping to have at least one up on him, I ask him if he had ever flown the legendary Piper J–3 Cub. His eyes flashed and the very polished and distinguished Captain turned into a proud little kid and stated boldly, "You bet!" We two kids then spent a few very enjoyable moments talking about our J–3 experiences.

Ice in Forbidden Places

We had a test stand that we used for the static running of engines. It was used mostly for breaking in or testing the smaller Continental type engines. Mounted on one side of its frame was a small control panel with a few of the basic engine controls and gauges that were used for power settings and engine monitoring. The gauges were interesting because they had their makings in Japanese, a relic from the war I guess. The stand, if I remember right was a welded unit mounted on skids. When it needed to be moved, we hooked it up to the old Dodge truck and dragged it out to a handy location, usually in front of the main hangar. With the main hangar doors open, the shop personnel could keep their eye on the operation of the engine being tested. To make sure no one accidentally walked into its turning propeller, we cordoned off the area with drums, ropes or whatever. Once everything was ready, the engine was started, set at a specific rpm and then periodically checked.

When breaking in an engine, we used a special propeller that we called "The Club." Its diameter was smaller than the standard flight propeller and its cord was rather wide. It was designed for moving high volumes of cooling air over an operating but stationary engine. The short blade also had the benefit of lowering the mounted engine, providing easier access. A cowling was never installed on an engine being tested and the non-standard exhaust system used were simple short stubby exhaust pipes that directed the exhaust gases down and away from the engine. A little noisy, but they did the job.

One day we had a Continental engine running on the stand. Occasionally, Chad would walk over and check it out. On one check, I noticed that Chad was studying the instruments a bit more intensely than on his previous checks. At one point, he even crawled under the engine and scanned its underside. Being a bit curious as to what the problem was, I wandered over.

"Ever seen carb ice before?" he asked loudly as I approached. Carb ice was a common expression heard around the airport. I knew that at times, under certain conditions, ice could and often would accumulate in the throat of a carburetor. If not checked, it could continue its build-up, eventually choking off the air supply and shutting down the engine. That was about the extent of my knowledge on the subject. To me, ice inside a carburetor was never seen, but occasionally something worried about. My answer to "ever seen it before" was a cautious "No."

He pointed to the running engine and shouted at a volume that could be heard over the sounds of the exhaust and propeller cutting the air, "There's ice in the carburetor; take a look." I knew the ice was in the carburetor, and I knew the carburetor was hanging on the bottom of the screaming engine. I just stood there, and I guess he could see that I was a little hesitant to crawl under the running engine. He assured me all was okay.

Still seeing reluctance (if not fear) written all over my face he got down on his hands and knees. Then looking at me to make sure I was watching, he casually rolled over on his back, maneuvered to a position under the engine and looked up into the throat of the carburetor. He did it almost as if he was crawling into bed! Then scooting out, he rolled over, got up and brushed himself off.

Then looking at me he said in a casual sort of way, "Go ahead, take a look." I looked at the running engine and all the wild forces that surrounded it and without a lot of enthusiasm mumbled, "okay." My response was without emotion, and I doubt if he even heard. I guess it was mostly a personal commitment. I knew there was no way I could look at him and tell him that I was too busy, or seeing ice is not that big of a deal, or even, "Sorry, but I'm chicken!" Even I'd consider myself a "dork" if I refused!

I remember the anxiety running through my body as I approached the roaring engine. I'm not an experienced mechanic, but judging from all the noise it was producing it must have been running at full speed. And I was supposed to crawl under the belly of that angry engine, into that confined space with all that thunder, turmoil and heat? Chad's invitation presented many challenges with few rewards.

I moved in slow motion, trying to keep as much distance as possible between the hot engine and myself. I even tried a little self-psychology hoping to get my mind off all the forces coming in at me. But it's hard to put a screaming engine into the background when it's right in your face! Boy, the convenience of just accepting Chad's word that the ice was in there and in fact did exist. I'd believe!

Half on my back and half on one shoulder, more ready to jump up and run, I was in position to scoot under the mighty Continental. The propeller blade or club was whirling a mere twelve inches from my head. The hot pulsating exhaust stacks, a mere foot away, were blowing the hot gasses of the engine's internal combustions directly at my body.

I wiggled more to the engine's underside with my eyes half closed. Then I looked up at the bottom of the dark power plant. Dominating my attention was the oil sump hanging from the bottom of the engine, almost touching my body. Higher up was the massive induction piping that we called "the spider." An invisible propeller was cutting air just a few inches away. Screaming sounds, sounds of a wounded Banshee were produced by the engine, sucking air up through the carburetor. The sights, sounds and sensations that were tearing at my body could never be described. Seconds passed. I slowly forced myself to tolerate the adversities. My concentration settled in on the carburetor. Slowly, my eyes adjusted to the dark throat opening. I studied the interior shadows. Gee what if the ice had already melted?

But there it was, a growth of cloudy white ice that had built up on a section of the throat's perimeter. The growth looked alive, offensive. Simple ice, but during flight it could have such dire consequences. For a few seconds, I found it difficult to turn my attention elsewhere.

However, enough was enough, and my full attention turned to the movements required to get me out from under and away from the screaming exhaust and hurricane winds. I shimmied, rolled and then looking up and seeing sky knew that I was finally clear. I stood up, took a step back and looked at the engine with some caution.

Then realizing there was space between me and the engine, a good feeling swept over my body as if I had just won some kind of contest. Most people could only talk about something that I had seen. And ya know, it wasn't all that bad after all.

One Up on Mother Nature

Chad and I were up in the 172, just kind of going nowhere when he looked over at me and said, "Want to see something"? I looked back at him a little unsure of what to expect but cautiously replied, "Sure!" He told me to loosen up my seat belt so I had plenty of slack. A little puzzled, still I did as he requested.

He leaned forward to get a clearer view of the outside and then made a clearing turn while scanning the sky for traffic. Satisfied the area was clear, he cut back on the power and dropped the nose of the Cessna into a glide. The air speed quickly climbed into some higher numbers. After a few seconds, he pulled back on the wheel and applied power. The nose lifted above the horizon into what I thought was a set up for a stall. Then just before the stall broke, he pushed the nose down into a parabolic arc. As soon as the nose started to drop, I could feel my body lift off the seat. I was floating, just as you would in outer space! I loosened up my belt a little more so I could feel more of the effect. My head was within a quarter of an inch of the cabin's headliner, and I was definitely a couple of inches off the seat. The Cessna's key chain and its tag were hanging straight up. I could see dirt and bits of whatever from the floor floating at a level just below the panel. I had an empty pop bottle in my hand and releasing my grip, it slowly drifted clear. Chad could control our floating by the amount of pull back on the wheel. He made several adjustments, changing our floating state by varying degrees. All total, we must have been in that zero gravity state for five or ten seconds, maybe more.

But like all things fun and good, we were soon running into a problem. The fuel in the wing tanks was floating just as we were. The 172's fuel system is the gravity feed type. When the fuel is floating up against the top of the tanks, it was not flowing into the fuel lines located near the tank's bottom. Fuel was not getting to the engine!

The engine sputtered once or twice, the prop flipped unevenly through a couple of compression points and then abruptly stopped. The only sound left was the whistling of the wind. I looked at the backside of the propeller with its pitted antiglare paint and bug smears. I had never been behind a dead engine before and seeing the prop just sitting there put a little fear of God into me. Looking over the side, I was glad that Chad had done the little demonstration while over some good open fields where we could land if we had too. However, without any concerns, Chad discontinued the arc and eased the aircraft into a rather steep glide.

Once the glide had been established all the negative forces were gone and the fuel was once again on the bottom of the tank where it would flow. The sound of the wind picked up and the prop made a little movement, then it hit a compression point and stopped. As the force of the wind continued to build, you could see the prop trying to force itself through the hard spot. Then in somewhat of a triumphant flip, the propeller broke through the hard spot and began to windmill freely. With the switches on and the throttle set, you could hardly tell where the wind milling stopped and the power took over. Chad pulled back on the wheel and eased in on the throttle. The engine rpm's swung up and the familiar sounds of power once again filled the cabin.

He repeated the procedure, and we again experienced the same zero gravity; and once again, the engine came to a full stop. He again put the Cessna into a glide. Then pulling the starter handle, the engine sprang to life. I guess he was showing me that he had a backup in case the air start didn't work. Either the air start or the starter would get the engine running again. If both of those methods of starting failed, he could have made a landing on one of the fields below.

He smiled and gave me a few words of caution, "Never try this in a J–3," he stated in a casual sort of way. "The Cub will experience all kinds of serious structural problems long before you get enough airspeed to turn the prop, and no one has fully figured out how to physically prop a J–3 while in the air, at least gracefully." Then he added with a grin, "Especially with only one person on board!" I came unglued at that statement.

Chad turned the controls over to me, and I put it through four or five of the outside arcs. Total, we went through the gravity thing about seven or eight times. Each time we put it through an arc we tried to experiment in ways that were a little different from what we had done before. It didn't take long for us to get a good feel for the controlling of gravity and fuel flow. I suspect that if you spent a little time practicing you could really fine-tune the experiment. When we finally headed for Utah Central I felt I had a good handle on gravity, at least in a playful way, in the 172.

Delta Adventure

I had my first duel cross-country flight scheduled to Delta, Utah with Max as my instructor. However, between the heavy work schedule and the short days of January, I was beginning to wonder if the trip was just wishful thinking. Every time I was free, Max was tied up or just the opposite. On top of all the scheduling problems, I had the nagging feeling that Max was not all that interested in making the trip. It was common knowledge that Max was not a big fan of the Piper Cub. For Max a short trip around the pattern was one thing but confinement within its cabin walls for hours on end, well that was something else. I don't know if Max was too big for the Cub or the Cub was too small for Max or maybe it was a combination of the two, but there was definitely a compatibility problem.

Then unexpectedly, Max approached me, and in his typical firm voice told me to drop what I was doing as we were leaving in five minutes. I made a quick pre-flight, gathered up a few things and threw them back onto the lid of the baggage compartment.

When the wheels of the yellow Cub finally broke ground we were several hours behind our scheduled departure. However, I wasn't complaining, we were on our way and that was all that mattered. There was however a possible problem, the return trip would be pushing daylight hours and the Cub was not set up for night flying. If we found ourselves fighting darkness, I guess we could spend the night on the trail somewhere. I wondered what Max would say about that? Some questions are best left unasked.

Once out of the pattern, I put the Piper in a lazy climb and kept a watchful eye on the altimeter and the developing mountain range on the south end of the valley.

As we approached the little town of Herriman in the southwest corner of the valley, the mountains, or more properly large foothills stood out boldly, almost in every direction. Slowly the brush and rock on the massive hills eased towards us, gathering in detail and color. With our low altitude, there was a sensation of increasing speed as we approached its peaks. I had never flown over mountains before and found the experience kind of fun.

With the hills still drifting out from beneath our tail, Max shook the stick, indicating that he was in control. He immediately cut back on the power and simultaneously pushed the nose down into a rather steep glide. The Cub's flight became solid in the fast moving air. The down-side of the mountain was passing to our rear at an exciting speed. Out front, the flatlands of Cedar Valley, a huge expanse of desert.

Max leveled out thirty feet above the valley floor, and with our excess speed we were whizzing along at a lovely pace.

Out in the distance I could see a heard of sheep peacefully grazing in the brush. With a few minor adjustments, Max had the Cub headed directly towards the herd. I couldn't help wondering what he had in mind. Shortly we were there, and they were suddenly very much aware of our presence. Panic hit, mud, dirt and snow flew in all directions; sheep climbed, jumped, slipped and pounced over one another in an attempt to clear our path. The massive carpet of wool split, with half fleeing to the left and the other half dashing to the right.

Off to the right, nestled in some Cedars, I got a glimpse of a sheepherder's wagon. If he saw us, I hoped that he could appreciate our playful spirit.

We had no more than crossed over the herd of sheep when Max pulled back on the stick and opened the throttle. My body pressed heavily into the seat as the nose of our Cub lifted high into the sky. The ground dropped away, and the altimeter swung around to new heights at an unbelievable rate. Then the little Cub went into labor, and our airspeed immediately started to drop off. With our airspeed nearly at stalling, Max pushed the stick forward and our bodies lifted against our seat belts. Once the Cub was nearly level, Max trimmed it for a shallow climb. He then indicated the controls were mine.

We flew on in silence, both taking on the role of tourist, just relaxing and looking around at miles of nothing spread out across a vast empty desert. Shortly Max told me to get my map out. There I was one up on him, as it was partially open and spread out across my lap. He smiled, threw a couple of unconvincing "good-old-boy" comments and turned around in my direction as much as he could.

Taking the map, he studied it for a moment and then held it up in a way so we could both read it. He gave me a quick refresher course on visual and dead reckoning navigation, making numerous references and comparisons between the map and the ground. Some of the items he talked about were statements of experience, things you just don't get out of a book. He also covered a variety of subjects, such as things to be aware of, verifications, mistakes to avoid and procedures to follow if lost.

Then he paused and studied the horizon out to the west and glanced back at the map. He brought my attention to some very distant mountains. I followed his directions, bouncing from one landmark to another until we were both looking at the same mountain.

The miniature mountain range seemed almost at the edge of the world and nearly hidden in the distant haze. But way out there, at the very edge of what could be seen, I could make out what he was talking about. "Yes I can see it," I commented, almost thinking out loud. Then he held up the map and pointed to a mountain range. I quickly glanced at the map, and then stared out to the

west. He was pointing to, and I was seeing mountains in Nevada. It was only
the nearby adjacent state, but it could have been light years away. Somehow,
I felt I was seeing something that could only be seen by people in high flying
aircraft, like our Cub.

We continued to study the west horizon for a moment longer, and then
apparently Max began finding things a little boring. He briefly scanned the
horizon in different directions, and still not seeing anything of interest, he
began twisting and looking around the interior of the Cub. I knew right off
that he was trying to find a good spot to curl up in and sleep the trip away. He
wiggled around trying to stuff his body parts into the best position possible.
Soon he stopped moving and sat there in a somewhat peaceful state.

Then he instructed me, in an almost sheepish voice, "Climb to seven thousand five hundred feet, try not to get lost, don't bend the crankshaft on any
rocks and wake me up after we land." His six foot three inch frame then made
the best of a bad situation. Like a squirrel, he adjusted his position once again
and was soon asleep.

Like I said, Max, because of his size, was not a big fan of the J–3, but it was
a job and he was building time. Still, I've never understood how he could sit
in the Cub's front seat, let alone sleep there. His head was resting against the
plexiglas and his right hip was pushing against the Cub's door. Without really
putting forth any effort to see, I couldn't help wondering how he had his legs
curled up. Then looking at the way his neck was cocked, I began wondering
if mine was starting to hurt.

The J–3 has never broken any climbing records, but with patience, you
could eventually get up to a desired altitude, if your goals weren't set too high.
Both Max and myself were pretty big guys and with our combined weight it
seemed as if the Piper was climbing slower than ever. Still, with each passing
moment, I was flying higher than I had ever been before.

Not wanting to wake Max up with the news that I was lost, I made
continual visual checks between the map and the ground. It was simple
enough. There were lots of uniquely shaped mountains that could be related to features on the map. I soon had confidence that there would be no
navigation problems.

I reached my altitude, trimmed the aircraft for level flight, leaned back
and divided my time between traffic watch, navigating, sight-seeing and

just thinking.

The Cub's engine was turning at 2,300 rotations per minute. In my books, that's fast! How fast are the pistons moving when they come to an abrupt stop and then reverse directions? How does a screaming engine stay together for hundreds of hours doing that kind of stuff? And what about all the sounds the Cub was making while it was moved through the air? I found that if I listened intently, studying and concentrating on a particular noise, I could isolate it. With some serious concentration, I could hear just about anything I wanted or didn't want to hear. There were the sounds of misfires, metal-to-metal grinding, deep thumping noises, even sounds like parts whipping around in the wind. It wasn't long before I was wondering if I had checked the pins in the rudder and the ailerons? The bolts, what about all the bolts, did I check all of them? I was soon wishing that I had done a more thorough pre-flight inspection, maybe something a bit more detailed, like a 100-hour inspection. Gee, maybe I should wake Max up and get a second opinion on all the noises. Boy, would that be stupid!

Glancing down at the earth, I wondered how I would fare if I did have an emergency landing. There were numerous flat places, but soft sand; outcroppings of rocks and brush were everywhere. Boy, I don't know!

Then looking out over the nose I could see the propeller turning in its big gray arc, not much more than a shadow. It was turning without a flicker, without hesitation, not paying any attention to my childish thoughts. The Cub was doing its thing, as always, as expected. Doubt became trust, apprehension turned to confidence, and I relaxed. I began to appreciate where I was, high in the sky, at the controls of an aircraft and on a long cross-country flight. I suddenly found myself thinking almost out loud, "Ron, enjoy what you're doing, relax and take it all in."

The desert is repetitious; everything looked like everything else, all colored in the drab shades of desert brown and winter grays. Even the Cedar trees that dotted the landscape were absent of the bright greens of summer. Maybe the heavy dark overcast has a way of depressing bright colors, I don't know.

Leaning forward, I could see a solid, uneven layer of broken clouds slowly drifting by the upper portion of the windshield. At our altitude, the clouds appeared to be moving much faster than the earth below. Then, for no real reason, I leaned back, relaxed and watched, even studied the clouds as they drifted by the window in the top of the cabin. It was a view I had never paid much attention to before. Somehow their movement seemed to have a calming effect.

I could pinpoint Delta's airport's location long before I could actually see its features. I cut the power back and started a long descent. The change got Max stirring a little. Turning his head against the plexiglas, he stared out at the world for a second, but seemed little impressed. Curling into a slightly different position, he was soon asleep again.

I flew high over the airport looking for traffic; there was no activity anywhere. Circling wide, I eased down to pattern altitude and rolled over into the Down-Wind Leg. The airport was small and like Utah Central had narrow runways, but unlike ours, they were asphalt. Judging from their bright black color, I suspect they had been resurfaced only a short time before.

After our gravel runways, the shock of the Cub's tires grabbing the hard asphalt surface was somewhat unanticipated. It was the first time I had landed on anything but dirt or gravel in a long time, and then I was a passenger. It was fun hearing the tires chirp as they hit the hard surface. And feeling the smooth roll without the sounds of the country gravel road rumble was kind of nice too.

I taxied over to the gas pump, revved the engine up and cut the mag switch. The engine was still unwinding as I undid the side door, hooked the window up on the wing, and dropped the door. Undoing my belt, I sat there for a few seconds, noticing for the first time just how stiff I was. Looking at Max, I knew his bones were also stiff, probably more so than mine.

Swinging my legs over the side, I slid down to the hard concrete. Then feeling the numbness in my legs, I stood there for a few seconds looking around while waiting for my legs to return to normal. With a little hidden amusement, I watched Max slowly uncoil. Appearing rather stiff, he pulled his knees up near his chest and swung his feet over the side. Then holding onto the overhead structural tubing of the cabin, he slid down. We both stomped our feet a couple of times trying to get the stiffness out.

With our legs returning to normal, we headed over in the direction of a small office located in a corner of the main hangar. We pushed the door open and stepped inside.

It was the typical FBO office. Off to our left there was a door leading out to the hangar area. A warm, wood-burning stove was located over in the far right hand corner of the room. A bulletin board covered with all the typical postings of a small airport was mounted on a nearby wall. I scanned the clutter that included a snapshot of some people standing near the front end of a DC–3. Another photo was that of a student who had apparently just soloed and judging from the grin on his face he was one happy guy, a typical reaction! There were also several posters stating airport information and several recipe cards with hand-scribbled or typed notices listing aircraft for sale. One ad that stood out was that of a J–3. It stated that it had an overhauled engine and new fabric with a listed sales price of fifteen hundred dollars, or "Best Offer." I bet he got the best offer! Who in his right mind would pay a price like that?

Off to the side, along the wall near the hangar entrance door stood a homemade table displaying a small selection of candy randomly placed in a box. Nearby was a small tin can where one made payment for items purchased. A short distance from that table stood an old refrigerator with a sign on the door indicating the soda pop on the inside was for sale at the prices listed.

Not far from where we were standing, there was a counter that doubled as a sales display case, very similar to ours at Utah Central. It displayed a variety of charts, a couple of textbooks, an E–6B Circular Computer, a navigational plotter and logbooks.

Behind the counter, an elderly man stood sporting a friendly smile. He greeted us in a warm way and as a matter of conversation asked where we had come from and where we were headed. We filled in the answers, but he seemed little impressed with our long flight.

We each got a bottle of soda pop and a candy bar. Then we sat down in a comfortable, but very old and rather deep couch located near the center of the office. As I was sliding down into its worn-out depths, I remember wondering what might be the easiest way to get back up with out looking ridiculous.

However, even a deep, worn-out couch was a welcome change from the confined space of our J–3, and I soon found myself completely relaxed. Nibbling and drinking, I began a mental comparison of our airport facilities with theirs. Except for the blacktopped runways and the fact that we seemed busier, the Delta airport was very much like ours. Yet with no reason that really stood out I somehow preferred Utah Central, probably because it was home.

With the few remaining daylight hours slipping by, we didn't dare spend too much time relaxing. Max was soon up and taking care of the fuel bill while I wandered outside and headed towards the Cub. I happened to glance to the north, in the general direction from where we had come. There was a rather skimpy barbed wire fence, along the north side of the ramp. Just over the fence was a small dirt access road. I wandered the short distance to the fence, passed through an opening, paused and looked north. Spread out before me were the vast flatlands of the desert covered with shrubs and grasses of varying shades of gray, dull gold and drab green. In the distance was a range of dusty, blue mountains topped with snow that accented the gray skies.

To me, it was almost unbelievable on how we had gotten to where we were. Just a short time before, we had climbed into a small airplane, at a location far beyond the distant mountains that I was looking at. We had traveled, not across the surface of the land laid out before me, but in the endless space above the desert and mountains, above where the birds were flying, near the base of the clouds. More than that, it was my hands on the controls. My hands had guided us across the heavens to this distance place. I had detached feelings; somehow it was more dream than real.

Like the landing, the take-off was just a little different. I remember thinking that the tracking of the Cub was a little strange, like being on a borrowed pair of roller skates.

The flight to Delta had taken about an hour and a half, and the layover at the airport was about twenty minutes. So when we got back into the Cub, it wasn't long until we felt like we hadn't been out at all. Poor Max, as broken down as that Delta couch was, I bet he wished he had brought it along with him. I wondered if he ever had the desire to kick out the firewall and stick his feet out on the Cub's engine. It would be a win-win situation, extra legroom and warm feet.

Time passed and he just sat there with his arms folded and staring at the panel.

It was a picture of total boredom if not defeat. After a time, he stirred, straightened up, looked around while rubbing his short gray hair. It was obvious that he had given up all prospects for sleep or even rest. I don't think he was all that tired; he just wanted to be somewhere else until the flight was over.

Max opened up the door and window hoping the cold air would bring new life into his cramped body. It was the middle of January, but the outside air was not that cold. It felt good, even in the back seat where I got the bulk of it.

He sat there for a moment. Then he casually looked up at me in the rear view mirror. He was looking, thinking and maybe even analyzing. And me, I was looking back into his eyes and wondering what he was thinking. Then without comment or explanation, he shook the control column, indicating that he was taking over. A little surprised, I cleared my hands and feet.

Cutting back the power, he put the Cub into a steep glide and headed down towards the desert floor. Twenty feet above the tops of the Cedar trees he leveled off and applied cruising power.

It was like a rebirth. We were winging across the scenery; the earth was everywhere, not at a distance below but to the left, the right, the rear, out to the front and occasionally above. Features on the ground were no longer remote, unreal, but vivid and alive. Each stone was distinct, each bush had texture and each tree had a personality. We flew up with the ground swells and down with the depressions, lifting a wing here and dropping a wing there. Birds would flutter off to the sides as they frantically cleared a path for our strange beast. On we flew, first winging over in the direction of a scampering rabbit and then away from a flock of birds taking wing. Smells of the winter desert were strong and real, the dampness of the sand, the musty smell of winter grass, the fragrance of the Cedar and the aroma of the lowly Sagebrush were all there.

Motion and excitement dominated our flight, the deafening sound of the exhaust, plexiglas rattling, wind whistling through the struts and clothing fluttering from the rush of wind twisting and churning through the open door. Even the earth made a special effort to move to the rear, almost in long streaks. Adventure was at every quarter, the rocking of the craft, the door swinging on its hinges as we banked to and fro, and areas of vegetation drawing closer and then silently flashing to the rear. The Cub seemed to be running better, even eager, like a young puppy running around the hills. The engine was tugging at its mounts, yearning to show us its stuff. We were part of the excitement, wide-awake, alert, feeling everything, hearing everything and seeing everything.

More than the excitement of our surroundings was the anticipation of what was over the next ground-swell. The flight had suddenly become one of exploration, of seeing new things and having the satisfaction of knowing we had been somewhere and were going somewhere.

The Cedars cleared, leaving an area of Sagebrush and rock-covered flatlands drifting up a long gentle slope. Max dropped down proportionally closer to the ground. Ahead, a depression in the earth, a huge gravel pit. He flew over the edge and dipped the plane down a little as the earth suddenly dropped out from below.

A car parked in the middle of the gravel pit, a convertible with its top down. Sitting on the front seat was a couple of teenagers, a girl and a boy. They had their arms around each other and were engaged in a very passionate and private kiss. In a flash, we were passing by their windshield. I don't think they were thirty feet away. I guess you could say they caught our attention by the way we were hanging out of the Cub's open door. Thank the Lord for seat belts. The guy had his back towards us and never had a chance to so much as flinch. The girl, who was facing us and partially visible over his shoulder still had her dreamy eyes closed, then pop, they were open, wide open, like big round silver dollars. She was staring up at us, and we staring down at her. That was it, and we were gone!

Max applied full throttle and yanked back on the stick, the Cub flared, gained a hundred feet and leveled off. He paused, staring straight ahead for a few seconds without comment or movement, apparently wondering if everything seen was real. Then turning around, he looked at me. We both had the stupid look of utter disbelief written all over our faces. Then we both passed through a grin and started laughing. We laughed and laughed until we couldn't see straight. Our sides hurt, our eyes watered, and our faces burned. Max finally wiped the tears off his cheeks and nosed the plane down a little closer to the ground. We both wanted to turn around and take another look but decided that if the guy had a gun we'd be history.

Our Cub wandered over the Jordan Narrows with the highway somewhat below our right wing and the hills of the military reservation climbing above us on our left. As soon as the narrows began to spread out into the valley, I dipped the left wing and our little Cub drifted over into a northwest direction.

The valley spread out to the north, with fields slowly giving way to a network of farmlands, farm houses and little dirt roads. A hundred feet to our left were some high power transmissions towers that circled around the southwest corner of the valley and then headed north.

Max turned around and indicated he wanted me to follow the towers until we were near Utah Central. He then paused, I guess wondering if I had any question and then without any added comments turned and drifted off into his own world beyond the confines of the cramped cabin.

I climbed some, keeping the power lines just below and off my left wing. We wandered over some farmlands, pastures and the quiet little houses of the people who lived off the land. At our altitude, you could see activities on the ground quite clearly. We wandered by six or seven kids playing Tin Can Hockey in a pasture. Not far away, a milk cow was walking rather lazily towards a shed. A man drifted into view walking from his car towards a young girl who was running towards him with outstretched arms. The young girl's excitement was plainly visible even from where we were. Then we wandered over a young woman throwing a pan of foaming water out onto the ground. Off to the right, a lifeless swing hung from the branch of a hibernating tree. Near its hanging branches, a couple of contented horses were eating from a busted bail of hay spread out across the ground. Warm lights and friendly interiors were plainly visible through several passing windows. Occasionally, our Cub would wander through the aroma of a cloud of rising chimney smoke, bringing with it the thoughts of dinnertime.

The surface of the land was drifting by in light and shadows. It was a display of soft images, so real, so unreal, something seen, yet imagined. Was it real? Or was I looking at a model of a community, all laid out on a huge table? Would it be possible to reach out and sweep all the toys away?

We loped along towards a developing sunset through alternating shafts of shadow and sunlight. Far to the north, Salt Lake City was displayed in its somewhat isolated cluster of city lights, sparkling like diamonds spread across the ground. To our left and front, heavy dark peaks standing tall against the western sky with an occasional opening to the retreating sun. The evening was giving birth to one of its spectacular winter sunsets. Just a stone's throw from our windshield, clouds were spread across the heavens in all their never-ending glory. Churning ever so slowly, clouds that were drab and lifeless just moments before were now alive with color and movement, bathing in their heavenly glory. How could anything be so perfect, so quiet and so majestic? Where does all the color and life come from? What would it be like to fly west at the speed of the turning earth and be in a single sunset for hours on end?

Highways, fields, lakes, everything was slowly developing into the familiar landmarks surrounding Utah Central. The unmistakable lines of buildings and runways emerged. Everything looked so deserted. My thoughts turned to Max. For a second, I was thinking of waking him but decided against it.

I was a little low. I eased the throttle forward. Unlike us, the engine was alert and instantly obeyed with the familiar sounds of power.

I crossed over the airport above the pattern, checking for traffic and noting the wind tee. No traffic, no wind, I would land on Runway 16.

I cut the power back and eased the nose of the Cub down. After an extended period of power settings, the pounding and screaming sounds of the engine were no more. The silence was overwhelming, such a drastic change and so unexpected. Only the purring of a slumbering engine, surrounded by a mild whistle of our Cub moving through the soft evening air, unchallenged. The struggle between the brute forces of man and nature were put on hold; machine and nature were at peace, one with another.

I began to lift my left wing into a turn but paused for a last look at the sunset. Somehow, I felt guilty for turning my back on such a collection of colors and light. What a waste!

I eased the stick over, rudder depressed. The Cub's nose drifted towards the airport's pattern. Shadows and golden light slid across the cabin's interior and then like a final salute, the instrument's glass caught and flashed orange, reflecting a last view of the still burning sun.

The earth tilted, and the runway drifted into position in the center of the windshield. The air was cold and as smooth as anything I had ever experienced. Soft evening shadows had washed out all earthly colors leaving only shades of gray. The world moved in a trance-- something experienced more through body sensations than sight. We were drifting through a dream, settling through silken air on our out-stretched wings.

Flight fading; the Cub feels its way through the soft air towards the earth. Ground shadows sliding silently to the rear in long quiet streaks. A touch of aileron, a touch of rudder, more and more elevator as the earth nears and ground shadows progressively gain more and more magical speed.

The Cub's power is at idle, elevator, rudder and ailerons making final adjustments; airspeed and lift are on a steady decline as we settle towards the earth. The Cub, wanting to stay airborne, eases back on its axes to grab more lift, but the descent continues. Stiff gears reach out, knowing the earth is near.

Tires grab the hard surface of the frozen runway, a sharp jolt and the Cub shudders. The humming sounds of tires racing across gravel are everywhere--in the air, the airframe, the fabric and the plexiglas. The Cub sways and rocks as it races in and out of ruts and the imperfections of the runway's surface--rudder flipping back and forth holding the Cub to the runway's center as the ground speed bleeds off. We ease to a stop. The Cub sits in the middle of the runway, without motion, its destination. The propeller turns sheepishly. Power applied, flickering propeller blades disappear into a soft haze. The Cub begins to move towards the taxiway.

Max stirs, not fully awake, but somewhat aware, looking around, trying to make sense of his surroundings. His body twists slightly, trying to move out of a bad position, but the effort gives no rewards.

The last of day's-end fueling was in progress with several aircraft spread around the gas pit. Nearing the pump, I cut the switch and with a silent engine coasted the last five feet to a spot just behind 308. Except for distant voices and fueling activities there was only silence.

Max and I sat in place for a moment, studying familiar surroundings. Then feeling the pain of prolonged sitting, I made an effort to exit my seat. My belt was still fastened. I flipped the belt's quick release, struggling a bit, making more noise than usual, my tired limbs moving awkwardly against the stick, the seat and the walls of the cabin. Then half-sliding, I slipped through the door opening, my foot awkwardly hitting the struts, banging noisily as I worked my way down to some very hard ground. The earth felt strange, but each passing second brought relief. Looking over at Max, I seriously wondered if he would be able to get out by himself. There was no humor in his movements. His exit (like mine) was noisy and awkward. But after a bit of a struggle, he too was on the ground.

We were near the Cub's door, stretching our tired limbs, when Chad and Mel Reeves approached. They made a couple of humorous comments concerning our feeble movements. Then after some idle airport talk, Max and I directed the conversation towards the gravel pit and our two friends in the convertible. Of course we ad-libbed the details as much as possible. We all laughed, then there was some humorous speculation on just what the young couple's impressions were concerning the incident.

It was dark with the only light coming from distance pole lights mounted near the office and hangar. We pulled our few belongings out of a dark and noticeably warm cabin. In January, with the setting of the sun, temperatures drop rapidly. With each step, we could hear the crunching sounds of frozen gravel breaking up beneath our feet.

I checked the Cub's oil as Chad finished up the fueling. Then together we pushed it over to a tie-down and secured the ropes.

The yellow Cub sat there in the stillness of the evening as Chad and I walked away. The only tangible record that the flight had ever taken place would be a brief, overly simplified notation in my logbook indicating date, aircraft, dual flight time and destinations. But for me, the occasional future readings of the simple notations would forever open volumes of memories.

Experience Gained, Dignity Lost

Pilots had been calling in most of the day asking if the weather was clear enough for flying. But just as soon as one rainstorm began clearing out, another one came rolling in. Even a couple of the most determined pilots, who had spent most of the afternoon dividing their time between the lunch counter and the window had finally given up and headed home.

However, Mother Nature, being in another one of her unpredictable moods, had seen fit to clear out the storms just before sundown. Gray clouds dominated the heavens but the clearing was wide and high enough for flying. I was among the many who had been hoping for the break, but unlike the rest I was still at the airport. I hopped into the tan Cub, feeling almost triumphant that I could shoot a few landings before darkness.

I headed towards the take-off position on Runway 34. Through the open door, I occasionally studied the soggy ground and watched the front right tire splash through numerous puddles. The outside air was cool, even cold and filled with the heavy moisture of the early spring rainstorm. I pulled my jacket up a little tighter against the chilled air. Still, it was quite enjoyable being outside in the aftermath of the rain.

I lined up on the runway, applied power and after a short run I was in the air. While climbing up into the pattern I scanned the gray sky. In every direction dark, heavy clouds dominated. Between the late hour and threatening clouds, it definitely would be a short pattern flight. I had no problem with that.

I made a couple of rounds doing lazy take-offs and landings. At the completion of the third landing, I pushed the Carb Heat in and applied power for take-off. The engine hesitated and rumbled while trying to get up to full power. I leaned forward and pulled the Carb Heat to the "On" position. Then I continued to wander down the runway for a few seconds waiting and listening for the ice to clear. After a few very long seconds, the engine began picking up its rpm's. The engine sounded and felt solid once again. I pushed in the heat and we lifted into the sky for another uneventful trip around the pattern.

I've had carb ice on more than a couple of occasions and although an irritation it had never been a serious problem, except maybe the time I was with Happ. I had always chalked that up as inexperience and part of my learning curve. In fact, I liked to think I had learned a fair amount about carb ice since my early days.

While flying around the pattern, I remember wondering if a person ever gets to the point of not being concerned with the sounds of a rough running engine? I never considered carburetor ice to be in the same league as engine failure. But for me there was a little anxiety connected with it. I've often wondered whether Chad and our instructors worry about ice. They always seemed so relaxed and laid back.

I finished the trip around the pattern, applied heat, cut power and turned onto Base. There I applied a little power to clear the engine, everything normal. I cut the power back to idle and made the final turn onto Final.

The J–3 settled down to the runway, the wheels touched picture-perfect and I rolled a short distance. With everything under control, I leaned forward and pushed in the Carb Heat to the "Off" position and opened the throttle. The engine bust into power and we were again on our way.

What must have been only a few seconds later I could feel the power dropping off. I was about fifteen feet in the air with a good part of the runway behind me. Out front, I could see 2100 South and a row of power lines.

I quickly pulled the Carb Heat to the "On" position. The engine rumbled and the rpm's dropped off some more. I paused and listened while waiting for the ice to clear. The engine continued to rumble. Then it began to show signs of picking up, but I could see that it wasn't happening fast enough! With questionable power and a raised highway lined with telephone wires out front, I decided not to take a chance. I quickly pulled back on the throttle. I expected an immediate loss of air speed, altitude and a normal landing.

The Cub, seeming almost unaware of the power cut-back was content to glide merrily along. I nosed it down to the ground and tried to flair out. The Cub, still with plenty of good air on its wings, lifted eagerly back into the sky, to nearly its original height. I still had too much speed! How do you lose air speed in a hurry?

About that time, the prop flipped to the ten o'clock position and abruptly stopped. Seeing that fixed blade made me feel more committed than ever. The Cub, however, was paying little attention to my problem. It just kept floating along. Each time I tried taking it down and forcing it into a three-point landing; it lifted back into the sky.

Out front, the highway and power lines. They were noticeably closer than they had been just seconds earlier.

Back down again, I got the main gear on the ground and began to apply some brake. The Cub started slowing, but I could feel the tail lifting and I didn't want that. I eased off the brakes, held back on the stick, dropping the tail and hopefully slowing us down. But again, the Cub lifted back into the air.

Once more I worked the mains back down to the ground, again applying the brakes ever so slightly. The tail seemed to be holding level, but the Cub was still running along like a rabbit. A little more brake, again the tail lifted.

"Was there no happy medium"? I eased off the brakes and the tail settled. Again I softly eased in on the brakes. The Cub showed signs of slowing, be it ever so slightly. But the highway was still out front, approaching much too quickly! I slowly increased the pressure, looking for that perfect medium. Everything felt good. I eased my heels down a little harder. Things still looked good, I was slowing down. The tail was behaving. The highway was looking to be a little less threatening.

Then without warning, the tail began swinging up fast. The seat of my pants was telling me that I had lost it. I had gone too far! In the technical language of the designer I had slid over to the wrong side of the curve and into the shaded area marked "Nonreversible Danger."

In layman's terms, "Hey buddy you've screwed up and now you're in big, big trouble!"

I had reached a point where all the solid forces outside the flight envelope were dictating what my Cub would and would not do. The tail was going up and there was nothing I could do to stop it.

In a crisis, with no working options, one tends to fall back on instinct. I pulled back hard on the stick. It was all wasted effort. Flight controls were useless, dead weight, unneeded baggage. I had made them ineffective through my incompetent input.

The lifeless prop started dragging runway dirt with a sickening hollow sound that resonated throughout the aircraft. Aggravated by the new resistance up front, the tail lifted higher and higher. Then the main gear lifted clear of the runway into free air. The little Piper's tail slowly moved up until the Cub was standing on its nose, nearly vertical to the ground and still moving. I sat in the cockpit silent, still pulling on the stick and bracing my feet against the pedals with every ounce of strength I could muster.

I hung there, frozen in position, wondering what fate would decide. I never felt in danger; I never felt fear; I never felt much of anything, physically or emotionally. It was almost as if I wasn't there.

The rotation of the aircraft slowed down and then stopped, with the aircraft vertical to the ground. It sat there balanced on the crankshaft for what seemed an eternity. Mouth twisted and wide-eyed, I stared at the earth spread out in front of my windshield.

Then I felt movement. The J–3 was tipping back, back in the direction from which it had come, towards its gear, slowly at first, then a little faster. It was not going over on its back! It eased down, hitting the main tires and then bounced softly back and forth between the nose of the aircraft and the tires. With the last of the energy gone, it settled down to a three-point position, left tire, right tire and nose.

Almost before it had stopped bouncing and rocking, I had my belt off, feet out the door and sliding down to the ground. I really don't remember undoing my belt, or dropping down, or even why I was in such a hurry. I just suddenly found myself standing on the ground.

Then all was still, no movement, no sound, just the Cub sitting on the main gear with its face in the dirt and me standing there in a "this-can't-be-happening-to-me" stance.

For some reason, the tail of the Cub caught my attention, and I looked up at the unfamiliar sight. I was more than a little surprised about just how high it stuck up into the sky.

The Piper Cub reminded me of a little kid who had stumbled and landed face first in a mud hole. However, unlike the kid who is able to lift himself up and run home crying the Cub was without options. It just sat there--a monument to pilot error?

There was still some runway left. If only I hadn't been so foot-heavy on the brakes, we might have made it. Then again, when something bad or terrible happens even a complete idiot can stand back and realize he should have done things differently. Who knows, with my luck I might have been embedded in some car's door by now. Yet with all the unknowns, I wished that I could try the landing again. Or better yet, I wished it hadn't happened.

For a few seconds I just stood there, incoherent, numb, almost as if I were waiting for someone to wake me and tell me it was all a bad dream. Then without conscious thought, I turned and started walking towards the office, hands in my pockets, head down and thinking terrible thoughts.

Something made me look up. A short distance away I could see the entire airport staff headed in my direction, some running, some walking, but all in a hurry. Then for whatever reason, I looked to the north. There were a couple of cars parked on 2100 South. The occupants, some standing near their cars and others sitting in their cars stared over in the direction of my upended Piper. All must have been wondering, "What in blazes was that kid doing to get that airplane in such a predicament?"

When Glen and the rest of the crew got to the Cub, someone climbed up and looked into the cabin. He could see I had somehow neglected to turn the mag switch and fuel off. Reaching in, he turned everything off, canceling my neglect.

Eventually everyone heard my explanation as to what had happened. Carb ice was my best guess. Everyone agreed. Why the engine quit was understandable. Why the Cub was sitting on its nose was not quite so clear.

Moments later, crew members took positions to lower the Piper to its proper sitting position. With a couple of men on the nose and a couple under the fuselage, they worked the tail down to the ground. I stood back, content to let others right my wrongs. I had done enough already. Luckily, the prop was the only part that had sustained damage. One blade had been bent back until it had broken. The cowl was undamaged.

Of note, no one joked with me or asked why I didn't do something differently. I don't think I could have taken that. Questions and a rather shallow defense would come later.

After jockeying a few parked aircraft around, they pushed "my Cub" into the hangar for the night. Because of the late hour, the lights were turned off, the doors closed and everyone headed home. I paused on the way out and took one last look before leaving. A busted propeller on an airplane sure looks awful!

When I arrived at work the next morning, first thing, even before checking in at the office, I headed over to the main hangar. I guess I was hoping that the propeller had been replaced and everyone had forgotten the accident.

As soon as I passed through the shop door, I could hear people working out in the hangar area where the Cub was located. I headed in the direction of the noise, ducking under a wing or two along the way. In the middle of the hangar, I could see bright floor lamps. Then I could see Wally working on the front end of the tan Cub.

All the bolts had been removed from the prop hub, and as I ducked under the Cub's wing I noticed he was in the process of pulling the busted prop off the shaft. He looked in my direction and broke out in a warm smile that nearly spanned the width of his face. Apparently, he already knew who did what to what. I was still feeling a little down about the whole thing and had a little difficulty forcing even a fake smile.

With the busted prop cradled in his arms, Wally thrust it towards me in an almost ceremonial fashion. But as I (almost subconsciously), reached out to receive it he changed his mind and pulled it back. Then with a grin he began a monologue that emphasized the humorous side of busting up airplanes in general and props in particular.

Don't ask me how he did it, but he had me feeling almost good about the stupid thing that I had done! It was just pure art in the use of words, expressions and humor. Then with me grinning from ear to ear, he presented me with the

broken prop as if it were a coveted trophy. With the presentation came ap-
plause and cheers from Chad who was working a short distance away.

That little ceremony would always stand out as a memorial to the class of
people I was working with.

A shining new metal propeller was installed on the little tan Cub, and in the
opinion of most, it was a perfect marriage of prop and airplane.

I kept the broken souvenir for years, but somehow lost track of it.

One Man's Wings

You didn't have to talk to Lou Pangman for any length of time to know that
he loved aviation, aircraft and flying. It was in his blood. For whatever reason,
he started taking flying lessons a little later in his life, but one flight was all it
took. He was one hundred per cent committed.

If I remember right, Lou told me he had learned to fly in an old Aeronca
Champ. After getting his private license, he purchased an Ercoupe. As soon
as he had his own aircraft and put aside a little money, he purchased some
charts and began the planning of a cross-country flight.

With his tanks all topped off, his luggage on board, Lou and his wife
climbed in and fastened their seat belts. His destination was New York. The
trip would cross most of the country. His wife had the required charts neatly
folded on her lap. Except for refueling stops, Lou really didn't expect to use
them all that much. He was, by profession a truck driver, and he knew the
land like the back of his hand.

He taxied out to the run-up area, checked out his engine and then pulled
out onto the runway and opened up the throttle. They were on their way. The
initial part of the run was slow, but soon he was moving along at a good pace.
The aircraft felt a little heavy, the heat of the sun and his baggage load were
definitely affecting the Ercoupe's performance. Still, he was confident that
there would be no problem. The seconds ticked away and more of the runway
drifted to the rear. Confidence waned, doubt became fear and everything felt
wrong. He wasn't going to make it!

He pulled back on the throttle and hit the brake. The nose of the little
airplane dipped down hard, compressing the nose wheel strut. The sound of
tires skidding across loose dirt filled the interior of the aircraft. Gravel and
dirt flew up, bouncing off the Ercoupe's underside making rumbling and

banging sounds. The Ercoupe quickly used up what was left of the short strip and continued onto the over-run. Dirt flew into the air as the little wheels tore deeper into the softer earth. The Ercoupe bounced hard across the uneven ground and slid into weeds, then through a patch of scrub brush. A dirt road, lined with a derelict fence, loomed out front. Lou pushed harder on the already fully depressed brake. Just when he thought he had had made it, a single broken fence post appeared and then disappeared beneath his wing. A sickening thud echoed through out the little Ercoupe as the post slammed into the fabric and metal of the wing. The aircraft bounced, rocked and came to an abrupt stop. Lou and his wife watched anxiously as a heavy cloud of dust settled in on top of their aircraft.

How much damage had the wing sustained? The fence post looked so short and old, maybe there was more noise than damage, but that was wishful thinking. For Lou and his wife, the trip was over.

Discouraged, not Lou. He couldn't stop thinking of flight and aircraft. That's all he dreamed about.

An aircraft banked and turned towards Utah Central's pattern. But unlike most of the local aircraft around the airport, it carried a much heavier sound, a very distinctive sound. As it approached the pattern, the shape took on the lines of a World War II trainer, a Vultee BT–13. Sunlight flashed off its unpainted metal wings as it banked and turned into the pattern. The wings leveled out on Final and the tail dropped a tad as it settled down towards the strip and bounced lazily at touch-down. The big silver plane coasted to a near stop. A little throttle, a burst of power, a cloud of dust and the aircraft was once again moving down the strip. It continued to the next turn-off and made an exit onto the taxiway.

Taxiing to a position near the edge of the ramp, the BT eased to a stop. The pilot revved up the mighty Pratt and Whitney engine. Sound waves echoed back and forth between the parked aircraft, buildings and then bounced around some more. He cut the switches, the thunder ceased and the propeller coasted down. Then, silence.

The pilot paused, placed his arms on the canopy rails while studying the area. Shortly, he unbuckled his belts and slipped out of their confinement. Raising himself up in the cockpit, he lifted his leg over the sidewall and onto the left wing. Cautiously he took the few steps to the wing's trailing edge and hopped down.

A few onlookers began to assemble around the big Vultee. The pilot approached one individual standing nearby and asked in a rather friendly tone, "Hi, where can I find Lou?"

Lou had bought a BT–13. He was making a jump, a huge jump, from a "puddle jumper" to a big military trainer. He was a low-time pilot who had done most of his flying in small, low-powered aircraft and most of that was in an airplane with non-standard controls. It was a giant step from a small, easy-to-fly nose-wheel Ercoupe to a high-powered BT–13 military trainer with a tail wheel. In more than a few circles, people said Lou was sticking his neck out not just a little, but a full country mile. Lou knew of the rumors going around the field, but he was one of those people who did what he wanted and paid little attention to what others were thinking or saying.

While the BT–13 was an impressive aircraft, it did, for many, have a dark side. Norma, one of our instructors had a pilot friend killed in a BT–13 accident. He was a former test pilot and the accident occurred while in the pattern. Accidents like that seemed to add fire to the BT's reputation. At times, for some, it could be deadly.

I've talked to several people concerning the BT's so-called "unpredictable flying characteristics." None could give me a satisfactory answer as to what the BT's problems were, if indeed there were any. One individual told me the wings were too small for the aircraft, another told me the wing's airfoil was all wrong. Still another individual told me that the military wanted tricky, and hard-to-fly training aircraft. Hard-to-fly aircraft sharpened the pilots' flying skills. Then when the pilot graduated to the higher performing and more expensive aircraft there were fewer accidents. Bottom line the government saved money.

Was there a problem, I don't know? However, many people seemed to agree, that under certain conditions, at the most unexpected time, the BT could simply roll over and fall out of the sky.

For those flying the BT–13 aircraft, the rule seemed to be, "you have to be with the aircraft every second or it will take you down." Lou had heard the stories and he knew of the trainer's reputation, but it didn't so much as make him blink. World War II pilots who had trained in the BT were for the most part very young. If those kids could do it, he certainly could! It was a personal challenge, and he looked forward to the experience. When it came to flying, fear was not in his vocabulary.

Lou paid fifteen hundred dollars for the BT. As part of the sale, the owner said he would check Lou out in the trainer. Unforeseen circumstances made the promise impossible to fulfill.

Lou made calls to the area airports, hoping someone could give him some dual instruction. None could be found without an extended waiting period. While waiting for an instructor, Lou decided that he might as well spend some time getting acquainted with his newly acquired airplane.

He found a Pilot's Manual in the map case. Lou later told me that when he first opened the BT's manual, everything was new, almost foreign. He read the manual continually, at home, on the job and as much as possible while sitting in the BT's cockpit. He read, studied, read again, memorized and practiced.

The little Continental engines on the "puddle jumpers" offered little experience in the operation of his big Pratt & Whitney radial. The start up, shut down, cold weather and flight procedures were each listed in their own section of the manual. At first, the information and procedures were overwhelming. Every operation seemed so exact, so precise and required such specific step-by-step sequences. But the procedures were a challenge to his liking. He spent hours in the cockpit with his hands on the controls pretending to move them as if the aircraft was operational. Instruments were studied, their makings and functions. If the markings were vague, he would make clarification notes on tape and stick them in a conspicuous place.

A control column or "stick" had replaced the familiar steering wheel of the Ercoupe and there was also a big set of rudder pedals to replace the single brake pedal in his Ercoupe. He spent extra time with his eyes closed, pretending he was taxiing on the ground or making turns in the sky. He practiced rudder and stick movement and coordination until he was bored. Eventually the stick and pedals became second nature and the Ercoupe's steering wheel was put deep in the back of his mind. Lou later told me, with a smile, that early in his training he had found himself trying to move the stick to the left or right for turning, a carry-over from the Ercoupe's control system.

After a time, the engine and aircraft's operation, procedures and limitations became second nature. The words in the book became redundant; he could quote the procedure and mimic the control movement properly before he reviewed any given page! The book became an "after-the-fact" verification.

His next step was to get the feel of his Vultee trainer while under power. He spent a considerable amount of time taxing the big BT up and down the lonely parts of the airport.

A few days later, he felt he knew the controls and handling characteristics well enough to graduate to a world that was just a little faster. He and his BT moved out onto the runway. He started out slow then gradually increased his taxi speeds to a point where there was enough forward speed or wind to lift the tail. Each time Lou could feel the aircraft getting lighter, near-lift off speed he would ease back on the throttle. The engine would wind down permitting the trainers' speed to bleed off, down loading the aircraft's weight back onto the landing gear. He practiced until he could feel exactly what the aircraft would do at what speed.

Still anxious and with no Check Out Flight in sight, he began thinking about the next step. With just a little more airspeed, he would actually be flying. He wanted to get the wheels off the ground, even for a few seconds. He felt he was more than ready.

Lou sat at the end of Runway 16 in takeoff position, canopy open and engine at idle. He looked down into the cockpit, first at the controls on his left, then across the panel, pausing at each instrument and then making a quick sweeping glance across the right side. Then a final check on the movement of all flight controls to ensure they were all free.

Out in front of the windshield, past the radio mast and the big massive cowling that shook softly under idling power, the runway beckoned and waited. The huge cowling obstructed most of the view directly ahead, but the view slightly off to the front quarters was more than adequate. Lou leaned his head out from behind the protection of the windshield. A steady breeze from the big loping propeller carried a slight and an almost sweet smell of burned fuel and oil from the engine.

Beyond the idling propeller lay the runway. Its long path looked as if it reached to the swell in the distance valley floor, far to the south. Lou knew the narrow runway was not nearly as long as it appeared.

The position of the pilot's seat caught his attention, and he made some minor adjustments, first to his seat, then his belts and then he paused. His entire body tingled with excitement as he thought of what he was about to do. On that day, at that time, he was to make his first flight in his BT–13. It would be a very short flight. He would lift off; fly a few seconds and then land, all before the end of the runway. It was to him, the next natural step. If everything went okay, the next day would be a full flight around the pattern.

He looked down the runway and for the first time could feel shadows of doubts creeping in, not in his ability but in preparation. Had he forgotten anything? Had he done every thing possible to prepare for the flight? He looked around at his huge aircraft with all its mass and power. Maybe a few more practice runs, a little more time, even a day, even an hour. The doubts faded, deep down he knew he was ready and more ground time would not improve his performance. He could do it; he knew he could. He was ready.

He took a deep breath, again noting the position of the throttle, the prop control, the mixture, the trim tab and the flaps. Satisfied, he eased the throttle forward. The big nine cylinder, 450 hp, Pratt and Whitney power plant broke out of its slumber spitting flame and thunder. The sound of the roaring engine was deafening. Power surged through every part of Lou's body like some huge electrical charge. His hands could feel the power in the throttle and through the stick. His body could feel it through the seat of his pants and his feet could feel it on the rudder pedals. The cowling twisted and trembled, the canopies shook in their tracks and the airframe was alive with the power from the anxious engine. Army pilots had nicked named the husky BT–13, "The Vibrator," and for good reason.

The four thousand plus pounds of aircraft started moving. Lou, his confidence at an all-time high, alert, leaning slightly forward watched and waited as the forces in his aircraft grew. The big prop, little more than a haze, clawed at heavy air and threw it violently to the rear. A chill swept Lou's body and every sensation in his being was telling him he was at the threshold of the greatest adventure of his life.

Clods of dirt and gravel were ripped from the runway's surface by the angry propeller blast, pulverized and scattering it in the wind. Slow at first, but with each revolution of the wheels, the aircraft moved faster. Wind passing the open canopy was tugging at Lou's shirtsleeves. Intently, he viewed the runway on the left and then the right side of the protruding cowling, making sure the craft was tracking properly down the narrow strip. A giant dust cloud, growing in size, was racing to the rear as the trainer gained more speed. Seconds passed and Lou pushed the stick forward, heavy and unwilling. But as the airspeed indicator moved across higher numbers the tail grew lighter. Then it lifted clear, free of the runway, higher, until the aircraft was in a near-level position. With the tail up, the rushing runway was fully visible over the weathered and pitted anti-glare paint of the cowling. Lou sat in the cockpit, tension losing out to excitement. Subconsciously he was making adjustments in rudder and elevator while waiting for the aircraft to tell him it was ready for flight. The wide track gear was tracking true, making it easy to hold course. Lou eased back on the stick. He could feel the full weight of the aircraft in his arm, but the pressure was easing. Hard, friendly air slid over the wings faster and faster. More and more the weight of the aircraft was moving from the landing gear up to the wings. The aircraft was getting lighter, transforming from an awkward piece of earthly machinery to a graceful aircraft of flight.

Space appeared between the free spinning tires and streaked earth. The uneven rumbling of the ground ceased. A second of flight and one of the aircraft's wings settled. An extended landing gear eased down, touched the ground and then broke clear of a final cloud of earthly dust. Lou pressed the toe brakes and the spinning wheels stopped their rumbling. Then there were no earthly sounds. Lou sat in the BT's cockpit, shaking mildly with excitement. He was surrounded by what he loved, instruments, controls and the sounds of powered flight. Even with all of the thunder, they seemed to be moving without effort, without restrictions, in their element.

At flying speed, the small dirt strip was quickly being used up, and Lou wanted that short flight and landing before a full trip around the pattern. He had what he wanted; his thoughts turned to the landing.

He pulled back the throttle. Without power, the will of flight was lost and the air suddenly became almost an invisible net dragging on every part of the aircraft. Lou was pulled forward, pressing against his seat belts, almost as if his BT had flown into a curtain of molasses. Immediately the aircraft began to settle. The quickness of the descent caught Lou off guard. He cussed himself for not easing back the throttle a little slower. He knew better! He reapplied power but his altitude was gone and his trainer was not much more than shaped steel and aluminum. The main tires hit the runway in a two-point landing position. Dirt erupted from beneath the wheels. The plane started a nose-up bounce, but Lou caught it with forward stick movement, forcing the main wheels back down solid to the ground. The airspeed bled off and the tail settled heavily to the ground and bounced. The trainer rumbled down the strip and rolled to a stop.

Lou sat there for a few seconds, his body ready to burst with excitement and pride. He had done it, the BT was his mount; he its master.

He applied throttle; the Pratt and Whitney burst into power and the aircraft moved forward. He taxied down the runway until he neared a taxi turnoff where he backed off on the throttle. Easing in on a left brake and rudder, he made the turn to the taxiway and headed back to the ramp. It would be difficult to convey the excitement that Lou was experiencing.

When Lou described his first flight to me he was almost incoherent. He fumbled for words, but none seemed to describe what he had experienced. Using his hands continually, he tried to explain his feelings. Lou was just like all the other pilots around the airport, to talk of flying was work for the hands. Words were a background to what the hands were describing. One old pilot told me "If you cut off a pilot's hands, he would be a babbling idiot!"

Every weekend Lou was out at the airport tinkering with and flying his big BT. On most of those weekends he had his wife at his side. When Lou took the BT up, she was usually in the back seat. I don't think she enjoyed it quite as much as Lou, but she must have enjoyed it some.

Generally, his weekend flights lasted about an hour. If I remember right, at the end of the flight I would top off his tanks for about fifteen dollars. On one occasion, while refueling his Vultee, I spent some time comparing the cost of his flight with that of a Piper Cub. Jokingly I said to myself that I could fly a Cub for a week with the fuel the BT burns in an hour. Yet standing on the big wing of the BT–13, I felt Lou's money was well spent.

I've heard that leaky landing gear struts and fuel tanks were often a big maintenance problem for many BTs, but I don't think Lou had problems of any kind during the time he owned the aircraft. Lou's BT–13 was quite economical to own and fly. It was just feed it and fly it.

Glen, and some of the other employee didn't view Lou and his big military aircraft with quite the same enthusiasm as me. To many he was "Hot Shot Lou." His airplane and his sometimes wild flying around green students in Piper Cubs was a combination that Glen would just as soon not have. He said it sent the wrong message to students. I always felt that Glen was just a little prejudiced. But, as I grew older, I could see more clearly Glen's point of view.

Lou knew that I loved his BT. Many times he had extended an invitation for me to go up with him. And I've got to admit that I wanted to go up in the worst way. At the same time, there were people on the field who cautioned me not to go. "He's always pushing it and one of these days he's going down."

Maybe it was my youth or inexperience or maybe the others were a tad over-protective. Still, the decision turned out to be a bit of a struggle. The BT finally won out. I approached Lou one day and asked if his invitation still stood. He grinned, and I had an airplane ride.

With more than a little excitement, I climbed up the side of the BT, swung myself over the sidewall and dropped down into the seat. The rear cockpit was huge when compared to a Cub. Massive structural tubing, controls, push rods, brackets, knobs, instruments, radio and dials, there was something everywhere. My feet rested on two boards like panels that were some distance above the bottom skin of the aircraft. After the Piper Cub, it was a feeling of sitting in a big boiler room. Out beyond the open canopy, the distant wings stretched out, looking almost like the wings of another airplane. And from where I was sitting, the wings' construction appeared heavy, almost boilerplate.

The starter engaged with its high-pitched whine. Leaning off to the side, I could see the tips of the propeller blades flickering in the sunlight. Then the engine caught, at first with a rumble, then with the power and thunder that shook every corner of the airframe. My body jumped with excitement and anticipation.

The throttle eased forward, the power level of the engine gained prominence and the massive trainer began moving across the ground. The Cubs, with their small lightweight frames and balloon tires seemed to emphasize the swells and depressions of the earth. The big BT on the other hand, with its extra weight and size did a fair job of smoothing things out. The ride over to Runway's 27's take-off position felt more like a bus ride on a well-paved road.

The engine and flight controls in the rear cockpit are linked directly to the controls in the front cockpit. So when Lou made control movements or an adjustment up front, I, for the most part, could see exactly what he was doing. It was kind of fun to watch and even anticipate his input.

As we were taxiing out to take-off position, I couldn't help but think of all the power contained in the BT's engine and the fact that it was all being passed off to the relatively small two-blade propeller. That propeller somehow had to claw and grab enough thin air to pull all of the weight of the aircraft forward fast enough to lift the heavy trainer. I guess all the calculations said it would do what it does, but man! As I looked around at the mass of that aircraft, it was almost impossible to imagine that the air we breathe could lift and support that massive structure.

One thing stands out in my memory of that flight, aside from the brute power and massive size. It was the view looking forward at Lou over the rear instrument panel. The curved plexiglas canopy and its framing created a nearly half-circular tunnel leading to the front cockpit where Lou was sitting. Between my panel and the back of his seat was a cluster of tubing or rollover bars. Lou seemed so far away and unconnected, so vastly different from a Cub. He was wearing his familiar and somewhat old and faded baseball cap. An old set of military type headphones were draped across his hat and down on his ears. He sat tall, alert, dividing his attention between the displays on the inside and all that was drifting by on the outside. A friendly wind from the open canopy was playing with his shirtsleeves. I studied him and his surroundings for a time, wondering how he felt up there in front doing what he so much loved to do. Without question, there was pride and satisfaction in every fiber of his body. Ironically, we were but feet apart in the same aircraft, in nearly identical cockpits but a world apart in our status. I envied him; his place seemed such a neat place to be.

It was a short flight, just a few trips around the pattern. I think Lou was aware of the peer pressure I was under and made a special effort to mellow out even the so-called normal maneuvers. I would always be thankful for the ride, even as short as it was, but man, would it have been neat to fly around the world in his BT.

Late one afternoon, a Waco YKS biplane moved up towards the gas pump. It was a big aircraft with its two sets of wings and big radial engine. Like most aircraft of days past, it was all fabric except for the area around the engine. It was orange in color, with a narrow black stripe down the side of the fuselage.

With its size, color and age it stood out boldly and demanded more than its fair share of attention.

With heavy rpm's, its movements were somewhat suppressed with squeaky brakes as the pilot inched the aircraft up onto the blacktop surrounding the gas pit. Brakes applied and the aircraft eased to a stop. The pilot then revived up the big 245 hp Jacobs radial engine and cut the switches. The unwinding engine was inundated with the sounds of sucking, blowing, compression kicks and metallic push rods clicking as they did their thing with the valves. Then the Jacobs shuttered and twisted on it mounts, almost like a wet dog shaking off excess water. It finally came to a compression point that stopped the big, polished two-bladed propeller short of a free unwinding. It's easy to see why some people referred to the old Jacob engine as "Shaky Jake."

Silence, then the sounds of seat belt buckles clinking against metal and cushions, followed by the shuffling sounds of feet moving across carpeted floorboards. The door handle turned and the door swung open revealing the pilot. He stepped through the opening, took a few steps across the wing, paused and jumped down to the ground. He looked around for a few seconds before ordering fuel. Then thanking me, he headed over towards the main hangar.

I was unwinding the gas hose while admiring the big Waco when Lou's BT, which had also just landed, came rolling across the ramp. It was obvious that Lou was in a hurry as he normally didn't taxi quite that fast. He pulled up to a spot some distance behind the Waco and before his propeller had completely unwound, stood up in the cockpit, swung himself over the edge, bounced across the wing, jumped down to the ground and headed towards the Waco's pilot. I found out later that Lou had seen the Waco some thirty-five miles out and had followed it in.

When Lou finally caught up with the pilot, he immediately asked him if he was the owner of the Waco. The pilot identified himself as the owner and a long conversation was in the making. The Waco owner continued in the direction of the hangar with Lou right at his side. Lou was asking all kinds of questions about the Waco, What was its horsepower? What was its cruising speed? Was it maneuverable? How did it fly? What's its stall like, having two wings? The last thing I heard as they disappeared into the shadows of the open hangar doors were Lou's words, "What do you want for it?"

Lou had made a comment some time back that he might be getting rid of his BT. Glen had expressed some relief when he heard the news. I guess Glen would always feel that Utah Central would be better off without Lou, his big airplane and occasional grandstanding. Somehow, while looking at the dark entrance of the main hanger, I could feel Glen's spirit sagging.

Later, I walked by Lou and the owner and they were still deep in discussion. From what I could hear of the conversation, it sounded like Lou was a Waco owner if he could sell his Vultee.

Lou's BT–13 was put up for sale, and a short time later it was gone. The speed of its sale didn't surprise me; it was one cherry airplane. If I had the money, I would have grabbed it myself.

Before Lou's first Waco flight, its former owner and Lou spent a considerable amount of time walking around and discussing its attributes. They removed the engine's cowling and Lou got a good briefing on the workings of a Jacob radial engine. Judging from the time they spent pointing and looking, I was wondering if Lou was getting a Jacob's familiarization talk or boning up for his A & E Mechanic's license.

Then into the Waco's cabin, where there was more talk. After a time, the engine was fired up, and then more talk and then they went flying. They spent some time out in the practice area and then the two made a series of takeoffs and landings.

The Waco was a super aircraft, but still, I used to wonder if Lou didn't like the BT, or what? Why or how could anyone sell an aircraft like a BT–13? Yet, as I got to know him better, I could see that he had a hankering to own or fly everything he could get his hands on. Since he couldn't own them all at once, I guess he figured the next best thing was to own them all one at a time. Everything flying was his favorite.

I got checking around and as near as I could tell Lou's Waco was built in the mid 1930's; in my book that's old, but not ancient. Still, I never realized how much things have changed in aircraft design until Lou invited me inside the cabin and showed me around. The Waco's cabin was antique in all of its most beautiful forms. The instrument panel was more artwork than display. The steering wheels were huge. You couldn't compare them to the ones in our Cessnas. And unlike the more modern aircraft, where the control wheels are mounted on a shaft that penetrates the panel, the Waco's steering wheels are mounted on a husky "Y"-shaped post mounted to the floor. Just by looking

at the shape of the seats and their upholstering, one could tell he was looking at something bred at a different time by designers who were part of a
much different world.

Lou offered me a ride in his beautiful Waco. I guess the BT ride had broken the ice. I had flown with him in one of his magnificent airplanes and
the experience was just too memorable. I knew those aircraft wouldn't be
around forever, and I didn't want to miss what might be my only opportunity. Did I thoroughly enjoy the flight? You bet! It would be my only ride in an
antique biplane.

Times do change. At sunset, instead of hearing and seeing the big BT–13
banking into the pattern with the sun flashing off shining metal, the sun
would be reflecting off the biplane's fabric wings with the unmistakable orange that seemed to blaze in the sky.

The Triumph of Being

The seconds ticked, the minutes drifted by, but the hours seemed to die a
slow death. The entire school day was spent, first looking out the window
daydreaming, and then glancing up at the clock to see if the big hand had
moved. Outside the sky was blue, the air was cool, flying would be at its best,
but somehow the classroom walls made flying seem so very distant.

That day after school I would go to the airport, not to work but to fly. I had
a nice little trip planed over to Promontory Point. That was where the historical Golden Spike was driven back in the late 1800s. It was not a long trip, just
a little flying beyond the confines of the pattern.

Originally, I had planed a trip up north to Pocatello, Idaho. Glen had put
the stops on that flight saying he didn't want a Cub tied up that long. He then
suggested a little shorter trip, maybe to the Point. While in the middle of his
verbal suggestion, he was scribbling my name on the schedule, under the date
of his preference, with just enough time allotted for the flight of his suggestion. Being somewhat boxed in, my choices were somewhat limited.

I guess for personal satisfaction, I took a quick look at the wall map to see
if anything jumped out as more interesting but found nothing. With no
alternative, I accepted the flight suggested. Looking on the brighter side, I
knew that with Glen's blessings the flight, be it a bit abbreviated, was almost
guaranteed. And to be honest, things had been a little busy around the field,

so any flight would be a good one. Bottom line, I was going flying and the "where to" really didn't matter!

Plans made, permission given, schedules verified, aircraft allocated, but no one ever said it's a perfect world. When I got to the airport, my scheduled J–3 was out with a student and being my double lucky day, the other Cub was also out. Can't blame Glen, business is business. However, he assured me that both Cubs were scheduled back shortly and the first one back was mine. I wandered out to the gas pump, sat down on the stool and scanned the sky hoping to see an approaching speck that would be my Cub.

After what seemed an eternity, the tan Cub finally entered and wandered around the pattern. Finally, it dipped down behind the distant brush as it made its way down to the runway. Then after some more waiting, it trudged up to the gas pit, parked, sat there, and then finally shut down.

I pushed the Cub over to the north side of the pit where it couldn't be seen from the office, at least without some effort. It was a selfish act, but it just might give Glen the impression that I had already left and that would be fine with me. With both Cubs due in at about the same time there was always the possibility that he might give mine to a student. The last thing I wanted him to say to some Johnnie-come-lately was, "Boy are you in luck, if you hurry you can take up 308; Ron is getting it ready for you as we speak."

I quickly topped off the tank and moved the stool back near the pit. Then pushing the Cub a little further to the north, I checked the oil and did a quick preflight. Without any fanfare, I got Chad over for a quick prop and headed out towards the runway. I could have been wearing blinders when I passed by the office area, as I wouldn't have noticed if the place was on fire. Sorry, but I really wanted to go flying.

I cleared the field in a somewhat short pattern and without any real conscious intent; I set up a course to the north, northwest. With that heading, the Cub's tail pointed right at the airport. Returning would be my decision and that decision was definitely in the future!

True to my daylong anticipations, the sky was perfect; visibility was unlimited with just a few white fluffy clouds spread across the blue. The air was cool and super smooth. I was bundled up in heavy clothing, and comfortable even with the door and windows open. The Continental engine purred and the passing air made the familiar sounds of a Cub in flight! I can remember making some final adjustments in my sitting position and then leaned back completely relaxed.

I found myself listening to the engine, the wind, maybe even studying their familiar sounds. The sights were there too, an empty front seat, the somewhat distant instruments on the panel, struts, even the fabric tape on the bottom of the wings. Simple things, even dumb things, maybe. But together they make up the wonderful world of being in a Cub high in the sky.

With the ETA (Estimated Time of Arrival) and flight times completely gone on my Promontory Point schedule, I decided to just point the nose at whatever looked interesting. I would continue to fly, putting time in the sky until the coming dusk forced me to make the inevitable one-eighty and head back.

I had never tried to get very high, just for the sake of higher altitudes; one reason, the Cub was not famous for its ability to climb. It took time. Moreover, I guess things were always interesting enough near the ground. However, on that day there was only distance lake water and the huge expanses of the desert, all of which presented something less than captivating scenery. With not a lot to look at, climbing just to be climbing seemed to be a good alternative.

Off to the northwest, I could see Antelope Island with its peaks slowly drifting in front of the distant horizon. The February colors of the island were mostly the gold shades of hibernating grass. Even rock formations seem to have taken on the lifeless winter colors. Then smiling a bit, I got thinking of my Piper Cub, its faded, nondescript and oxidized tan was a perfect match.

A cloud formation was resting above the island. I studied the mass and figured its base to be about 9,000 feet, not far above my altitude. In movies, clouds are often used to represent the unknown or even adventure. Who hasn't looked into cloud-filled heavens and wondered what it would be like to wander through the white, fluffy mist? I certainly have. At that moment, everything that seemed adventurous, mysterious and exciting in life was just a short distance to the northwest.

I put the little Cub into a wide left turn and continued climbing. The mass of clouds drifted slowly to a position in front of the Cub. Steadily, I continued closing in on the formation and with each passing moment, I could feel the excitement building. The mass grew, extending its presence in all directions.

I studied the mountainous shape; somehow it looked much too massive, too dense and too heavy to be floating around in the sky.

As I passed the flat expanse of the bottom, I suddenly realized that I was looking at something I had never seen before in my life, clouds between the earth and me.

Then, almost unnoticed with the distance closing, the Cub seemed to be picking up speed. The cloud was moving in faster and faster.

My shadow bounced into the formation, then eagerly crawled up the side of the twisting billows and zoomed up over the edge. It was a sensation of climbing out of a body of water onto a beach. I eased the nose of the Cub down to level flight. It was strange, different, like looking at another world.

There were areas that were laid out in bumpy, twisting billows. Here and there were stacks of huge out-croppings of mist, like odd-shaped trees, even hills covered with snow or cotton candy. Deep caves; fissions and huge crevasse penetrated the mass, twisting into deep shadows that were enticing and beckoned to be explored. Depths and swells appeared, disappeared and then reappeared. Misty formations in the shapes of animals, some appearing almost vicious, while others seemed cuddly and friendly. Off to the sides were distant forms, watching with curiosity while other nearby shapes were playfully reaching out at my little Cub as we passed.

The Cub passed over an opening, a vertical shaft, a deep canyon lined with massive gray jagged clouds, sealed in place with dark forbidding shadows. Through the twisted opening, I got a flashing glimpse of the western shore of Antelope Island, thousands of feet below. For some unknown reason the fear of heights flashed through my body, and then the view was gone. Once again, there were only the gray clouds streaking to the rear. The Cub's shadow, surrounded by its glowing halo, was bouncing, dancing wildly up and down, bending back and forth, near and far.

I nosed the Cub down to within a few feet of a relatively flat area, then lower until the landing gear and the lower half of fuselage were periodically buried in the mist. A world of white sped towards me and then flashed to the rear. The sensation of speed was incredible.

A little rudder and a wing tip cut through a column. Billows rushed up and then were gone. Mist played at the cabin's open door, swirling, teasing at arm's length, almost pausing, seemingly wanting to reach inside and then flashed to the rear. The Cub rolled over into a steep bank and passed between two vertical formations without touching either. Banking steeply in the opposite direction, I watched a vertical stack of clouds pass near the top of the cabin. Leveling out, I slipped through some twisting billows, forever disfiguring the formation. The propeller cut through yet another column that draped the cabin with flickering shadows. Back down to the level and again the J–3 cut a path as it plowed through the mist.

Aileron, rudder, elevator, the Cub soared in and out, up and down, streaking across the surface of the playful mist. One second I was near a weightless state, then a second later I was pressed firmly into my seat. We leaped, we dove, we turned and we played. The Cub and I, not one giving directions with the other obeying, but two acting as one, having fun doing what they both loved.

Then my faithful shadow streaked out over the edge of the cloud mass and unseen, hit the lake water many thousands of feet below. All sensations of speed were lost. The Cub once again seemed stationary and very alone, content with making noise but lacking noticeable speed. Applying power, I lifted the nose up once more to continue my quest for higher air.

The sun was nearing the western horizon, and its position put a little bit of a kink in my subconscious dream of a never-ending flight. It was February and it's easy to forget just how short the days are. Staying up in the sky for the duration of my desires was no longer my decision.

Still I had a little time, I could climb through a wide arc on my way back. A little rudder and aileron and the aircraft gracefully banked left into a new heading to the southwest. Slowly the north end of the Oquirrh Mountain Range moved into a position out in front of, and below the nose of my Cub. I settled back and studied the distant mountains.

To my left and above, I caught sight of the tail of a long white contrail drifting out from behind the leading edge of my wing. I depressed a rudder; the Cub swung off to one side enabling me to follow the white trail to a four-engine aircraft. It was a B–29 or maybe a B–50, as I assumed that most of the B–29s had been retired. Yet, looking closer, I could see that it was a 29. I studied the shapely lines of the outdated bomber no longer wanted by the Air Force. Every line contributed to its still modern beauty and sleekness. It was hard to imagine that the friendly giant up there in the heavens, was just a few years before one of the most efficient machines of destruction know to man. Yet, I was seeing only beauty and grace in flight. Whatever its past, however outdated, at that moment the mighty bomber was at peace and a beauty to behold. Would it, or could it ever look old? I doubted that!

It was close enough so that I could see a round blister on the side of the fuselage; exhaust stains along the sides of the engines and even a bit of glass on the nose. A short distance behind the trailing edge of the wings the racing contrails swiftly sped to the rear, giving it speed in the still sky. The big bomber with its four mighty thunder-producing engines, turning their huge four-bladed propellers moved in silence. The only sound in my part of the sky was the very noticeable thunder of my Cub, with its little four-banger engine chewing away at the sky with its little two-blade propeller.

The bomber passed behind my wing leaving only the white contrail visible. I depressed some rudder and once again the bomber moved into view. Man, wouldn't it be something to fly alongside that beauty! What if? I knew I couldn't catch up, even if it stopped and waited. Ignoring the obvious, I pulled back hard on the stick and hit the rudder to swing the Piper up and around into the direction of the giant. The Cub, caught almost by surprise, immediately started shuddering and rebelling, refusing the request by threatening to stall.

I pushed the nose back down into friendlier air. Once more, I looked up at the mighty Superfortress surrounded by all its forbidden airspace. Somewhat content with having seen the giant from such a special vantage point, I swung my J–3 to its previous heading and continued my climb.

The J–3 inched higher, but progressively each foot of altitude gained was at a slower rate than the last. The Cub has no rate-of-climb instrument and it got to the point where the altimeter didn't seem to move at all. I was beginning to wonder if my only gain, (what little there was of it), was the result of fuel being burned off. If that were the case, I would reach maximum altitude only if I kept on climbing until my tank ran dry. How high could I get anyway? Now there's a question worth thinking about! Should I try for the ultimate altitude, stupid probably, but fun definitely! Man, wouldn't that be something. And when I did run out of fuel, I would be high, and I mean high. I bet I could glide for an hour, maybe more. That alone would be worth the effort!

Moreover, with all the salt flats in northwestern Utah, finding an emergency field would be no problem. Sadly, almost any landing in northern Utah would come with a three-day walk to find any signs of life. And then there was Glen--what would he say? Being over thirty, he probably wouldn't understand!

I stared at my altimeter again. It had hardly moved. I really didn't know what higher altitudes take away from engine performances, but something was definitely being lost. Still, that little Continental might not be doing what it was capable of doing at sea level, but you couldn't tell with all the noise it was making.

Looking down, I gazed at the hazy earth. There seemed no movement at all. I felt stationary. It was almost as if some cruel individual had a rope tied around my tail and was holding me back.

I leaned over towards the door opening. Looking down, squinting my eye, I sighted across a point on my right tire and lined it up with a building far below. After a few seconds, I could definitely see some movement. Somehow, I felt some satisfaction at the confirmation.

Then leaning further out into the wind, I glanced back in the direction that I had just come from. The cloud formation still looked to be parked right over the distant island. I applied a little right rudder to get a better view. From where I was, the adventure of the cloud formation still beckoned, and somehow, I could feel a yearning to return and continue to explore its mysteries.

A moment of heightened satisfaction, the hand of the altimeter was finally indicating 13,500 feet. It was a goal I had set sometime earlier. At the time, I was not sure that I could reach that seemingly forbidden altitude.

The Oquirrh Mountains were directly below. The Salt Lake Valley spread out to my left and beyond. On the far side of the valley were the majestic Wasatch Mountains. Although not so obvious, I was above their highest peak that reached up to something just under 12,000 feet. I was looking down on some mighty mountains that I had been looking up at all my life.

The valley floor was somewhere around four thousand plus feet. What if I were on the coast where the ground was near sea level. That would put me an additional four thousand feet above the ground. Wow! That would really make it a long ways down! The thought made me feel like I was almost in outer space. Then still excited about my personal altitude achievement, I thought of Mount Everest the highest mountain in the world. I tried to imagine what it would look like if it were sitting in the middle of the Salt Lake Valley. Now that would be a mountain! It would be towering many thousands of feet higher than even the mighty Wasatch Mountains. In comparison, they would appear as mere foothills.

Then disappointments flew in from every direction. I remember thinking, almost out loud, "I'm not even up to the top of the ground yet!" I suddenly felt as if I was flying down an irrigation ditch, suffocating in its depths. How does one put size into perspective? What is really high or big? The world is big. Then there is the universe. Maybe the world is small. And if it is, what does that make me? I didn't even try to come up with answers. But at that moment I was beginning to feel like the smallest of the small. There I was, trying to imagine myself in near outer space, while in reality I was just bumping along the ground.

A cold chill suddenly swept across my body. Heavy winds battered my winter coat, beating the material almost like a flag. My breath came in heavy white wagging swirls. As soon as the vapor appeared, the beating, frigid wind swept it away. All of a sudden I felt very cold. Why are the windows and door open? I had felt that I was playing out a once-in-a-lifetime adventure and closing up the cabin would distance me from the experience. Experience? Adventure? What experience? What adventure?

I sat there feeling discouraged, thinking empty thoughts and looking, but not seeing. I felt very alone. Maybe I've been in the thin air too long. For the first time in my life, I couldn't reach out and touch someone. Utah Central, it was out there somewhere, buried in the distant haze. If it were light years away it wouldn't have seemed any further.

Long growing shadows were reaching out across the valley from the mountains on the west. Night was closing in, separating me from the airport. Why was it so cold? I was asking myself questions, questions I couldn't answer, "Why was I up here? What was I doing here anyway? I don't belong here! I'm trespassing, violating this space." I turned, groping, hoping to find something familiar, something I could hold onto. But there was only the beating of the cold wind and a vast emptiness.

The lake and the expanse of the desert look to reach out to the very edge of the universe in a profound stillness, like a huge painting. There was nothing, anywhere that moved; a lifeless cold beauty that defied human description.

Beyond the horizon and partially hidden behind burning clouds, the setting sun reached out in long misty streaks. Golden light reflected off the salt flats and clouds, reaching up to the bottom of the Cub's wing and into the cabin. Even with the frigid wind scouring the insides of the Cub, I suddenly felt the sun's warmth and comfort. With a new awareness, I relaxed and studied the calm beauty. There was a greatness out there, and I suddenly felt very much a part of it.

Goosebumps pricked my skin and I felt a surge of excitement, even triumph in what I was doing. The cold, the shadows, the loneliness and the setting sun were all part of it. I was seeing and feeling something that would be with me all my days.

5

Dusty Wings

October Flights

While I was working at Utah Central, the Air Force was selling off a bunch of its Beech C–45 and AT–11 aircraft as obsolete and surplus. I guess there were a lot of them coming out of Hill Field (Hill Air Force Base) up north near Ogden, Utah. Years before, you could drive by the base and see what must have been hundreds of B–25's, C–45's and C–46 type aircraft in open storage. I guess the government figured they would not be needed again or maybe it was just time to sell them off. We never saw any surplus C–46's or B–25's come through, but there were dozens of the Twin Beech aircraft.

In its day, the Beech C–45, or simply "Twin" as we commonly called it, was a top-of-the-line aircraft. When the government began selling off the Beeches as surplus, more than a few individuals felt some of them had a few good years left. Investors flocked to the government sales hoping to pick up a couple at rock-bottom prices. Buy 'em low, clean 'em up and dump them at huge profits seemed to be the general line of thinking. The question we were asking around the airport was, "Who was buying them at jacked up prices when they were available at rock-bottom prices?"

Gordon Theurer, brother of our boss Roy, was a frequent visitor at Utah Central and he was always talking about ways to make money. He had heard about the surplus sale and on one occasion he told me "it was a golden opportunity." I also talked to several individuals who hoped to pick a couple up and start a charter business. There was a lot of interest to say the least.

There was yet another side to the Twin's buying frenzy. Many of the BT–13s had been converted to spray planes and needed replacements for worn out engines. And the old Stearman bi-wing trainers also made excellent spray planes when refitted with the Twin's bigger and more powerful Pratt and Whitney engines. It was no surprise when one of my fellow workers told me that many of the surplus Twins were being purchased solely for their engines. Pratt and Whitney engines were being used up at a phenomenol rate.

The AT–11 was the same basic design as the C–45 but with some eye-catching differences. It has a large plexiglas nose to accommodate a student bombardier. To gain access to the nose position, the right side of the instrument panel had been designed out.

In the rear cabin of the AT–11, the passenger style seats were replaced with some small bench-type seats mounted along the sides of the fuselage. If I remember right, the AT–11 had two small bomb bays in the fuselage. All of the bomb racks were still in place.

Years before, when I was eight or nine years old, my friend and I used to spend a lot of time at the Salt Lake City Municipal Airport. We spent hours walking up and down the aircraft parking area near the old terminal building on the east side of the airport. Back then, United, Western and Frontier Airlines all shared parked space with private and executive aircraft. Wandering up and down the line, we could examine the big DC–3's, DC–4's and Convairs along with a variety of business aircraft. Often during slow periods, the airline personnel would take us up in the cockpits of the airliners and talk flying.

On one occasion, while we were wandering around the area near the terminal building, a Western Air Line's Convair 240 was positioning itself for passenger unloading. All of a sudden, there were the hollow sounds of popping glass and tearing metal. The Convair's right wing tip had torn into the top of a parked Beech D–18S (D–18S was the C–45's commercial name). The wing tip was just inches into the Beech, but it was enough to make a mess out of the top of the pilot's compartment.

The pilot immediately shut down the big Convair engines as mechanics, line workers, and spectators rushed in from all directions to inspect the damage. Being kids and knowing we were not part of the official spectator crowd, we hesitated. Nevertheless we quickly worked our way over to the damaged Beech.

After all the commotion had settled down, we struck up a conversation with a Western Airlines' mechanic. He took us up near the front of the Beech and explained about the damage and what would be required for its repair. I guess things were a little slow at the moment, because when he finished talking, he led us over to the Twin's entry door.

As we walked under the wing and headed towards the door I remember looking at the side of the fuselage and seeing our image in the bright aluminum skin, it reflected like a mirror, and just about too bright to look at. Pausing at the door, the mechanic opened it, and stood off to one side. My friend and I hurriedly shuffled to the opening and looked inside.

Up front in the cockpit area, we could see the leading edge of the Convair's wing still embedded in the upper portion of the Twin's cabin. As kids, we were looking at the shattered area almost as if it were battle damage and felt special for being able to see it. All of the twisted framing, shattered glass and busted plexiglas spread around the complex cockpit held us spellbound. Yet as interesting as everything was up front, our attention was soon drawn to the plush interior furnishings of the cabin area. The paneling, carpet, executive seats, fixtures and the cabin lining was nothing short of unbelievable. We had no idea that there was that level of luxury anywhere in the world. I could never express the life-long impression that cabin's interior made on me. That Twin and others like it were the top-of-the-line aircraft of their day. Money, no matter how much, just couldn't buy any better!

The military had literally hundreds of the dependable little Beech aircraft in their inventory. However, time is cruel, even for the favored. The Twins soon found their design more and more outdated and unwanted.

The Twins were declared surplus. But, for whatever reason, the government wanted to hold onto them for a time. Each aircraft was prepared for open storage. I'm not sure what all that entails, but "pickled' is a common term that we used for the process. Extended outside storage is harsh on anything, especially complex equipment such as aircraft. Engine and mechanical workings become gummed up, plexiglas turns yellow, paint fades and the bright aluminum skin oxidizes leaving a dirty, dusty chalk-like film.

The surplus Beech aircraft that were coming through Utah Central were all Air Force veterans in their standard military configuration. The military stars and serial numbers had been removed and assigned civilian serial numbers had been hand-painted on the sides of the fuselage.

Getting the Twins ready for flight, even with the minimum preparation required for a one-time Ferry Permit, must have been challenging. Aircraft engines are at their best when they are operational and properly maintained. I've
heard that in some cases, getting even those dependable Pratt and Whitney
engines turning over required top of the line magicians, and keeping them
running was something akin to a miracle. Nevertheless, to the credit of both
engine designers and mechanics, into the sky they flew.

Yet, after seeing a few of the aircraft that came through Utah Central, I've
often wondered if some of the people involved in the aircraft's preparation
had their fingers crossed as their aircraft took to the sky. At any give time,
we had a couple of the Twins parked out in the tall weeds, just south of the
East-West Runway in what we called "long-term storage." Several were there
for weeks and some even months, awaiting decisions, parts and/or work to
get them back into the air.

Some of the pilots coming through must have been a little new at the controls of the Beech aircraft. I saw a couple of landings that were rather hard. I
remember watching one Twin make what I thought was a very hard landing
where some damage must have occurred. However, after shutting the aircraft down, the unconcerned pilot grabbed his bags and headed for the office
without so much as a passing glance at his aircraft. Being a little curious, I
wandered over to take a closer look.

Surprisingly everything looked good, but the main starboard tire caught
my attention. The tire looked like a huge gob of grease saturated with dirt
and other gunk. During the aircraft's storage, engine fluids must have leaked
down onto the tire. It was impossible to tell what was gunk and what was tire.
It looked terrible! I had an urge to kick it just to see what would happen but
was a little fearful wondering if it could withstand even the blow of my foot.

Yet, it had just come through what I would call a very hard landing with
flying colors. For that, I had to give it credit. Whatever brand name the tire
carried, stamped somewhere under the gunk, it had earned my respect.

Gordon did get involved in the "buy 'em low and sell 'em high" fever. Over
a period of six or seven months several of his Twins came through. On one
occasion, Glen had me do a little "clean up" work on one. I took out the passenger seats, oxygen systems and cushions, all of the "non-essential items."

After the clean-up, I had quite a pile of "junk" stacked out near the tail of the aircraft. An effort was also made to remove the white "pickle" paint from the cabin windows. However, the paint had penetrated the plexiglas. It was decided to let it be. For some reason, the glass around the cockpits, and the plexiglas nose of the AT–11's never seemed to be painted.

On one occasion, a C–45 was grounded with a starboard engine that was being a little stubborn. (They couldn't get it started!) I remember several mechanics standing around discussing what may or may have been the problem(s). I watched from a distance wondering what their thoughts were. How does a mechanic look at a troubled engine that had just come out of extended storage? Where does he even begin? After some discussion, the Twin was towed over into the weeds and parked. I never did hear any theories as to what the problem was or might be. Money seems to be the motivating force that moves airplanes best; maybe the owner never had the immediate cash to solve the problem.

A week or so later, Glen told me that someone wanted one of the cylinders pulled on the stubborn engine. He looked at me with a smile and stated that I had the job.

I grabbed my beginners tool box, placed a ladder between the engine and the fuselage, climbed up near the row of cylinders and then feeling like a real mechanic I began removing the "jug." Boy, did it make me feel big time.

After a bloody knuckle and a few words stated to the engine, I was finally able to slide the finned cylinder off the piston. Pulling a cylinder is not a big deal for a real mechanic, but for me it was a huge feeling of accomplishment.

After the cylinder had been removed, I wrapped it up in a rag and covered the exposed area of the engine. I took the cylinder over to the office and gave it to Glen. He examined the insides for a moment or two, and then thanking me, he placed it on the counter. The aircraft sat around for another week or so, and then one day it was gone.

Occasionally when one of the Twins was started up or moved, I was able to be up in the front right seat. On one memorable occasion I was able to taxi one a short distance.

After work, under the stars of the evening sky I would occasionally climb up into the left seat of one of the Twins, lean back, relax, look and dream. To my young and inexperienced eyes, the cockpit of the Beech was a technical jungle. I would try to put all the controls, knobs, dials and instruments in perspective, giving each of them a function or purpose. Wally or Chad would have been more than happy to brief me on everything, but it was too much fun to explore and try to figure everything out on my own.

I could flip a switch and the panel would light up like a Christmas tree. The old Air Force Instruments had radium markings on their faces that not only reflected light but the markings actually glowed. Heavy layers of dust from months of outside storage covered everything, but those glowing instruments brought life to the cockpit that would put most Christmas trees to shame. It was a beautiful sight.

The cockpit was fascinating to sit in and God only knows how many great and wonderful dream flights I made. The only thing that could have been added was the coveted thunderous sounds and exhaust smells of the powerful Pratt and Whitney engines, giving life way beyond the lifting of the instrument needles off their pegs.

Kay Andersen belonged to the Naval Reserve over at the Salt Lake Municipal Airport. Along with their SNJs, PV–2's and TBMs, the reserves had a handful of JRBs. JRB is the Navy's designation for the Twin Beech. Kay had time in the JRBs, and because of his experience he was in demand to ferry the surplus Twins around the country. He often made stops at Utah Central and occasionally we would cross paths.

Late one evening, I was in the office while Kay was finishing up some paper work. Stacked and piled at his side were flight bags, clothing, some business forms and a manual. I happened to notice that the manual on the counter was a Pilot's Manual, a restricted official government publication for the Beech type aircraft. I eagerly asked Kay if I could browse through it for a moment. He must have got a kick out of my enthusiasm for he smiled and quickly answered, "Sure."

I've studied our Piper and Cessna's manuals, but they were pre-kindergarten primers compared to that official government publication of Kay's. It was filled with dozens of high-quality pictures and descriptions of each control found in the C–45 type aircraft: Fuel Management, Emergency Procedures, charts, Cautions, and Warnings were also covered. I had never seen such a book. I guess with my interest in the manual Kay was wondering if he would get it back. And to be honest, I had serious doubts as to whether I wanted to give it back. The manual, obviously in many ways meant more to me than it did to Kay, but he needed it and I only wanted it, so back it went, be it a bit reluctantly.

The pilots hired to ferry the Twins from the government disposal areas to their new destinations came from everywhere. Some, like Kay were local people, while others were strangers from who knows where. Occasionally, strange faces became familiar and after a time, I could put a name on a few. Yet for most, the only indication that they had ever been through was a line on the Gas Sheet.

All of the pilots were friendly, and I've got to admit that it made my day a little brighter to have them hop out of a Twin and strike up a lively conversation. They talked a lot about flying and airplanes, the things that I liked to talk about. It was during this time that I began to realize that people, even more than aircraft, made aviation what it was.

One day, while refueling an aircraft, I was watching an AT–11 during its final phase of landing. Instead of leveling off near the ground, the pilot actually continued his glide path straight onto the ground, no leveling off, nothing. The Beech hit hard, kicked up some dust and then found solid air once again. If its glide slope was just a little steeper, boy I don't know.

The pilot got control of the aircraft, brought the power back up and continued around the pattern for a second attempt. I watched, intently wondering if there might be further problems.

The pilot flew around the pattern and onto Final. He established a normal glide and made a beautiful landing. It was nothing short of textbook perfect, like there had never been a problem in the first place.

He pulled up near the gas pit with both engines roaring. I recognized him as one of the ferry pilots who had been through several times. He shut down the engines, and then went through a final cockpit check. Even from where I was standing, I could see that he was still a little shaken up.

He got up from the pilot's seat and wandered down the aisle to the cabin door. I ducked under the wing and was standing near the door ready to receive his service instructions.

The cabin door opened and he hopped down to the ground. His face was somewhat flushed and he was clearly embarrassed. Without a single inquisitive word on my part, he apologized and went into a detailed explanation of what had happened.

The exterior of the AT–11 aircraft looks nearly identical to the C–45, except for the nose. The nose of the AT–11 is much bigger, room enough for a student bombardier. The C–45 on the other hand has a much smaller nose, which is empty, small and pointed. When sitting in the cockpit of the C–45, the nose gradually slopes down from the windshield. On the other hand, the nose of the AT–11 goes straight forward, and then abruptly drops off at the plexiglas nose. The ferry pilot who had blotched the landing was well qualified in the C–45, but when he got into the AT–11, apparently for the first time, the straight, oversized nose threw him a bit. During the flair-out, the nose of the AT–11 gave him the impression that he was in more of a level flight or even a nose-up attitude than he really was. It was a major shock to him when he made contact with the ground as he did.

I guess the pilot's detailed explanation of the landing was almost a confession. By the time he had finished, he had calmed down and we were both laughing about all of our self-inflected bad days.

I had never compared the nose of the AT–11 with that of the C–45 or considered what effect it might have on the pilot's judgment during landing. However, the more I compared the two aircraft, the more I could appreciate his experience. I've heard stories of wartime ferry pilots who one day were flying the tail wheel B–17 aircraft and the next day, or even the same day, would be flying a nose-wheel B–24. One ferry pilot recounted, that to keep things in perspective, he would be mumbling "flag" words all the way through his approach and landing, words like, "B–24, nose wheel, nose wheel, nose wheel." I guess the design quirks of individual aircraft best be kept in mind.

Bob (I'm not sure that's his name, I just can't remember), one of our former part-time instructors pulled up to the gas pit in a nice looking C–45. He had bought it surplus some time before, but what I was then looking at was a very nice looking executive aircraft. The Beech looked brand new. It was beautiful!

During our ensuing conversation, he told me that he had a thriving charter business in New Mexico. He smiled as he stated that he was hauling Air Force Generals around in one of the government's surplus aircraft. From the way he was talking, he was doing quite well. Bob's charter business was one of the few real success stories that I've heard concerning the use of the surplus Twins.

While I serviced his aircraft, we spent some time talking about his business and changes around Utah Central. He had me put some fuel in the wing tanks and I was just getting ready to check the oil in the starboard engine when Bob stated with a bit of humor,"Skip the check and just add oil, lots of oil." While I was putting the oil in, he stated that the oil problem was the main reason he was in Salt Lake. His starboard engine needed an overhaul, big time.

Bob smiled and explained, "I made a stop for gas a while back, and the engine needed some oil. I turned my head for one second and in went detergent oil, the wrong oil. Never did see it go in. Would have changed the oil right then and there if I had known!" Then he added with a tone of regret, "True to my luck, it didn't take long till the detergent was doing its thing." Then looking at the engine, he stated with some sadness, "That engine has a big oil sump, but I can hardly make it from one airport to another." Bob felt bad, because it was such a simple error, but for him a very costly one.

Back then, there were basically two types of aviation oils on the market. One was classified as "detergent" and the other as "non-detergent". Other than what the name implies I know nothing concerning the technical make up of the two types. But I've been told that detergent oil, if used, best be introduced when the engine was new or "low-time." If on the other hand, someone had been using a non-detergent oil for any length of time, it is best not to change over to detergent, as in Bob's case. Switching from non-detergent to detergent oil has a tendency to clean up, or break loose deposits or gunk that has accumulated in the engine. Then more likely than not, it thereafter has a tendency to either leak or burn oil, sometimes both and often quite a lot.

Then changing the subject, Bob began talking about some C–45's that were being parted out at the Ogden Airport. The owner of the junked Twins had offered Bob any parts that he could use, free of charge. Bob was on his way up to see if he could find anything of value. He paused and then asked if I would like to go up with him. I was "all feet," running around getting permission from Glen and making sure Chad could cover the line.

I took my place up in the right front seat. It was my first, and ultimately my only opportunity to sit at the controls of a twin Beech aircraft in flight.

I followed his every movement and compared it with knowledge, or assumptions, that I had accumulated over the past several months. If something didn't fit or make sense, I asked. I probably kept him more than a little busy with my questions. However, there was a certain excitement in his voice as he answered my questions, like when you hear a father talk about his child. During our conversation, the statement I remember most was almost a summary of the Twin's flight characteristics. "It is an aircraft that should be taken very seriously or it will get away from you," he stated as a matter of fact. "It wasn't forgiving like the little Cubs, but once a person got to know her, it was all love," he said.

After we were airborne and at altitude, Bob asked if I would like to take the controls. I couldn't say yes fast enough. I slid my feet forward to the pedals, put my right hand on the wheel and the left hand on the throttles. It felt strange. The Cub and the Twin were both aircraft but that's where the similarities end.

I don't care how much you know about an aircraft or where you sit in it, or how close you are to the pilot's seat. Until you are in that seat, with your hands on the controls during flight, you are just a spectator! The aircraft is "there" and you are "here." It flies and you watch. There is a gap with no bridge. However, once your hands are in place and in control, communication is established; there are no lines of separation.

At first, the movements of the controls were heavy, stiff, foreign and strange. Co-ordination was difficult. The aircraft was skidding here and slipping there. Power control seemed awkward and even lagging or non responsive.

But after moving the seven thousands pound of aircraft around some, I developed a bit of a feel. I made a couple of level turns and then I rolled around into some gentle climbing and gliding turns. I pushed forward on the throttles and lifted the nose up. The big aircraft, with its big radial engines of some nine hundred horses instantly obeyed.

Free of passengers with less than a full load of fuel the Twin Beech eagerly lifted higher into the sky and climbed like it never wanted to stop. From where I sat, the entire sky was filled with its power and dominance. There is no way you can separate that kind of energy from a pilot. Nor would any pilot ever want to be isolated from it. I can easily see why pilots are in such keen competition to sit in the left seat of such aircraft.

Approaching the Ogden Airport, I turned the aircraft back over to Bob. With my feet and hands clear of the controls, I just watched, even stared at the panel and controls in front of me. The wheel and pedals moved per his input as he made adjustments with the controls on his side. It seemed as if the controls on my side were moving magically, by some unknown and unseen force, a little like an old time player-piano.

He cut the power back and went into a descending turn. The panel became alive, flight and engine instruments all moved to respond to and verify his new settings. My wheel turned, rudder pedals moved, dials spun this way and that, some fast, some slow but all with precision, indicating exactly what the aircraft and its engines were doing. Then he leveled out and applied power and each instrument repositioned accordingly. Not man and aircraft, but of two working together for a common purpose.

Out of the right window, I could see the huge cowling moving briskly over the backdrop of farm fields. Under the cowling, tucked in snugly was the big Pratt and Whitney engine, powerful and smooth. There was a light gray shadow of the propeller just in front of the cowling, such a soft and subdued indicator of all the might and power being produced by the engine.

Yet, beneath the cowling was something else, huge volumes of air rushing through the carburetor, twisting and turning through induction piping, past the hammering valves and into the red-hot cylinders. Metal against metal, spinning, sliding, moving and pushing. The only insurance against almost instant self-destruction was a thin layer of red-hot oil. Behind it all, sadly, in the case of the right engine, a thin trail of light blue smoke peacefully streaming back as far as the eye could see, caused by the mistaken addition of the wrong type of oil.

There were six C–45's at the airport, all had been stripped and thoroughly picked over. Engines, instruments, landing gears and most of the interiors were gone. Even the tail wheels had been removed. If you could get it off with a screwdriver or wrench, it was probably gone. What few control surfaces remained were damaged beyond reasonable economic repair. Without breaking down the main wing, fuselage, and tail components, only airframe skin remained.

Without their gear, the aircraft were lying on their bellies in a trampled-down patch of dry weeds-- a picture of complete abandonment. After having been so impressed with a sister aircraft, to see others of the same type, in such pathetic shape was sad, to say the least.

We went through each of the gutted aircraft, but it was obvious that Bob was one of the last of many looking for parts. I could see the disappointment written on his face as he entered each aircraft, looked around and departed. We were hoping he could find something that would make the trip worthwhile, but it was not to be. When he climbed back into his Beech, his total take was a handful of knobs liberated from one of the aircraft's engine control pedestal.

He commented on the fact that the trip was a waste of time and money, and I felt some sadness in his disappointment. Yet for me it was a trip of a lifetime. I would be forever grateful for that few moments in the right-hand seat, flying such a magnificent aircraft.

Gremlin's Paradise

Driving west on 2100 South, I could see an aged and somewhat tired looking ex-Air Force C–45 approaching the airport on Final. I turned off at the airport entrance and pulled into a parking spot near the office. Once out of the car, I paused to watch the Beech as it sailed over the highway and then crossed over the end of Runway 16. To me, no matter how old, or dirty with age, or even how mechanically unfit with even smoke trailing from tired engines, an aircraft in flight is still graceful, beautiful and fascinating. I watched the aircraft on its Final until it began to level off for its landing. Then it settled below the brush line making it impossible to see clearly.

I had checked in and was walking out to the line to start my duties. Once outside I was expecting to see the Twin moving around somewhere on the ramp. I looked around, but there was no Twin. A little puzzled, I paused and searched the airport property to the southwest. Off in the distance, I could see the upper portion of the Beech behind the brush line. For some reason, its location looked out of place. I stared for a moment. It was not moving. Then off to the side, I could make out an individual walking through the brush. Apparently, it was the pilot of the C–45, and for whatever reason he had left his aircraft sitting out on the runway and was hoofing it in.

He was still a long ways away but there was something about his walk and build that reminded me of Kay. I called over to Chad who was just inside the main hangar. Together we studied the figure of the individual. He agreed with me on the probable identity of the individual and added that something was definitely wrong. Chad went into the hangar, got on the squawk box and called Glen over in the office. He told him what we had seen and then stated that we were driving out to see what the problem was. A moment later, Chad and I were in my Olds and headed in Kay's direction.

Kay was working his way through weeds and brush--bent over and struggling with a heavy load. He had his chute slung over one shoulder, a clothing bag draped partially over the other shoulder, an overnight bag in one hand, a flight case hanging low under another arm, and headphones mounted awkwardly on his head. It was a picture of a man who had obviously had a long day. I don't think he was aware of our approaching vehicle until he heard our car moving through the sagebrush.

I pulled up, and he took a final few steps to the car. Chad jokingly asked if he could use a ride. He smiled and replied, "I sure could."

With all his equipment and baggage, he was having trouble getting anything undone. Seeing him struggle, Chad and I both hopped out to give him a hand. As each item was pulled off, it was placed on the back seat of the car. Once everything was loaded on the back seat, there didn't appear any space left for Kay. However, he did a little reshuffling, and in a few seconds he was in.

Even during the best of times, Kay was not a great talker, and at that moment he had even less to say. He did casually mention however, that his Beech had a flat tire.

We decided to continue out to the Twin to get some idea of what it would take to get it back to the ramp. On the way out, we further questioned Kay on what the problem was. In his modest and somewhat reluctant speech he finally stated, "Right brake locked up... ground looped... blew a tire."

When we arrived at the site, we could see the aircraft sitting some distance off the runway. Everything about it looked sad, abandoned or even haunted. Kay had left the door open and the aircraft was leaning heavily to its starboard side in weeds and brush. The aluminum skin was ghostly gray with oxidation. Cabin windows were covered with odd patterns of preservative paint. The once proud Air Force markings had been removed and the assigned civilian serial number had been hastily scrawled on the side of the fuselage. It was a picture of an aircraft that had seen better days.

The Twin's tire tracks in the soft earth indicated a severe ground loop. Looking at the blown tire, I could see a shapeless mass of rubber piled against and around the wheel. Judging from its shredded condition the tire must have really taken a beating.

We had been there only a few moments when I noticed Chad eyeing the lower part of the starboard rudder that was hidden behind some brush. He wandered over and began kicking away at the growth. With the weeds and brush cleared, he stopped and gazed down at the bottom of the rudder. From the elevator down it was bent inward about thirty degrees. Without so much as a comment, Chad moved over to the side of the fuselage and began clearing away the brush from the area near the tail wheel. With most of the heavier brush cleared away, it was obvious that the tail of the Twin was sitting on or very near the ground. I dropped down to my knees, and together we cleared away the last of the weeds. The tail wheel assembly had been damaged and was lying almost flat under the fuselage.

We grabbed a flashlight from my car and headed for the cabin door. Climbing into the rear of the fuselage, we jockeyed ourselves around until we were in a position to view the inside of the tail cone.

The tail wheel assembly had been completely ripped away from its mounting brackets. There was also extensive damage to the aircraft's skin, brackets and stringers in the area of the tail wheel's mount.

Shortly, Glen along with a couple of mechanics and a few flight instructors drove up. Before long, there was a fair-sized group milling around the C–45. Most of the people at the site had worked around aircraft a good part of their adult life and idle speculation wasn't part of the conversations. Damage was discussed in a professional manner, along with the best way of getting the aircraft back to the shop where the true extent of damage could be evaluated. Many were wondering if the old bird would ever be air-worthy again. Surplus Twins were just too cheap to buy and too expensive to fix.

The pros and cons of the locked tail wheel were also discussed. It was standard procedure to have the Twin's tail wheel locked in a neutral and non-swivel position during takeoffs and landings. That procedure was in part, intended to prevent ground loops. It was the general consensus that in the case of Kay's blown tire, even with the damage that had occurred to the tail; the locked tail wheel probably prevented a much more severe ground loop and even more extensive damage. Max casually remarked that, "if the tail wheel hadn't been locked we'd probably still be trying to get Kay out."

While everyone was wandering around, I got my camera out of the car and took a few pictures. I tried to get Kay in one but he wanted no part of it. I guess he felt bad about the accident and was probably hoping the whole thing would turn out to be a bad dream. At the time, it was no big deal, but I would always regret that I didn't push him a little for a photo, as I would never have another opportunity.

A couple of the crew pulled a wheel off one of the Twins parked over in the extended parking area. Changing a main wheel on a rather heavier aircraft can be a challenge, especially when the crew doesn't have access to all the proper equipment. A variety of jacks, blocks, planks, even oil drums all combined with a lot of well-thought-out teamwork was required to get the Beech on proper footing. Once it was sitting on some good rubber, everyone's attention turned to the tail. They got it jacked up and placed a trailer-like dolly under the aft end and presto, the C–45 had a new tail wheel, sort of. Then with a truck pulling on the mains, a pickup pushing the tail trailer, much coordination and a fair amount of coaxing the Twin was again moving.

With the repairs required on the tail, it was decided to park the Beech near the southwest corner of the main hangar, handy to the shop. The tail-end dolly was removed and a padded sawhorse was placed under the tail. The Twin looked rather awkward supported by an old sawhorse. The dangling tail wheel and the bent rudder added little to the aircrafts' former glory.

As we were putting away our equipment, a mechanic paused, and looking at the damage around the tail wheel mounting he mumbled half to himself and half out loud, "Glad that's not my job."

For several weeks, the broken Twin sat there unattended and seemingly forgotten. I was beginning to wonder if the owners, whoever he or they were, had written it off.

Then one evening, Dick, Max and I were checking out the line making sure everything was tied down for the night. As we were moving around, we looked over at the main hangar. The shop door was open, lights were on and the sounds of hammering could be heard. Everyone stopped. We all knew that none of our people were in there. Someone said, "Who's that?" We all glanced at each other and then over in the direction of the shop. Without so much as a word we were headed towards the open door.

Inside, we found what I at first thought to be a mechanic banging away on Kay's damaged rudder. Scattered around the floor were pieces of sheet aluminum, a can of rivets, some tin snips, bits and a drill, a chisel, a hammer and an assortment of bucking bars. Some of the damaged aluminum skin had been removed and about half of the damaged ribs and spar had been roughly hammered back into place. To reinforce the repairs, there were some hastily placed brackets and patches riveted to the damaged areas. I hated to judge, but even with my limited experience the workmanship didn't look all that professional.

A partially torn down C–45 brake assembly was lying on the floor a short distance away. The complexity of it caught my attention. Unlike cars and our Cubs, it worked not on the principle of the familiar brake shoes but discs, and there were lots of them. I tried to make sense of how everything fit together and functioned, but it was way beyond anything that I had ever seen.

We all paused in silence while looking over the damaged rudder, brake and tools lying around on the floor. The mechanic (or whoever) looked up at us and said, "Hi." He then went into some involved explanation of what he was doing. It was obvious that he was embarrassed. I think he knew that his workmanship was poor and the fact that some of the people he was talking to knew more about what he was doing than he did. We listened to the explanation and then turned and walked away.

Once out of the hangar, Max stated that whoever was doing the work was doing a pretty shoddy job, "You can get away with work like that on a Cub, but on a high performance aircraft like the Beech, it's suicide." I'd never seen him so critical.

The C–45 was gone a few weeks later. I never did see the repairs completed on the rudder. Nor did I ever see anyone working on the aircraft in the area of the tail wheel. What was done and how it could be completed so quickly has always puzzled me. Maybe the damaged tail section was just removed and replaced! With all the surplus Twins around, it might not have been hard to find one. That probably would have been the fastest and cheapest. The aircraft must have made its destination, wherever that was. I never heard any more about it.

For months, the Twin Beech aircraft were an active part of the airport's environment. Most were just passing through and some spent time at the airport undergoing repairs. For a while, the Twins were everywhere. Then, there was only an occasional fly-in. The few we had sitting around slowly began to disappear. So many Twins--then there were none.

6

Wings, Places and People

Wings

Getting a Pilot's License in the 50's was a relatively simple matter, or at least that was pretty much the middle-of-the-road opinion. Simple or not, a Pilot's License was a very big thing in my life.

When it came time for my Private Pilot's Examination, like most people, I was a little nervous. On the agreed-upon day and time, the Official FAA Examiner, Walt McClain stopped in at Utah Central and together we sat at the lunch counter for the oral part of the test. He was an older individual, who like Glen had a crew-cut and graying hair. I knew little of his background, but it was soon obvious that he was no newcomer to the field of aviation.

He drilled me for over an hour on all aspects of Weather, Rules and Regulations, Navigation, Instruments, Aircraft and Engines, Emergency Procedures and Airport Traffic. Being around airplanes day in and day out, I, at first, thought I knew most of what I needed to know and the rest I could bluff my way through. It didn't take long to see that wasn't going to happen. He wasn't happy with a simple, partially-right answer. He kept digging until he knew how much I knew or didn't know about a given subject.

About the time I thought his questions would never come to an end, he suddenly stood up and grabbed his jacket. "Come On, lets go flying," he stated, full of enthusiasm.

I grabbed my coat and hurriedly put it on. My charts, plotting equipment, E6B Circular Computer, along with several pencils and a notebook, were scattered around on the counter. I, like most of the students on the field didn't have a flight case so I gathered everything up the best I could. Walt was half out the door before I had everything secured.

He paused just a few steps beyond the door, turned around and asked, "What airplane are we using?" I pointed to the tan Cub.

I threw my equipment on the baggage compartment lid and then hurried over to his side where he was patiently waiting to begin the Pre-Flight. Together we walked around the Cub, going through the motions, with me doing a verbal explanation of what I was checking. He didn't seem to be paying attention to what I was saying or looking at, but I knew that if I said something wrong or missed something, it would develop into an extended line of questioning.

As near as I could tell, the aircraft pre-flight was going smoothly. Then without a word, he left me standing alone, almost talking to myself. I turned my head just in time to see him swing himself into the front seat of the Cub. His entrance was smooth, like he was sliding in on silk, that guy is either a ballet dancer or he grew up in Cubs. His entrance had me wondering if it wouldn't have been to my benefit if he had just stood there and asked me what seat was his and what was the best way to get in.

I walked over to the front of the Cub, put my hand on the prop and stated as positively as I could, "Switch Off." I don't know how many times I've propped a J–3. It's a simple procedure, but at that moment my head was just spinning trying to make sure I wouldn't forget even some small but essential detail or procedure, something that would make a negative difference in his eyes.

We got it started and nothing happened to cause me regrets. Then walking briskly under the wing I grabbed a strut, swung around in the direction of the cabin door and climbed up into the rear seat.

We sat there for a moment while the Cub was warming up. All the while, he was asking questions and scribbling comments in a little notebook.

After we started taxiing, along with the standard "S"-turns, I did a lot of leaning and moving around trying to make it obvious that I was alert and paying attention to possible ground traffic.

In the run-up area, I went through an elaborate check of all controls and instruments, explaining verbally everything being done and why. He seemed-little impressed and asked very few questions. Then I made the clearing turn, making sure I was giving myself plenty of time to look around. With the area clear of traffic I moved out to the center of Runway 34, held a second, and applied throttle.

Once out of the pattern, he told me to head out to our practice area. When we got out over the dry farms he told me to do some "S"-turns over so-and-so road and then he had me to do some Figure Eights. He seemingly didn't pay much attention to the maneuvers, but continued writing. He then requested that I go up to my normal altitude for practicing stalls. Once there, he requested that I do some stalls in various configurations. I made a mental note of leveling the wings with the rudder and not the ailerons, as that had been one of my early bad habits. All I needed to do was fall into one of my old bad habits. After the stalls, there were other requests. I was holding my breath, but the flying part of the test seemed to be going well.

He then told me to plot a course to Naples, put the Cub on a proper heading and give him the numbers. Pausing a second, he then added a fictitious wind speed and its direction. Gee, I thought, that's easy enough.

The Cub does not have a lot of handy storage space for much of anything, even little stuff like navigational equipment. After a little leaning, extended turning, bending and probably doing a lot of unintended maneuvers with the Cub, I had everything out from behind me and positioned where I could use it.

I placed the chart on my lap and began unfolding it. While unfolding the map I started thinking about where I was going. Then it hit me like a brick wall, Naples, Naples. Where in the heck is Naples? I've never heard of such a town! Was it west of Salt Lake, or south, or east, or maybe even north? Was it even in Utah? Darn it, I should have paid more attention to my geography lessons. Maybe it's a trick question. No, he wouldn't do that! I've got to look and hopefully find it.

There's no city listing or locator on aeronautical charts. I guess they figure that if you don't know where your destination is you shouldn't be going there. I was on my own! I rattled the chart in frustration then turned it over a couple of times. There I was, spending precious time trying to find some little town on a very big map, while patiently waiting was a Federal Agent who was probably wondering why I was having so much trouble coming up with a simple compass course.

It must be a small town, I thought. Maybe it was a big town just over the border, and by some quirk I hadn't heard of it! No one knows the names of all the cities or towns in a given state, do they? But, there was such a matter-of-fact tone in his voice, as if he expected me to know where it was! But I didn't! Would it be best to come right out and ask the dumb questions, "never been there, never heard of it, don't know where it's at, could you help me, Please"? Somehow, the obvious quick solution made me feel like the airline pilot going back and asking his passengers where they were going.

I kept looking, top to bottom, left to right, bottom to top, right to left then around in a circle, no Naples, where in the devil could it be? I didn't have a full set of charts for the state; maybe it's not even on my chart. But he knew what I had. He wouldn't request the information if I couldn't plot a line to it. Would he?

I knew exactly what he was thinking, "That deadbeat doesn't even know how to plot so much as a basic course!" But I did, I just didn't know where I was going. After a few very long moments, he, sounding very impatient asked, "Well?"

In the most apologetic way I knew, I came right out and said that I didn't know where Naples was, but I was looking.

"Have you got an Aeronautical Chart?"

That question was designed to make me look dumb, or feel dumb, or both. He knew I had the charts! The question was cold and unsympathetic and it put me down a big notch. "Look on the chart, its there!"

More hours seemed to go by and I could feel the frustrations building in both of us. "Find it yet" was his next belittling question. "No, not yet," I replied, while trying to hide my embarrassment. "It's in eastern Utah," was his next cold statement. It had undertones of "how much help do you need for crying out loud"?

In all truthfulness, I didn't know what he was thinking. But looking back, all I can see is humor. First, there is the Federal Inspector waiting patiently for a simple compass heading. Secondly, sitting just behind the Federal Inspector there is this teenager, a Student Pilot with aspirations of becoming a real Private Pilot. He is holding a rather large map that covered a good part of the state of Utah. The map is spread out curving up the sides of the cabin and occasionally rattling on the back of the Federal Inspector.

The frustrated student has a plastic navigational plotter clamped under his arm. There is also a pencil tucked in behind his ear and an E6B Circular

Computer partially tucked in his open shirt. A notebook is resting precariously on one leg and occasionally slides off to an awkward spot on the floor. The Student Pilot's mind is overloaded with two questions. Where is Naples, and what is the inspector thinking?

After what seemed an eternity, I spotted Naples. It was a very small settlement near Vernal, Utah.

With a lot of effort, and not a little noise, I quickly refolded my chart to a more manageable size. With my plotter and pencil I then run a pencil line between Utah Central and Naples. I wasn't sure if he wanted a plot from our present position, which was a fair distance southeast of the airport or from Utah Central but no way was I going to ask. I was trying desperately to make up for lost time, while still doing everything as accurately as possible. I took a heading, factored in the wind, the magnetic deviation and a correction for compass error. That number was my best guess, as the faded numbers on the panel-mounted card were not all that readable from the back seat.

A column of numbers appeared on my pad, and then the number I had been looking for. Knees off the control stick, hands and feet all back in their proper places on the throttle, stick and peddles. I made a smooth turn towards my new heading and rolled out with the numbers right behind the wire indicator of the compass. Once my heading was established, I stated in apologetic boldness that the Cub was on a heading for Naples. He asked me a few questions to verify what numbers I had used and how I had come up with my answer. Referring to the numbers on my pad, I went through the steps. With no reaction I was left hanging wondering if he had even heard me. After a few seconds, he pointed down. I cut the power, rolled over into a new heading and started a long decent back towards Utah Central.

I suddenly found myself making mental plans on how to improve my next Flight Test, after the obvious failure of the one I was on. I quickly cussed myself out for thinking such thoughts. There was always a chance I could still pull this one off, if I could just keep a clear head and maybe calm down a little.

On the Downwind Leg, he told me to shoot three landings. The first one was fair, maybe good. Going around for the second landing he kept asking me questions:

"Is this your normal pattern altitude?"

With no wind, what runway would you use?
What about the Wind Tee?
What if you had an engine failure? Now!
Is this your normal gliding speed, why?"

To make matters worse, he seemed to sit tall and wide. He was always in front of whatever I was trying to see. If he was trying to get me frustrated, he was doing a very good job.

Nearing the runway on the second landing, he suddenly asked me to do a short field landing. I did and it bounced a bit, not hard, but in a rather funny way. It took me half a second to get things under control, but the humor would always be a part of the landing. Then he said in a rather loud and an almost terminal way, "Take me in!"

I taxied over to a spot near the front of the office and shut the engine down. When I went to undo my belt, I realized that I had not even done it up. While I was trying to figure out how I had missed something like that, Inspector McClain climbed out and without a word headed towards the office. I wish he had looked at me even with a slight smile, or a frown, or anything. For some reason, I felt like my world had just come to an end.

The test was apparently over. For days, I had been hoping that at its completion I would be walking on Cloud Nine. However, I really had no idea of how to act at that moment. Without enthusiasm, I tied the airplane down and then reluctantly walked over to the office. It was a short distance, but it was one of the longest walks I could ever remember making. Maybe it was time to start thinking about my next Flight Test. The turning of the doorknob made my body cringe.

I pushed open the door and took a step inside. Walt was standing in my path holding a piece of paper in my face. I looked at him for a second then at the paper, it was a Temporary Pilot's License, with Charles R. Furden listed as its holder. I had somehow passed! A piece of paper had never made me feel so happy in all my life. What put the frosting on the cake was the fact that he was smiling and seemed happy to be giving it to me. It was a real struggle not to give him a big hug.

Glen later told me that while Walt was filling out the papers, he asked him how things went. Walt had told him that he could feel the tension building throughout the flight, but he felt that I was "plenty safe."

Snow Bird

I had arrived at the airport extra early anticipating some major work in getting the walks and aircraft cleared of snow. However, with the extremely cold temperatures, the snow was light and dry, making it very easy to shovel. I could shovel a walk just about as fast as I could walk. And much to my delight, clearing the snow off the aircraft was almost like dusting furniture. In fact, I could grab a wing tip or a strut; shake the aircraft, and most of the white powder would simply slide off and float away. Clearing off the remainder wasn't much more than a gentle sweep of the broom.

I had cleaned off the yellow Cub and was headed over to the tan one when I got wondering what it would be like flying from a snow-covered runway. If the snow had been wet and slushy I wouldn't have even considered it. But it was dry and only four or five inches in depth, enticing to say the least.

I continued over in the direction of 308 but the desire to fly just wouldn't leave. I paused, turned, looked back at 234 and then headed back in its direction.

I untied the tie-down ropes on the wings and checked the rope on the tail. Opening up the door I checked the mag switch, and then walked around to the front of the engine where I turned the prop through a couple of times. Back to the cabin, I turned the switch on, primed it a couple of shots, walked to the front of the Piper and flipped the prop. It caught, and I wandered back to the door to check the oil pressure.

When it's really cold, I don't care how much warm clothing a person has on, walking through or standing in a propeller blast is almost an unbearable experience. I remember standing at the door, window hanging against my back, while waiting for the oil pressure to work its way up. I leaned into the cabin as much as I could, but I still felt like I was standing there without so much as a shirt on.

After a few seconds (it seemed much longer), the frozen goo started pushing its way up into the instrument. I quickly backed off and closed the cabin door and window, subconsciously thinking it might preserve or even gain some precious heat.

Swinging my broom over my shoulder, I once again headed off in the direction of the tan Cub and the job of removing its burden of snow.

Once the tan Cub was cleared, I headed back in the direction of the yellow

Cub and untied the tail. Before climbing in, I took a few seconds and brushed off the snow from my pant legs and shoes. I threw the broom off to one side, opened up the door and hooked the window on the bottom of the wing. Then stomping my feet a few more times I climbed into the back seat. The engine was warm and the force of the prop blast was soon on the far side of the closed door and window. With my heavy clothing, I felt rather comfortable.

I leaned forward, reaching for the cabin heat but stopped somewhat abruptly; it was already on. I smiled to myself thinking that it had probably been on since the previous winter. I set the altimeter and checked the gauges again, buckled up and applied power.

A huge white cloud lifted from the ground and spread itself across several parked aircraft. The frozen ground and dry snow offered little resistance and the Cub smartly moved out across a blanket of white. Habitually looking around for non-existent traffic, I headed out towards Runway 36.

The area of the taxi strip and ramp were pretty much a white flatland. Everything blended together making it a little difficult to distinguish what was where. However, with a lot of searching "S"-turns and more than normal concentration, I was able to keep the Piper somewhat on the established path. At least I didn't bounce across any drainage ditches.

Nearing the end of the taxiway, I passed into the first rays of the morning sun. The brightness, both from the sun and its reflection off the dense white snow, was almost blinding. Scratches in the plexiglas side window caught the light making a sunburst that was almost too brilliant to look at. I remember lifting my hand up to shield my face from the diffused sunlight; it was such a drastic contrast from the darkness that I had been working in most of the morning. With the sun came warmth that seemed almost a revelation of what a beautiful day it would be. My body tingled in the sun's brilliance.

I did the engine check while on the move and then locking up one wheel, I half spun and half slid around a somewhat enlarged circle, doing a final traffic check. As I circled around, a portion of a rather large snow cloud (created by the prop blast) settled down over the Cub. Thousands, maybe millions of minute frozen flakes tumbled and turned, each catching and flashing its prize of captured morning sunlight. I locked my wheels and slid to a stop, pausing, looking, fascinated with the glittering dust-like crystals. Slowly the cloud drifted off to the side and settled on the snow.

I taxied out to the open area that I judged to be the center of the runway and coasted to a stop. The area was a huge expanse of white, everything was hidden under the snow; none of the familiar landmarks were visible.

I studied the surface for tell-tell signs of what was runway and what was not. Off to one side, I could see a line of uneven snow indicating the stubble weeds at the edge of the graded strip. Then using it as a reference it was easy to identify the edge of the runway on the opposite side. The left, the right and distant center, everything fit. I applied a little power and eased the Cub over a few degrees to a more perfect runway alignment. Centered on the runway, I paused.

Everything I was seeing was such an extreme contrast. The sky was of the deepest frozen blue, the front end of the Cub was the purest yellow and the snow was a most perfect white.

I eased the throttle forward. The rpm's swung up into higher numbers, loping exhaust sounds jumped up the scale to a dominating roar. An unseen propeller was screaming, cutting thick air and unmercifully blowing it to the rear. A cloud of snow erupted into a white dust storm and began its rolling journey to who knows where.

Without anything to hold it back, the Cub eagerly moved forward, gaining more and more speed, almost as if it had been waiting for that moment. My body broke out in goose pimples and I began to shiver--from the cold, from the excitement? I don't know.

Faster and faster the Cub streaked through the unblemished powder. Spinning tires, disrupting, plowing, splashing snow in artistic, wake-like patterns, leaving a path in the once peaceful blanket.

I began to feel life in the controls and eased the stick forward. The tail lifted and the nose dropped. A field of white moved higher up on the windshield. Off to the sides, I could sense (more than see), snow going crazy trying to get out from the path of the speeding Piper. My speed continued to build. Faster and faster we raced along, propeller turning at maximum, showing nothing but a soft gray haze.

Then, approaching the assigned magic numbers, wheels got lighter, lifted, tracks became mere streaks across the white powder and then disappeared altogether. A white cloud drifted aimlessly above a path once traveled and then settled to the blanket of snow, unnoticed, in silence.

The Piper's wings were cutting through cold, rock-solid air, lifted ever higher into the waiting sky of blue. I rocked the wings, kicked the rudder and jockeyed the elevators in excitement. Oh how I loved it!

...and worth every penny!

I, like everyone else who had ever put his hands on the controls of an airplane, dreamed the common dream of bigger, better and faster. Yet I knew that in reality every dream has a downside. In the case of bigger, better and faster, it was money!

When I first hired on at Utah Central, I did a little calculating and found that at the time it cost, in a general sort of way, around eleven cents a mile to fly just about any rental airplane in the area (the big and fast and the little and not-so-fast). The smaller and slower aircraft gives a person more flying time over a distance traveled; bigger and faster aircraft gave a person less flying time over the same distance traveled--plus, I guess, gaining experience. It's a terrible equation! However, a fact of life it was, and I couldn't see any way of changing it. With that, I had decided the more flying time in the smaller Cubs was preferable (to a bearable degree) to the prestige, speed, excitement, experience, and not-to-be-forgotten higher cost of the more advanced aircraft. That decision would not have held up if the Cubs were not so much fun.

Nevertheless, Glenn and Chad both had stated on several occasions that I really ought to get checked out in some other company aircraft. They were always stating the advantages of flying multiple aircraft types. It was an ongoing temptation! I knew that professional and military pilots all have aircraft without numbers listed in their logbooks. I really didn't want to be called "Ronnie-One-Plane" the rest of my life, but I did enjoy the "extra" hours of flight time. So even with their prodding and suggestions, it was for the time being, more flying time for fewer dollars.

There was the future however, and it would definitely include, the bigger, the faster, the better and yes, the more expensive!

Then near quitting time one evening, Chad and I were doing a final walk-around check on the aircraft for the night. He glanced over at the Piper PA–12 Super Cruiser parked not far away, and again, almost as a matter of conversation suggested that I really ought to check it out.

"What could it possibly hurt?" was his ending statement. I paused and looked over at the red Piper with the big 92505 numbers across its fuselage. I studied its size and graceful lines for a few seconds and thought about Chad's words. I had admired the Cruiser, fueled it, washed it, pushed it, sat in it, and had even been up in it but never as its pilot.

Somehow, even at dusk, I was seeing the Cruiser in a different light. My budget (and maybe common sense) took a step back into the shadows and the Cruiser boldly stepped forward. I began mulling over all the arguments that I could possibly think of. What if I didn't like it? (as if that were possible), it would be money down the drain. And what if I fell madly in love with it? That still didn't mean I could afford it!

Leaping from the Cub's $8.50 an hour to the Cruiser $12.00 an hour is quite a jump! What then, smarty? But, I took a little pride in the fact that I had a little discipline when it came to money. Maybe, if worst came to worst, it would be the Cubs most of the time, and the Cruiser some of the time! Would that be so bad?

At the first opportunity, I grabbed Dick and set up an appointment for my Super Cruiser's Check Out Flight. Then I read the rather skimpy PA–12's handbook several times, mostly because it fueled the excitement and anticipation of the upcoming event.

On the day of the flight, Dick and I gave the PA–12 the once over. As we walked around the Cruiser, he made comments explaining this and that. It was almost a carbon copy of the J–3. Then he put me in the pilot's seat and explained the controls of the Cruiser and some of the flight characteristics that were above and beyond its little kid sister, the Piper J–3 Cub.

Even though the J–3 and the Super Cruiser were pretty much the same airplane, kind of, there were a few physical differences. The PA–12 had a full-size door mounted on vertical hinges that made cabin entry and exit much easier. There was however, a bit of a shuffle required to get from the door opening to the pilot's seat. The front seat appeared rather small in the wide cabin, quite a contrast to the J–3. However, even with the extra cabin width I could still see over both sides quite comfortably. Behind the pilot, there was a seat wide enough for two people. Moreover, unlike the J–3 pilot who sat in the rear seat, the Cruiser pilot sat up front. And from the front seat, all of the controls were within easy reach of the pilot. There would be no grunting with the long, back-to-front stretch.

And the view from the pilot's seat was definitely improved. For the first time, I could lean forward and see the leading edge of the wings and there, right in plain sight, was the top of the cowling. Beyond the cowling there was a piece of real estate that had always been a hidden spot in a Cub.

The PA–12 was also equipped with a full electrical system. And with all the wires and battery came a little button located near the lower center of the panel marked "Starter." Press it; even with a single little pinky finger, and the propeller would turn over all by itself.

The movement of the control stick has a bit of a heavier feel, even while the aircraft was stationary on the ground. Around the field we referred to the PA–12's control stick as "spring loaded." The spring-like tension was enough to keep the stick in the neutral position even when the aircraft was not flying. In flight, it gave the elevator controls the feel of a larger aircraft (or so I've been told).

The smaller and somewhat more visible, behind-the-panel nose tank of the Cub was gone. The Cruiser's tanks were in the wings, one in the left and one in the right, with a total fuel capacity of something like thirty gallons.

Not to be outdone by the J–3, the PA–12 was also equipped with a set of dual controls; the rudder pedals and the control stick being duplicated in the back for the rear passenger. I suspected, though, that it would be a little bit of a trick flying from back there with the restricted forward visibility.

Up front, the trusty little Continental had been replaced with a bigger and smoother Lycoming power plant rated at 108 hp. I guess as far as the "big and powerful," 108 hp is not that big of an engine. However, after the Cub's seventy-five horses you've got to call it a step up. Then again, I remember thinking; there was another way to look at it. Small engine, small airplane, big engine, big airplane, how do you plug that in--what difference would there really be? I sure didn't know, but I was becoming more and more anxious to find out.

Once buckled in, I checked with Dick, making sure he was in and secure. Then I began to flip the switches that would bring life to the Cruiser. It was procedure for the pilot to poke his head out the side window and yell, "Clear." You never had to do that in a Cub! However, I quite enjoyed the clout that came with the warning.

Then with my eyes half on my thumb and half on the backside of the big aluminum propeller, with its somewhat pitted antiglare paint, I pressed the little button marked "Starter." Gears engaged, parts whined and life was created. The cowling shook and the prop disappeared, leaving only a haze. A light breeze drifted in from the open side window with the familiar sweet smells of exhaust. A wave of excitement drifted across my body. I knew right then and there that my budget would need an overhaul.

I sat there a few seconds, content, just looking things over while the oil pressure and temperature came up.

Opening the throttle, I could feel a smooth power surge through the airframe and the big red Piper eagerly moved out of its tie-down spot. A check of the ground traffic and I headed down the taxi strip towards Runway 34.

I couldn't believe how the Piper Cruiser handled. It felt like I was taxiing a bomber. With its extra weight and size, the swells in the ground were not nearly as noticeable as with the smaller Cubs. The feel of power, the rudder control, the visibility, and its mass; it was nothing short of a dream. I must have had a grin on my face a mile wide, just like the little kid who had found a B–17 on some abandoned airport and was taxiing it home to show his mother.

Excitement--even a thrill--surged through my body as I taxied out towards the center of the runway to the take-off position. It was the beginning of something special and I knew it! Positioned, I applied brakes, bringing the Piper to a stop. That Cruiser, just somewhat bigger and somewhat more powerful than the traditional Cub would be the beginning of a new chapter in my world of flight!

I looked out beyond the sounds of the loping engine, beyond the Cruiser's red cowling, beyond the flickering propeller and out along the runway. The runway and what lay beyond dominated my thoughts. In a way the view was like looking into the future. Stillness rested peacefully along the vast emptiness of the graveled strip. Yet, I could see my PA–12 racing down its expanse with me at the controls. What sensations I would then be experiencing, I knew not. However, I knew that it would be an experience long remembered. The Cruiser faced into a light breeze, poised with its engine at idle, seemingly ready, waiting patiently, for me...enough!

I eased the throttle forward; the rpm's leaped without hesitation. The Cruis-

er was suddenly alive with an excitement that reverberating through its airframe. Wheels started turning, the aircraft began moving faster and faster,
almost as if it was trying to rid itself of the little dust storm it had created at
its tail. I could feel my body easing back against the seat cushion, as more and
more runway went streaking to the rear.

With the passing of each fraction of a second, the ailerons, rudder and elevator were gaining more of their authority. I eased the control stick forward,
the tail lifted nearly clear of our dusty trail. Like a little puppy, head lowered,
streaking across the ground the Piper raced. There was power, not just noise
and vibrations, but real power coming from every direction. I could feel it;
my eyes could see it, and I could sense it through every fiber of my body.
It was as if the Piper Cruiser were putting me in my place for doubting its
ability. Small engine, small airplane, big engine, big airplane--there is a difference. Argument settled!

Then, at a time defined by someone in nature, the numbers of weight, lift,
drag and thrust shifted, setting up new parameters, creating flight. The air
become solid, the controls well established and all 1600 pounds of steel and
fabric found it easier to become airborne than to remain on the ground. I
didn't know all the numbers of the equation, but I was enjoying the results.

I lifted into the sky, higher and higher, a little movement on the controls, a
turn, wings level, another turn, level again, and up to pattern altitude. Some
throttle and trim adjustments, a second of "Wow, this is great" and I was suddenly aware that most of the Down-Wind Leg was behind me. I glanced at
my airspeed, 103 mph. A few seconds to take in the sights and it was time to
think about turning onto Base. Compared to the PA–12, flying around the
pattern in a J–3 was a little like cross-country.

Before the flight I had wondered about the landing. Anyone can take an airplane off, but landing--that's a little different. The Cub is somewhat unique,
as far as small private aircraft go. Sitting in the back seat, aft of the landing
gear, most of the cockpit, the engine (what you can see of it), the wings and
most of the wing struts are visibly spread out in front. And be it somewhat
subconsciously, you are viewing a good part of the aircraft and what it is doing. With the PA–12, the pilot is positioned on top of the gear, much more
to the front of the aircraft. There is a lot less of it in view.

I had wondered in a weird way if seeing things from a different perspective would affect my judgment on landing. I knew my concerns were just shadowed thoughts of the unknown, and in reality there would be no problem. Still, I was more than anxious to see how my scrambled theories on landing would pan out.

I could sense the Cruiser's bigness as I rolled out of the turn onto Final. The controls were not what you would call heavy, but in command of more. Up front, the big Lycoming was resting with a somewhat different purring sound than the little Cub's Continental. Even the wind sliding across the wings and fuselage seemed softer on the Cruiser's cleaner design. Everything was so easy, too easy! I kept looking for something amiss, something out of place, something overlooked, something that needed correction. Yet, everything was in its proper place, at the proper speed, at the proper slope and at the proper alignment, all seemingly put in order by the aircraft to the satisfaction of the pilot.

The Piper sailed over the end of the runway and held steady a few feet above the earth. The higher landing speed of the Cruiser was much more pronounced with long ground streaks racing by, almost in silence. The nose gently lifted as the soft sounds of the wind dissipated. The tail settled and the craft slowly drifted the last few inches to the ground. Then the tires touched the earth with their little skidding sounds.

We rolled down the center of the runway for a time without power, bleeding off the excess speed. A bit of a pause, then a little throttle and the engine burst into life; and we were moving under power towards the runway's exit.

I looked back at Dick, he had pulled the control stick out of its socket and was holding it up to his eye, like a spyglass, looking at me and smiling. I smiled back--holding back some laughter and much satisfaction.

Pegleg

Somewhere along the way Roy had purchased a Piper J-3 Cub for the school. Apparently, it had at one time belonged to Mel Reeves. Just in front of its door, near the cowl, was a circular logo made up with Mel's initials, "MR." We never did get around to removing it, and I guess more than one student had wondered what it meant. However, the Cub was unique in the fact that it was our only J-3, maybe the only one in northern Utah with a nose wheel.

Mel, or someone, had reversed the main landing gear, left side to right and right side to left. That little gear-switching had moved the location of the main tires back enough so that the Cub's sitting weight shifted from the tail-wheel to a nose-wheel position.

Piper J–3 nose-wheel conversion kits were available from several different sources across the country. Maybe the design was something Piper was experimenting with, and its success led to the Tri-Pacer.

The major structural members of our J–3's nose-wheel strut were tied into the motor mount at the firewall. However, unlike most nose wheel aircraft that I've seen, where the nose gear was long enough to give the aircraft a little bit of a nose-high, tail-low, sleek ready-to-fly look. Our nose wheel Cub had a shorter nose gear, which gave it a bit of a nose down, tail high, not so fast, hold on, lets think about this for a moment appearance. I've often wondered why the nose gear wasn't a bit longer. Was it because of structural limitations, or did the designer just want the Cub to have a better view of the ground? Good question, but no one would even guess at an answer.

Often, to describe the airplane, students would often ask for a scheduling in "The J–3 with the Nose wheel" or "the Cub with the tricycle gear." Those handles were awkward and wordy. Soon nicknames began to emerge, some being more humorous than others. At the beginning, nothing appropriate really stood out. The name "Stinky" (apparently from the tail-high stinkbug's attitude while it was under stress) was popular to some. We did, however, have affection for the little bird, so that name was played down as much as possible. Over time, and without a lot of thought or debate, our nose-wheel Cub eventually picked up the name "*Pegleg.*"

As soon as it went on line, it was in demand. It seemed that everyone, including me, wanted time in it. With it being so busy, I as an employee had a hard time finding an open spot on the schedule. Several times I was scheduled but got "bumped" by some anxious customer. Then one day, it was just sitting there looking ready to go with no customers lined up. I grabbed Dick and asked if he would check me out. He looked at me and then at *Pegleg*, parked a short distance away. Without a lot of background or even an introduction, he started in on the quirks of nose-wheel aircraft. After about thirty seconds of talking, he paused and then studied me in silence. With a blank look on my face and no immediate response, he added, "Well what are you waiting for, go!"

My first flight in *Pegleg* was quite memorable. I guess the big thing for me was the fact that I had never flown a tricycle-gear aircraft before. Taxing it out was such a different feeling; the view out front was unbelievable, even to the point of putting some adventure in the trip out to the runway.

The initial part of the takeoff run was also an eye opener. I even got a kick out of lifting the nose wheel off the ground and racing down the runway in that nose-high position. And the landing? It was almost too easy. For me it was love at first flight!

In the aftermath of one particularly bad rainstorm, there remained one rather large puddle just southwest of the gas pit and pretty much in the middle of our main East-West Taxiway. There was ample room to go around and many aircraft did. But for whatever reason, most students in the Cubs preferred to go right through the middle. I guess to Piper's credit, the tail wheel J–3's had no trouble getting through the expanse of mud and water. And I guess you could say that to some degree, it was a little dramatic and looked to be lots of fun. The main wheels would hit the water and the propeller blast would catch the splash, whip it up into a frenzy and then blow it off into space. To students, the mud, water, splash and spray seemed to hold some special fascination. And I've got to admit that even I thought it looked kind of neat.

A student pilot was taxing *Pegleg* out for a flight. He had undoubtedly watched a couple of the tail wheel Cub's splash across the expanse of the puddle, and apparently, he had decided that if their Cubs could do it then his Cub could do it!

Armed with curiosity and inexperience, he entered the brown liquid. Almost as soon as the little nose wheel hit the water it started cutting into the soft goo at the bottom, dropping the nose down just a little more than the student was anticipating. He soon realized that his tri-Cub was reacting differently in the puddle than the tail draggers. Concerned, he hit the brakes. The main wheels locked and the little J–3 slid forward to an abrupt slowdown that shifted *Pegleg's* weight forward. The short nose-wheel strut compressed while forcing the narrow tire yet deeper into the soft mud. The tip of the propeller blade, which was very close to the surface of the water as it was, hit the liquid with a slapping vengeance. Water spray was everywhere, and the slapping sounds were almost deafening. Thinking the worst and almost in a panic, the student pilot quickly shut the engine down.

The engine and propeller wound down, the aircraft relaxed, the nose tilted up a few degrees and the Cub came to rest. Dirty water was running down the fabric, the plexiglas, the cowling, and dripped unnaturally from its belly. Added to all of the decorations, a light cloud of steam was drifting off the engine cooling fins. Ripples on the surface of the puddle were silently drifting away from the hapless little Cub. It was a sad picture.

Very concerned and totally embarrassed, the student sat stunned for a few seconds. Then, calming down, he leaned out of the open door and studied his surroundings. Sensing there was no damage to the Cub, he relaxed. Then realizing he was surrounded by water, looking to be about six inches in depth, he again began to feel some anxiety. It was apparent that there was no easy way for him to get back to friendlier ground with dry feet, and he intended to keep them just that way. Sitting somewhat on the edge of his seat, he began looking around for outside help.

Two or three of us had gathered on the perimeter of the pond and stood there staring at the stranded Cub. In a way, it was almost amusing seeing it parked in the middle of the water with a dead engine. Then again, all of us were fully aware that getting the Cub and the student back to dry land was our responsibility. It was also obvious that all those standing on the perimeter of the pond had about the same "wet-feet-not-me" attitude! We all wanted to help. But…! Hands in pockets, everyone was staring at the water, hoping someone (over there) would run in and retrieve the hapless Cub.

Understandably, the student was becoming increasingly aware of his predicament. Moreover, he sensed that he was the center of some unsolicited attention, if not amusement. He failed to see the humor and was fast becoming irritated. He wanted out, and an extended wait was not an option.

Then someone with a rope came over to the edge of the pond. All others just stood in place, watching out of the corner of their eye, hoping he would continue with the initiative. With rope in hand the individual studied the water, apparently thinking about the prospects of cold wet feet. Then he took a deep breath and started in. At first, he tried running or tippy-toeing, hoping to minimize the wetness. After about four steps he realized he was just wasting energy and slowed down to a fast walk, dragging his feet along in a sloshing manner.

Approaching the tail of the J–3, he looked around for the best place to secure the rope. Seeing the fuselage handhold, he looped one end around it and made a quick knot. Then uncoiling the rope from around his shoulder, he splashed back toward the pond's edge. Once out of the water he looked down at his shoes, probably for a reality check. Then he stomped them a couple of times producing some rather funny squishing sounds.

His attention then went to the rope wrapped around his arm. Eagerly, we all rushed to his side to help. Each of us grabbed the rope in a convenient spot and secured our grip. With more than a little effort, the crew started pulling the little craft back to friendlier ground. The Cub resisted our every effort by seemingly cutting deeper into the muck. Seeing our struggle, the student pilot quickly broke out in a grin. We continued to struggle. Grunts and perseverance paid off and *Pegleg* finally let go and followed our lead to higher and dryer ground.

On May 21, 1957, a pilot by the name of Dick Larsen was out brushing up on his flying skills when suddenly *Pegleg's* engine quit. He quickly checked the mags and then the fuel valve, but the prop was dead in the wind before he had much of a chance to do anything else. He did however have enough altitude to give him time to get control of his senses. Dropping the nose, he established a glide, cut the switches, determined wind direction and started looking around for a good place to land. He was over a patchwork of dry farms, uncultivated land and some plowed ground. He scanned the area and decided that a patch of freshly plowed ground would be best.

Being eastbound and near a highway, he continued on course a few more seconds and then made a ninety-degree turn to the south. There were some power lines running along the south side of the road. Dick held his breath as the lines passed just above his windshield. Clear of the lines he again diverted his attention to the target field. The plowed ground had a gentle up slope to the south, with the furrows running parallel to his path. Everything looked as good as it could, under the circumstances.

A bit nervous, he nevertheless was able to do everything by the book as he drifted towards the ground. He rotated the nose of *Pegleg* progressively higher as his airspeed bled off. The main gear slowly settled down towards the freshly turned soil. Then contact.

There was some rather wild left and right jerking of the Cub as the wheels fought their way along the badly spaced furrows. The plowed ground was soft, but the Cub's big balloon tires held their own as they rolled, plowed and bounced along the soft earth.

Dick was just starting to pat himself on the back for a successful emergency landing when *Pegleg*, losing speed, began rotating its nose downward. It wasn't long until the front tire was skimming across the tops of the uneven earth. But, unlike the big main tires, the front tire was small and narrow. As it continued down, it began cutting into the freshly plowed ground like a hot knife cuts into butter.

Before the pilot knew what was going on, he felt himself being pressed forward, hard against his seat belt. The nose wheel continued its cutting, ever deeper into the freshly plowed ground. Then it swiveled off center and began dragging through the soft black soil like an anchor. Immediately, the overstressed nose gear collapsed. The hapless pilot watched as the front end of his little Cub headed down, directly towards the black earth. With the propeller in a near horizontal position, the cowling hit the soft earth and dirt began flying.

Dick braced himself against the pedals, hit the brakes and pulled back on the stick with all his might. But Murphy's Laws were already in place and all the brake pushing and control movements were wasted reflexes. The nose plowed harder and deeper into the soft unyielding earth. All forward movement ceased. But the Cub's energy still needed an outlet. Its tail continued to lift higher into the sky, to vertical, then beyond. Dick watched with a frozen expression, as dark earthly furrows swung up towards his windshield. Then the earth was everywhere.

The J–3 landed hard on it back, bounced a few inches and then settled down to a death-like stillness. All energy, momentum and life were gone from *Pegleg*.

Instinctively, the pilot, hanging upside down in his seat belt wanted to get out as fast as possible. Without thinking, he hit the seat belt release, and completely unsupported he fell like a rock into the headliner. Dazed and with his body rolled up in a very awkward position in what was once the top of the cabin, he struggled against the door trying to find its release. Once found, it took him a few seconds to figure out which way the up side down handle turned. The door and window finally popped open. He half crawled and half rolled out onto the wing. Then, he continued to scoot and crawl until his hands felt the soft earth. He stood up, stumbled, found his footing, ran, and stumbled again. Feeling that he was clear, he turned and backed a short distance away from his upended Cub.

There he paused, staring blankly while trying to clear his head. Odd sounds coming from the Cub caught his attention. Studying the hapless Cub, he could see fuel gushing out from *Pegleg's* inverted nose tank and onto the freshly plowed soil. There were also signs of black oil oozing out from the cowl.

Not long after the accident, we were headed towards the site with a flatbed truck loaded with tools. As we approached the area, we could see people milling around on the side of the road. As we had only a general address, the crowd was a good indication that we were there. *Pegleg* was a hundred feet or so off the road and partially hidden behind yet another group of people.

We parked our truck on the side of the road and wandered out onto the field. The freshly turned earth, with deep, uneven furrows, was a little awkward to walk across to say the least.

Moving through the crowds, we could hear people talking about the accident, some stating rather convincing probable causes and pilot's performance evaluations. Then I overheard one elderly woman saying, "What is the world coming to with airplanes falling out of the sky every which way?" Sorry, but what she said made me smile.

A couple of FAA officials, apparently finished with their work, were leaving the area. I was headed in the direction of the pilot to see how he was doing. As I approached, it was obvious he was in the middle of an interview with a reporter from the, the Deseret News, a Salt Lake newspaper. I overheard him say (in some colorful words of the day), "I was flying along when suddenly the engine just conked out."

Apparently, the pilot was suffering from a mild headache, but overall he was feeling fine.

My first full view of *Pegleg* was a shock. I had never seen an aircraft flat on its back before. My first impression of the Cub was almost of compassion, yet I could also see a bit of humor. For some reason, *Pegleg* lying on her back conveyed certain vulnerability along with a lack of grace and dignity. With its landing gear sticking straight up, it had the same physical appearance as a dead cow. Sadly, maybe even a little like seeing a deceased family pet.

After looking at the depression in the headliner, caused by the pilot's head as he slipped out of his belt, I felt that he was more than just a little lucky. He had just missed a cross-brace located behind some very thin fabric. The fabric headliner has some give, but the structural tube would have probably given him more than a mild headache.

To load the Cub on the truck it needed to be dissembled. To take the Cub apart, we preferred it be in an upright position and on some firm and level ground, preferably on the road, near the truck. To do that, we first needed to get the Cub back on its gear so it could be moved.

To upright a Cub is not hard but it best be done with four or five people and some long ropes. A couple of workers would do the initial lifting from the tail. A second team would lower it from its vertical position and those on the ropes would be there to help lift, lower and steady. The ropes were not only there for lifting the Cub up and over, but they were insurance against unknowns, such as a sudden gust of wind.

With it sitting on its own gear, everyone paused to look at the sad aircraft. With the collapsed nose gear, *Pegleg's* nose was right in the dirt, and its sitting position was way beyond its normal, slightly high-tail attitude. It was a sad picture that somehow made you smile.

Once on its gear, we tried pushing the hapless little Piper over to the road. But the freshly plowed ground was just too soft and all we were doing was repositioning dirt with our sliding feet. Another alternative, disassemble the aircraft and carry each part across the freshly plowed ground to the distance truck. That, also, was something we would rather not do.

Luckily, there was a spectator on a horse watching the activities with a smile. We looked over in his direction. His smile broadened. He knew what we were thinking and we knew what he was thinking.

One of the crew went over and stood by his horse, looked up at the rider and asked very politely, "Could you give us a hand?" He smiled bigger than life and reached for the lariat hanging on his saddle while stating in typical cowboy slang, "Be mighty glad to."

We tied one end of his rope around the propeller, near the shaft; the other end was secured to the cowboy's saddle horn. With the full crew pushing, the horse pulling, and the rest of the crowd waving, yelling, cheering and throwing hats into the air, we were soon moving.

The newspaper photographer was right there to capture the triumphant occasion. You guessed it; the picture of the horse pulling *Pegleg* made the front page of the local section of the newspaper. And you know, I can't really be positive, but I think the horse was smiling just about as much as the rider!

We moved the aircraft to a spot near the truck and unhitched the proud old horse. We all thanked the Cowboy several times. I could tell by the look on his face (the cowboy) that it was a day he would not soon forget. He acknowledged us in a friendly way and patted his horse on the neck.

We got out our tools, undid the control cables, fairings, struts, pins, and bolts. Once we had broken the Cub down to pieces of manageable sizes, we carried everything over to the truck and loaded them for the trip back to Utah Central.

After we got back to the shop the engine was torn down to determine the cause of its failure. The problem was later related to me in a single phrase as only a mechanic could describe it; "The engine had swallowed a valve." The shop did a complete overhaul on the Continental.

Between the condition of the fabric and damage caused by the turnover, it was decided to go through the entire aircraft. We stripped off all the old fabric and with some minor airframe repairs, rebuilt her to near-new condition. The nose wheel strut was bent enough to be reclassified as junk. There was talk of replacing it but the price tag on a tail wheel was somewhat less than a new nose gear, and you can probably guess which direction that went. So Ol *Pegleg* was relegated to memory and logbook entries. We must have sold it soon after, as I have no recollections of it being on line after the accident.

In the Eye of the Beholder

Late one summer, Valley Airmotive sponsored an air show at Utah Central. It wasn't a big show, just the small town airport type, something to let people know we were in the area. Advertisements were made and posted at various locations around the airport. We also sent out flyers to nearby airports.

Days of hard work were spent in its preparation. Everything we could think

of was done to spruce up the airport. We cleaned and then re-cleaned everything again. We swept and even dusted the main hangar. Every aircraft was
vacuumed, washed down and polished. Engine compartments were cleaned
with solvent. I even went so far as to hand-polish the Cub's oil sumps. Weeds
were pulled out in some areas and cut in others. Tumbleweeds were removed
from around hangars and out from under forgotten aircraft. Lawns were
mowed, trimmed and given extra moisture.

We parked our aircraft in a grouping that we hoped would represent
the best of the modern and the ultimate in fun flying. Positioning and
lining up the aircraft was done with precision. You know, "you're too far
forward, pull it back a couple of inches, not that much, hold it, yah, that's
fine, it looks good."

Hand-written signs were strategically placed on horizontally positioned
propellers, stating or advertising the benefits of the particular aircraft.
Other signs were posted, listing all the things that we as a company could
do, like charter flights, aircraft rentals, rides, private pilot classes and, of
course, flight instruction.

It was held on a Saturday, and somewhat to my surprise there was a good
crowd. People were everywhere. With the large crowds, every airplane on
the field was on display (even a few that should have been hidden behind
closed doors).

And we had our share of top-drawer experts wandering the field, stating
opinions, making claims, listing extensive experience in type, discussing the
pros and cons of each aircraft, climbing on, shaking wings, banging rudders,
flipping ailerons, kicking tires; yanking, turning and shaking props. And a
couple even made a fair attempt at poking holes in fabric.

We had several flying demonstrations. Once they started, everyone's attention was focused on the participating aircraft. There were flour bombings,
spot landings, ribbon cutting and a few mild acrobatics. We even had a P–51
do a fly-by. The crowd smiled, wooed, clapped and on occasions, cheered.
You could tell by their expressions that the crowd was favorably impressed
with both the aircraft and the ability of their hometown pilots.

Parachuting was a major part of the show. Since a parachute club was located
on the field, they were right at home. Some jumped with smoke trailing from
smoke bombs attached to their ankles, others made spot landings. Others

formed up in groups, creating interesting formations. They were super!

Before the big day of the air show, some airport crew members got together with members of the parachute club to discuss ways to make the air show something unique, something that would make it stand out among all air shows for all time. Suggestions were made and the pros and cons were evaluated. Most ideas were quickly dropped; others were discussed in detail. One, the one that stood out among all, was eventually chosen.

During the night, a jump suit was filled with watermelons and cantaloupes. Everything possible was done to make it resemble a real live parachute jumper. Then the "dummy" was secretly loaded into the jumper's aircraft. Next day, as the very last scheduled jump of the air show the crew threw out the jump suit packed with fruit.

It looked realistic floating down towards the ground, tumbling and rolling in its free-fall. Shortly, the crowd could see that things were just a little different than had been on earlier jumps. The jumper looked a little limp, even out of it, and he seemed to be waiting too long to pull the cord.

"Why doesn't the chute open?

What's taking him so long?

Is something wrong"?

Eyes got big, mouths opened, then widened. There was silence everywhere. Then the dummy hit the ground, and I do mean it hit! It looked real, even if it was a little too graphic. It bounced high and appeared to disintegrate with pieces flying every which way, in living color. We in the know were splitting our guts laughing. We knew what was going on and no one else did. It was great innocent fun! We felt the crowd would really appreciate the excitement, the tension, the build-up and the final eruption. It was a super event, a demonstration that would be remembered by all, forever.

Boy, we sure got into a lot of trouble over that stupid act!

Two Wings and a Mag

Several of us were headed towards the office when we heard the sounds of an aircraft's engine cutting out, followed by several loud backfires. We all swung our heads around just in time to see Lou's climbing Waco backfire one last time before the engine quit. Then except for the whistling of the wind, there was silence.

The big Waco was taking off on Runway 34. He had about 150 feet of altitude, maybe a little less and was over the intersection of the East-West and Diagonal Runways.

Lou promptly stuck the Waco's nose down, steep, and made a hard right turn. A mili-second later, the big bi-wing rolled left trying for what looked like the East-West's taxi strip, which was on the north side of the runway.

I stood there holding my breath, watching the big Waco wind its way through its violent turns, fighting off stalling conditions while looking to be headed straight for the ground. With his turns eating up so much altitude, I wouldn't have bet a penny against a dollar that he could have successfully made it. Then as I watched, I remember new thoughts creeping in; somehow, maybe, he just might pull it off. I knew it was going to be close.

With the ground nearly in his face, Lou abruptly lifted the nose of the Waco. The bi-plane immediately stalled out and hit hard in a flat three-point attitude. It made one bounce, rolled a short distance and came to a stop. A heavy cloud of dust swirled around the Waco, then slowly drifted off. He hadn't made perfect taxi strip alignment, but with his short ground roll, what little space he had was enough.

Behind me someone remarked, "That was too close! He should have held his heading and landed on the north side of 2100 South." I think most would agree that at Lou's altitude and position over the runway, he probably should have made the emergency landing directly ahead.

We were all at the side of the Lou's Waco when Chad opened up the cabin door. Lou was still in the pilot's seat, apparently still trying to collect himself. Chad asked if he was all right, Lou gave no response. He just sat there without motion, a little on the pale side and seemly unaware of our presence.

After a few seconds, he undid his belt, slid around in his seat, stood up and shuffled towards the cabin door. There he paused and looked out at us. He then climbed out onto the wing and jumped down to the ground. His legs were a little rubbery and he was shaking a bit. Other than that, he seemed to have taken his ride in stride.

There was some discussion on what had caused the engine to shut down. Lou said it had just quit cold without any warning. The fuel and mag switches were checked and all were at their proper settings. There was plenty of fuel in the tanks. Based on the way the engine behaved when it quit, the consensus was either a fuel or an ignition problem. For some reason the big Jacobs just couldn't keep the fire going.

Then wondering about damage, we all did a visual walk around inspection of the aircraft's exterior. If the hard landing had caused any internal damage, it would probably show up in the form of wrinkled fabric or metal. There was no visible external damage. Apparently, Lou had just made a rather hard emergency landing for reasons unknown. The next step in solving the problem would require more than a discussion and a leisurely walk around.

Someone asked Lou, in a rather nice way, why he didn't continue straight ahead. Lou stated rather quietly, "The ground ahead was pasture but there were too many cows and the land was way too bumpy." He felt that he had enough altitude to make the East-West Runway. He then reluctantly admitted that the turns ate up much more altitude than he had anticipated, and he felt lucky to have made the taxi strip.

It was close and no one knew it more than Lou did. Although his Waco was getting along in years and was even considered an antique by some, it was new to him and he would do just about anything to prevent it from being damaged. Thinking of the plane before procedure has gotten many a pilot into serious trouble. However, for Lou, it was a judgment call and with the possible alternatives, you can't argue the results. I might add something to Lou's credit; he didn't flip coins trying to come up with a decision, it was instantaneous.

After all the conversations had died down, we all spotted ourselves around the aircraft and pushed it over to its tie-down. The big Waco was secured, and then the crowd departed.

Lou had a short stepladder that he kept near the aircraft's tie-down. He flipped it open and stood it up along side the engine's cowling and undid the fasteners.

Once he had undone the big cowling, I helped him lower it to the ground. Then we both stood there in silence staring at the massive assembly of shaped steel that was a Jacobs Engine. Seeing Lou was deep in thought and beyond conversation, I wandered off to other duties.

Just before entering the main hangar, I turned around and glanced back at Lou. His head was bobbing back and forth around the rear of the engine. I wondered what his chances were of finding the problem. Later, when I walked by, Lou was still checking the engine out.

A few days later, Lou grabbed me by my arm and pulled me over to his car. Then opening up the trunk, he lifted out a rather bulky item wrapped in a cloth. Holding it out in a position just to the front of me, he rolled it out of its cloth wrapping.

"This is the magneto off the Waco," he exclaimed excitedly. "That's where the problem was!" He went on to explain that unlike modern aircraft engines his Jacob's engine has only a single magneto. When that magneto shut down, with no secondary or back-up, the engine quit cold.

A very detailed explanation was given on just how he zeroed in on the mag as the problem. It was mostly the result of intense and prolonged inspection. Having found the problem, a loose wire, he described in detail the steps taken to fix it. His enthusiasm was overwhelming. It was like listening to a little kid in a grade school "Show and Tell" class. He couldn't have been more excited if he had discovered flight. He then added, somewhat reluctantly, that he would have a mechanic check it out and pass off his work. However, you could tell by the way he talked; all the credit and glory would be his-forever.

Lou wrapped the mag back up in its cloth and put it in a cardboard box. I took the boxed mag and he grabbed his toolbox and we took everything over to his Waco. I watched as the excited Lou started the job of getting his mag back on his Waco.

Later, I could tell that the Waco was nearly ready. All of Lou's tools had been gathered up and he was walking back and forth studying the Waco's engine while wiping his hands on a rag.

I wandered over and stood at his side. He glanced in my direction, grinned and said, "Ron, it's ready." Then causally, he took a few steps over to the big propeller, paused and with one hand on the blade looked up at the Jacobs. He studied it for a few seconds, almost in reverence, like he was communicating with it. Then seeing a smudge of grease on the big wide metal blade, he wiped it clean and then polished the spot.

Walking around the wing, he climbed up and opened the cabin door. He looked a little nervous as he crossed the threshold into the darkened interior. Knowing him, he probably felt both his mechanical aptitude and reputation were on the line.

He took a step or two forward, slid into the left seat and paused a few seconds while looking the panel over. Seeing everything was to his satisfaction, he repositioned a few switches, leaned his head near the open window and hollered, "Clear."

The electric starter whined, the compression from Jake's big cylinders resisted. The big prop turned hard and heavy and appeared to be turning unevenly, and then it began to turn faster. It caught solid, belching blue smoke and then smoothed out into the familiar roar of a mighty Jacob's.

The engine was run for a time, first at low rpm's and then up to near full throttle. The aircraft shook and roared full of vigor and stamina. Lou listened intently to its pulse and heartbeat. He studied the instruments, and then looked at the haze of the propeller for a sign of a blip that might indicate something not quite right. However, every sound, every vibration, every instrument and every human instinct pointed to perfection.

I looked up at Lou sitting there in the subdued light of his Waco's cabin. He was surrounded by images of yesterday, the unique cabin enclosure, soft contoured fabric, the heavy upper wing with struts mounted between it and the lower wing, the classic landing gear struts with their huge tires, the massive round engine with its big polished metal propelled arc reflecting soft evening colors. Everything there belonged to yesterday, everything stood out boldly, proudly, maybe even flauntingly. Like the great sailing ships and the mighty steam locomotives of days past, classic aircraft were being phased out, replaced with "newer, better and more efficient machines." As beautiful as the modern Beechcrafts, Cessnas and Pipers were, sadly, somehow--something almost spiritual was being left behind.

Then there was Lou, sitting up there at the controls, smiling from ear to ear in all his glory. Could any words describe his feelings?

Lou calmly reached out his hand and repositioned a couple of switches and the big Jacob began its journey into mechanical hibernation. The big prop wound down into silence, leaving the aircraft resting at peace, reflecting the colors of the setting sun. Whoever said, "A picture is worth a thousand words," must have been looking at Lou's Waco and seeing what I was seeing.

Lou climbed out of the cabin, jumped down to the ground, walked around front to a position just below the cooling radial and looked up at the uncowled engine. He was beaming with pride and admiration, not for himself and his accomplishments but for his beloved Waco. There was really a bond between the two.

We discussed the beauty of the big old radials for a few moments, and then I helped the happy owner/pilot/mechanic get the cowling up and secured in place.

You've got to give him his due; the old girl never missed a beat after that.

Friends not Known

Gene and his son Terry spent a fair amount of time at the airport. Terry was about my age, a football-player-type of guy who sported a winning smile and a great personality. I don't know if you could call them wealthy, but they definitely had an edge on most of the people I knew. One of the more visible signs of their good fortune was the fact that they owned a new Cessna 172. It was something to behold, no exhaust stains, no oxidation and the seats and door panels still had their protective plastic coverings in place. It was almost a misfit at Utah Central.

Apparently, the father had been flying for some time. Terry was at the time taking flying lessons and was a natural in the left seat. I used to watch him climb into that new Cessna, and it would just about turn me inside-out with envy.

They had some kind of business in California and made frequent trips back and forth. Justifying a nice new airplane didn't require a lot of debate, "Business Travel you know," Terry had once told me with a smile. On another occasion, he added a little color to their business travels in the Cessna, "… it's big enough for comfort, plenty of room for luggage, fun to take off, fun to land and just plain pleasurable in between." It had me wondering if life could possibly be any better for two people.

I guess I had always been a little curious about the line of work Gene and Terry were in. You know, the money angle! Yet probing into one's source of wealth can be an awkward line of questioning. There never seems to be a good entry point. I had pretty much accepted the fact that it would remain an unasked question. However, one day a lengthy conversation led to me inquiring.

Terry kind of smiled, and then stated that years before his dad had invested heavily in what some were then calling "worthless California real estate." Then with the California land boom, the land was worth a fortune almost over night. I sensed that Terry was almost embarrassed about just how easily money was coming their way.

At the time, California Real Estate needed no recommendations. If you owned land in California, you were wealthy. If Gene and Terry had California real estate before the boom, their Cessna probably came out of the Petty Cash drawer.

Money, money, lots of money, lots of easy money, it got me thinking about the real estate thing. Boy would it be neat to buy a piece of land for next-to-nothing and then in a couple of days sell it for a huge profit. Hey, I could handle that!

Who was I kidding? I couldn't even afford to hitchhike to California. Yah, I guess I was a bit envious.

Then returning to work after a couple of days off, Chad approached me and asked in a rather inquisitive way, "Did you hear about Gene and Terry?"

I thought for a second, and answered cautiously, "No."

"You haven't?" "Do you know where they went when they flew out on their little trips?" Chad asked rather briskly.

Well, I knew the answer to that. "Sure," I said, "California, they own a bunch of land over there!"

Chad knew my answer before he heard the words, "Well the California part is right, but they were not involved in real estate! They were robbing banks!"

"Uh Uh," I answered dumbly.

"Yep, its true!" Chad came back, "They would hop in their airplane, fly to California, knock off a bank, hop back into their airplane and fly back to Salt Lake".

"Really?" I answered, sounding a little unsure of what I had just heard.

"Yah, there're both in jail now," Chad boldly stated, trying to make the unbelievable sound believable.

"You're kidding me, right," I asked in total disbelief.

"Nope, all true," he answered.

The entire story seemed incredible. Chad was not one to fabricate anything for any reason, but Gene and Terry, bank robbers? Come on! The words didn't make sense, but I had to believe him.

Trying not to give him the impression that I was questioning what he was saying, I made a couple of inquiries, mostly to convince myself that I understood what I thought I had heard. "Are you sure its Gene and Terry, our Gene and Terry?

"Yep."

"They really don't have land in California."

"Nope."

"They were robbing banks and using their Cessna for their get-a-way?"

"Yep."

"The brand new Cessna that's based at our airport, Utah Central?"

"Yep!"

Then he added, "It's in all the papers. Glen has spent hours talking to the FBI, almost an open-and-shut case. It's true alright, no doubt about it"!

How could I dispute it? Yet nothing made sense. How could it be true, with or without the facts? It was if I had just discovered the world was in fact flat, and China wasn't down there after all. The whole round earth thing was a simple "typo error."

Somehow I felt sorry for Terry. And thinking about it, I guess I felt a little sorry for myself. I had envied those guys, and now. If all facts were known about anyone, how many people would really feel comfortable walking around in their shoes. What did the wise old Indian say?

"You've got to walk in a man's moccasins for many moons before you really know him!" Smart Indian! Dumb me!

Truth in, impressions out!

The Five Penny Flight

Mel Rozema, like me, was taken flying lessons while working at the airport. When it came time for his Solo Cross Country training flight, he scheduled the PA–12 for a flight down south to Richfield, Utah. And he, like me, often had to do some fancy footwork to squeeze his flying into some of our busy days.

Nearing his scheduled departure time, unforeseen problems appeared then reappeared. However, once clear, there was still time enough for a nice leisure flight down and return.

The trip down was uneventful, except for the fact that he couldn't get his left wing tank to feed. Every time he switched the fuel selector from the right tank to the left tank the engine would cut out; fuel starvation. After a few tries, he accepted the fact that he wasn't going to get any fuel out of the left tank. That was not a serious problem as Richfield was well within the range of the Cruiser's right wing tank. However, the usable fuel in the functioning right tank would be marginal for his return trip back to Salt Lake. Luckily, the charts indicated fuel was available at the Richfield Airport. Mel could fill up and be on his way with a minimum delay--or so he figured.

He landed and pulled up near the gas pump. No one came out to greet him. The field was deserted except for a mangy old airport guard dog that did little more than open one eye as Mel stepped over its lifeless body. As he neared the FBO's office, he could see a pay phone mounded on the outside of the building and nearby, a sign posted on the front door. It listed an after hours telephone number to call if fuel was needed. Then something made him think of money, money for the fuel. Mel was not one to have more than a few dollars in his wallet at any given time, sometimes--most times, much less. He knew he had a problem and went into a semi-state of shock. He pulled out his wallet and after a quick examination his worst fears were confirmed. Not a single dollar anywhere! It was a blow like he had never felt before. He was at a strange airport. He was a long way from home, and it was getting late. Never had he felt so alone in his life.

Wondering what he could do, he wandered over in the direction of his Piper. Then he noticed an older man with two young boys wandering over in his direction. All three were eyeing Mel's airplane with interest. As the three individuals neared, the man commented that they had seen the airplane land, and the kids had expressed a desire to go for a ride. The older individual then asked Mel if he gave airplane rides. Mel, a student pilot, was at first a little reluctant to say yes as he was not licensed to carry passengers, let alone paying passengers. Then thinking of everything that had gone wrong and facing the prospects of sleeping with a mangy old airport dog, he put on his best face, smiled and smartly answered, "You bet!"

The PA–12 had a passenger seat in the rear wide enough for two people. The boys hopped in and Mel tightened up their seat belt. Then he crawled up into the pilot's seat, started the engine and they were on their way. The flight was a short one over the city, and the kids appeared to enjoy every moment. When they climbed out they couldn't have been more excited if they had been to the moon. Mel made five dollars on the flight. Not a fortune, but it would buy enough gas to get him back to Salt Lake.

With gas money in hand, he eagerly headed back towards the telephone. He

had some fears that the manager might refuse to come out for a measly five
bucks worth of gas, but he figured once he got him here, he would apologize
for the short sales after he had fuel in his tank. As he approached the telephone, he reached into his pocket for change. No change of any denomina-
tion. He frantically reached into his other pocket. Nothing! Stopped in his
tracks, he searched every pocket in his trousers. Nothing--not so much as a
quarter, a dime, or a nickel. Nothing. He had five bucks but not one lousy
nickel for a phone call! He went through his pockets a second time, even a
third time, still nothing. No coin, no telephone call, no fuel. Why didn't he
charge the kids $5.05, or even $4.95! Now what!

It was getting late and he had no experience in night flying and he had no
desire to spend the night at a strange airport. Then he thought of his Flight
Plan. If he didn't get it closed, the FAA would assume he was down somewhere. Without a nickel he couldn't even close that! The thought of expensive
search-and-rescue teams flying all over the country, looking for his lost aircraft sent chills up his spine. Boy, heads would roll over that, all for the lack of
a lousy nickel! He had to get back. Somehow he had to get some fuel.

He had currency, and the highway wasn't all the far from the airport.
Maybe he could get change. Even better than that, maybe he could hitchhike to town and buy some fuel. Buying the fuel from an in-town gas station would save him time, the airport gas boy would probably take hours
to get him serviced.

It didn't take long for Mel to flag down a ride. As a conversation developed,
Mel was asked where he was headed. Mel casually told him about his airplane
and the problem with the fuel. The driver gave Mel a somewhat questioning
if not an outright look of disbelief. It was obvious that he thought the story
was made up and everything Mel said was to be questioned.

Mel felt some relief when they finally pulled up at a gas station. He thanked
his still puzzled driver and hopped out.

Mel needed a couple of five-gallon cans for the gas. He hated to spend good
gas money on cans that he would probably never use again, but he was in a
hurry and there was little else he could do. Another problem, automobile fuel
contains lead and is not recommended for aircraft engines. Hopefully, a few
gallons of car gas mixed with the aviation fuel remaining in the wing tank
wouldn't cause problems. It was a relatively short flight back. The next day he

could address the problem of the remaining car fuel in the wing tank.

While the station attendant was filling the gas cans, Mel looked at them and began wondering about the particulars of his fuel problem. How much fuel did he really need anyway. His young energetic mind began analyzing his needs.

First he needed enough for the flight back, plus some reserve. He began flipping numbers: consumption per hour, fuel burned on first leg of the trip, flying time required for the return trip, all factored into the cans the attendant was filling. Then there was the useable fuel remaining. How much was in the wing tank anyway? What were his actual fuel needs, in gallons? He began searching for the numbers, whatever they might be to plug into the formula, whatever the formula was.

Then again, there was the nighttime factor. The rules stated that a good pilot should have a greater fuel reserve at night than required for the same daylight flight. It might be a good idea to follow what rules he could. Then again, he felt there would be no problem finding his way back, since there was one long highway connecting Richfield and the Salt Lake Valley. The highway was almost a guarantee that he wouldn't get lost. Then crossing the Salt Lake Valley, he could read the lights and they would lead him to the airport, or at least the general area. So he wouldn't need all of the standard nighttime reserve. But... Somewhat discouraged, he decided to buy all the fuel he could and if he was running short he would land at Provo, or somewhere, and then bum a ride to Salt Lake.

Getting a ride back to the airport was a little harder with the two cans of gas, but some fellow in a truck finally took pity on him. Mel threw the cans into the back of the bed and hopped in. He was glad the cans were in the bed of the truck. If they were up front the driver might have asked Mel what the gas was for and Mel wasn't in the mood to go through that explanation again.

Once back at the airport, Mel grabbed an old stepladder and placed it near the leading edge of the wing. Then he grabbed a can of gas and climbed up the ladder. He removed the fuel cap and began pouring the precious fuel into the wing tank. The can of fuel was heavy and awkward. A nice big funnel would have been handy.

True to his luck the first gush of precious fuel missed the tank opening and ran down and off the trailing edge of the wing. Mel backed off and began pouring slower. He wanted every drop of fuel in the tank. Dumping in the first can of gas must have been a learning experience. He didn't spill more than a drop or two from the second can. He secured the gas cap, jumped off the ladder and set it aside.

Then he glanced at the fuel gauge on the bottom of the wing. It indicated more fuel in the tank than he had dared hope for. Feeling somewhat triumphant, he ran over to a hose and quickly washed his hands. Then while running back to his Piper he dried them on his shirt. Quickly checking the surrounding area for obstructions, he swung the tail of the Piper around so he had a clear path to taxi. Then he did an abbreviated Pre-Flight and another quick look around the area. Everything was ready.

Climbing in, he quickly did his belt up, positioned the throttle, checked the fuel valve, set the altimeter and checked the carb heat's position. Then sticking his head near the open window he yelled, "Clear" and hit the starter. The engine caught and roared to life. Mel opened the throttle and the rpm's leaped up. Feeling the aircraft move was one of the most beautiful feelings he had ever had in his life. He was finally on his way!

Looking out over the tops of the parked aircraft, he could see the sun sinking mighty low in the western sky. "What a heck of a night for a beautiful sunset"!

His take-off must have been one of the shortest in the history of the Richfield Airport. He cut across the parking area, through a brush covered medium with wings rocking and the engine blowing dirt, dust and weeds. Once Mel was near the runway, he made a wide circle to check for traffic. The tail wheel was nearly clear of the runway's surface as he swerved to the center of the northbound strip.

He went through a short pattern, turned his aircraft to the north and lifted the nose up into a shallow climb. Then eyeing the highway off to his right, he moved his Piper's flight path just to its left and parallel to it. That highway was not only his path home, but with the lack of night flying instruments and his inexperience, it was a good reference to keep the ground down, the sky up and the aircraft level in between.

Then as things settled down and with the Piper on course, he started thinking about the possibility of more problems, like an engine failure. It would fit right into the pattern of things, but he quickly brushed the fears aside. He had lots of faith in the solid roar of the Lycoming. With everything done that he could do, he leaned back in his seat and tried to relax.

Relax he tried, but there were just too many unknowns out front. Then the oncoming dusk caught his attention. Lights, aircraft position lights; he had better turn them on. There was small electrical panel on the right side of the cabin. He groped in the shadows at the panel switches, trying to make out the markings and just where the "Off" and "On" positions of the switches were, but it was too dark. He fumbled with the switch, even putting his face down near the panel trying to see something that would indicate its position.

A flashlight would have been handy. He played with the panel while periodically looking out at his wing tips to see if there was any indication of lights. Most modern aircraft have little plastic tabs hanging down from the wing tip lights to visually indicate when the lights are on. His PA–12 lights lacked these indicators. After countless efforts, and not really sure what the switch's positions were when he started, he made his best guess, positioned the switches and put it out of his mind. He cussed himself for not knowing his airplane better and vowed never to have that problem again. The Cruiser continued north. It might not have surprised Mel had he been able to see that his position lights were still off--and dark.

He had been looking forward to some nighttime flying since he couldn't remember when. And there he was on his first night flight, the flight of his dreams, scared and knees shaking. How nice it would have been if someone, preferably a qualified flight instructor, had given him a few pointers or even a hint or two before being kicked out on his own.

Then thinking of all the problems, he had to admit that the flight had given him a vast amount of experience. Never had he learned so much on one flight, if he could make just one more successful landing.

Meanwhile, at Utah Central, Glen was beginning to get a little concerned. Not knowing what was going on, and unable to contact Mel, he decided to make what preparations he could, just in case. With evening approaching, he called the airport staff together and told them of his concerns. He instructed us to get our cars, park them on the west end of the ramp, and wait. If Mel buzzed the airport, we could in a moment, have our cars out on the edge of the strip with some runway lights.

We moved our cars out on the ramp and shut the engines down. Then in

near silence, we all congregated around one of the vehicles, all eyes scanning
the southern skies for Mel's aircraft lights.

Following the main highway to the Jordan Narrows, Mel then moved his
path west, to trail the automobile lights along Redwood Road, a north-south
highway on the west side of the valley. Soon the narrows opened up into the
Salt Lake Valley.

Mel studied patterns, making sure he could identify them before his eyes
moved on to the next groupings, never trusting himself to assume or relax.
Whenever possible, a nearby pattern was identified and compared to the
known pattern. Each known position was a simple, but important milepost
leading to the ultimate destination, Utah Central.

Approaching a cluster of lights, he immediately recognized as the little community of Granger. There was the traffic along Granger's main street, 3500
South. A little farther north, he could see the streetlights of 3100 South. To
the west, sky reflections on Kennecott's Duck Pond and a car or two along
3600 West. Following a path straight east, he could see the sky reflections on
the surface of Decker Lake. Then there was the traffic moving along a distance
2100 South. Everything fit. Between all the recognizable landmarks was a
huge dark area, Utah Central Airport, his destination.

The airport property was huge and well defined, but the runways were small
and buried in shadows. If he missed his runway, he would be in some rather
lumpy brush. It would be nice if Utah Central had runway lights, or if he had
a radio or if it was still light. Wishful thinking, he had to do the best he could
with what he had.

Studying the darkened area, he felt some concerns and a little nervousness. He
knew he was facing a challenge, yet he was also confident that he had the ability
to get down safely. He just needed to be cool, positive, alert and focused.

Cutting back on power, he started his descent to pattern altitude. He opted
to do a full landing pattern, using all available references to establish and keep
him on track. If he could fly a proper pattern, it would put the runway out in
front of the Cruiser on a near perfect Final. He hoped!

When he got nearer the ground, he was sure the runway would be visible. If
not, well, he'd decide when the time came.

His little Piper entered the Down-Wind Leg, slightly to the east of 3600
West, then the left turn onto Base, followed by the turn onto Final. Even

without all the visual landmarks, he knew he was on track. The runway was there even if he couldn't see it.

He eased back on the power, adjusted his glide, and cut back on his airspeed as much as he dared. A long and narrow gray line slowly emerged. The line was faint, washed out, almost to the point of being an illusion, Runway 34. Mel was jubilant. All of his checks and balances had put him right where he wanted to be. A little power, some minor adjustments and he had perfect runway alignment. However, in the dark he could see that the numbers on depth perception were going to be a little harder to sort out. He drifted down while easing the throttle back to idle. The runway grew in his windshield. A few seconds passed, and he cautiously pulled back on the control column. The nose lifted, the aircraft continued to settle. The landing gear reached out towards the earth. Hopefully, it was in the right place. Right or wrong, Mel was 100 percent committed.

On the ground, our conversation had given way to silence. We milled around our vehicles, looking and waiting anxiously, hopeful that we would soon see Mel's lights. His Piper PA–12 had no bright landing light, but it did have some good strong wing lights. They could be seen for quite a distance. Mel's wing lights would be the key to giving him the runway lights he needed.

Eyes played tricks in the darkness and several times someone would say "there." However, aircraft lights failed to materialize. Someone had seen a star or even imagined a light.

Then, engine sounds, the drone of an aircraft engine--Mel's aircraft? Our silence deepened. We gazed at the black sky until our eyes watered. We all heard the sound, but couldn't determine where it was coming from, or even what it was. There were nearby highways on the north and west sides of the airport. On occasions, heavy trucks traveling by would sound like aircraft.

We continued staring, straining our eyes, looking, imagining until we didn't know what we were looking at or seeing. There was nothing out there indicating an aircraft, nothing that could be Mel in his Piper. Someone discounted the sound as a truck. The rest agreed, and we dismissed it from our minds. We looked for more positive signs.

Then, a hollow bump sound. Silence. Then another bump, more silence then several smaller bumps in quick succession. These sounds were coming from the direction of our runways. It couldn't be an aircraft, could it? We didn't know what it was or what to think. Someone jokingly stated that one of those Texas Jack Rabbits had probably taken up residence on airport property. A couple of us laughed. Most probably hadn't even heard the remark. We continued our gaze into the darkness searching for the red and green lights of Mel's Super Cruiser.

Roaring sounds, an engine, something cutting air, the source still covered in darkness. A point, a smear of reflective lights, an emerging image without a distinguishable shape was moving towards us. Lines were vague but slowly taking shape as the image emerged from the darkness. With the images came the sounds, sounds that were growing, intensifying, echoing.

We all stood there in silence, arms hanging, mouths open, eyes bulging and minds blank. Nothing should be there, how could anything be there? Was it an airplane, no way, impossible! Then we could make out a big shimmering propeller arc, an engine cowling, the spread of wings, a set of landing gears and then unmistakable plexiglas reflections. "Well I'll be, it's a Piper, a Piper Cruiser, its Mel!"

The somewhat dark and shadowed aircraft continued towards us, growing in size and detail with its distinctive Lycoming engine sounds. Then from behind the propeller arc and plexiglas reflections, we could make out Mel. His face was lit up like a light bulb, displaying a smile that went from ear to ear. Was he happy to see us, or was he feeling good after his first successful night landing? I wasn't sure, but it didn't really matter.

Tall Tale Roger

Roger Kunz was the kind of guy you would walk a mile just to say "Hi" to. Unquestionably, he was one of the easiest people to like and talk to that I have ever met in my life. He was a little older than I, and his physical appearance could not be described as anything but jolly. Always bright, bubbly and fun, he dominated any conversation that was going on anywhere, simply because he was fun and interesting.

He was a member of a small flying club based at Utah Central. The club flew a little tricycle gear, mid wing, two-place homebuilt called a Stits Flut-R-Bug. Everyone around the field called it the "Bug." The Bug, like the Piper Cub, had tandem-mounted seats in a narrow fuselage. With a rather large nose wheel, it was right at home on our dirt runways. The aircraft was almost entirely fabric and its short stubby wings were mounted mid fuselage. To enter, you climbed up onto the wing and then dropped down into the pilot or passenger's seat. Powered by a 65 HP Continental, it like most aircraft on the field had no electrical system and no starter.

Late one Saturday afternoon, several of us were sitting around the lunch counter in a rather laid-back bull session. Roger came in and after listening for a time related the following experience. His expressions are impossible to put on paper, but the story that follows is pretty much as he told it.

"It was a beautiful day for flying," he started out. "The kind of day where you feel no matter what you do, it just cannot go wrong. I untied the Bug and checked the gas and oil. There was no one around to give me a prop so I decided to do it myself, done it a million times! I know I should have left the tail tied but no one was watching so I thought it would be okay.

"I checked the switches and turned the prop over a couple of times. So far so good, everything was going great! Then I turned the mag switch on. That's normal and all went okay there too. The day was having a great beginning. I spat on my hands just like the big boys do, took a step closer to the propeller, reached out my hands and placed them on the blade, just so and so. Wanting everything to be perfect, I leaned forward to the proper position, lifted my right foot up to the square, all of which indicates the proper balance and power. Then flexing all my arm and back muscles to their fullest, I gave the prop a good hard flip. It started right up, not a bit of trouble, on my very first flip, you know what I mean.

"But it sounded a little bit loud, like maybe it was at full throttle! The sound and visual effects were terrific. It would probably surprise you, but it's a real wakeup call to be standing a foot or two in front of a spinning propeller, one that is starting to move towards you. Now there was a problem, there wasn't anyone in the cockpit who could hit the brakes, pull back on the power, cut the switch, or even scream at.

"A millionth of a second after it started I was backtracking, hopping, kicking and paddling air trying to get a little space between me and that very angry propeller, ya know what I mean? Movements brought about by panic will only lead to a fall, and that's what I did.

"A 'fall' might be an overly graceful way of putting it. I mean I dived, and I hit face first. I bounced and slid along like a common dirt plow. Next thing I remember I was spiting grit out from between my teeth and clearing my eyes of dust while trying to roll onto my feet for some kind of control. While doing all the flopping and maneuvering, I was trying to keep clear of the Bug.

"Being around an airplane on the loose is not a good thing, and no one knew that better than I. Somehow I had to tackle it, rein it in, or even throw a rock at the propeller, anything to gain some control. However while maneuvering for position, I couldn't sense up or down, or here or there or this or that. I couldn't even scream. All I could do was make wild groaning sounds while trying to determine its whereabouts.

"But I could tell by the sound of the screaming engine that it was in the area somewhere and very close. And ya know, without even seeing it, or knowing for sure where it was, I somehow knew that it was headed right for me. And ya know, I was right--is that a sixth sense or what? I turned my head and there it was, my Bug with its head lowered, spitting flame out one side and smoke out the other, and it was headed right for me.

"I still wasn't fully up on my feet and I guess that was good because being half up and half down made it a little easier for me to dive into the dirt again. Again, I hit the ground hard with a loud grunt. While in the middle of a bounce, I was blindly swinging my arms hoping to grab a wing strut, a gear, or something, but all I got was lots of air, the wing had already passed over.

"Off hand, I don't know of any Federal Regulations stating that it's illegal, not right or even not proper to send an aircraft into the sky without its pilot, but somewhere, there has got to be a paragraph or even a sentence stating that it's not recommended. What was I thinking; the Feds were going to give me ten to twenty on every single law in every law book ever written!

"So much for my legal problems, but for right now, I had a more pressing problem, my run-away-airplane. I again got my body parts operating collectively and somehow I managed to stand upright, somewhat. Off to the side, I saw my Bug bouncing happily through the brush, but it was over there and I was over here! It had to be a dream, a very bad dream. Yet I knew it wasn't; there was too much noise and dirt. On top of everything my normally calm disposition was giving way to a real bad nervous condition.

"It still wasn't going real fast, but even in my mental state, I could see that it would be long gone before long. Stumbling and kicking dirt and weeds in every direction I was after it. My body, being short and husky is built for comfort, not speed. Nevertheless, out of the corner of my eye, I could see that my short little legs were moving so fast that they were a blur. If only my old high school coach could have seen me, it would have brought tears to his eyes.

"The Bug, Oh Yah, it was still bucking, jumping and rocking across the landscape. And me, I was right behind, bobbing, stumbling, screaming and waving my arms. I think I might have even cussed it out once or twice, not sure. But even with all my wild uncoordinated romping and jumping, I was somehow closing up the distance between us. Then success! A little anyway! I finally got hold of its bucking tail feathers, and I held on for dear life with my little pinkies. It must have been a miracle; my body was keeping up with my fingers--to some degree anyway."

"My fingers might have found some security in holding on, but I was fast losing control of my feet. I was stumbling more and more with every giant step taken. Then like some divine revelation from heaven, I realized that I couldn't possibly hold on and tag along forever. The Bug wanted to go flying, with or without me! I had to do something, and fast!

"I tried and tried to hold it back but just couldn't get any good footing. Then with an effort way beyond anything I've ever exerted before, I began working my way up towards the cockpit. But as expected, my feet were having trouble keeping pace. I think they were beginning to accept the fact that the race was lost. But I fought and clawed, hand over hand; half-running, half-stumbling, half-dragging, I managed to work myself around the tail and up near the fuselage. By then my Bug was really moving. The length of my stride was unbelievable. Maybe, judging by my speed, I might have even looked like a real athlete, but I knew that wasn't possible.

"The Bug was screaming and bouncing through the brush and I was bouncing and screaming right at its side. Boy, were we having fun, just like a couple of wild horses in a Wild West movie.

"Slowly, I continued to inch forward until I had a handhold on the corner of the cockpit opening. Now the plane was going so fast that it was getting more flight time than taxi time. Have you ever wondered what thoughts run through a pilot's mind when his airplane is about ready to break ground and he only has two fingers inside the cockpit? Don't ask, cause you won't like my answer.

"And to add a little humor to misery, have you ever tried climbing up on a wing when the airplane is moving just a little faster than your top speed?

"I stumbled onto the secret; it was just a matter of throwing myself into the air, as much as I could under the circumstances and dragging myself up. I kept pulling, grunting and crawling, trying to work myself higher up on the wing. Somehow I had to move forward so my arm could reach into the cockpit. If I could reach into the cockpit, then, hopefully, I could reach a throttle, or switch, or something that would get me out of my mess. Boy, I wished that I had an anchor to throw out.

"Looking out the corner of my eye, I could see that we were actually more airborne than not. Hey, if a pilot is flopping around on the wing of his airborne aircraft, is that flight time entered in his logbook under the Pilot In Command column? Oh Well.

"Finally, thank my lucky stars, I got hold of the ignition and shut it off, hard. Then I grabbed the stick. I don't know why I did that, maybe I was hoping to improve upon whatever type of landing the bouncing plane was about to make. Would you call that wishful thinking or what? I can't make a good landing even while sitting in the pilot's seat. What chance did I have while lying on the wing? I couldn't even see the ground!

"You can't even imagine what kind of landing it was. The Bug bounced and tossed until I was unable to hold on. Then with a form that was a little less than graceful, I flew off the wing kicking, waving my arms and screaming.

"I hit the ground hard, making more funny noises than a hippopotamus doing a belly flop from a high dive. The Bug and I bounced around together for a time, each in our own little personalized cloud of dust and flying weeds. Then, except for a few of my moaning sounds, stillness.

"I guess I must be a better pilot than I had originally thought because, I was still alive and the Bug was still sitting on all three's."

Roger paused a few seconds and then added with remorse; "Looking back at all the things that were stacked against me, that's probably the best landing I've ever made…. and I wasn't even in the airplane."

We were all rolling across the counter, stools and floor in fits of laughter and pain. All the while, his expression was one of somber confusion, like his experience was traumatic, and he simply couldn't understand why everyone was laughing.

Rattling the Pearly Gates

Once we had made the run-up, check out our controls, Chad moved his tan Cub out checking for pattern traffic. With no traffic, he moved out towards the runway's take-off position. I applied a little power and followed. Chad eased to a stop just to the left of the runway's center. I moved up on his right and positioned my Cub a length behind his. We both paused; giving ourselves a few second to make sure all was ready. Then Chad looked back at me. I gave a little nod.

Chad's prop arc flashed from a flickering shadow to a light gray haze. The Cub's balloon tires slowly started moving across the runway's packed surface of dirt and gravel. I opened up my throttle to hold my position at his side. Increasing sounds of rushing air and tires moving over dirt and gravel added to the excitement of the roaring Continentals. The aircraft swayed and bounced lightly, giving references to the runway's surface. I could see a line of light gray dust trailing from behind his tires. As our speed increased, I began picking up some of his turbulence. I eased over to the right.

I watched Chad's Cub intensely and noticed with interest the amount of rudder play it took to keep it in line. Slowly his tail lifted to near horizontal, and I nudged my stick forward. Two Cubs racing along together, tails held high, engines roaring, wind humming and a cloud of dust marking their path--what a beautiful picture.

The trail of tire dust ceased as he broke free of the earth. My wheels lifted clear at about the same time. Chad's tires spun in the air and then locked and hung still. In the spirit of unity I tapped my brakes. Again, I began picking up turbulence, so I eased off to the right a couple of extra feet.

Chad held a few feet off the ground to let our speed build up. Then easing back on the stick, he pointed his Cub up into the sky. I held position as the numbers on our altimeter increased. Easing in and out of turns, we wandered through the pattern and then took up a course to the southwest while still holding formation.

Once at altitude and over the practice area, I looked over at Chad. He was grinning in a mischievous sort of way. His Cub suddenly flipped over on its side showing off its full bottom (I made a quick mental note to get its belly cleaned up). Rolling out, he started into a climbing turn. I flipped my Cub over and followed. We had ourselves a game of tag. I had him lined up in my windshield for a few seconds. Then he was gone. His Cub was every where, first to the left, then to the right, then dropping down below the nose of my Cub, and then he shot back up into altitude. With both of us banking, turning and rolling in different directions, he sure looked like he was having a wild ride.

Chad wandered over a flat stretch of clouds. I was still hot on his tail, occasionally drifting across and bouncing through his turbulence. Then dropping his nose, he slipped down between two vertical walls of clouds, almost a canyon. At the end and some distance out, another billowing wall stood in his path. He could have rolled out to the left or right. Trying to anticipate his next move, I deducted that he would swing to the right. I went into a mild right turn.

He surprised me by flipping hard to the left. Having lost some advantage with my wrong turn, and trying to read where the clouds would take him, I looked for and saw an obvious short cut. I lifted the Cub's nose up into a climbing right turn towards the shorter side of the cloud. Then I rolled over into a left climbing turn over the top of a cloudbank. Once over the top, I eased into a diving turn to the left and followed the wall of the cloud in a mild left turn. I fully expected to see Chad's tan Piper out in the clear.

Like a clap of thunder, my entire frontal view was filled with Chad's Cub. I was headed right for him. My Cub's position was something like two o'clock high, relative to his. His Cub was at twelve o-clock, slightly high and dead in my path. We were looking at each other, almost as if we were sitting on opposite sides of a table. It was almost like looking at a picture of Chad. I could see his plaid shirt with papers in his pocket behind his partially unzipped jacked, the texture of his stocking cap, his hanging jaw, and oval eyes filled with stark surprise.

He and his Cub seemed to be everywhere, at all destinations. We were on a collision course and seemingly no way to avoid it. In my mind, I was seeing the full range of all the terrible things that were about to happen. Aircraft ripping into and through each other, explosions and then countless unrecognizable parts flying out in all directions--twisting, tumbling and floating to earth in a thousand crazy patterns, like so much confetti.

I can't remember taking evasive action, but as suddenly as Chad appeared, he was gone. Then I was aware of heavy "G" loads. I weighed a ton! I remember being pressed down in my seat, while wondering if the wing spars would be able to withstand the load. I twisted and rolled my body back and forth trying to get some reference to the ground while asking myself all kind of questions. Where was I? Where was Chad? Did we hit?

I looked down and could see only blue sky beyond my right landing gear. I turned and twisted in my seat. Finally I found the earth above and behind me. I rolled the stick and kicked the rudder trying to get the gear pointed down. Negative loads, a cloud of vaporized fuel erupted from the fuel tank, spread across my windshield and disappeared. I rolled out into level flight.

Still no Chad! He seemed to have vanished! A feeling of fear and desperation swept over me. I continued to circle--looking, hoping but still no Chad. The only things I could see in the sky were clouds. They appeared almost as motionless spectators, watching with amusement.

Then far below I saw some movement. It seemed almost too small, too far away, but it just might be him. I cut the power, pushed the nose down, and rolled into a descending spiral. It was an airplane, a Piper, a tan Piper Cub, Chad's. He was still in the air and everything appeared to be all right. Never have I been so relieved in all my life. I moved in on his wing, wide. Then he saw me and we closed up. He looked drawn and thankful, like I felt.

The near miss had taken the fun out of what we were doing so we headed back. For young people, that kind of stuff, you know collisions and dying is not that big of a thing and it is soon forgotten. However, over the years, I've thought about that incident many times and wondered, how could we have missed colliding, we were so close? Why didn't we hit and what if we had?

Lesson learned, you bet! Every experience leaves rewards. The one for that day; "Don't bet the farm on a gut feeling substantiated by smoke patterns and blowing leaves. And, Oh Ya, Stay away from clouds"

Utah Central Airport
...baring unseen circumstances it would be there for a long time.
Picture courtesy of the Glen Dellinger Family

Glen F. Dellinger
His flying career was terminated at the completion of a very normal spray run.
Picture courtesy of Glen Dellinger Family

Chad Jenkins with a Ford V8
...and I guess Chad could probably tell it's designers a thing or two about its workings.

Piper J-3 Cub
"Then it hit me. He was turning me loose".

Lou Pangman
He was making a jump from a "puddle jumper" to a big military trainer.

A Waco YKS
...somthing almost spiritual was being left behind.   *Andy Heins National Waco Club*

Beech C-45
"Right brake Locked up...ground looped...blew a tire."

The author with a T-50
..."but I did, by myself make the landing".

Douglas C-54
The Douglas transport drifted over the fence, looking almost like the tail would take a strand or two of wire off the top.

The author with the companies' PA-12
How many times have I had that dream only to have it aborted at daylight?

Sam Buttars
...it could have been just another day, passed over and forgotten.

7

A Teenagers' World

Like a Cub, Almost

Our company had a Cessna 120 on line that was available for students. For whatever reason, flight training at Utah Central started out in the J–3's and then after building up some time students were checked out in the Cessna.

The Cessna 120 is a good-looking airplane and in most ways was years ahead of the Piper Cub. It was a two-place airplane, but unlike our Cubs' tandem-seating the Cessna's was side by side. It had the traditional tail-wheel and the engine was still the dependable Continental, but it was rated at an honest eighty-five horses and was hidden under a nice streamlined metal cowl. Obviously, the exposed jugs design of the J–3's was fast becoming outdated. The fuselage and tail feathers of the Cessna 120 were a bright shining metal, but the 120 retained the traditional fabric-covered wing. Interestingly, we at the airport called the fabric-covered wings of the Cessna 120 "rag wings."

The 120 had a relatively thin wing (Bruce referred to it as a "high speed wing"), giving up some of its lift for a little more speed. Between the cleaner design of the aircraft and the additional horsepower, it was faster than the Cub. The books list the cruise speed of the 120 just over 100 mph.

The Cessna is much easier to enter, as airplanes go, with its two individual side doors, one on the left and one on the right. Inside the cabin were two small steering wheels mounted on shafts that penetrate the panel. I had always preferred a control stick, partly because the traditional military aircraft like the Thunderbolts, Mustangs and Hellcats had 'em, and also because the stick was fun. To a lesser degree, I had always looked at steering wheels as something designed for business people. However, the Lockheed Lightning had a steering wheel so what can I say.

The 120 had side-by-side seating, which to me is both a plus and a minus. The view out the left side was terrific, and to the front it was also much improved over the Cub. But the pilot's right side, well that view wasn't quite up to par with the Cub's. The real advantage of the side-by-side seating was one's ability to listen to, talk with and watch your instructor or friend sitting at your side. I guess to that you can add another advantage, when you looked at the panel; you saw instruments, not someone's back. The Cessna was a neat airplane!

Up at the Logan airport, Roy had both the older Cessna 120s and the newer 140 aircraft. The 140 looked almost identical to the 120, but 140 does have some updates, like rear windows, wing flaps and an all-metal wing. Some claim that the 120 is a little faster than the 140. If that's true, it's probably the extra weight of the metal wing and flaps that slows the 140 down. That could be a perfect example of what Bruce referred to as "trade offs--that is the gaining of a nice metal wing with flaps while losing some coveted air speed. One airport acquaintance told me that there were some production overlaps with the two models. If he knew what he was talking about, some early 140 features were incorporated on some late 120's before the model was officially changed.

I had always wanted to fly the Cessna and the day came when I said, "Why not, why not today?" I grabbed Sam and he agreed to check me out.

Like it was yesterday, I can remember climbing through our respective doors and sliding onto our seats. It seemed that our bodies collided somewhere near the centerline of the airplane while parts of us were still not entirely within our allotted cabin space. Sam was built like a football player, and I came in at just under two hundred pounds. Well, it was a friendly fit to put it mildly.

Buckling up our belts had to be the highlight of the day. His left belt and my right belt were nearly on top of each other. Traditional courtesy demands that one individual leans to one side while the other does up his belt, and then the other politely follows with a sweet "Thank You."

It's not always done that way. Occasionally, as it was on that day, the domineering instincts of individual males each demand the lead. Not to be outdone by the other and with a somewhat manly attempt to emphasize our individual strength, a friendly contest was in the making. The little cabin was filled with flying elbows, the sounds of grunts, cute little remarks, faked injuries and moaning sounds.

All the while, the little Cessna was rocking back and forth, as if it was in some kind of windstorm. For young people, especially young males, second place is a disgrace, a slot not to be tolerated under any conditions. I'd like you to believe that I won the contest. But Sam would probably smile and respond, "Come on Ron."

Once buckled up and at peace, Sam explained some of the particularities of the Cessna 120 as we went over the panel and controls. There's not a lot of difference between the controls of the Piper and those of the Cessna. The Cessna's cabin looks different and the location of the controls are different, but they all did the same thing. With everything in place and accounted for, Sam leaned a bit to the center of the cabin and closed his door and then I took my turn.

I got an all clear and pulled the starter giving the engine life. After watching the engine instruments for a few seconds, I turned my attention to possible ground traffic and the windsock. Moving out of the tie-down spot, I headed for Runway 27.

I went through the ground checks and then lined up the little Cessna on the center of the runway. Easing the throttle forward into full power, the little Cessna headed towards the sky.

I guess each aircraft has its own personality quirks. There might even be a difference between aircraft of the same make and models, like our two Cubs. Maybe most of that is in the rigging, could even be the props, or the engine on one could be having a bad day. If the differences are not too great, I guess most people really wouldn't notice.

However, the Cessna--to me, everything about it was a little different from the Cub. I could feel it in the controls. I could feel it during its take-off run and even during its lift-off. Not a "bad" difference, just a difference.

I reached pattern altitude, made some adjustment on the throttle and trim; leaned back and took in some of the attributes of the Cessna. Piloting an airplane in the air (while flying straight and level) is always a laid-back experience. Everything is in slow motion, peaceful and simple. It's a time to relax and enjoy the aircraft as it moves through the sky. An aircraft in flight is always at its best.

Around the pattern we went, then onto Final. As the runway was growing in the windshield, Sam was quietly feeding me information about the landing. Right hand on the throttle, I eased back with my left hand on the wheel. Out front, the runway was sliding by faster than in a Cub, but speed is a good feeling and I thoroughly enjoyed the sensation. When I found the ground, the wheel was full back and a good three-point landing was the result. With any good landing comes an abundance of pride, especially in a strange aircraft.

I made two more landings. The first was a little better than the others (beginners' luck), but they were all fair-to-good landings. After the third landing, Sam turned me out on my own. I then made five solo landings. It was still a somewhat strange airplane, and I felt a little uncomfortable in it, especially during the landings. To me, it ran differently, climbed differently, floated differently, stalled differently and sadly, even bounced differently. On my second solo landing, I missed the set-up and it bounced around a little. I'm sure the reason was I was flying the Cessna while expecting it to behave like a Cub. The bouncing woke me up! With a renewed determination, I made a couple more landings. Although not perfect, they still left me feeling good.

Sam signed my Log Book and I was officially checked out in the Cessna 120. I've got to admit that, for a while, it wasn't the familiar old shoe feeling of a Cub. However, after some additional time, my favorite airplanes were the Piper J-3, the Piper PA-12 and the Cessna 120 (along with a whole bunch of other aircraft that I hadn't flown).

Devil Winds

Just a few miles southwest of Utah Central was an abandoned airport that we referred to as Airport No. 2 (now South Valley Regional Airport). During the war, it was part of Camp Kearns, and at the time it was used as a primary training base for Army pilots. Frank Kelsey, one of the partners of Kemp and Kelsey Flying Service had once told me there were more Stearmans based there than one could count in a day.

After the war, the government tore every thing down--hangars, shops, offices--and just walked away. For many years, it sat there pretty much as a weed farm. Left behind however, were some exceptional runways. Area students and pilots often practiced take-off and landings on the old strips. And with the activities there were a few accidents. I've heard some say that at times there were some tricky south winds coming off the dry farms. I really don't know if those "tricky winds" did in fact exist, as I never encountered any. But there were accidents, so who knows?

I've often wondered, with all those nice wide and long runways, why someone didn't go out there and set up some kind of flight operation. I don't know if the government had wrapped the property up in red tape or if the location was just too remote.

As far as "tricky winds," if green army pilots could fly Stearmans, with long legs, tail wheels and big double wings, then surely green civilian pilots could fly tame little Pipers and Cessnas off the same field. Yet, while I was working at Utah Central, Airport No. 2 just sat there--not totally closed, but not really open either. Tumbleweeds were king.

One day, one of our students had taken the yellow Cub over to practice take-offs and landings. After several successful efforts, he decided it was time to call it quits and head back. Since he was nearer the far end of the strip, he decided it would be to his advantage to give himself a little more runway for his take-off run. He checked for traffic and then started into his one hundred eighty degree turn. He recalled later that he had just completed his turn when, "I was on my back, no warning, no nothing, I hardly knew what had happened, I was just there."

He had either neglected to, or was a little late getting his stick forward. With his elevator in the up position, the tail wind had gotten under his tail and turned his Cub over.

When taxiing a tail-wheel aircraft, it's proper and natural to hold the stick back to keep the tail down while taxiing into the wind. However, when taxiing with the wind (that is, the wind coming from your backside) the stick needs to be held forward. That takes a little training. Putting it another way, holding the stick forward drops the elevators down while taxiing with a tail wind. It's the only way to keep the underside of the elevators from being exposed to the wind. It doesn't take much of a breeze under the Cub's light tail to lift it up and over. For many new students (even some not so new), holding the stick forward gives one the feeling of putting the controls in a position to force the airplane over on its nose, which while taxing with a tail wind is not really the case.

Luckily, our student was not injured and he was able to hike a fair distance northwest to Kearns, a small community that was then growing out of the old army camp. After a long hot walk, he saw a woman hanging clothing out in her yard. Approaching quietly, he said, "Hello."

The one word greeting nearly scared the daylights out of her. After calming down, she was able to tell the student that "nothing ever comes from the south, except dust, weeds and lizards."

After she apologized for being so startled with his sudden appearance, he asked for and received permission to use her telephone. She then overheard the end of the conversation in which the student pilot confessed that he had "crashed his airplane" and needed help.

That caused her more discomfort. "You crashed your airplane?" she mumbled in disbelief. It was almost as if she had never seen or even heard of airplanes before. The student pilot began to wonder if she thought he was some kind of alien from outer space. "I really don't think she considered people who flew airplanes humans. She looked extremely up-tight until the moment I left."

Upon my arrival to work that afternoon, I checked in at the office. Then without talking to anyone I continued over to the main hangar. As I passed through the shop door, I could make out the image of a disassembled airplane off in the southeast corner of the hangar. Low in profile and covered with heavy shadows, it appeared almost to be in hiding. In the shadows, I didn't recognize it as our yellow Cub until I was just a few yards away.

Not really knowing what was going on, I cautiously approached the disassembled Piper. It was obvious that it had been in some kind of an accident. There was torn fabric, damage to the top of the rudder, the struts and the upper wing tips. One tip of the propeller had been sheared off and the other bent back. The wings were lying on the floor with the struts off to one side. The fuselage, lacking its gear, was lying flat on its belly. Off in the corner, the Cub's landing gears were leaning against the wall with the tires up. While the Cub had lain on its back at the accident site, oil and fuel had drained out of the sump and tank, leaving heavy residue and stains on and around the cowling and windshield. Like a magnet, dirt, dust and weeds were attracted to the oil residue. Between the oil and dirt, it was really a mess. Residue oil was still oozing out from around the cowling and forming puddles on the concrete floor. It was the saddest thing I had ever seen in my life.

I guess it's not good, or even natural for humans to get sentimental about non-personal objects made out of wood, fabric and steel. But looking at the broken Cub smeared with dirt and oil in that dark corner brought a lump to my throat.

At first, I had fears that maybe the damage was so extensive that the Cub would be written off, junked. But, after walking around and studying the scattered parts for a few moments I felt better. The damage was not all that extensive, but I could see that it would have an extended stay in the shop.

Then for some reason, my eyes fixed on the tail number, 88234. It boldly stood out, almost like the aircraft's personal name. How many logbooks does that number appear in? Would anyone even dare guess? I doubt it. It was a number, along with all of its students, pilots and instructor that would be forever a part of aviation history.

I pulled out my pocketknife and carefully cut around the numbers 234, a souvenir.

The yellow Piper was already overdue for a recover, and the accident had just upped the schedule a bit. During the next few weeks, we tore the fabric off the wings, fuselage and tail surfaces. Some parts needed replacing while we were able to repair other parts. The metal tubing and fittings were all sandblasted and coated with Zinc Chromate Primer, and painted. We cleaned and varnished all the wooden parts. The entire Cub was recovered with yards of fresh new fabric and doped. Originally, the yellow Cub had an enamel finish that sported a very nice shine. But the new fabric would be finished with butyrate dope, not quite as glossy but much easier to work with. The little Continental engine that gave power to my solo flight was put on the bench, torn down and rebuilt. A new metal propeller with a beautiful luster finish was lifted up and bolted to the crankshaft flange.

The little Cub rolled out of the hangar and into the daylight as pretty much a new airplane. Most noticeable were its new colors. The yellow "Cub" color was history and in its place was an overall toned-down, red-colored aircraft with bold cream-colored serial numbers along the sides of the fuselage. It was sure good to see old 234 out on the flight line again. I might add that it was one very good-looking airplane.

Yellow Piper Cubs, like the black Model A's started out with their respective colors of yellow for the Cubs and black for the Model As. In mid life, many

J–3's were painted in a variety of colors just to be a little different. However, as the Piper Cubs became classified as antiques, most would then come out of the shops in their traditional Cub Yellow colors. Somehow, I feel that's the way it should be. A shining black Model A or a bright yellow Piper Cub, you just can't beat the basics.

After the accident, Glen put some restrictions on the use of the abandoned airport. I don't think he was so much concerned with the so-called "tricky winds" as he was with the fact that if someone was involved in a serious accident, it might be difficult to get immediate medical help if needed.

Two Guys With Wings

Mel and I were both holders of crisp, newly issued Pilot's Licenses, (or at least slightly worn temporaries). It wasn't long before we were talking about pooling our resources and making some long adventurous flight beyond distant horizons.

We soon found out that it was a little more involved than just "Hey, lets go!" He had his schedule to work around, I had my schedule to work around and the airplane of choice, the Piper PA–12 was scheduled out more than just occasionally. Several times, everything seemed clear, and then at the last moment something got in the way. We kept checking with Glen, the shop, and the Cruiser's schedule, looking for a window that would let it happen.

Then late one afternoon in the middle of November, Glen informed us that if we still wanted to go the next day was available. When we got the word, we both looked at each other and almost in overlapping words stated, "Yah!"

There was a map of the western half of the United States pasted on a portion of the south wall of the office. The overall map covered most of the wall from floor to ceiling and was made up of Aeronautical WAC Charts.

We hadn't talked about where we wanted to go and to some degree; I don't think either of us cared that much. We just wanted to go on a nice, semi-long cross-country flight.

We ran our fingers over the smooth surface of the chart, crossing over the contour lines, the blues of the waters, the greens of the low lands and the browns of the mountains. Images, wandering lines, printed words, flat colors, together they represented an almost nondescript images that were in reality majestic mountains, sparkling lakes, endless deserts and rolling hills that wandered to the horizons and beyond.

We studied the map trying to visualize what an area along a purposed route would be like. We debated destinations, comparing distance and time against schedules and money.

"Better not go there, that's too far, don't have that much time nor money."

"Uh Uh, that's not far enough, we can do better than that."

After studying several options, trying to get the parameters to fit an adventure into the squares of the schedule sheet, we finally settled in on Rawlins, Wyoming. Not exactly a New York to Paris flight, but it looked fun and it was about as far as we dare go.

We didn't have the charts in our office covering the route; so late that evening we hopped into Mel's old '53 Ford truck and headed over to Thompson Flying Service located at the Salt Lake Municipal Airport. Once we had the charts, we made a second stop over at the Weather Bureau and verified that there would be no problems with Mother Nature.

That evening, we had already loaded up the hangar before we got word that we had the next day clear for our flight. As fate would have it, the PA–12 had been left outside. During the past week, morning frost had been the norm so wanting the morning of our trip to be a flying and not an aircraft defrosting experience, we decided it would be best to move the PA–12 inside. It wasn't an easy decision as several aircraft had to be moved to get ours in the hangar and accessible. It was a little work and we never really appreciated our decision until the next morning. Being right always has an upside.

Next morning, we rolled open the big hangar doors. Then taking position on the main struts of the Piper, we pushed it out into the cool morning air. Once clear of the hangar we made a big wide turn and continued pushing it over towards the gas pit. The bright red Cruiser was a stark contrast to all of the frosted and almost ghostly-appearing aircraft scattered around the field.

Once at the gas pit, we each wandered around the Cruiser doing the preflight, checking fuel, oil, engine compartment, hinge pins, struts, tires, fabric and safety wiring. We then moved the fueling stand over and we cleaned the windshield. The tanks had been topped off the night before; but we figured with the cooler temperatures the fuel in the tanks would contract some. We figured right. It didn't take a lot of fuel but somehow there was some satisfaction in knowing it was in there. I guess we were both thinking of Mel's previous trip to Richfield and his wing tank that wasn't feeding.

There had been reports that there was a shimmy in the tail wheel. We had checked it out the night before and found that there was a little play. It didn't look too serious though, so we decided to let it be. We did however, tighten it up the best we could and then greased the daylights out of it. We were both aware of the potential problem and we each made a mental note to take precautions on take-offs and landings.

Both satisfied that everything was ready; we pushed the aircraft clear of the pit and swung it around to a clear path to taxi out. It sure looked good sitting there in the early morning light.

The night before we had flipped coins to decide who would fly the first leg. The call had put me up front on the trip over.

We then wandered over to our respective vehicles and gathered up the few items that we were taking on the flight.

I opened the PA–12's door and climbed into the front seat. With only a light jacket on, it felt good to get out of the cool damp air. I placed my maps on the dash and slid open the left window. While I was settling in, Mel climbed in and took his position. It was quiet except for the occasional shuffling sound of maps, cold seat cushions and belt buckles clicking. After a moment or two, I turned around and we nodded to each other.

I cleared the panel, leaned my head near the open window and yelled, "Clear." With the expected no response, I put my thumb on the starter button. A short metallic whine, and the engine came to life. I made a slight adjustment to the throttle, cutting the rpm's back to a more comfortable idle. Then I turned my attention to the engine's oil pressure. A little cold and reluctant, it nevertheless began its movement up into the green.

Then something happened that I had never seen before. A continuous trail of vapor, much like one's breath on a cold day, suddenly began trailing off the tips of the propeller blades. It unwound like a giant coiled spring and slowly drifted back around the fuselage. I called Mel's attention to it and we both watched, fascinated by the spectacle. I applied a little throttle and the vapor trail disappeared. The Piper moved forward, and we were on our way.

I don't know how Mel felt, but sitting in the center of the runway with the engine running quietly at idle was a moment like no other. I was very much aware of my surroundings, the sounds of the engine, the rhythm of the aircraft, the early morning light and the adventure beyond the mountains to the east. How many times have I had that dream only to have it aborted at daylight?

I looked out over the bright red cowling through the almost invisible propeller arc and slowly, very slowly I eased the throttle forward. It was a time I wanted to remember, an experience that I wanted to be part of my life forever. With me high in the front seat, the aircraft began inching forward. Its track was straight and positive as more and more runway rushed to the rear in progressively longer streaks. Slowly I began to feel life in the stick and rudder peddles, and then the tail lifted. I held that position for a few seconds and just raced along. I eased back on the stick. The adventure was beginning.

I lifted clear of Runway 16, climbed and then eased through the turns and clear of the pattern. I put the Piper in a long, shallow, climbing turn towards the northeast while crossing the valley. When we reached the Wasatch Mountain Range, we had good altitude and I dipped the right wing bringing us on a new heading to the east. Emigration Canyon was directly under the nose and slowly drifting our way. I was happy to see that the high broken clouds were blocking out the early morning sun.

The vast desert stretched out ahead as far as the eyes could see. It was a land of sand and clay all laid out in the flat dusty colors of brown and gray. The skimpy vegetation scattered around in bits and bunches seemed almost to blend in with the terrain.

The view below and ahead was endless and would be repeated many times over. I guess when you're high above just about any desert; a little sightseeing goes a long way. However, I was going to enjoy every moment of it.

I cut power, dropped a few numbers off my altimeter, leveled off at an altitude corresponding to our heading and trimmed the aircraft for cruise. Then settling back, I made myself comfortable. It was time to enjoy the passing of time and scenery.

So far from everywhere, yet here and there, spread out across the desert were traces of less-than-successful mining activities, crumbling shacks, mining holes, off colored piles of overburden and occasionally some rusting equipment. All left behind by men who must have concluded that somewhere else things had to be better.

Off to my left, about 10 o'clock, something moved, something sliding across the horizon. It was an airplane, a twin-engine military aircraft headed in our direction. Instinctively I lifted into a climbing right turn. The big aircraft nosed down a few degrees and continued on its course. It was an Air Force A–26C and apparently we had seen each other at the same time. As he passed underneath, I could see the pilot looking up at us. In a flash, the big silver bomber was gone. I guess if we hadn't seen each other, there was at least a fair chance that we might have collided. One wonders how, hours from nowhere, in all that empty space, two courses could converge at such a nondescript point.

About three quarters of the way to our destination, Mel got a call from Mother Nature. Uncomfortable, and not having many options, he began looking around. The rear seat of the Cruiser does not have many built in solutions for that kind of problem. However, being in need and resourceful, Mel began looking at the rear control stick. It was just pushed in its socket and friction was the only thing keeping it in place. He unceremoniously yanked the stick out of its socket. Then using it as an extension to reach out through the partially open door, the problem was solved. We laughed hysterically as only teenagers could laugh.

Flying from altitude, the landscape moved unbelievable slowly, even in our rather fast-moving Cruiser. The lack of apparent speed made me think of an acquaintance that flew a Piper J–3 Cub back east to Ohio. Boy, that must have been an eye-opener.

Rawlins slowly appeared on the horizon. At first it was hardly noticeable, only a scattering of something on a barren landscape. Then a few off-colored images took shape that slowly developed into patterns of roads and buildings. As we approached the airport, trees and grasslands stood out boldly in green, much greener than I would have thought possible. The green was such a sharp contrast to the vast expanse of drab desert that we had just crossed. Maybe the cloudy sky was the tail-end of a series of area thunderstorms.

I dropped down, but still held high above the pattern. The area of the airport spread out below. Big and impressive with some nice black top runways. Yet in most ways it was comparable in size to Utah Central.

I've read or heard somewhere that Charles Lindbergh had once made a flight over Rawlins during some national tour back in 1927. I spent a moment wondering how things looked back then and how neat it would be to see the *Spirit of St. Louis* flying alongside our little red Piper.

I drifted across the airport while looking over the runways and searching for possible air traffic. Clear of traffic, I then checked the windsock and tee and picked out the appropriate runway for landing.

I eased back on the power. Engine sounds and wind noises drifted to the rear as the Piper settled down through its altitude.

Once in the pattern, I applied power and winged my way through the turns until I was on Final. The thought of the tail-wheel popped into my mind. I remember thinking that it might be best if I made one of my better landings. You know, like smooth. Yah? However, even with a fair landing, the tail wheel gave no indication of any problem.

I taxied up to the gas pump located out in front of a rather large hangar. Rawlins Municipal Airport was painted across its front. It was positive proof that I was at the right airport! Once positioned near the pump, I shut the engine down and all was still.

It would be an overstatement to say that anybody rushed out as part of a welcoming committee. We sat there for a time in silence and took in the newness of our surroundings. Then we subconsciously undid our belts. They fell to the side of our seats making abnormally loud noises as the metal buckles banged against metal tubing and the wood flooring. I opened the door and Mel slid out and I followed.

A middle-aged man appeared and engaged us in a rather shallow conversation, sounding almost like a prepared statement for transients. We exchanged information; the usual stuff on who we were and where we were going and then added in a few casual remarks concerning the weather.

Shortly he was dragging the hose and stand over to the Cruiser. With fuel gushing into a tank, we wandered over in the direction of the office. We each got a soda pop and a Twinkie. Then we slumped down into some old but comfortable lounge chairs. The change in seating sure did feel good. We relaxed, drank, ate and studied the office décor in silence.

Wanting to stretch our legs a bit, we went outside and wandered around the tie-down area looking over the parked aircraft. Most were typical of all airports. However, like most airports, there were a few older models mixed in with a few of the newer ones. Occasionally we would see a type that was new to us; or at least we hadn't had a chance to study it up-close. We would stop, walk around the aircraft studying its lines while making a few comments. It was interesting to study the unique construction of the older aircraft or the innovative design of the more modern ones. And I guess on more than one occasion, we would wonder why aircraft designers of the past couldn't see a more modern approach that was so obvious to us. It was unfair and we knew it, but it made us feel knowledgeable in our field. Invariably, whenever we looked at an aircraft that was unique, new or old, we would discuss its flight characteristics and our ability to fly such a craft.

"Hey, I could fly that"!

"Yah, me too"!

But when we came upon a Globe Swift; we were both captivated by its lines. The Swift is a little side-by-side, two place, low wing, retractable gear and conventional tail wheel aircraft. When it came to performance and beauty, it was in a class by itself. We studied the aircraft in silence and awe. We both acknowledged some modest reservations as to our ability to hop in and fly such a hot and probably squirrelly aircraft. Yet our final words were, "But man, would I like to try!"

When we returned the PA–12 was all fueled and waiting. We took care of the bill and made a trip to the rest room. Then together we made a quick pre-flight.

I climbed into the rear seat. It had been a long time since I had been back there and it was a little strange to say the least. Between the fact that the front seat was higher and the plane was sitting on the ground, tail low, I actually felt like I was looking up at everything. Happily, in flight, the tail was brought up to level, putting me a little more equal with the world.

Mel climbed to altitude and we both settled in for the flight home.

I watched Mel and admired his attention to the details of the flight. He was looking at his charts constantly. Not just to verify his location, but also to pinpoint his exact path over the ground. I don't think he was ever more than five feet off the centerline of his plotted course. He was a good pilot, and I had no doubt that someday he would see the insides of some impressive aircraft.

On the way back, an old twin engine Cessna Bobcat passed below. It was at a lower altitude and parallel to our course. Mel being in a little bit of a playful mood opened up the throttle and even put the Cruiser in a shallow dive trying to keep up, but it was just a little too fast. We would see it later at Utah Central where it would be taking on fuel.

The tops of the Wasatch Mountains were hidden in tall vertical clouds that towered well above any altitude that we could reach. Occasionally an opening appeared, but they were always small and unpredictable. Mel searched to the south, then to the north and then back to the south again for a suitable opening. Several times, he approached what appeared to be a good-sized opening only to see it cave in. So back and forth he continued to wander, hoping, looking and waiting. We had plenty of fuel and daylight so there was no real problem.

Then suddenly, without fanfare, the clouds moved aside, creating a mammoth hole leading into the Salt Lake Valley. Mel made a steep bank to the west and we crossed through with ample daylight on all sides. For some reason, the thought of Moses and the parting of the Red Sea crossed my mind.

My logbook entry for my half of the trip was two hours and fifty-five minutes.

An Act Unplanned

About 11 o'clock and low, a little gray cloud was moving my way. Not a big cloud, maybe a hundred feet across and thin, thin enough to see through. It was the only cloud in the entire sky.

With no adjustment in course or speed, I waited for just the right second and then rolled the PA–12 into a diving turn. The cloud drifted to the center of my windshield. I leveled my wings and continued downward. My airspeed began moving into higher numbers as the spreading mist grew in size. The controls tightened and the sound of the wind grew in intensity. Then with the airspeed needle in some very respectable numbers, I flew into the mist. Almost like a silent explosion, it was everywhere, enveloping everything, patterns of shadows and light, flickering and flashing. Then it was gone, leaving only bright sunlight.

Still diving, I could feel the air getting rock hard against the wings and the airspeed was approaching the Cruisers' red line. Not wanting to get on the wrong side of the maximum speed of the aircraft, I began a slow pull-up. My body pressed into the seat as the nose slowly lifted up toward the horizon.

With the extra airspeed, it would be a waste not to turn it into some good altitude. I passed level flight attitude and continued moving the nose up higher into the sky, putting the airplane into an ever steeper and steeper climb. I continued easing back on the stick, lifting the aircraft higher into the arc, forty-five, sixty, seventy-five degrees above the horizon. The earth slowly moved to the rear of the aircraft. The nose of the Piper Cruiser continued to lift until it was pointed straight up, ninety degrees relative to the ground. I pushed the stick forward, moving the airplane out of the sweeping arc and into vertical flight. The earth was directly behind me. I still had good airspeed, but it was dropping off at an unbelievable rate. I held the vertical attitude.

For a second, I was thinking of alternatives, "Should I loop, roll off to the side, drop the nose down to level or just continue in a vertical climb?" However, words of daring and adventure were all that I could hear, "Why not." Go for it! My grip on the stick firmed up. I couldn't help wondering what was up at the top. The Cruiser continued its flight upward.

It was a little weird to look back over my shoulder and see the earth lying flat beyond the tail of the aircraft, then looking down at my gear and seeing the horizon at such an odd place.

The airspeed continued bleeding off, faster and faster. Up to that point, the energy for the climb came solely from the momentum of the dive. That momentum was fast disappearing. I eased the throttle forward. The rpm needle swung into higher numbers, the engine noise increased. The propeller grabbed and sliced at the mushy air and threw it to the rear. The feel and sound of all the raw power was encouraging, but the airspeed continued to drop. It was a simple fact of flight; no Piper Cruiser could do what I was asking it to do! The propeller just couldn't grab enough air to sustain the Piper's climb, and I knew it. There was nothing left to reverse the trend. The inevitable was just a short distance ahead, whatever it might be.

I held firm, the controls remained in place, but they were fast losing their feel, getting soft, mushy. Then thinking about what was coming, I eased the stick forward a degree or two. If I stalled out, and I knew I would, I wanted the nose to drop forward, not backward which would put the Piper on its back.

The rate of climb needle was nearing neutral. The airspeed was moving towards the failure of flight, stalling speed. "Stalling speed." To some, stalling speed is a rather bad choice of words. At that given air speed, the aircraft falls more than it stalls. What is the "stalling speed" of a PA–12 in vertical flight anyway?

The Piper still had the heart and determination; you could hear it in its screaming sounds. It was not about to admit defeat, almost as if losing was not an option. But, the laws of physics are all written in stone. No man, no aircraft violates the laws of physics!

Then everything felt different, everything felt wrong! The senses in my body were going wild, flashing red, flashing danger; something beyond my wildest dreams was about to happen. The PA–12 was in forbidden airspace! The air sounded different. The controls felt soggy, wimpy and dead, as if they weren't connected. The flight instruments were all in areas they shouldn't be. The physical rules of sustained flight were all behind me; they were back there, simply left behind. The aircraft was still pointed straight up. The engine was still screaming, but it was only noise.

Then my body lifted slightly, rather softly from the seat. I was in a state of weightlessness, floating. For a fraction of a second, the Cruiser was parked in its vertical position. It was almost as if it was pausing, waiting for a new set of flight rules to kick in and take effect.

Then the uncomfortable feeling of my safety belt pressing firmly against my mid section, the Piper Cruiser was sliding back, sliding straight down towards earth, tail first. I pulled back slightly on the stick lifting the elevator up into the on-coming tail wind. Then, with what felt like the speed of light, the nose dropped one hundred and eighty degrees down, from vertical straight up, to vertical straight down in less than a mili-second.

Loud and strong, the sound of the wind and engine once again dominated all my senses. All flight instruments jumped up into the green, we were alive again. I cut the power. The airspeed continued to build at a breathtaking rate. Pulling back on the stick, I could feel the forces of gravity weighing in on my body. The plane arched across the bottom of a curve and like a shooting star it shot up into higher altitudes. I held a medium climb as the air speed bled off. Then nearing cruising speed, I leveled off and applied cruising power.

The unmistakable aroma of raw fuel filled the cabin. Instinctively, I glanced out at the fuel indicators on the wings. They indicated normal for my time in flight, but apparently, I had lost some fuel during the stall.

On the way back to the field, I had a moment to reflect on what I had done. I felt good, like you wouldn't believe. Yet, way down deep I knew that maybe I had pushed it just a little. Would Glen condone what I had done? I think not! What about my friends? I've got all kinds of friends who have done stupid things, almost at the risk of life and limb. Without a doubt, each of them would praise my actions. To the person, I could hear them saying, "That's what life is all about, take a little risk now and then, enjoy life, grab it by the horns, you're only young once!" Maybe the echo of their voices was a little self-justification, I don't know?

Over the years, my thoughts occasionally return to that day, the excitement, the thrill and even some of the things that may have gone wrong. I sometimes ask myself the question, if given the opportunity, would I do something like that again, in the same airplane, at my age? I don't know, but I think I might!

Tracks Well Laid

You could feel something was in the air. Out in the southwest part of the valley, clouds were building in size and intensity. At first, there was some hope that the ominous clouds would stay "over there." However, that was not to be. The huge black mass developed and grew, spreading darkness across every corner of the valley.

Driven by a breeze, little white flakes began to drift diagonally across the landscape. Then with the passing of the front, the snowstorm took on Christmas card proportions. Snowflakes grew in size and number. It was one of Mother Nature's finest with huge white flakes, big and heavy, drifting, circling in artistic silence. Visibility dropped down to a hundred feet, then less. Aircraft and buildings became shadows or simply disappeared behind a gray curtain. Brush and grassland were the first to pick up the white coating; soon even the warmer flatlands were being covered.

Somewhat surprised by the sudden severity of the storm, we found ourselves running around in shirtsleeves, pushing aircraft here and there. One by one, we moved what aircraft we could inside the main hangar. Even as we were moving them in, the accumulated snow was melting, dripping from the aircrafts' upper surfaces, forming puddles on the concrete floor.

The snow continued to fall, covering the land with a white stillness. When it had finally run its course we had a blanket of white on the ground--four, maybe five inches deep.

It was early evening when the heavy dark clouds parted, leaving only scattered formations congregating along the mountain tops. It was a perfect set-up for a beautiful winter sunset.

Earlier, the radio announcers had been forecasting a late afternoon clearing. A couple of pilots, using the predicted clearing as a pretense, had been sitting around the office drinking coffee and fine-tuning their flying stories. When the dark clouds began breaking up, their conversation turned to the possibility of flying.

The pilots wandered outside dragging their feet through the soft snow. One, looking out to the southwest and noted the clearing skies, said to the other, "Looks like we got ourselves some flying weather. Want to take em around a couple of times, be fun in the snow."

"Well, I really should go home and shovel the walks," remarked the second. "Yah, me too," followed the first.

Then silence as they studied the sky trimmed with billowing clouds. Looking at each other, they smiled and stated almost as one, "Let's go flying."

It was late and they didn't have a lot of time so they just shot some take-offs and landings, but I suspect they thoroughly enjoyed the evening. More than once, I glanced over at the circling aircraft pictured against the evening sunset and paused almost in disbelief--the cloud formations, the colors, the sunrays and the sensations. It was a picture that any calendar would be proud to display.

Glen couldn't get the snowplows out that evening but had them scheduled for the next day, around mid-morning.

While we were closing up the office we got a call from Roy. He needed our Cessna 120 in Logan bright and early the next morning. It sounded like a good trip so I volunteered to take it up. However, there was a problem with the return trip. The only aircraft he could spare for my return flight was a Cessna 172 and, sadly, I had not yet been checked out in it. Not surprisingly, he came up with a workable solution. I would fly the 120 up solo, and then fly the 172 back with an instructor, logging it in as duel cross-country. It must have been a good idea as I was about to suggest it myself. I had been looking forward to a little 172 time. Dick, standing nearby, "volunteered" to go with me as "baggage" on the flight up and return with me as my instructor. That sounded great to me, as he was always fun to be around.

Early the next morning, I did my clearing turn and moved out to the center of Runway 34 and positioned the Cessna for take-off. However, the runway that stretched out before me was different from anything I had ever seen before. Tire tracks, frozen tire tracks from the previous evening's flying were everywhere.

Any other time, I would be happily rolling down the strip. But that morning, I just sat there, looking at the frozen scars and wondering how they would affect the Cessna's take-off run. Dick was silent, but I knew he was thinking along the same line. I think we both knew it was going to be a handful. We sat there in silence, looking, thinking and evaluating.

Knowing the challenge might be more than my ability; I stated in a somewhat subdued voice, "Would you like to take the controls for the first little bit?" Without any acknowledgement, he continued staring straight ahead, but slowly he reached out and put his right hand on the wheel and then his left hand on the throttle. With his hands in position, I removed mine from the wheel and slid my feet back.

Dick eased the throttle forward and we started moving, very slowly at first. He moved over to the left side of the runway where the strip was relatively free of tracks, for a ways anyways. Seconds into the run, we hit a frozen track that almost stopped us cold. Dick pushed the throttle to the full open position, and the little engine roared out in determination. The Cessna busted through the ice and continued. A second passed, then another frozen track. The Cessna ungracefully bounced over it with wings rocking wildly. Faster and faster, the little Cessna raced on, in, out and across the unpredictable ruts. Each frozen ridge of ice had its own little vicious personality; some we bounced over or through, others grabbed our spinning wheels, sliding and pulling us off to the side.

Yet others seemed almost as barriers that shook the little Cessna to its core. Probably the most awkward of ruts were the ones that ran almost parallel to our path. They at times seemed almost in full control and were the hardest to break free of. Our eyes studied each approaching rut, while subconsciously bracing against its unknown impact. Dick eased forward on the wheel, and the tail lifted.

Then there appeared a clear stretch of beautiful white snow, free of ugly scars. It was a time of running smooth and the gaining of precious speed. Then another sharp jolt as a tire slammed into another frozen ridge. Dick's feet were moving faster and faster. The jarring became sharper. Ridges of ice sent shock waves up through the spring landing gear causing a chatter that penetrated the very soul of the airframe. Pieces of fractured ice flew off like shrapnel, some banging into the skin of the aircraft making bone-chilling noises. Our bodies continued to be thrown one way, then another, bouncing off each other, then off the sides of the cabin.

Then the little Cessna hit a solid ridge of ice and bounced. The aircraft staggered into the air a few inches. Not yet ready for flight, it hesitated and then began to settle, tail hanging low, main gear reaching out bracing against more punishment. Then, dragging its gear across the top of the snow and ice ridges, it somehow held.

More and more you could hear the sounds of flight as the wings moved faster through the cold morning air. Dick eased back on the wheel. Triumphantly, the Cessna lifted higher, up into its rightful place in the sky. The air was frigid and smooth. The smoothness of flight was an unbelievable contrast to the beating we had just experienced.

"Here, take the wheel! I've had enough!" Dick stated in a somewhat forceful tone. I broke out of our pattern and held a northwest heading to clear Salt Lake Municipal Airport's Control Zone.

With all the aircraft in the area not equipped with radios, pilots had, over time, set up imaginary physical boundary lines to keep them clear of the Salt Lake's Control Zone. To the west of the Salt Lake Airport, it was near the shore of the Great Salt Lake. To the east, the line was Redwood Road. To the south, be it a bit hazy, the boundary was defined somewhere between 1700 South and 2100 South. Our pattern was right up against or even extended into the Salt Lake Airport's Control Zone. However, as long as we at Utah Central flew a predictable pattern on the north side of our airport, the Salt Lake's Tower knew what we were doing. With that, there never was a problem.

We flew on a short distance before making a lazy turn to the east. Our path took us through an acknowledged corridor that was uncontrolled by both Hill Field to the north and the Salt Lake Municipal Airport to the south. Near Farmington, we made another ninety degree turn to the north, placing our flight path near the western edge of the Wasatch Mountains. That course kept us to the east and clear of Hill Field. We continued north, watching the majestic mountains dwindle down to foothills. Soon we were over the farmlands of northern Utah.

Just below my window, I couldn't help but notice the left landing gear and its tire as it drifted across the face of the white landscape. A few days before the snowstorm, there had been a thawing period with lots of mud. All of our aircraft tires had been carrying around varying degrees of mud from the field. After that morning's take-off through the frozen snow, the Cessna's tire was polished to a new squeaky-clean black, looking more as if it had come out of a hospital's supply room. Obvious also, was a fair amount of heavy snow packed in solid around the area where the strut connects to the axel and tire.

The runways at the Logan Cache County Airport were quite different from those of Utah Central. They were wide, long and blacktopped. And even at that early hour, they had been plowed. There were alternating patches of clear black, even dry asphalt and other areas of packed snow scraped smooth by the plows. After what we had been through, Logan's plowed runways sure looked good.

I flew high above the pattern and checked out any possible traffic. With little or no wind, I opted to land on Runway 28. I made a wide turn and dropped down into the pattern. On Final, I couldn't help feeling a little lost with the bigness of everything in front of me. Jokingly I thought that maybe I should continue flying for a while to cut down on the taxi time.

We sailed over the road, a fence, across an area of flat land covered with snow and then crossed over the end of the strip. I slowly lifted the nose as our airspeed and altitude bled off.

We touched down in a near perfect three-point attitude on a large patch of scraped snow that made the landing super smooth. There was no jarring, no squeak, nothing but smoothness. We half-rolled and half-slid a short distance across the glazed white surface. Then the little Cessna hit a patch of black asphalt. Uncharacteristically, the Cessna jerked to the left. Then we crossed onto another patch of scraped snow. With a little rudder correction, the course was again true, straight and smooth. Then, more bare asphalt and another sharp jerk to the left. Again the Cessna found another patch of smooth, scraped snow and again straight and smooth. I found myself staring at the next patch of cleared black top with some anxiety. Sure enough, the Cessna jerked sharply to the left when it hit the black and then relaxed as soon as it crossed over onto more scraped snow. Then more patches of black and more pulling to the left.

Each patch of black top was pulling the Cessna more towards the left side of the runway. I had my hands full just trying to keep it headed in the general direction of the runway; getting it back to the center of the strip was out of the question.

More clear black top, more jerking, then a patch of smooth snow and some correction. The Cessna was slowing down, but more and more we were traveling down the far left side of a very wide runway. Then another patch of black top, more jerking and we were right on the shoulder. Then there was another patch of scraped snow then another patch of black top. Again we jerked to the left, slid off the edge of the concrete and plowed into the dirt and snow. The Cessna spun wildly, throwing dirt and snow as it tipped heavily to the right. The rocking was violent, almost as if the Cessna was jumping. It finally landed flat and hard, the propeller flipped to an abrupt stop and then no movement, only stillness.

We both sat there in silence for a few seconds, in almost total disbelief. Then I could feel some movement from Dick. Without conscious thought, I cut the switches.

Dick looked over at me and stated in a very serious tone, "Did you happen to notice if your wheel was turning?" In my state of anxiety, thinking he was serious, I answered, "No, I didn't." Dick laughed. I laughed. We unbuckled and climbed out.

No one likes to ground-loop an airplane as it quite often causes damage to the aircraft. On any aircraft that had ground-looped, Roy, our boss was always concerned with the possibility of damage to a wing tip or a wheel hub. They were the areas that most often were damaged and most expensive to fix. I guess with that in mind, Dick and I wandered over to the right wing tip and inspected it for damage. There was none, no signs of ground contact whatsoever. We then inspected the right wheel hub and found no damage there either. I was still on the good side of the boss.

Checking the left wheel, we found it was indeed locked up. Dick explained that some snow had probably found its way into the brake assembly. With the heat generated by the brakes during take-off, the snow had probably melted. Then the cold air encountered during the flight had frozen everything solid. Why the ice didn't break loose when we hit the runway's dry patches was something neither of us could understand.

We pushed the aircraft this way, then that way, the locked wheel just slid across the dirt and snow. I knelt down and tried turning the wheel by hand, but all I accomplished was getting myself cold and wet. While down on my knees, I pulled out my pocketknife and cleared away what packed in snow I could from around the axel and hub. Then we both took turns kicking the tire, but the added effort seemed to be just wasted.

Not wanting a long walk to the hangar, and not having other options, we just kept banging away with blows from the heels and toes of our shoes. After a while, I was wondering if there wasn't some kind of mechanical blockage.

Tired and a little discouraged, we paused for a moment. I suggested that it might yet be faster just to bag the whole thing and walk back. Dick, with a renewed determination said, "Let me try one more time." He steadied himself with one hand on the wing strut. Then he took a second to ready his body, making sure everything was set for the best possible effort. With what must have been every ounce of strength he had in his system, his foot shot out and hit the tire with a good hard whack. The little Cessna seemed to shudder under the force of the impact. Then he repositioned himself and whacked it a couple more times, again very hard. The impacts were solid but still nothing to indicate the blockage had given way. He paused, too tired to kick any more.

Hoping for a miracle, we positioned ourselves on the aircraft and gave it a little shove. The wheel turned freely, without effort, like there had never been a problem. Dick broke out in a smile and me, I couldn't resist a smart remark. "Dick you really missed your calling in life, you should have been a mule," I stated with a grin.

We took positions, one on each side of the elevator and with a little foot-sliding and grunting we were able to drag the little craft through the snow and onto the hard surface of the runway. Then kicking and stomping, we cleared what dirt and snow we could from our feet and clothing. Satisfied, we climbed into our seats and buckled up.

The engine had stopped rather abruptly while the Cessna was bouncing around. With all the bouncing maybe something might not be right. We might yet be in for a long walk. I flipped the mag switch, positioned the throttle and paused. Then with a hopeful tone in my voice I yelled, "Clear" and pulled the starter. The little engine caught and was running factory smooth, good ol Continental. I made a clearing turn for traffic and we headed for the hangar.

That evening back at the office, I was standing at the display case, filling out my logbook. Dick took note of what I was doing and wandered over to my side. He paused and watched while I filled in the information relating to our Logan flight. Then without a word, he reached around and added a question mark at the end of the entry.

A Perfect Time, A Perfect Place

It was a picture-perfect day, blue skies, a light breeze and just enough clouds to give it that postcard look. If you could have ordered perfect weather, it couldn't have been better than that day.

Occasionally, early in the week, things were a little slow around the airport. With not a lot of activity I got permission from Glen to go up for an hour or so.

I was removing the ropes from the PA–12 Super Cruiser when Dick wandered out of the office and headed in my direction. He's not a great one to kill time gracefully and to say he was a little bored would be an understatement. I suddenly found him following me around as if he was my shadow, and he was in one of his corny moods. He commented on about everything that I looked at or touched, as only he could comment.

"Is this the aircraft that everyone's been complaining about, dirt in the fuel tanks or something like that?"

"I've got a funny feeling about the main spar attachment bolts. You know for some reason or other they just won't stay torqued. They've had so many problems with 'em that the FAA has issued an AD (Airworthiness Directive) requiring the bolts to be re-torqued before each and every flight!"

"Wow, the fourth rib in your left wing feels a little funny. It feels serious enough that I think you ought to check it out. The only way you can really verify its condition is to cut away some of the fabric. Wanna borrow my knife?"

"Oh my gosh, will you look at this; metal filing on the wing fabric. That's not dirt and dust; look closely, it's metal filings. There have been reports of some funny grinding sounds coming from inside the wing. There must be some loose parts in there grinding back and forth. That's where all the metal filings are coming from. As soon as you get back, the very first thing, I'm going to have Chad condemn this aircraft."

"Hey look, this aileron goes up and the other goes down. That can't be right!

It'll make the aircraft spin."

"Oh Boy! Will you look at this? This aircraft has an illegal left-handed propeller mounted on a non-standard right-handed crankshaft."

"Oh no! This propeller has a cruise pitch! Doesn't that just beat all! You can't possibly climb with a prop like that; you'll never get off the ground!"

"Good grief, I think the engine has a cracked block. Here, right there, look real closely and you can see the crack. There, the paint is covering it up so it isn't quite so obvious, but it's there."

Each time he made a comment, it got to me a little more than the last. As much as I was trying to act serious and even pretend that he wasn't there, I was fast coming apart at the seams.

His humor was adding to an already perfect day. The very best of everything was at my feet. I was young, healthy and working with a great bunch of guys doing what I loved. I had not yet entered the world of heavy adult responsibilities; and yet I had access to some of the best adult toys known to man.

While walking around the Piper Cruiser, I could feel its prominence. It sat there displaying grandeur with its huge wings; speed with its sleek lines, and power with its massive size. It might not have been on the cutting edge of all modern technology. But to me, it was big, fast and beautiful, and I had more than a little pride in my ability to fly such a craft.

In spite of all Dick's teasing distractions, I finished the preflight. Walking by the front end of the aircraft, I patted the cowl with the flat of my hand as a final jester indicating something akin to, "Its ready! I'm ready! I'm outta here!" Dick took note of me slapping the cowl and made a final and seemingly very serious remark.

"Careful, the last guy that did that got charged for an overhaul."

The windsock indicated Runway 34, and I had just taxied out of the tie-down spot when I happened to look over at Dick. He was standing at attention, eyes straight ahead, right hand placed firmly over his heart and he had a very sad look on his face, maybe even tears, couldn't tell for sure. I had to laugh!

Emerging from between two parked aircraft, I happened to glance over toward the office. There were two young kids standing near the gate. They stood there in silence, watching, even staring as I taxied by. Hair uncombed, shirts half in, half out, and clothing looking like they had been on the road most of the day. At their side, their bikes lay discarded on the grass. I wish I could count the times that we as kids had stood on the ramp at the Salt Lake Municipal Airport watching the pilots in their big beautiful aircraft taxiing in and out. Our imaginations went wild thinking of all the great adventures those aircraft had had or were about to have. Seeing those kids was like looking into the past.

One of them waved, the second hesitated and then he waved. I smiled and waved back.

I was climbing out and nearing 2100 South, when I looked over towards the office. The kids had wandered over near the Wind Tee to watch me take off. I waved and wiggled my wings, they responded instantly. It made me feel like a million bucks.

I cleared the pattern, put the nose into a shallow climb and wandered onto a course to the northwest in the general direction of the Great Salt Lake.

Without intent or reason, I lifted a wing, pushed the nose down a few degrees and turned east towards Antelope Island. The horizon lifted higher up the windshield and the mountains grew in size and detail. I rolled into a mild turn to the left and then, without pausing, gently rolled over to the right and lifted the Cruiser's nose higher into the sky.

From the ground, one may see an airplane as something gracefully diving, turning and soaring through the heavens. A pilot's world is one of scenery drifting across his windows. Yet for him there is more, so much more. There are the sounds and forces of unseen air; the sensation of throttle movements and the power they command; the howling roar of the engine moving in and out of its power cycles; interior shadows sliding around the cabin; the movements and shifting of one's own body, lifting, leaning and pressing, as the world moves around the aircraft. There is also the paramount feeling of being master, in control of an earthly object, moving freely through the heavens.

I continued to play, diving this way, rolling over that way and then climbing higher into the heavens. Nothing dramatic, I guess it felt something akin to a young colt kicking and running across fields of green. It just felt good!

BAM! My stomach flew through the roof!

A sharp, very loud pop, almost an explosion sounded throughout the aircraft followed by the sound of a high-pitched screaming wind. Something was out of place. Instinctively, I pushed the nose down to level attitude and cut back on power to slow the air speed as much as I dared. The whistling sound subsided some.

Except for the whistling or wind noises that seemed to be coming from the lower front of the Cruiser, everything seemed normal. I leaned forward, almost standing, until my head was against the plexiglas windshield. Straining in a very awkward position, I gazed down at the left side of the cowling hoping to see something, anything that would explain what had happened. There was nothing that I could see to indicate any problem. I repositioned myself on the right side and gazed down the best I could. Something there was different.

I could see that the lower rear edge of the engine access panel was bulging out. The forward edge was too far under to see. The PA–12 had a cowl, or panel sections on the sides, hinged along the upper edge and fastened along the bottom. Some of the fasteners on the side paneling must have worked loose, allowing it to flip into its present position.

At first, I was a little concerned that the panel would work itself loose and cause some further damage. But the more I studied the twisted panel, the more confidence I had that it was wedged in tight. Hopefully, if the panel remained in place, there was no danger of anything else going wrong.

I made a slow wide turn back towards Utah Central. Then I cut back on the power a little, trying to set up a descent that would put me just about pattern altitude when I reached the airport. I had plenty of altitude, so even with a little power my trip back would be almost a long extended glide. Occasionally, I would open up the throttle, in a rather cautious way, to keep the engine clear.

There was no airport traffic so I made a normal downwind entrance into a somewhat wide landing pattern. Then turning out of the Down Wind Leg onto Final in one large turn I was lined up with the runway. From there, I eased down to the ground for a normal landing.

I toyed with the idea of shutting down the engine and checking out the problem as soon as I was on the ground but decided that it would only be wasted effort. I taxied over to the ramp and pulled off to the side, near the front of the main hangar. I cut the switches, undid my belt and climbed out.

The twisted cowling was still there and I felt good about that. One or more of the cowl or panel fasteners had worked loose. The wind had then pushed the forward end of the panel up into the engine compartment. With the front of the panel inside the compartment, the trailing edge had nowhere to go but out, and that's the part I was able to see.

I grabbed the lower front corner of the panel and tried to pull it free, but it was really wedged in solid. I worked on it from one angle and then came at it from a different direction, all without results. About that time, Chad, who had been working over in the hangar noticed me yanking and pulling. Being curious, he wandered over.

He studied the panel for a few moments, smiled and casually remarked, "Well I'll be, here let me try." He grabbed the rear end of the panel and tried to pull it clear. No success. He then grabbed it from a different position, and with a little more effort tried to yank the front edge clear of the engine compartment. Still nothing. He paused, studied it again for a few more seconds, smiled and quietly mumbled, "How did you do that?"

"Hey Chad, you know me, straight and level Furden, it just happened," I responded while wondering if the statement was even a little believable. We both laughed and then I explained what I had been doing and some of my concerns.

Moving in closer to the engine compartment he said, "I can't believe that it's in there as tight as it is!" He then got serious with both hands. The cowling material on the PA–12 is not that heavy, but the panel was jammed up in such a way that it was locked in tight. Moreover, it was in a rather awkward location. If it was out in the open with clear access, Chad could have torn the thing off with two fingers.

"Boy, I don't know," was his next remark, spoken almost to himself.

Our interest in the cowling got the attention of Bill, a part time mechanic who had also been working in the hangar. Curiosity got the best of him as well, and he was soon standing at our side. We all put our heads together and tried to figure out something that would work. There had to be some simple approach to do the awkward task.

Without new inspiration, we all took positions and grabbed the wedged panel the best we could. Things were a little snug with the three of us standing in one very small circle. At a given signal, we all started pushing, pulling and wiggling. None of us could really put our best efforts into the task. But, with the three of us working together pushing and pulling the panel in different directions, it finally popped free. Chad looked over at me and said, "I don't know what you were worried about, this thing wouldn't have broken loose if you had flown into a mountain."

Dick must have been away from the office. In a way, I wish he could have seen what had happened and the work involved in getting it clear. I'm sure he would have made a memorable remark or two that would have had us all rolling.

That day would always be a perfect day!

"You're not what?"

Al Rowley, a middle-aged businessman and gentleman pilot had just bought and taken delivery of a brand new Cessna 180. There were not a lot of new airplanes based at Utah Central and I probably would have thought any of them were beautiful, but that 180 was something else. The metal skin shined like the aircraft was built out of mirrors. There were four seats in its roomy cabin, all plush like a fine car. The instruments and radio with their high tech look were nothing short of beautiful. Just looking at the panel made you feel important. The tail sported a tail wheel that gave it the ability to land on dirt strips that the newer nose-wheel aircraft wouldn't dare dream of. Its lines were graceful, and yet the aircraft conveyed a solid look that radiated muscle and speed. Moreover, it was hot! Most people that I've talked with said the 180 was one of, if not the hottest aircraft on the civilian market. The way it sat on the ramp, tail low, nose high, gave one the impression that it was a machine ready for flight, anytime, anywhere, with or without a ground run.

Al was a low-time pilot with all of his time logged in smaller eighty-five horsepower puddle-jumping aircraft. Al, more than anyone, knew his Cessna was hot, and he was not ready to pilot such a high performing aircraft. Part of the purchase package included some dual instruction and a check-out flight. Understandably, Al, like anyone with a new airplane was anxious to get his hands on the controls.

Not long after taking delivery of his Cessna, Al noticed Wally walking by, and hit upon an idea. He was always going up with people. Maybe Wally could give him a few pointers on how to tame his dragon. It would give him a head start. Or maybe even get him officially checked out. Al really didn't care who checked him out; he just wanted to fly his new airplane. Shortly, Al was asking Wally if he had a few moments to go up with him. Wally was more than happy to oblige.

As they headed over to his new Cessna, Al gave Wally a rundown, maybe even bragging a little on some of its finer points. Wally was obviously impressed. They climbed into the aircraft, Al on the left and Wally on the right. Al was excited and even anxious to show Wally that, even though he was a low-time pilot and his Cessna was a little more airplane that he was accustomed to flying, he was proficient in what he did know.

Al took off with only minor errors and it boosted his spirits to see that Wally seemed satisfied with his performance. His Crosswind Leg was maybe a little wide, his altitude was probably off a little, the Downwind Leg was possibly a little long, and some minor maneuvering was required to get runway alignment on his very first approach, but still, so far, so good.

Al had no doubt that he could take his new airplane off, flying straight and level and there certainly was no problem making turns. The landing, that was the part that Al wasn't quite so sure about. However, he was willing to try. He had full intentions of making the landing all by himself, or a least trying.

Wally was right there, just inches away from the copilot's controls and could take over if there was even so much as a hint of trouble.

Then Al began the mind games:

Boy we are sure going fast.

That's a mighty big engine out there.

The landing gear sure does stick down a long ways.

The tail--can I keep it back there where it belongs?

Am I really ready to land this hot potato?

Confidence waned, fear blossomed and Al suddenly found himself not so sure about attempting his very first landing without a little tutoring. Al turned to Wally and stated, "Why don't you make the first landing, I'll follow you through, just to make sure."

"Huh! What do you mean? I don't want to fly," was Wally's quick and questioning reply. Then he added, "I don't want nothing to do with flying this airplane, that's your job. I'm here for the ride."

Al looked over at him a little puzzled and quietly mumbled in almost apologetic terms, "But I don't know how to land it! I wouldn't dare try to land this thing without a little dual instruction first!"

"What do you mean you don't know how to land it? This is your airplane isn't it? You've got a license, don't you?"

"Well yes," Al began matter-of-factly, but drifted off into doubt. "Well, yes, I mean, yes I do, but I've only flown little airplanes, not this one. It's so big and fast; that's why I brought you along." Pleading with more than a little anxiety, he added, " I was hoping you could help me get checked out."

Wally's face radiated surprise, astonishment and concern. Then he stated clearly his position in the aircraft. "I'm here for the ride; I just came along because I thought you had a mechanical problem or were showing me your nice new airplane. I am not a flight instructor! I am not a pilot! I do not know how to fly this or any airplane! I do not want to learn how to fly! Believe me; if I had known you needed me to land this thing, I wouldn't be here now! I'm a mechanic; you know wrenches and pliers and stuff like that. I work on airplanes while they are on the ground! Now please take me down, right now"!

Al was suddenly aware that a terrible and wrong assumption had been made.

Once the gravity of the situation had been established, most of the runway was behind them and the possibility of making any landing had been long lost. Al gave his powerful new Cessna a little throttle and it briskly lifted higher into the sky, leaving behind the runway and safety.

Pattern flying is simple as far as flying goes. But sadly, flying around a very small runway does little to prepare a nervous and inexperienced pilot for an upcoming landing. There is ample time, however, to think of the dangers of hot aircraft in the hands of the inexperienced!

It was interesting that two different people, from two very different backgrounds were thinking almost the same thing. Both knew they were in a modern and high performing aircraft, both knew there was no one on board that was qualified to land such an aircraft safely, and both were wondering what the final outcome would be.

All things considered, Al did a fair job working through his jitters and setting up his next landing attempt.

Again, everything looked good, at first, but the landing gear hung down even further than he had allowed for. He was just getting ready to level off when the long stiff, gear hit hard, spread wide and flipping the 180 back up into the air, scaring both occupants half to death. The bounce and Al's awkward recovery did little to calm fears or instill confidence in either Al or Wally. Shaken and somewhat rattled, Al poured the coal to his powerful new aircraft. With wings rocking and elevators being a bit over-used, the big Cessna lifted into the security of free air. Al and Wally had yet more time to dwell on past mistakes and what lay ahead.

Glancing over at Wally, Al noticed his white knuckles gripping the edge of the seat's upholstery. Al was about to caution Wally about damaging the material but quickly decided against it. Besides, Al's own grip on the control wheel and throttle was itself rather rigid. Al wondered if he would ever be able to let go of the controls, even if he did get down safely.

On the trip around the pattern, Al tried to force all negative thoughts aside. He knew his attitude had to be positive. It was only another airplane. He was, after all, capable of landing an airplane; he had done it many times before. The Cessna 180 was just a little bigger, a little faster, and a lot different.

Wally just sat there, eyes staring but unfocused. Many airline passengers have over-blown fears concerning highly qualified airline pilots who could land an airliner on the roof of an outhouse. Who could blame Wally, or even Al for being a bit nervous?

Al again made his standard, if not abnormally long approach while trying to rehash every comment that he had ever heard or read about landing an airplane. But negative thoughts kept popping up. Then he began forcing himself to think positively. "People no better than I were landing Cessna 180s every day, why am I so nervous? I sure do wish I had an instructor with me!"

Consciously trying to clear his mind he made his best effort to get back in control. "The runway is coming up fast--think, its just another landing," he told himself. He leveled off with the intent of making a wheels landing. That little decision got his mind out of the shadows and focused on what he was doing. Again, he misjudged, and the mains hit the ground prematurely. The Cessna bounced, although not nearly as hard as before. Al's muscles tightened up like steel and Wally's body flipped stiff.

Then the big Cessna began to settle, but the descent looked and felt familiar. Al had been through similar bounces before, although, maybe not quite so pronounced. The 180 wasn't all that different after all! For the first time, Al could feel confidence building. "I think I can!"

He eased back on the wheel, simultaneously applying a little power to slow the descent. His mind focused, his fears drifted to the background and he felt positive and in control. Everything looked and felt right; the runway was in position and coming up slowly. The big aircraft seemed in the right attitude!

His input had done the job!

Then, to Al's surprise, the Cessna stalled out and dropped to the ground hard. It went into a series of awkward bounces, but the bounces were not that severe. Al fought his way through with rudder, elevator and ailerons until all unwanted momentum was gone.

The shinny new Cessna rolled to a stop, somewhat off to the side of the runway. The Cessna was down, sitting still and without damage. Al was relieved, almost ecstatic. He was safely down and he had made the landing. Maybe it wasn't a professional and actual Check Out, but he had actually taken his big Cessna 180 off and landed it by himself, without help from anyone!

Wally was just glad to be on the ground. He had his door open and was about to jump out and walk back, but at the last second he changed his mind. What else could possibly go wrong? Without question, all of his bad luck had been played out.

It was a few weeks before Wally and Al could look each other in the face again. Thereafter, whenever they passed each other, they would both break out in a grin and Wally would shake his head.

The Pilot's Best Friend!

For some time I had wanted to take Dave Dowdle up on some little round-about flight. We'd known each other a long time, since way before either of us could remember. Dave was what I would call an All-American kid. He was strong, healthy, athletic and always ready for adventure.

At first, I was going to make the flight in a Piper J–3 Cub. The Piper Cub was open and fun and everyone seemed to enjoy it. Then I got thinking about the PA–12 Super Cruiser, it wasn't so open, but it was much faster and he could see more country. It was a toss-up and, for whatever reason I decided upon the Super Cruiser.

On the big day, I brought him out to the airport and showed him around. After a short tour of the field, we headed for the flight line and the PA–12.

It sat there in silence, big and bold, alongside the smaller Piper Cubs. I proudly pointed out the aircraft we were going up in. He seemed quite excited and immediately began asking questions about its speed and altitude capabilities. Seeing his excitement brought back memories of my first airplane ride. I also felt some additional satisfaction in being able to take him up with no cost on his part. My first airplane ride had cost me dearly in allowances.

I opened the cabin door, explained a few things about the aircraft, and then had him climb onto the back seat. I took my place up front and promptly started the engine. Occasionally, I turned around to check on him and make sure that everything was okay. To my delight, he seemed eager and excited about the upcoming adventure.

Everything checked out, and we were soon on our way. I cleared the pattern and we headed out to see the country.

The air was cool, so flying was almost like zipping around on a silk blanket. First we headed toward the southern shore of the Great Salt Lake to view the old Saltair Pavilion. Then we headed out over the water at the south end of lake, mostly just to be over the expanse of water.

At first, my turns and banks were steep, you know the fighter pilot image; but I could see that bothered him, so I backed off my exhibitionism a little. After the flight over the lake, I winged around and headed back for the southeast shore to view some of the old pavilions and concession sites along the shore. When we were younger, the Great Salt Lake was a popular attraction, and as kids, we had been out there on many occasions.

We took a turn to the southeast, to check out the remains of a section of the ancient Lake Bonneville shoreline. Then we rolled over onto to a new westerly heading toward Grantsville and eventually south, out over the desert. As young teenagers, Dave and I had spent many a pleasant hour rabbit hunting in the area.

I dipped my wings and took up a new heading to the southeast. Then near the west side of the Oquirrh Mountains, I rolled over into a southern heading.

I guess we were still on the south leg, somewhere east of Vernon when I turned around to bring his attention to something of interest on the ground. He was sitting back there in the middle of the seat, eyes straight ahead without movement or expression. His complexion was a tad on the pale side and he appeared not to be interested in anything on the ground, or the in the airplane or anywhere for that matter. I had gotten him airsick!

There was probably only one place in the world that he would rather be, and that was anywhere else! I became concerned and asked him how he was feeling, obviously a dumb question. He tried to smile, then mumbled that he was okay. After a few seconds he added, "But don't move the airplane so much."

I cautiously made a very large and nearly flat ninety-degree turn to the east, crossed over the foothills and then north through the Jordan Narrows. I remember sitting in the cabin staring out through the propeller arc towards the area on the distant horizon where Utah Central was located.

Repeatedly, the words rolled over in my mind, "I wish this crate could move faster. I wish we were closer to the field. I wish we were on the ground. I wish. I wish." I felt like a heel for not taking it easier. I kicked myself time after time for being a hotshot pilot. Even an idiot knows how easily people get sick in the air, especially if they hadn't been up for a time. Maybe even the boxed-in atmosphere of the Cruiser's rear seat added to the problem, I don't know, but it really didn't matter.

When we were finally on the ground, he seemed much improved and that made me feel a little better. Sensible flying with passengers does make a difference. It was a nice trip made bad by hot-shot me. It was a flight that both of us would always remember, for all the wrong reasons!

One Long Dirty Day

Early one afternoon the phone rang and Dick answered, "Good Afternoon, Valley Airmotive"

"Dick, this is Sam. I crashed! Come get me."

A bit shocked, Dick responded, "Are you hurt?"

"No," replied Sam.

"Is the airplane damaged," Dick asked.

"No," Sam answered.

It didn't take long for Dick to realize that whatever had happened had taken some of the shine off Sam's normal happy self.

"Then you didn't crash, you made an unscheduled landing," Dick stated with a bit of relief in his voice.

"No I didn't, I crashed! Come and get me," Sam stated.

The conversation continued for a few more seconds while Sam detailed his location. Dick listened, hung up, shook his head and said almost to himself, "I guess there was a lot of dust when he landed!"

Sam had been out spraying most of the morning. One more run was required to finish the job. But it had been a busy day and his fuel reserve was in question. Still, he felt that he could finish the job and have enough fuel to make it back to the airport, but it was marginal and he knew it. If he did finish his spraying, and his tanks ran dry on his return flight, would that be so bad?

The return flight to Utah Central was over mostly desert and open fields with numerous good landing spots. Sam weighed his options, and felt that with a little planning, a forced landing wouldn't be much more than an inconvenience. Besides, there was better than a fair chance that there would be enough fuel for the spray run and the return flight. He decided to finish the spraying and take his chances.

He dropped his last load and then climbed a couple of hundred feet to give him a little maneuvering room.

Sam was feeling good about his chances of making it home when the engine of the Super Cub missed, coughed, sputtered and began to unwind rather unevenly. He quickly eyed the landscape out front. A made-to-order flat area lay dead ahead. With just a little additional help, he would touch down in a more favorable spot. He unlocked his primer and quickly pumped a couple of shots of fuel into his nearly dead engine. There was just enough fuel left in the line to make a difference.

The engine burst to life for a second or two, coughed once and then stopped cold. Except for the sound of the wind there was only silence, but the spot was right where Sam wanted it to be. His gear reached out and touched down in a near perfect three-point landing. The plane bounced across the less than perfect surface, rolled and wandered a short distance through the brush and came to a stop in a drifting cloud of gray alkaline dust.

While the cloud of dust drifted off, Sam sat in his cockpit mumbling quietly about his bad luck. He was so hoping that he could have made the airport. It had been a long day, it was hot, and he was tired.

He swung open the window, dropped the door and locked the window up against the bottom of the wing. Then swinging his legs out of the cabin, he slid to the ground and stood in place and looked around. He was disappointed at how far he was from everything. Yet, good or bad, it had been his decision and he had no one to blame but himself.

Sam made a quick walk around his Piper looking for damage. Other then a heavy layer of dust covering his aircraft the only thing of note was a slightly bent spray boom. Apparently, some brush had snagged it, bending back the outer end of the pipe and damaging its support bracket.

He spent a moment evaluating his location and the direction that would be the shortest walk for help. His best bet was a group of buildings on the distant horizon. He could see that it was a fair walk, but he would have no problem making it.

He removed his helmet and gloves, placed them on the front seat, did a final check on the switches and closed up the Piper. Looking out across the flatlands, he took a deep breath and headed out into the dusty alkaline desert.

Distances on the desert are a little deceiving, as the buildings were farther away than what they had appeared. The dusty brush, the soft alkaline soil and the burning sun were all there to add to his already long day.

It was after Sam got back to the airport that we got the full story from Dick. Dick added a little color to the details but even his humor was somewhat depressed. The story would be told later in its more humorous version.

The immediate problem was getting Sam's aircraft back to the field. I guess Sam had worked out all the details while walking around in the brush thinking.

Sam told me to push the yellow Cub over to the pump and top it off, "as full as you can get it." Dick was asked to pick up a gas can and a siphoning hose from the main hangar. Sam then got a soft drink and flopped down on one of the stools at the lunch counter. With his drink gone, and thinking of the task ahead, he headed for the ramp where he met Dick waiting at the Cub.

Dick climbed into the back seat of the J–3, and Sam took his place in the front. I stood by the Cub's door with the gas can and hose in hand. Sam, a bit anxious to get going and probably not thinking with a clear mind, grabbed the can along with the hose and put it on his lap.

I should have held on to them until after he had buckled up. With the can sitting on his lap, there was no way he could do up his belt. He tried putting the can down on the floor, at his left side. It made lots of hollow banging sounds as he attempted unsuccessfully to work it into a space that was much too small. He then tried to put the can on the floor between his feet, no room there either. He pulled the can up, banging and making more noise than ever. Seeing all the commotion, I grabbed the can and held it while a rather frustrated Sam buckled his belt.

With his belt secured, he took the can and hose from my hands and placed them on his lap. Then looking straight ahead, he said rather anxiously, "Let's get out of here!" I gave them a quick prop and they were on their way.

They had lifted off Runway 34 and were headed up to pattern altitude when Sam, anxious to get his sprayer back, told Dick to cut the pattern short and "head out." Dick causally mentioned there were a couple of FAA Inspectors on the field and they might get the wrong impression with a short pattern. Sam grabbed the stick and overpowered Dick. Dick later jokingly said he tried to slouch down in the cabin and hide himself the best he could, hoping not to be seen by anyone, especially the Feds. The inspectors either hadn't noticed the short pattern or they didn't think it all that important as nothing further was said. The little Piper J–3 Cub, with its two occupants, was on its way to the "Crash Site."

Dick landed the J–3 a short distance from Sam's PA–18. They siphoned fuel from the Cub's tank into the can. Once it was full, they hoofed it over to Sam's aircraft and dumped it into one of the wing tanks. After a few trips, they figured they had enough for Sam's return trip. Sam had also brought some wire along to tie up the spray boom for the return flight.

The sprayer was sitting on a piece of land that one would call a good emergency strip but not exactly an approved runway. Nothing dangerous stood out in front of the sprayer, but there were more than a few dusty bumps and a scattering of brush. Both Sam and Dick knew the sooner the PA–18 got into the air the better.

Dick climbed into the J–3 and Sam gave him a prop. While Sam was walking over to his sprayer, Dick taxied over to his take-off position and held. Sam put on his helmet and gloves, climbed into his airplane, did up his belts and started his engine. Sam had more than a little experience flying in and out of short fields so getting his Super Cub into the air was no problem. Dick began his take-off run as soon as Sam broke ground. The two then joined up for the flight back to Utah Central.

I was standing at the gas pit when Sam taxied across the ramp and turned in my direction. A big roaring propeller arc cutting air pulled the Piper up to the edge of the gas pit. Aircraft brakes squeaked, then locked, tail lifted, bounced and the aircraft came to a stop.

The aircraft, like Sam, was showing signs of a very long day. All leading edges of the Piper were well defined with a black fuzzy layer of mosquitoes. One wing had a new dent in its leading edge, caused by some duck that had gone on to obviously friendlier skies. A good part of the brown and yellow color scheme had been covered with the dusty color of alkaline dust. One spray boom was bent and hanging by a hastily applied strand of bailing wire, looking almost to be tied in a bow.

Behind the haze of the propeller arc was a windshield coated with bugs and dust. And behind all the bugs and dust on the windshield, I could make out the image of a very tired Sam who was in the final stages of shutting down his engine. Then switches cut, the sounds of the engine drifted off into silence. Fully aware of my observations of the clean-up work that he was bringing me, a smile crossed his face and he made an apologizing gesture. I could only smile back.

I topped off his tanks, checked the oil and then pushed the plane over to the wash rack near the main hangar.

The dent in the leading edge of the wing, like a couple of others already there would wait for a recover job. The bent spray boom--an easy-looking job that turned out to be a little harder than anticipated. The boom was in reality a steel pipe. After working on it for a time, I found that I just didn't have the grip to secure it while bending it straight. With my frustrations building and still not accomplishing anything, I found myself saying "enough." To relieve some of my accumulated frustrations, I threw the pipe wrench into the dirt and headed for the hangar.

By the time I found Chad, I had pretty much calmed down. Still, I think he could tell that I was a little frustrated by the way he smiled at my explanation of the problem.

Soon, both Chad and I were walking out towards Sam's sprayer with a second pipe wrench. Between the two of us, one holding and one bending, we were able to straighten out the spray boom. While Chad was there, we did some preventative maintenance on the spray pump, mostly cleaning and lubricating. For whatever reason, the pump had had fits of not working properly during the past few days.

I gathered up some tools, a piece of flat metal and fabricated a bracket to replace the bailing wire on the spray boom. With the new bracket in place, the boom was secured and in alignment. Things were looking good.

Next came the wash job. I soaked and scrubbed and then soaked and scrubbed again. After I had the outside looking good, I spent some time cleaning up the interior.

With everything done that I could do, I stepped back and took a good look at Sam's Piper. It was beautiful! It couldn't have looked much better the day it had come off the production line, except for maybe a couple of distortions on the wing's leading edge and the somewhat faded paint.

Walking back towards the tail, I splashed through several large puddles of standing water. I was about to lift the tail up to push it over to its tie down spot. Then I got thinking about the work and effort that I had put into the sprayer's clean up. I paused. I guess I was thinking that it was my turn to enjoy some of the fruits of my labor.

I pushed the Super Cub over to an area where the ground was dry. Then cleaning my feet off in a patch of grass (weeds), I hopped into the Piper. I checked the throttle and applied a little pressure on the brakes. Then leaning towards the open door, I hollered "clear" and hit the starter. The engine caught, and was soon idling like a purring cat sleeping on a fluffy pillow. It's amazing, how much better an aircraft runs after a good wash job.

Easing the throttle forward, I taxied through the puddled water and over to the dry apron. I passed by Sam's tie-down spot, circled wide around the ramp and then headed back towards his tie-down. Once positioned over the ropes, I eased in on the brakes and the Piper moaned to a stop. Then I just sat there with the engine at idle, listening, relaxing and looking. Everything about the airplane felt clean, even refreshing in the hot afternoon sun. I got thinking of the way it had looked just a short time before and the way it was looking now, and I felt good. Pride comes easy when you're working with aircraft.

Slow Flight

Several of us had gone over to Salt Lake Municipal Airport to see an air show. One of the main attractions was the Utah Air National Guard, which, at that time, had about 20 North American P–51 Mustang fighters and about a dozen of the twin engine Douglas A–26 Invaders in their inventory.

It was in between acts and spectators were finding ways to kill time. Kids were running here and there; adults were talking or moving around looking at about anything that caught their attention. A few had wandered over to the concession stands to pick up a drink or a hot dog.

Off in the distant sky, minute flashes of light, sun reflecting off wings as aircraft banked into a turn towards the crowd. A few people took note and stopped what they were doing to study the distant objects. Seconds passed and the specks became shapes. A father pointed out the objects to his young son; another individual was explaining the upcoming event to his girl. Some eyes watered in the bright sun, some lost focus with the distance. Still everyone was staring. "Look," someone said, "Here they come," said another.

Excitement grew. The very young followed the example of their elders and stared at the objects. Then unimpressed with the distant forms, they looked up at their parents for verification.

Shapes continued to grow, sounds intensified, sounds seemingly without a source. Eyes fixed, bodies without movement--waiting. A teenager, watching intently, mumbled, "A–26's and Mustangs, the sky is full of 'em." Those who knew the growing images could feel their bodies tingle with excitement.

Suddenly, the entire sky was packed with huge flying objects. Every sense of every body was inundated with their presence. Some women held their hands over their ears, ducking their heads. A few of the children began to cry. Men gazed up in excitement. A few men trembled in reverence and tears, remembering. Young children stumbled back, some almost falling, as they tried to work their way behind their parents.

There was so much more than what many had expected. Large aircraft were flashing by at incomprehensible speed, each leaving in their wake the sounds of heavy powered flight. Flashing shadows, broken by sunlight raced over the concrete in long blurs.

Spectators, with heads swinging back, and forth attempted to study, to take in all the details of the screaming aircraft--big engines, markings, exhaust stains, glass enclosures and pilots. But there was too much to see, too fast to study and their ear-splitting thunder was just too distracting. One young lad was hanging on the arm of his friend, while jumping up and down and squealing "Look, look, do ya see 'em, do you see 'em"?

Proudly, each aircraft screamed on by, with the sounds of pulsating thunder, then trailing off, leaving a wake of upended sky.

As the last of the group roared by with all of the clout of the pack's leader, the crowd stood in silence, watching, fanned by the breeze created up by the flight. How many spectators were wishing they were up there--probably more than a few.

I watched the shapes in the sky diminishing in size. Then, by chance, I turned my head to the south, in the direction from which they had come. There in the distance was one lone aircraft turning towards the crowd. It was a Mustang, a P–51 Mustang, looking to be a leftover from the huge formation that had already thundered by.

However, a Mustang is a Mustang and it was headed our way, guaranteed renewed excitement. Many of the guard pilots were ex-combat veterans with extensive Mustang experience. They were the very best. The pilot in the approaching Mustang was obviously among the best of the best. He had been saved for a one-man show. Man-O-Man, I thought, we're going to see some flying now!

I readied myself, confident that something super was in the making. Yet, while studying the approaching aircraft, I couldn't help but notice that it seemed to be moving rather slowly. Perhaps he had throttled back to give the last flight ample time to clear the area. Once he had the crowd to himself I was sure we would see a new standard for flying excitement! I waited. Still, it seemed to be moving so slowly.

Maybe there was a problem? Nah, no way! Yet, I found myself mumbling impatiently under my breath, "Come on man, get moving and show us your stuff, the power, the speed, the thunder."

Still, it looked to be doing more hanging than flying. I waited. "That thing must have 1,500 horses under its cowling and I bet he's not using fifty of em," I mumbled impatiently. Then as a final insult, I added, "If that's all the power you're going to use why don't you hang a Continental on the front end? Man, think of all the gas you'd be saving!"

The Mustang pilot paid little attention to my thoughts. His aircraft drifted over North Temple, then over the fence and finally near the viewing area. On the positive side, while he was crawling along, I was able to get a good look at it, the big gray prop arc surrounded by a yellow band, light and dark shadows sliding across its underside, the big air intake, the gun housings, gear up, flaps up.

"What's going on? A Mustang all set up for speed and yet it's not even up to slow motion! Mr. Mustang pilot, what is wrong with you? What a waste!"

I remember mumbling a final statement meant for the pilot, whom I hoped could read my mind, "You've got the power, and you've got the ability, use it or get out! Move it man; speed's the name of the game. It's the throttle man.

Yah, that thing in your left hand, move it, push it forward, hard! That airplane will move, I guarantee!

Better yet, get out and let me show you how it's done!"

Almost as if my unheard thoughts had cued him, Max, who was standing behind me, said to one of the other instructors in a very respectful and envious tone, "That's the most beautiful display of slow flight that I have ever seen in my life, by anybody!"

His statement struck me like a two hundred pound dictionary (filled with stupid words), falling on my head. In twisted attention, I stood without motion, hoping no one would notice the dazed expression on my face. I studied the Mustang as it moved across the sky and felt not a little anger and disappointment in myself.

Why hadn't I seen it? I've done my share of slow flying, in J–3's. But to be honest, it had never occurred to me that anyone would want to do it in an aircraft like a Mustang. I guess speed is a teen-age thing. But flying slow in an aircraft like that? With all that power and capability for speed--wouldn't that be a little like hauling manure in a sports' car? Yet, all that weight, the huge engine, the high-speed wing, how does one even develop a feel to fly so slowly in such a massive machine? I studied the shadowy figure of the pilot as he and his aircraft drifted by. Like me, I'm sure a good part of the crowd hadn't the foggiest idea what he was doing--but that Mustang pilot certainly did.

I guess when a person sees something as impressive as the Mustang's slow flight there is a desire to imitate, if that were possible. Almost daily for the next few days I was looking for an opportunity to try. Then one day I had my chance. Things were a little slow--I checked out the Cessna 120 and headed for the runway.

Most of my slow flight had been at altitude. Practicing short field landings has an element of slow flight, but this was a little different. I wanted to do more of what the Mustang's pilot was doing, as much as possible.

Since I was not nearly as proficient as the Mustang's pilot, I decided that it might be best not to try to duplicate his flying. He must have been about fifty feet above the ground, and I could see me getting into lots of trouble at that altitude. I thought about heading out to our practice area and trying it at altitude. However, up there, it would be a little hard to gauge my performance. I could gain or lose 30 feet and not really know it. I wanted to be a little tighter than that.

Then I remembered that someone had once told me how he had practiced slow flying over the runway.

"It's a good way to fine-tune your skills and the procedure is not all that hard to do," he had said. "You just fly down the center of the runway and establish the proper height, a foot or so above the ground. Once you've got the height, gradually cut back on the power, let your airspeed bleed off until you are right up against the stalling speed but still in the air and maintaining control.

"Then it's simply a matter of flying down the length of the runway, very slowly. It's simple and it's beautiful. If you gain a little height, it's easy to see and make corrections. Keeping the airplane in the air, at its slowest possible flying speed, at a constant height, without stalling out, that's the tricky part!

"If you do lose it, the aircraft will simply stall out and drop to the ground. Stalling out, from a foot or so above the ground is no big deal. Everyone has done it on dozens of blotched landings. When most of the runway has been used up simply apply power and go around for another try." He made it sound so simple, and it was exactly what I wanted to try.

I was hoping to use the diagonal runway, the longest one, but the wind was from the west so it would be Runway 27.

Right off, I found that practicing slow flight just off the surface of the runway, while trying to maintain that foot or so of height is not quite as easy as chewing gum while walking. I would set everything up, slow the Cessna down, hold it for a second and Bang!

I would be on the ground bouncing. And as you can probably guess, when the Cessna hits the ground under those conditions the fall is somewhat less than graceful. I don't know why, but the sudden drop-out and bouncing reminded me of the ballerina who reportedly danced off the stage and landed in the drum section of the orchestra pit.

My fallouts must have looked rather humorous, if not totally ridiculous. To a degree anyway, I guess you could say that I was slowly galloping down the runway, from one cloud of dust to another. Several times, I thanked the good Lord that it was a very slow day at the airport? Spectators, cheering crowds, thanks, but no thanks! I don't think they could or would appreciate what I was trying to do.

At first, my slow flying was essentially a series of set ups, stall outs, bounces, self-criticism, re-control and then re-trying. Not being an easy person to get discouraged, I kept on practicing. I must have made about a dozen trips around the pattern. And with each pass, I could see some improvement. I was slowly developing a feel for what I was trying to do. An added bonus, after a few bouncing runs, I felt more at home in the 120 than I had ever thought possible.

I was approaching the diagonal intersection on one very successful run when the Cessna suddenly dropped out. I fought my way through the awkward bouncing and was into a few seconds of smooth flight when I looked over to my right. There stood Vern Dedman at the door of his hangar. He shook his head, lowered it and then turned and walked into the shadows. I was in the left seat on the far side of the aircraft, and I doubt that he even recognized me. I was thankful for that!

Good grief, maybe he had been watching for quite some time. Man if he had, I can't imagine what he must have been thinking. There I was, not an expert by any means but feeling rather good about my progress. And he was probably seeing total incompetence. Touché! Maybe Fate was getting back at me for all the cute little remarks that I had made to the Mustang pilot.

I've got one final word about P–51s and flying. As much as I respect and admire that Mustang pilot and his magnificent slow-flying ability, if I ever get my hands on a Mustang, it's all stops out the window, with the throttle fire-walled, instruments pegged, exhaust screaming, rivets popping and Preston hissing. And there ain't no way I'm backing off till my tanks are dry!

8

Visibility Unlimited

A Day's-End Gathering

It had been a long and rather warm day. With the schedule clear, Chad began tying up the loose ends on his projects and I headed out to the line. I had just finished refueling the Cubs when Chad came out and helped me push them into the hangar. Once the Cubs were inside, we pushed the 172 in and closed the doors.

With that done, we wandered around the ramp, making sure all the aircraft were over a tie-down and secured.

Then, on our own time, Chad and I decided that it would be a good time to work on the cars for a few moments before calling it a day. The 172 was moved out of its spot at the front of the main hangar. Then our cars were pulled into its place under the lights. There we just kind of did the things teenagers do with cars. Things like checking oil, cleaning floor mats, straightening items in the trunk, polishing a hood or maybe a fender. Mostly there was silence, occasionally there was a bit of conversation that was not much more than teenagers thinking aloud.

I couldn't help but notice the Cubs, pulled in tight and facing the main door. With us working where we were, they were facing us. Like Chad and I, they seemed relaxed within the silence and cool of the evening. More than that, they somehow seemed curious, like a stable of horses watching their trainers from a distance, content, knowing they wouldn't be called upon to work until the next morning.

Pat, Sam's fiancée, had driven down from Ogden to meet Sam. As often was the case, he was with a student discussing some of the finer points of the day's flying lesson. Pat could see that he would be tied up for a time, so rather than wait in the office she wandered outside into the cooler evening air. Eventually she ended up at the main hangar with Chad and I. She was always hanging around with Sam, and we enjoyed her company.

We were soon involved in a lazy conversation about this and that and nothing in particular. Then somehow, the subject of her and Sam came up. How did they first meet? She blushed. A blush, what did that mean? I looked at Chad, Chad looked at me and then we both looked at Pat. What did the blush mean? What happened, what did Sam do to get her to blush? It would have taken some fancy footwork on her part to get away without telling us the story. We coaxed in a friendly but forceful way. She hesitated, smiled and finally consented to tell us how they first met.

Her words came rather slow and guarded at first, as if she wasn't sure how we would receive them. Maybe she was worried that the story would get back to Sam in a somewhat expanded and humorous version. Not us! Scout's honor! But soon she felt at ease and her talk came easy. It was obvious that she was telling us her all-time favorite story.

"Since I was a little kid, I've always wanted to fly. So sometime back I went out to the airport and signed up with Kemp and Kelsey for flying lessons. They had the Cessna 140s, and I thought they were cute. The Instructor assigned to me was Sam. He seemed like a nice sort of guy and he certainly knew his flying. Before going up on my first airplane lesson, we spent some time going over the basics and we hit it off real good.

Then came the flying part. He took me up in the airplane and told me to put both hands on the wheel."

Chad and I both looked at each other our eyes round with surprise. That wasn't the way it was done, it's one hand on the wheel and one hand on the throttle. What's going on? Sam should have known better than that!

The question somehow lost its importance as Pat continued.

"So I put both hands on the wheel, just like he said. Then he told me to hold the wheel tight, which I did. Then he told me that while flying, it was important not to be distracted or let go under any circumstance. I think he said concentration was a big and important part of being a good pilot. So just like he told me, I was holding on to the wheel very tight and concentrating hard on what I was doing and wondering what the next part of the lesson would be. Then he kissed me."

"Sam kissed you? Sam did that; our Sam did that, are you sure?" Chad and I stammered out the questions while fighting to control our emotions so as not to disrupt the story. "Yeaaaah, then he kissed me again and again," Pat added, her face almost glowing.

She was fascinating to watch. Her expression and emotions told as much about the story as her words. Her eyes were moist and would gleam and sparkle. At times, her lips quivered, and her voice broke and trembled as she spoke.

"I was scared to let go of the steering wheel, but it was real hard to hold the airplane straight," she continued. "I tried to move out of the way, but the airplane was so small there was nowhere to go. He kept kissing me, and I just kept moving here and there. The airplane was going all over, up and down, left and right, banking and turning. I just couldn't hold it straight, and I didn't dare let go of the wheel.

"I kept asking him to stop, but I guess the airplane was making too much noise for him to hear me. Finally, I got mad and he could tell that I was real mad and he stopped. I told him to take me back right now! He tried to apologize, but I was just too mad to listen.

"We landed and I hopped out and headed for the car. He followed, saying he was sorry, but I was too mad to even look at him."

"Sam is still around?" one of us butted in. "Didn't you tell him to get lost?"

"No," she said, stomping her foot. "I didn't want to do that," she exclaimed, "I liked him too much!"

"Weren't you afraid you would never see him again," was our next question? "He'd be back," she added, "he was too rude to not apologize. And he did come back, and he did apologize, and we dated, and we fell in love, and now were going to be married!"

I suspect that Chad and I were the first to hear her story in the manner in which it was told. However, the story was already part of her heritage, and I had no doubt that it would be repeated many times in the future.

Next to hear it would be her friends, maybe her parents and then their children and probably more than once. Then the grandchildren would get the still vibrant story from the gray-haired grandmother with a gleam in her eye.

I could almost hear the children's laughter and see the sparkle in their big eyes as they listened to the story of how their aged grandparents had started their lives together so many years before, in the cabin of a little Cessna, wandering to and fro, so high up in the sky.

Across the way, the classroom door opened and a figure stood against the light and called out to Pat. Pat wandered over to the edge of the hangar, acknowledged the call, smiled and headed over in the direction of the office. Chad and I being a bit curious glanced over to see what was going on. When the individual in the doorway saw us, he invited us over. We hesitated, looked at each other and then back at the classroom. It was filled with people. We weren't sure if we wanted to work on the cars or join the group. About then, a burst of laughter came from the open door and windows. The cars could wait.

We quickly moved our cars out, pulled the Cessna back in, buttoned up the hangar and headed for the classroom.

It was one of those rare days, when everyone had finished their work at about the same time. Instead of heading out to different destinations, the group had assembled for a little get-together.

Chad and I grabbed a soda, pulled up a chair and slid up to a table. Most all of the staff was there, talking, drinking pop, coffee or chewing on a candy bar.

A few jokes were told and easy laughter filled the room. The conversation went around in circles with every phrase, comment or word somehow being humorous. Then the conversation settled in on military experiences. Those stories were always fun. Pilots (like fishermen) are some of the greatest storytellers in the world.

Sam's girl fit right in, laughing and telling stories along with the rest. Sam and Pat seemed like the perfect couple. When you really like people, it's a good feeling to see them so happy.

Then the conversation turned to student pilots and their sometimes erratic behavior. After listening to some of the stories, I was quite surprised to find that students could be the source of so much humor. Based on the laughter going around the room, I was wondering if students should receive some kind of compensation for their entertainment value. However, I hung on every word, and I guess we all took our turns laughing at and being laughed at. After all, we were all student pilots at one time. Pilots and those associated with flying are definitely special people, and being part of that group was something very special.

It was one story after another as each participant told a story that seemed to top the last one. The stories would bring tears to our eyes and pain to our stomachs as we bent over with laughter. Below are a few of the stories that I remember from that long ago meeting.

A pilot was hired by a middle-aged couple to fly them to a town in southern Utah. The pilot could see that the woman sitting behind him was more than a little uneasy about flying. Throughout the entire flight, he was hoping that she wouldn't come apart before they reached their destination.

When their aircraft turned onto Final and she still appeared under control. It was if a great weight had been lifted off the pilot's shoulders. They had made it! He relaxed; the potential problem had not materialized. He quickly turned his full attention to the upcoming landing.

The aircraft touched down on the blacktop with its traditional jerking and screeching tire sounds. That jolt was all it took. The woman came completely unglued and let out a chilling scream in the ear of the unsuspecting pilot. The pilot flinched and jerked. His flinching caused the aircraft to balloon back up into the sky.

For the woman passenger, who appeared to have given up on making any destination alive, zooming back into the sky was definitely the wrong thing for the airplane to do. She was right on top of the flair-up with more screaming, still directed into the ear of the pilot.

With all the screaming, the pilot was beginning to question reality. What was wrong, what was the problem, was the airplane really coming apart? It was getting to the point where both the passenger and the pilot were in a near full screaming mode. To this day, the pilot still doesn't know how he made it.

Another story began about a student who had been turned loose by his instructor, and he did a superb job on his solo flight.

His patterns were perfect and the take-offs and landings were flawless.

After the flight, the proud student taxied back towards the parking area, forgetting completely that his instructor was still standing out in the middle of the airport. The instructor stood in disbelief as he watched his student and his airplane headed back to the ramp.

It was a rather long walk back to the office. The instructor later said he had never in his life come so close to flunking a student on a perfect solo, and making him do it all over again. But one walk back to the office was enough.

One pilot, shortly after receiving his pilot's license, took his favorite girl friend on a sightseeing trip. It wasn't long until he could see she was nervous, but he was hoping she would calm down as they got into the flight.

It didn't happen. The longer she was in the air the more nervous she became. Seeing things were not going to improve, the pilot thought it best to get her back on the ground. He was starting into his turn towards home when his girl went into a near panic.

After a few hectic moments, he found the only way he could calm her down was to keep the airplane straight and level. Every time he dipped a wing she would scream, every time he moved the controls she would scream; its not easy flying an airplane without moving the controls. Somehow they reached the ground without the pilot cracking under the stress.

Another student, after a few hours of flight instruction, got to a point where he just "hit a wall," so to speak. He had wanted to prove to himself and to his friends that he could fly. He had been under a lot of peer pressure and he had really tried. However, in reality, he knew it was a waste of time. It was a challenge, more than something he really wanted to do. He never did feel comfortable in an airplane.

Flying straight and level, he could handle. Taking off was something he could tolerate, to a degree. Landing an airplane was something he hated. After several miserable landing attempts, the student threw in the towel. He had had enough! He pulled over to the side of the runway, slid to a bouncing stop, shoved open the door, hopped out and headed for the parking area, on foot. He refused to even let the instructor taxi him back; he wanted no more of any airplane.

Way back in the very early days of the DC–3s, or so the story goes, a pilot working for Western Air Lines had a disagreement with the people in power. There was a heated argument. The pilot lost; and because he was unwilling to admit defeat, he was given notice.

On his last flight with the airlines, he walked up the aisle between the passenger seats with a bag of empty liquor bottles. Most of the passengers saw him walk up the aisle to the pilot's compartment and were aware of the sack, but were unaware of its contents.

After the flight was underway, the passengers heard laughter coming from behind the pilot's compartment curtain. After a time, the curtain parted and a hand could be seen with an empty liquor bottle. With a flip of the wrist, the empty bottle came skidding down the aisle between the passenger seats. The cabin curtains then closed and all was quite for a time. A little later, more laughter and again the curtains opened and another empty liquor bottle was flipped out. It, like the other, sailed down the aisle. Each passenger intently watched the bottle as it skidded by, and then all eyes were again focused on the closed curtain.

The attention of the passengers was undivided; each studied the curtain, waiting and watching. The little game continued until the entire sack of empty bottles had been thrown down the isle by the irate captain, who was progressively feeling better.

Before the landing, the captain did come out and apologize to the passengers and assured them that no one in the pilot's compartment was even a little under the influence. The passengers were in no danger.

It was probably one of the few commercial flights in history where no passengers looked out the windows. When the flight finally ended, the passengers scrambled out the door. The pilots calmly followed.

As the clock ticked away, the hour grew late, and the stories just kind of dribbled off. We just couldn't laugh anymore. There was silence, and then a few statements were made in reference to the late hour. We all looked at each other with red eyes. One by one, we quietly left the room. I followed the group through the building, turning off the lights and locking the door.

Time Frame

I've always enjoyed photography and on several occasions had taken photos around the airport. I guess Sam had taken note of my interest in photography, because one afternoon he asked if I would take a picture of him standing by his spray plane. He said that he wanted to give a copy to his girl, Pat. Taking a bit of pride in his request, I grabbed the camera from my car and headed for the sprayer.

Sam was already there with helmet in hand and was just closing up the door of his Piper. He placed the helmet on his head and then spent a few seconds trying to get it just so and so for the photo. Still not fully satisfied, he turned around and used the plexiglas of his swing window as a mirror for some final adjustments. Satisfied with everything, he leaned against the main strut, re-positioned himself and told me to "Shoot away." I stood in position, sighted and was ready to click the shutter.

"Hold it," Sam said as he started towards me. I guess he was thinking that he should put a little more thought into such an important photo. He turned around and studied his aircraft while trying to decide just what would make the best picture. Then moving his hands up, he made a square window with his fingers to frame what picture the camera was going to take, much like a motion picture director might do.

Once he found the perfect shot, he explained what he wanted. "Right here, this is what I want!" I stood at his side and he put into words exactly what he was seeing. "The Restricted sign in the window, I want that in the picture," he said almost business-like. Then he added, "And the round Davis County Mosquito Abatement Emblem on the cowling, get that too."

Then pausing, he stated with some satisfaction, "Yah that'll impress her." He again studied the scene a few more seconds. Satisfied, he moved over to the side of his Piper. He turned around, leaned against the fuselage and placed one foot on the tire. It was a perfect picture. I moved around until I had in the viewfinder exactly what I (he) wanted. Just as I was ready to snap the picture, he again said, "Hold it."

I pulled my eye away from the viewfinder and watched as he cocked his helmet to a corner of his forehead.

Everything about him reminded me of some adventurous World War I pilot. "That was more like Sam," I mumbled to myself as I snapped the picture.

Sam placed his helmet back on the front seat. Then glancing at the instrument panel he paused. "Ron, would you do me another big favor?" I moved over to his side and peered into the cockpit wondering what he wanted me to do. "Do you see anything wrong with that thing?"

I looked at his panel but couldn't see any problem. "Everything looks good to me," I cautiously replied. In a pleading tone, he asked, "Would you replace that Mickey Mouse Altimeter with a real one."

It was the old style altimeter with only one hand. I guess you could compare it to a clock with only the hour hand. It worked, but it left a little to be desired.

I told him he would have a new one before his morning flight. He reached over and rubbed the top of my head. Then smiling he said, "Thanks, I would sure appreciate it."

Ever since I had gotten my hair cut in a very short crew cut, Sam and a couple of the other guys would, on occasions, rub the stubble, as if my head were some kind of a good luck charm or something. Somehow, they all knew I hated it, although I tried not to show my annoyance.

I wandered over to the office and found an altimeter in the display case. It was the newer Sensitive Altimeter with multiple hands, a beautiful instrument, apparently, the only one on the field not in use. I talked to Glen about Sam's frustration and his desire to upgrade his panel, better there than in the display case. Besides, it had been in there forever. Glen agreed. I knew he would; he was pretty good that way.

Replacing the old altimeter took only a few minutes. Once in place, I set it to the field elevation and leaned back for an over all view. The new altimeter, with its crisp bright numbers stood out boldly. To a degree, it dated the other older and somewhat faded instruments. However, its very presence seemed to upgrade the entire panel.

Sam walked up as I was putting away my tools. As soon as he saw the new altimeter mounted in the panel, he broke out in a grin. For a second, I thought he was going to give me a hug. I've never seen anyone so happy over an instrument.

I replaced Sam's helmet on the front seat and closed the window and door.

The photo turned out great, although the restricted sign and the Davis County Emblem were washed out some. However, I'm sure Pat liked it. One thing Sam and I both missed during the photo session was his pant leg. It would have looked so much better if one pant cuff had been hung up on the top of his flying boot. That would be the real Sam.

As the Eagles Fly

There was a light wind blowing. The wind seemed to make the cold and damp more noticeable than they really were. We had been expecting rain on and off for most of the day, but as a sure thing it never happened. Even without the cold drizzling rain, the day was miserable.

It was late afternoon when Chad and I had finished our work. With not a lot going on we wandered over to the old wood stove.

We stood in our acknowledged favorite spots with our arms resting on the edge of the plenum openings where it was nice and warm. On a cold damp day, an old-fashioned wood stove beats a furnace vent hands down. It was time to unwind and talk about things that really didn't matter.

Neither of us had been up for a few days and it wasn't long before one of us popped the question, "Wanna go up?" The miserable weather was then debated. While standing by a warm stove one tends to minimize the cold outside, but in reality, we both knew how cold the Cubs could be.

For no apparent reason we wandered off the subject and started in on the next day's work schedule. However, flying was still on our minds, and it soon resurfaced as the central subject. We both wanted to go up but leaving that warm stove for the cold required fortitude.

The conversation then jumped over to the fact that there might be some money in designing a good heater for the Piper J–3. We both laughed. To make a Cub warm, we decided the most economical approach would be for Chad to take the rudder off and hold it, and I would take the prop off and hold it, while an interested third party with finances, redesigned and rebuilt everything in between. We again laughed!

Then it was back to flying, "With the wind blowing like it is, the air is probably bumpy," one of us said. "Yah," replied the other.

"Cold air, bumpy air, but have you ever had regrets going up under such conditions?"

"Don't think I have, now that you mention it."

Looking back on any flight, cold, or bumpy, it was remembered as a good flight.

"Come on, it'll be fun."

"Ya talked me into it!"

Chad grabbed his coat, gloves and stocking cap, and I put on my Field Jacket over a rather light jacket that I already wore. Together they were bulky but hopefully warm. Unable to find my gloves, I borrowed a pair from Chad. The only headgear I had was an old baseball cap. It wasn't all that warm, but it would be better than nothing.

Laughing and joking we walked out of the shop door and headed for the ramp. Chad headed for 234 that was tied down near the corner of the main hangar. He had the ropes off the wings and was flipping the prop before I had reached 308, which was parked southeast of the office.

Shortly, I had the ropes off the wings and was working on a stubborn engine without a lot of success. Chad had his engine running, and seeing that I was having trouble, headed over in my direction. Before I knew it, he was at my side telling me to hop in.

Chad's a pretty big guy and under normal conditions it didn't take a lot of coaxing for him to get a little Continental doing its thing. Even at that, it took a couple of good flips before the engine caught and was running--sort of anyway, putt, putt, cough, putt, putt. I guess sitting in cold damp air can have a negative effect on the old Continentals. Then there was always the possibility that I had over-primed it, something best not mentioned.

When Chad got back to his plane, he discovered that someone had taken the rear seat cushion out and had failed to return it. He wasn't about to sit on the bare canvas stretched over a metal frame, so he headed back into the hangar and grabbed an extra one.

While Chad was in getting his cushion, I swung my Cub around into an open space near the taxi strip to let it warm up. I had no more than gotten in position when Chad returned.

He placed the cushion in his Cub, untied the last rope from the tail and climbed in. After a few seconds, he had his doors closed and was moving out. I opened my throttle and started towards the end of Runway 34.

I checked out my engine at the run-up area. Its temperature was in the green and the engine was running like a top, be it a bit of a noisy one. Chad was about a hundred feet behind me, taxiing through some slow "S"-turns.

Still rolling through the clearing circle, I gave the engine full power and laid a long curving path out onto the center of the strip. By the time I was centered on the runway I was moving at a good pace. There was a fair breeze and I wanted to see just how short I could make the take-off run. I held the tail down and almost immediately, the J–3 popped up into the air. Once in the air, I dropped the nose down to level and watched the airspeed build. After a few seconds, I had some good speed and lifted the nose up into a steep climb.

For the past several weeks, I had been doing all my flying in the PA–12. Being back in the J–3 felt a little strange. Strange maybe, but good being back. Cold and slow, but nevertheless the Cub was second to none when it came to fun.

Shortly after getting airborne, I banked into a slight turn and looked back in time to see Chad start his take-off run. His Cub looked like a little toy airplane moving slowly down a miniature road. After a very short run, it lifted into the air, leaving only a shadow that seemed reluctant to be left behind. It was almost impossible to picture a human being, sitting inside that miniature Cub so far below.

I made a wide pattern to give Chad a chance to catch up, but he cut his pattern short and I found myself looking down at his tail, although I still held the altitude. I put the nose down and the Cub moved into faster air. By the time we were over the southwest corner of Kearns, I was on his wing and slightly above. He continued climbing and it wasn't long until we were looking across at each other.

We flew side by side for a time without direction or purpose while still gaining altitude. Shortly, a low, rather thin cloud drifted to a position out in front. Chad banked into a wide arc around its left side. My side of the cloud wasn't that high so I climbed over the top. Coming off the other side, I spotted him headed in the direction of the practice area. I rolled over into a lazy bank until he was centered in my windshield.

Once over the practice area, he made a clearing turn and went into a series of practice maneuvers. I guess I got feeling a little guilty watching him fine-tune his flying skills, or maybe the maneuvers looked more fun than my straight and level flight. Whatever, I moved over to a distant part of the practice area and went into a series of my own maneuvers.

I guess I did a couple of everything I could think of, even a few things that didn't make a lot of sense, but were fun. Then, I just wandered the sky, doing a series of mild maneuvers. I simply enjoy the feel of flight.

After 15 or 20 minutes, I became a little curious as to Chad's whereabouts. It took a little looking, but I finally spotted him, circling around at an altitude far above mine.

I pushed the throttle forward and lifted the nose of my Cub into a climb. I guess Chad saw me climbing and started to rock his wings. I leveled out, wondering what he was trying to tell me. Suddenly he pulled the nose of his little Cub up and rolled over into a spin. The little Piper spun around at an incredible speed, dropping straight down, almost as if it were on a shaft and in a vacuum. Then he rolled out just above me, circled once, and wandered over in my direction.

We again joined up and the two of us relaxed and flew on.

Chad's J–3, with a backdrop of broken gray skies, majestic mountains and open fields, had all the elements of a big-budget movie. It was a perfect picture of balance, color and movement, everything brought together by the wonderful world of flight.

His Cub moved silently through the air with ease, gracefully and artistically. At times, I imagined the sounds of a full orchestra accompanying the scene. In contrast, like a lowly spectator, watching from afar, my Cub seemed cold, noisy, windy and without the benefit of special effects. Even with all the noise, I felt suspended, without movement, without motion.

Then Chad rolled over in my direction. With no ties or restrictions, we slid in and out, bounced through each other's wake and exchanged challenges. We chased each other, laughing like drunken sailors. We flew across the sky with the grace of mystical birds. With the flick of our wrists, the earth tipped, twirled, rolled and spun. We climbed higher then rolled over in a dive while we taunted, teased and played with gravity.

Our engines moaned and groaned as we lifted our Pipers higher into the sky, and then ran free, with our props spinning in a dive. The winds played at our doors, rattling, tugging at, and then slipping away. We soared along in the wind with the heavenly music that gave lift to our wings. Like two young eagles just discovering flight we winged through the heavens, having everything and wanting nothing. We were in our universe. The planet earth simply didn't exist. The sky stretched out forever, and it all belonged to us!

Chad made a sweeping turn to the outside, banked and moved in close on my wing. We flew on for a few seconds, and then he motioned towards the earth with his hand. Below was the old abandoned military airport that we called Airport Number Two. I nodded affirmatively.

Chad rolled off into a gentle spiral, losing altitude as he circled. He leveled out at pattern altitude and entered the Downwind Leg. I flew wide before slipping into the pattern to give him plenty of room. The yellow Cub was just touching down as I rolled over onto my Base Leg. Shortly, my wheels touched concrete amid the weeds growing along its fractured surface.

Turning off the runway, I spotted Chad swinging his Cub around on a rather large aircraft parking area. I taxied across the ramp, swung around and positioned my Cub at the side of his aircraft. I locked my brakes and squeaked to a stop.

I was still undoing my belt when Chad walked over, pausing while watching me swing open the doors and climb out.

There was nothing there at the time, just bare black top, concrete and weeds. It was a strange feeling walking around alone where once there had been so much activity.

Under late evening skies, we walked to the east for a time, talking and stretching our legs. The sun was on the bottom edge of the sky, partially hidden behind broken clouds. The wind had died down and it was getting colder. Traces of our breath could be seen in the damp air. We talked about the Cubs, flying, having fun and the fact that we should do it more often.

An orange sun, setting in silence, is like a bugle call to the lowly VFR pilot. There was the need to head back and we both knew it. Chad was the first to speak concerning the late hour. I agreed, almost in silence. I was thinking the short trip back would only bring an ending. More than any day that I could remember, I hated to see this one come to an end. But growing shadows and cold damp air can't be ignored. My wishes and desires would change nothing. In silence, we walked back to our waiting Cubs. The Pipers sat together, untied, facing us, looking as if they also sensed their day was also ending.

We each propped our own plane and taxied out, side-by-side, to the middle of Runway 34. We positioned ourselves for take-off on each side of the centerline. Chad was in the lead with me just behind and to the right. He looked back, and seeing things were ready, eased his throttle forward. We started to roll. I held in position. Clumps of weeds, broken and cracked concrete began to slide beneath our wings, faster and faster. Thumping across the cracks reminded me of a rail car moving over the seams of its tracks.

Chad's tail lifted, not quite to a full horizontal position. Below his wings were long fleeting shadows and streaks. Then evening twilight slipped in below his spinning tires. Mine lifted clear at almost the same instant. The bungee shock cords on the landing gear relaxed and the wheels spun themselves out.

We eased through gentle turns as we wandered through the pattern. Then side-by-side, we drifted through the evening skies towards home.

From a distance, Utah Central looked to be in a state of hibernation. Highway traffic consisted of one lonely car headed east. The few pole lights around the hangar and office were on, but it was not quite dark enough for them to do their thing. The lone night-light in the office did little more than make the building look deserted.

I followed Chad, watching patterns of light and shadows all mix in with gold colors sliding across his fuselage and wings. He drifted down to the runway in almost slow motion. His Cub seemed to float for a time before touching down, about midway on the strip, giving me access to the near end.

I guess I was a little too relaxed. I hit a little hot and found myself in a long, ballooning, arc-like bounce. Unlike most of my bad landings, the bounce was long and graceful. As the little Cub began to settle, I applied a little power, slowly eased back on the stick and settled down to a perfect three-point landing. The flight and its day were over.

9

Days Without End

"Do you have an aircraft missing?"

I did my duty-walk from the office to the pump house, opened the heavy steel door, entered, turned on the main power switch, tidied up the stacked oil cans and wiped some of the oil residue off the shelves. Satisfied, I headed to the gas pit, pulled the refueling stand off the lid, and placed it to one side. I swung open the steel lid and casually looked down into the pit where the hose was wrapped around the recording gauges. Satisfied that everything was ready, I headed for the shop.

Sam usually left an hour or so before I arrived.

Glen and his family had skipped town and at the time was enjoying the beautiful cool forest of Yellowstone National Park.

Ray Daynes, our newly hired instructor, was due in at any time, and Chad was scheduled in shortly after that.

Dark clouds in the area gave me hope for the possibility of rain. A little moisture would cool the temperatures. I guess rain would bring some unwanted humidity. It would still be a pleasant change.

I opened the shop door and entered. The summer days were long and hot. But at that early hour, the hangar was cool--maybe even a little too cool. Could it be that the hottest days were past? In reality, thinking cool in July was little more than wishful thinking.

We had a J–3 that we had just finished re-covering and were in the process of putting it back together. The freshly covered fuselage was against the west wall, near the south end of the hangar. The night before, I had gotten the floorboards ready for paint. That was the first thing on my agenda that morning.

I rolled open the main doors to pick up a little morning light. The Cessna 172 was sitting just inside the hangar. To provide a little open space, I rolled it out onto the concrete pad at the hangar's entrance. I was glad it was the 172 at the front. Often, the 182 was the last in. If the 182 had been at the front doors, I would have left it. It was just a little too big and awkward for one person to muscle around.

Until Ray was in the office, it was my job to answer the telephone--an unwanted duty, mostly because the only phone extension in the hangar was located on the north wall of the shop. It wasn't all that far away, but to drop everything and run the length of the hangar was something I'd rather not do.

Shortly after I got into the painting, I heard a car drive up and park near the office. With paintbrush in hand, I walked over to the shop door to confirm that it was Ray and not a customer. It was Ray, so I quickly dropped the phone and office off my list of responsibilities.

A short time later, the phone rang, and I looked up and listened. After a ring or two it stopped. I felt some satisfaction in knowing Ray was there and doing his thing. I continued painting.

Suddenly, Ray came running around the corner and through the main door of the hangar. "Where's Sam's plane?" he asked, trying to catch his breath. Surprised by his sudden appearance, I hesitated, then responded that he had it out spraying.

"Where's he spraying," Ray asked. I didn't know exactly, and said so in an almost apologetic tone.

Ray then said, almost incoherently, that the Davis County Sheriff was on the phone asking if any of our aircraft were missing. One had apparently gone down up north, and they were trying to locate the owners. Without further explanation, Ray spun around and headed back toward the office on a dead run.

Stunned, I tried to evaluate Ray's words. My first rational thought was, "Do they think its Sam's plane, why?" I then stated, almost out loud, "That couldn't be possible!" I didn't know Sam's exact schedule as to where and when he would be spraying. It was still early; maybe Sam was still on route to the spray site. Maybe the ground crew was still getting him loaded for his first spray run. Still...

I dropped my brush and headed towards the "T" hangar. It was just to the east of our main hangar. I had hangared Sam's plane in there the night before.

Swinging open its man door, I partially stepped inside. No spray plane, only its tracks in the gravel. I then made a dash for the parking area, just west of the office, where Sam always parked his car, a two-door, red with black trim 53 Mercury convertible. It was there just like every other morning.

I then swung around to the south side of the office, peering out over the expanse of the airport, wondering if he could have had some mechanical problem and was somewhere out on the strip, trying to get a start. Again nothing. There was nowhere else to look, nothing else that I could do.

I dashed into the office, hoping Ray had some new information indicating the downed aircraft was not Sam's. He was in the process of locking up the north office door.

Unsure of what was going on; I asked if he had any more information concerning the missing aircraft. There had been an airplane crash near Centerville, Ray explained. He had told the sheriff that we might have a spray plane working the area. The sheriff then asked Ray if he would come up and see if he could identify the aircraft. Ray told the sheriff that he was on his way.

Looking at me, he added, "You too, I'm not going up there alone!" I was glad to hear that, because there was no way I was going to sit in the office, waiting and wondering.

Ray grabbed a piece of paper and began to scribble a note for Chad. Then, without looking up he stated, "Get out the 172, we're going to meet the sheriff at the Bountiful, Woods Cross Airport." I bolted out the door.

Thankfully, it was already outside. I turned it clear of the hangar. Seeing Ray headed my way, I ran back into the hangar and closed the doors.

By the time I was back at the Cessna, he had the engine revved up and was holding back with the brakes. I opened the right side door, climbed up on the step and jumped inside.

We took off on Runway 16 and headed east to Redwood Road and then straight north to the Bountiful Airport.

The sheriff was standing near the front of his car. He motioned us over, and we climbed inside.

On the way to the site, the sheriff gave us a quick rundown on what he knew about the accident. From what a witness had said, the pilot had been spraying an area two miles north of Centerville and east of Highway 91 (now I–15). He had made a spray run to the west across the target field, pulled up over the highway and was making a counter clockwise turn on the east side of the power lines that ran along the west side of the highway.

The sheriff figured that as he was turning near the power lines, he had diverted his attention from the lines to the next spray run. The bright sun may have also been a factor as it was low in the sky and there were times when it broke through the overcast.

The witness had told him, that the aircraft's right wing had actually slipped in between the power lines and may have been tangled in them. The aircraft's wing slid along the lines for a short distance before hitting the steel, truss-like transmission tower. The aircraft spun around, stalled out and hit the ground hard and nearly flat. The fuel tanks ruptured on impact, causing the aircraft to burst into flames.

Judging from the wreckage, the pilot had probably died when the aircraft hit the ground. The sheriff arrived shortly after the accident, but there was little he could do except pull the body from the wreckage and put out a few lingering fires.

We pulled up on the east side of the highway and parked on the shoulder. The wreckage was on the far side of the railroad tracks with the tail section being the only part visible from the road. It was the tail of a Piper aircraft. There was still fabric on the tail that had not been consumed by fire. I studied the colors against the distance, brown and yellow, a faded brown and yellow, Sam's colors.

It was a short walk from the car, across the highway, down and back out of a shallow ditch and then up and over the railroad tracks to the site. A few people were standing around looking and talking; some looked official, most were curious onlookers.

Except for the fabric around the tail section, the airplane had been completely consumed by the fire. Both tires were still smoldering with lazy wisps of blue-gray smoke. The scorched ground was covered with puddles of a milk-like liquid, (mosquito spay). Most of the aircraft was little more than a pile of twisted, almost unrecognizable junk. I stood at the edge of the wreckage for a few moments trying to convince myself that it wasn't Sam's airplane, but it couldn't be done.

Ray came over and told me the sheriff wanted to take us over to the mortuary in Centerville. I wasn't sure why, since by then I had dismissed any doubt that it was Sam. Before turning away, I looked into what had been the cockpit. Amid all the black and twisted metal, was the blackened instrument panel. It was almost unrecognizable, but I could make out the remains of the altimeter--the altimeter that I had installed just a few days before.

We took a short drive to the Union Mortuary in Centerville. Inside, off to one side we could see the body of an elderly lady, lying on a metal table. Except for her face, she was covered with a white sheet. The sheriff looked over in her direction, and then asked the attendant if that was "Mrs. so and so." The attendant, filling out some papers at a nearby desk looked up at the sheriff and quietly acknowledged that it was. The sheriff stated that he had known her all his life, and that she had been one of his schoolteachers.

The sheriff was unemotional in his statement. I guess when people deal with death almost daily it affects them differently. It was different for Ray and me.

The sheriff took us back to the airport and thanked us. We walked to the Cessna in silence and were soon in the air. Trying to take my mind off the accident, I remember looking up and studying the gray overcast sky. Maybe I was looking for a sign of rain. Neither Ray nor I said a word on the return flight.

On Final, as we approached the end of the Runway 16, our 182 had just started into its clearing turn before taking off. Upon seeing us, it pulled over to the side and waited. We passed over its top and I could see Chad and Dick in the front seat. There were people in the back seat, but I couldn't see who they were. We taxied over to the office and parked. The rest of the crew headed over in our direction as soon as our aircraft came to a stop.

Once everyone was in the office, we all assembled around Ray. He took a deep breath and told everyone what had happened and what the sheriff had told him. On leaving that morning, Ray had left a note explaining that Sam had probably been in a serious accident. Between the note and a few calls, everyone knew about all there was to know. But without the official word, there was still hope. Ray's words were those final and official words. As he talked, you could see the hope drain from everyone's faces. A few questions were asked and Ray answered them the best he could. The only real questions left unanswered were, "Why? Why Sam?"

Then there was a period of silence. Instructions were stated concerning things that needed done, and one by one everyone drifted off in different directions.

The sheriff had mentioned that his office would locate and notify Sam's next of kin. So that was something we need not worry about.

Dick said he would phone Roy in Logan and tell him what had happened.

Glen had been making check-in calls to the office each evening, but until he called, there would be no way to contact him.

The FAA was contacted and asked when their on-site investigation would be completed. They reported that their people were already on the scene, and we could begin clearing out the wreckage in a couple of hours. They also stated that they wanted to further examine the engine and propeller. As near as possible, they wanted them left "as is."

We spent the next hour or so making arrangements for a flat bed truck and collecting the tools needed to get Sam's plane back to Utah Central.

Getting the truck from the highway to the site of the accident turned out to be the first problem. The only road over the ditch and tracks was a mile or so to the north. Once we got across the ditch and tracks, we were on pastureland. Cattle were wandering the area and we had to travel up and down the length of several fence lines before we could find gates.

When we arrived at the wreckage, there were additional onlookers; many more than there had been earlier. While we were unloading our tools, one of the crew noticed a Cessna 182 circling overhead. It was the company's 182. "That must be Roy," someone said.

What I can remember most about the clean-up, aside from the sadness and pain, was the soot, ashes, filth, cables and wires. It seemed that no matter what was picked up, there was a cable or wire connecting it to something else. Working with the wreckage of Sam's aircraft was one of the hardest things I have ever done in my life.

Mel Rozema, a former student of Sam's and I found ourselves discussing the accident and the aircraft recovery some 40 years later. He remembered the clean-up vividly as, "…the hardest and dirtiest job I've ever had in my life."

The remains of the Piper were hauled back to Utah Central. The airframe was unloaded and placed in the open storage area between our main hangar and the rental T-hangar, the hangar where Sam's Piper had spent the night before. Four of us slid the engine off the bed of the truck and carried it inside the main hangar. We carefully placed it on a moveable bench that had been set up near the southwest corner of the Parts Room. Once the engine had been placed on the bench, a few of us paused to look at it, and then we all wandered off.

Like many threatening and cloudy days in the area, the clouds broke that evening and the day (Saturday, July 6, 1957) ended with what many would call a beautiful sunset. I can't remember if it rained or not.

For Reasons Unknown

Glen, still in Yellowstone didn't make his check-in call until Sunday afternoon. When the call came in, Dick was the one who answered the phone. He stumbled over his words for a few seconds. Then realizing he was making it harder for both Glen and himself, he paused and laid everything out, almost in technical language. Glen listened as Dick summarized the events of the previous day. When he finished, there was only silence. Struggling with words, Glen told him he was on his way home.

Monday, the FAA Inspectors showed up first thing in the morning. We opened up the hangar and led them over to the bench and the engine.

Very professional and business-like, the two examiners stood there for a time studying the carcass that had once been an aircraft engine. Since it had been brought in, residue oil from inside the case had drained, forming a large and unsightly puddle on the bench. The inspectors seemed unconcerned. They intently pored over the engine, occasionally moving to a new position, sometimes squatting down to the level of the table, other times leaning over for a closer look. Using pencils, they would move a wire or clear away some mud or ashes to expose hidden areas. Occasionally a quiet word or two was spoken, mostly without acknowledgement. Not for a second, did either of them give me the impression they were inexperienced or had no idea of what they were looking for. Everything on the bench seemed to be telling them something and they were very good listeners.

Satisfied they had seen all there was to see on the outside, they requested the engine be broken down. Chad and I had been standing by with instructions to help them in any way we could. At their request, we selected the appropriate tools from a nearby toolbox and stepped up to the task.

I remember approaching the engine reluctantly. Perhaps out of respect for Sam. I don't know.

Aircraft engines are normally clean, but what was laid out before us was anything but. Melted, torn and twisted pieces of aluminum, mud and oil were embedded or caked on the casing and cooling fins. On any other job we would have spent time cleaning things up, but on that occasion we cleared away only what was required for the engine's disassembly.

We first pulled the cylinders off and set them aside, and then we unbolted and split the case. Each item removed was placed relative to its removal. The inspectors stood by watching intently, occasionally stepping in for a clearer view. Their attention never wandered.

I guess we had some extra lights, probably portable shop lights, but all I can remember is working in shadows. Shadow filled with offensive smells, nauseating smells of oil, ashes and insecticide, mixed together and fouled by a consuming fire.

A damaged engine was being disassembled for the last time with no intentions of its ever being rebuilt. It was the last remaining and most recognizable part of a friend's aircraft, never to be functional again. What were we doing anyway? Something terrible had happened! And there we were trying to uncover the reasons why it happened, with the only player silenced. I couldn't help wondering what Sam's feelings would be if he were standing at our side?

With the main parts of the engine broken down, we were told we had gone far enough. We stepped back and placed our tools in the toolbox. The inspectors took their places at the bench.

Then, without expression, they surveyed the collection of parts as a whole and then individually. Always probing, they would scrape at a surface with a screwdriver, or wipe a part clean with a cloth. Everything was examined, some items more thoroughly than others. After examining the internal parts, they picked up each of the spark plugs, one by one, and examined them carefully.

Silently, they next walked over to the twisted propeller and carefully studied the deformities and damage caused during the accident. With their hands, they mimicked the distorted bends, theorizing on what the aircraft and engine were doing to twist it in such a way.

After a short conversation, the inspectors were apparently satisfied the engine had given up all of its secrets. The information taken from the engine would become part of the data collected on the accident and would be placed in a folder, a file. That information would then point to a probable cause as to why an airplane had been lost and a life taken.

They politely thanked us, and without another word, picked up their few personal items and walked out of the hangar.

For Those Left Behind

On the day of the funeral, we would pair off in two groups for the trip up to the Logan Cache Airport where we would meet Roy. Then together we would all motor over to Trenton, Sam's boyhood home.

Glen would take half of the crew up with him in the company's 182. Dick said that he could borrow a four-place airplane that was a little bigger and faster than our Cessna 172. Having an airplane that could keep up with the 182 and still provide a little extra elbow room was welcome news.

Next morning, Dick was first to arrive. Seeing he had a few moments to kill, he parked his airplane by the gas pump and headed for the office. He grabbed a soda and sat down at the lunch counter. One by one, the crew wandered into the office. Each was dressed up in his "Sunday best." It was like looking at a different group of people.

Glen, his wife Doris, Ray and Bob Miller were to go up in the Cessna. Chad and Mel Rosema were paired off with Dick and me.

As we all headed out to the ramp, Dick pointed to his aircraft, a Beech Bonanza. My heart skipped a beat.

The Bonanza was a top-of-the line aircraft and was pretty much in a class by itself. It had the lines of a fighter; big engine, retractable gear, low wing and a unique "V" tail. A few years before, I had been up in one of the older models, (in fact, it was my very first airplane ride), but Dick's Bonanza looked to be the latest model just off the production line.

As we headed out toward our airplane, Dick, a long-time Bonanza fan, commented, with more than a little pride, "Today we are going to fly in style." The words were hardly spoken when Glen took note of what aircraft we were headed towards and asked, "Dick, you're not going up in that thing are you?"

Dick turned, and somewhat apologetically answered, "Well yes."

"We're a Cessna Dealer," Glen said. "How is it going to look with half of the crew of a Cessna Dealership arriving in a competitor's airplane?" Glen had a good point and Dick's face fell. Glen then suggested we consider the Cessna 172 as an alternative. But someone noted that the 172 was out on a cross-country. By default, Dick would be forced to fly his Bonanza. Glen, looking a bit gloomy, turned and continued toward the 182. A bit of a grin spread across Dick's face.

Anyone in his right mind would admit that the Bonanza, in most ways, held the edge over the Cessna. However, when it came to prices, well that muddied the water somewhat. As much as I was going to enjoy the ride, I was hoping no one noticed that our airplane had its wing on the bottom and sported a rather funny looking tail.

The trip up was fun. Any time there were two or more of the airport gang together it was something of a party. We talked, laughed and enjoyed ourselves. Except for Mel, I was the youngest of the crew and to me it was always a special occasion when I was sitting in their midst.

There was, of course a downside. Thoughts of Sam kept popping into my head. With each thought came guilt, so much fun and laughter while headed for his funeral. But I got thinking of Sam and the type of individual he was. He wouldn't have wanted it any other way. I put aside my guilty feelings and laughed right along with the rest. Unknown to any of us, it would be the last time the "original old gang" would be together under such laid back circumstances.

Roy Theurer had a car rental agency operating out of the Logan Cache Airport. As soon as we landed, we all piled into a couple of the cars and headed to the Trenton LDS Ward Chapel. No one at the Logan airport commented on our Bonanza. That had to be a plus.

Walking into the chapel filled me with emotions that I had never felt before. It was almost as if someone was telling me--not just a feeling, or a passing thought, but someone making a profound statement-- "This is Sam's funeral. Sam your friend is gone forever."

Never had I felt like that before. I guess I hadn't yet accepted his death as a reality. I could still hear his voice, feel the warmth of his presence and sense the dynamics of his personality. Many times since the accident, I have looked up or turned a corner and fully expected to see him standing there with some uplifting remark. It was almost a surprise when he wasn't there. For me, it seemed impossible for something even as basic as death to bring to an end a personality such as Sam's.

The chapel was filled with people of all ages and descriptions. Some were sitting quietly, others standing around, some alone, some in groups. It was obvious Sam had been someone special to many people.

The casket was sitting up front near the pulpit. Several people were standing at its side talking quietly. On top of the casket was a photo of Sam in his Navy Uniform, the same photo used in all the newspapers. I tried to recall one of the many humorous military experiences he had talked about, but none came.

Pat sat off to one side, not far from the casket. Her head hung low. Even without seeing her face, you could tell that she was a changed person. She could have reached out and touched several people; but seemed very much alone. Maybe that's what she preferred.

I couldn't see her eyes but her cheek was red. There were probably no tears left.

Of all the people in Sam's life, she was the only one he had been destined to spend the rest of his days with. All others, friends, even relatives would move to the background. A few short days before, the world had been at her feet; there was nothing she wanted that she didn't have. Then very cruelly, it was all taken away-left only with memories that boldly stood out as a testimony of what she had lost. Maybe hardest of all was the prospect of wondering what might have been.

Many people spoke at the service. The talks were mostly upbeat, like Sam. There was even a story or two that was outright humorous, describing Sam's remarks or doings. Ray, representing our company, concluded with an aviation poem by Gill Robb Wilson, a writer for the popular aviation magazine, *Flying*.

After the services, we joined the motorcade to the Clarkston Cache County Cemetery. It was a bit misty, and dark clouds filled the sky, but they didn't look threatening.

All together there was quite a crowd at the burial site. Many people appeared almost lifeless with no emotions left. Other people cried, some softly, others quite openly. Others appeared to be fighting total disbelief. I stood there in sadness, trying to listen to the words that were being said; but time after time, I found my mind wandering. A picture of Sam at the controls of a large airliner, maybe one of those new jets.

The airlines, that's where he was headed. I had believed that someday, as an passenger, I would look up on the pilot's compartment door and see a plaque with the pilot's name, his name. "Hey I know you," and we could have talked about old times. Maybe he would even let me take a turn at the controls of his airliner.

Then there was Pat and all that he would have added to her life. It was hard to picture Sam as a family man, a husband, and a father, even a grandfather with kids hanging on his arms laughing. But he would have made one of the better ones, no doubt. Now dreams of the future would remain only as memories of the past. A marriage, a life and a family, something that only might have been.

Then there was the accident. That Saturday, it could have been just another day, passed over and forgotten. If only there had been a little tap on a rudder, a slight movement of the stick, or even a solid overcast to block out a possible piercing ray of bright sunlight. Any one of so many little things could have made a difference to so many people, if only, broken words.

After the interment, everyone was invited over to one of Sam's brother's house for light refreshments.

The room where refreshments were served was filled with pictures of Sam. Some were of him alone while others were of him with other people. All of the photos showed him dressed in suits or stylish sports clothes. Never had I seen him in anything but his flying outfit, with his pant leg tucked in at the top of his boot. There was nothing in the room to indicate that he had worked at an airport and that he loved flying. It was obvious that Sam's circle went way beyond his love for flying.

Sam had three brothers, and the more I heard one talk, the more I had the impression that he was a little more than sad about what had happened. His feelings were bordering on anger. I never heard him come right out and say what was bothering him, but something sure was.

There had been talk around the airport that the field Sam was spraying was too small, too tight, and never should have been put on the list to be sprayed by aircraft. Maybe Sam's brother had heard those rumors. On the other hand, maybe the brother had suddenly realized that he had lost his kid brother--forever. To him, Sam was a life-long friend, someone bigger than life. Someone special--lost while fighting insects, mosquitoes. There was something very painful about that!

The flight back was under dark, heavy clouds. It was early evening but it looked more like the sun had already set. The mood in our airplane, like the sky, was downcast and dark. There were no jokes, no laughter. Four people stuffed into a small cabin, each alone, each seemingly trapped in his own thoughts. Reality had finally set in.

Glen had taken off a few moments before we did, and he was out front on the horizon somewhere. I wondered if things were as gloomy there as they were in our group? Somehow, I suspected that they were.

Sam's burned-out airframe sat between the main and the rental hangars for a time. Then one day, Glen asked us to move it out to the dump. The dump was where old discarded aircraft parts, oilcans and trash were taken. It was located on airport property, about a quarter of a mile southeast of the main hangar.

After that, we never paid much attention to it, but we all knew it was out there. Then one day someone noticed that it, along with everything else was gone. Glen had called up a junk dealer and had everything hauled away. I had never been out near the burned-out Piper, but for some reason I felt some sadness in knowing that it was gone.

The Passing of a Time

Things seemed to be changing around the airport. It wasn't something you could put your finger on, but somehow things were different. At first, it was just an occasional feeling. After a time, it became more obvious. There didn't seem to be as many students as there had been in months past. Chad was the first to put it into words. After some discussion, we realized that we were both feeling the same way. Was activity really down, or was it just our imagination, or maybe a seasonal slump?

We talked to Glen and he confirmed it. He stated in rather cold terms that the G.I. Bill from the Korean War had pretty much run its course. Most of our students had been using it to help pay for their flying lessons. As the bill

was being used up, new students weren't signing up like they used to. Even
before Sam's accident there had been a decline. With the downturn in business activity came other problems. Roy was getting discouraged and talking
about getting out of Utah Central. We all knew what that meant--losing jobs,
looking for new jobs, all that fun stuff. Then Glen interjected a few words of
encouragement. He was out looking for business-oriented people to step in
when Roy backed out. He was having talks with several prospects and had
hopes that one of them might be interested.

After our conversation with Glen, Chad and I knew a little more of what was
going on. Even with the prospects of new partners stepping in, uncertainties
and rumors became part of our daily conversations. Every time we saw someone from the office, we would ask if there was any word.

Mostly, the answer was a simple, "Nothing, yet." Occasionally we heard
something-- a statement, a prediction or even a guess. But invariably it bor-
dered the extreme edges of pessimism or optimism. About this time, the company was dealing with a period of money problems. Paychecks were sometimes late. Sometimes there were restrictions or cautions as to when they
could be cashed.

Occasionally, Glen would appear on the field with an individual we had
never seen before. As they walked around the area, Glen was doing a lot of
talking and the individual was doing a lot of listening. We would watch from
afar, wondering in silence what was being said, what was being heard and
what impressions were being made.

After what seemed forever, a young man by the name of Earl Short appeared
and seemed very interested in the operation. An arrangement was eventually
worked out that involved Glen, Earl and Earl's dad. Glen would continue
as airport manager. Earl would be the on site owner with the final say. Apparently, Earl's dad had put up some of the money and would participate
as a silent partner.

When everything was finalized, Glen called us into a meeting and explained
the new organization. We had new owners, with money. It was like having a
great weight lifted from our shoulders. We even had a new company name,
Midwest Aviation. Things were looking good again.

Earl was ambitious and threw himself wholeheartedly into the job. He put
into place new shop and line procedures. The hangars were cleaned up and

weeds were removed from around the office and ramp. A few of the office rooms received an overdue coat of paint and there were even some decorations brought in.

Earl had a couple of family pictures taken of his employees and aircraft. The pictures hung in his office and it was obvious that he was very proud of the operation. Included in the airport personnel picture was Glen Dellinger, manager; Earl Short owner; Wendell Despain our flight instructor; Chad Jenkins, who continued doing most of the aircraft maintenance; Wally Wahlquist, the part-time A & E mechanic and me, who was there to do a little of everything. Gone from the roster were many of the old-timers who had wandered off to the four corners of the earth.

Like most people, Earl questioned the sanity of the individual who had come up with the flat, drab tan color for the 308 Cub. One day he entered the hangar, gave it a quick look and promptly told us to paint it, "Cub Yellow and quick." Yellow it became, with full size black numbers down the side of the fuselage. It was beautiful!

Earl and Glen also tried to bring in a little outside interest. One of their more notable successes was persuading a wing of the Civil Air Patrol to set up its headquarters in the east hangar that was part of Glen's residence. They had a Stinson L–5 and it seemed like there was always something going on at the hangar. On weekends, the L–5 was lucky to be on the ground long enough to take on fuel.

A new executive office was built in the west end of our office building. It was to be Earl's office. It was simple, but for Utah Central, quite impressive. It had some nice wall paneling, carpet on the floor (a first at the airport) and a real executive's desk. On the top of the desk sat a model of a P–51 Mustang. Earl told me that as soon as the operation got on its feet, he was going to buy one, a real one. I took note of that.

Sadly, with the construction of the office we lost the old lunch counter. Its removal was a good business decision, even I will admit to that. Food was never sold across the counter, except maybe for a brief period of selling sandwiches (unprofitably). In reality, about the only thing that crossed the counter were cups of coffee and wild stories. To that, I guess you could add that talk was cheap and the coffee was pretty much on the house. We did sell soda pop, but even there, the profit was negligible.

Good idea or bad idea, I sure hated to see the old counter go. So many of my living heroes were "airport bums." Old people, white haired people, people who in any other environment would be content to sit in the background in silence and leave their wonderful stories untold. But, at that old lunch counter, they did congregate, they did talk, and they did laugh. They stayed for hours, drank a lot of coffee and smoked a few cigarettes. For many it gave the airport a reason to exist. I'll be forever grateful that I was there to brush their elbows and enjoy a few of their life's experiences. Call me old-fashioned, with little or no business sense. I'm sorry, but that's the way I feel.

The spray contract with the Mosquito Abatement Commission would continue with Glen as chief pilot. A second PA–18 spray plane was put on line with Earl as its pilot.

When Earl's plane arrived, both his and Glen's were painted white with red trim. They looked pretty good.

Hoping to pick up some students who were seeking their Twin-Engine Rating, Earl had purchased a little twin engine airplane called a Cessna Bobcat. The Bobcat was both an excellent and inexpensive twin-engine trainer. It was one of the many surplus aircraft coming out of World War II. Painted a washed-out yellow with a golden brown trim, it was in its own right one good-looking aircraft. It had once belonged to the legendary Tom Johnson, a captain with Western Airlines. Dick Thomason had received his Twin-Engine Rating in the same aircraft while it was under the ownership of Tom. When Dick heard that we had purchased it, he was a little skeptical. He later told me that we had missed the boat. He said, "Everyone around these parts had already received their Twin-Engine Rating with Tom and since he didn't need it anymore, he sold it to us."

In its day, the Bobcat must have been one widely used aircraft. You could call it just about anything and probably hit on one of its names. It had quite a list. Some of the official names were the T–50 Bobcat, Crane, AT–8, AT–17, C–78, JRC–1 and the UC–78.

Some of the more often-used, and seemingly preferred nicknames were the "Useless–78, Double-Breasted Cub, Box kite, Rhapsody in Glue, Wichita Wobbler and the Bamboo Bomber." Obviously, there is some humor in the names, but a friend of mine owned a Bobcat based at the Provo airport. He affectingly referred to his Bobcat as "a Poor man's Twin." He loved that airplane!

The military listed it as a trainer, utility or a light transport. According to the books, it could carry five people, the pilot, the copilot/passenger and three passengers on a wide rear seat. The power plants were two Jacob radials that were rated at 245 H.P. each. Its wingspan was just shy of forty-two feet.

The Cessna Bobcat's construction was steel tube in the fuselage and lots of wood in the wings. There was a little metal around the engines, door and windows. The entire aircraft was covered with heaven-only-knows how much fabric and that was just about it.

After the war, hundreds of the little Bobcats were sold off as surplus, and I've heard every airport in the country had its own little "Bamboo Bomber Fleet." However, the aircraft had a real weakness, its huge wings with wooden spars and ribs. The wood in the wings had a tendency to develop dry rot, practically over night.

For a time, it seemed like everywhere you looked there was an abandoned Bamboo Bomber or two sitting out in the weeds shedding parts. It was a sad fact that, "Without lots of love, the Bobcat would disintegrate almost before your eyes."

I've heard that mechanics and FAA Inspectors were scared to death of the little surplus Bobcats. No matter how good all the massive wood in the wings looked during inspection, there was always a fear lurking in the back of their minds, that something had been missed and sooner or later the Cessna would shed a wing. With a smoking pile of rubble on the ground, the mechanics and inspectors had little doubt as to where all the fingers would point.

I've never heard of anyone making major repairs on the Bobcat; it was, in most cases, money down the drain. For a while at least, you could buy a used one for much less than about any repair cost. You could almost say that the little Cessna was expendable, buy it, fly it, junk it and re-buy. After a time, good ones were hard to find. Today they are very rare. However, ours was airworthy and ready to take on students.

Early one winter morning, Glen approached Chad and I complaining that the Bobcat had a dead battery and asked if we could get it started with a hand prop. I wasn't so sure, but good old Chad stated without hesitation, " You bet!" I'm glad Chad was there as I had never tried to hand-prop an engine that big.

First thing we did was kick away the snow in the working area of the port engine to ensure solid footing. After clearing away the snow, I remember looking at that big radial engine and its huge two blade metal propeller. I wondered what I'd do if I were alone. Yet I've seen pictures of the old timers hand propping aircraft like the DH–4. Some of those old-time aircraft were rather large with relatively big engines so I knew it could be done, but! The smaller aircraft like Cubs, with their little four-bangers, had a propeller blade that was relatively easy to swing. On the other hand, the Bobcat's engine was a much bigger with more cylinders; more compression and it had a much bigger propeller blade. With a little effort, you could prop it, but you could sure tell it wasn't a Cub.

Chad, as always, had the experience and he spent a few moments giving me some pointers on where to grab the big blade, how and where to stand, how to pull it through, where to be, and where not to be.

With everyone supposedly in the know, we got busy with the task at hand. We each took turns "flipping" (a bit of an exaggeration) the propeller. While one was on the propeller, the other would be supervising from the cockpit with a hand on the throttle, just in case.

The big Jacobs made a lot of clicking, sucking and blowing sounds and occasionally it coughed. Sometimes it even puffed a bit of gray smoke, but no way did it give me the impression that it would run during my lifetime. However, we were young, had plenty of time and giving up never crossed our minds. There was a positive side though. I don't know if it was the challenge or just fun, but I remember that I thoroughly enjoyed all the flipping and anticipation.

We would take turns "flipping" it through the compressions until we got tired. Then we would stand back and relax for a moment. On one occasion we discussed and tried to analyze the old Jacob and philosophize on just why it wouldn't start. We came up with two very good reasons; first, we couldn't flip it fast or hard enough, and second, it was ornery. We had no solution for either, so we just kept flipping.

Then, for some unknown reason, the engine caught and began turning on its own, somewhat. It belched smoke and made more funny sounds than any dictionary would ever dare to define. It actually looked to be running in slow motion--the coasting end of a bad flip.

It couldn't have been running on more than one cylinder, but the big blades just kept on going around and around while Chad and I watched in utter disbelief. The engine smoked, it shook, it coughed and I think it even burped on its own fumes once or twice.

It looked to be turning so slow that I was almost tempted to reach out and help it along. I watched and I waited for it to coast to a noisy stop with all of its funny chugging, burping, clicking and wheezing sounds. Yet it kept on turning, obviously unaware that it was not developing enough power to maintain life. Why, or how it kept turning, I'll never know.

Apparently friction and fire, even in small amounts, were enough to put a little life in its body. It somehow became a bit spunky and picked up another rpm or two. Then almost by design, or magic, or heart, or something, it cleared the cobwebs from another cylinder and put it on line, then another, and yet another. Slowly, the fire, exhaust and wind sounds all picked up in tempo.

The old Jacobs began acting and sounding like a real airplane engine. It stopped smoking and even smoothed out, as much as a Jacob's radial could. It had lots of heart and apparently she was just beginning to show us her stuff. Her rpm's continued to climb and the big metal propeller spun into a huge reflecting circle. Chunks of snow and ice were lifted from the ground and simply disappeared in a white haze. A white cloud of blowing snow formed behind the engine. The noise became nothing less than continuous thunder, and the air sounded as if it was being shredded.

There was nothing but intense excitement wrapped around that weary old body of fire and steel. It was all there, the thunder of its exhaust, the screaming of wild untamed and beaten winds, the trembling of the ground and the aircraft shaking and begging for its freedom. How could anyone be near a power plant like that and call it old and out of date. Is there anything more exciting and beautiful than a big old radial engine showing its stuff? I don't think so!

Occasionally, Earl took it up to sharpen his twin-engine skills and on one special occasion he invited me to go along. He spent some time out in the practice area doing this and that and then he shot a few landings. Above and beyond that, on the last landing, Earl turned the controls over to me. His hands were inches from the wheel and ready to spring into action, but I did, by myself, make the landing, and a fair one at that! It's a fun airplane to be around and gives the impression that it's much bigger than its five seats would indicate (which in a way, I guess it is).

I loved having the Bobcat at the airport. I was able to do a little minor maintenance on it and most of the fueling. Sadly, as Dick had predicted, we didn't have many students sign up for instruction.

Nothing around the field had really changed. We just didn't have the business to keep us busy. Days blurred together. Most were a little less that busy, much like the day before and you could expect about the same the next day. Occasionally a good day would come along where things looked better, and it had me wondering if maybe we had turned a corner, but it was just wishful thinking.

During my employment, I had developed a bit of a "feel" for the business, and it was obvious that more money was going out than coming in. And for the life of me, I couldn't see anything on the horizon that gave any indication that things would change for the better. Even I knew that things couldn't continue as they were.

It was impossible to visualize my name anywhere but on the very top of any layoff list. Would that be so bad? My Utah Central pay was not that great and it would be easy enough to duplicate or surpass it at any one of a dozen jobs. But duplicating the work and the environment, well that wasn't going to happen and I knew it!

Then the day came, the day I got my layoff notice. It simply stated that my services were no longer needed. Glen couldn't apologize enough. I would never blame him or even Earl for letting me go. It was something that just happened, and to me it was no surprise. Sadly, my name would only be one on a long list of former employees. The days of Utah Central were numbered. What remained were maybe a few years at best, maybe even months. No one knew the numbers but there was a number in place and counting, and I think everyone knew it.

One for the Road

I pulled up into my old parking place near the main hangar and eased to a stop. The morning sun was above the mountains, but it was having a hard time getting through some dark clouds, the tail-end of an overnight snow-storm. The air was cool, warm, damp and invigorating, sensations often felt in the wake of spring storms.

I turned the engine off and sat there for a few seconds looking and thinking. It was quiet, no movement and no signs of life. It had only been a couple of weeks since I had been laid off. Yet, somehow, I felt very much an outsider in some very familiar surroundings.

Chad's car was parked near the shop's door. It was in the same old spot where he had been parking for years. I had to smile while wondering what would happen if Chad came to work one day and another car was parked in "his spot." Would he even know how to handle it?

I got out of the car and navigated my way through the slush and standing water. Near the shop door there was a small concrete entrance pad, I paused and stomped my feet a couple of times. Then I looked at the closed door and hesitated. Was it proper for me to walk in as if I was still on the payroll? Boy would I feel out of place if I barged in on a group of people in the middle of a conversation. Maybe, I should I knock? But I quickly put the feelings aside knowing that I would know almost anyone inside.

Once inside, I felt completely at ease, everything was familiar, the heat from the old wood stove, the sight of tools and parts laying around, the workbench with its odd patterns of oil stains and paint blotches, the smell of fuel, oil, dope and coal and wood smoke. It was like being home.

Chad was standing at the bench looking over in my direction and grinning from ear to ear. Then he stated without braking his smile, "Well Hello Ron, I was wondering when you would stop in!" He wiped his hands on a nearby rag and turned away from a partially disassembled carburetor spread out on the bench. We shook hands like two misplaced persons who had finally found a familiar face.

Shortly, he asked me what I had been doing since I had left. I smiled and stated that I was working at an office supply store, and I made more money while working a shorter day, had weekends off and got paid for not working holidays. Pretty neat, but I'd trade for the old days at Utah Central in a second.

Chad shook his head and sighed with some sadness, "The old airport we knew doesn't exist anymore. The old-timers were few and far between. Many just seemed to have disappeared, and new students; well I haven't seen many of those either."

Another major problem that Utah Central Airport's builder and "prophet," Vern Carter, had foreseen many years before was Salt Lake's air traffic. The proximity of Utah Central's traffic pattern to Salt Lake's Municipal Airport's had raised new concerns with the FAA. The possibility of airplanes bumping into one another was being discussed in federal safety meetings almost daily. Needless to say, when Piper Cubs and big airliners were getting in each other's way, does anyone need to ask which would be asked to leave? Chad then stated that the only question unanswered was how long would it take the Feds to shut down Utah Central.

The conversation turned to more pleasant things, but I could see that Chad was busy and I got feeling a little guilty keeping him from his work. I bid him adieu, wondering if I would ever see him again.

Heading back to the car, I couldn't help but notice the PA–12 sitting over in Sam's old tie-down spot. The morning sun had broken through the clouds giving its snow covering a fairy tale luster. I paused and studied the bright red Piper Cruiser beneath its blanket of white. It was almost a Christmas card covered with all the best of the real world. I turned around and headed back into the shop.

"Hey Chad, has the Cruiser been up lately?" "It hasn't been up for two, maybe three weeks," Chad replied regretfully. I then asked him if it would be okay if I started it up one last time. He smiled and replied, "Go ahead, it will probably save me a hand start."

Picking my way through areas of snow, slush and standing water, I wandered over to the side of the Piper Cruiser. I ducked under the wing struts and unconsciously swung a little wide into the path of water dripping off the trailing edge of the wing. The sting of cold water across my back and neck quickened my pace to the cabin door. I opened it and paused a few seconds. The slight, but ever present aroma of aviation fuel, leather, oil and fabric was still there. Was it possible that I missed that dumb smell? You had better believe it!

The aircraft settled as I climbed up inside. The cold, stiff cushions moaned and creaked as I settled into the front seat. Then silence.

I sat for a second in the cool damp air looking at the backside of the snow-covered windshield. My own distorted reflection stared back at me in silence, looking almost to question the reason for me being there. However, the familiar, even good feelings of being in that front seat soon pushed all negative thoughts aside.

Unconsciously, I reached for the seat belts. Then catching myself, I paused and felt a little sadness in the fact that they were not going to be needed.

My eyes drifted across the panel, pausing briefly at each instrument. Typically, the altimeter was in an area where it shouldn't have been. I guess it was telling me that it too was aware of the snowstorm that had come through. I set it to field elevation. Somehow, there was satisfaction in making it right. All engine instruments were pointing towards something akin to a state of hibernation. Yet their very presence seemed to be begging for a wakeup call.

I unlocked the primer, pulled it back slowly, paused and gave it a good solid pump and—then another. I put my hand on the throttle and pulled it back, confirming the closed position. Then without pausing, I opened it a tad. Sliding open the left window, I hollered out the traditional "Clear." I paused and listened; nothing expected, nothing heard. My hand reached over to the mag switch and I caught myself remembering my first front seat Cruiser flight. It was my Check-Out Flight, and Dick was sitting behind me. It would be fun to know that he was back there again with a few good jokes. Man, how long ago was that?

The key clicked across the mag positions until it reached the position marked, "Both." I paused a second and then pressed the starter.

The Piper was suddenly alive. Metallic sounds of spinning and meshing metal parts cut sharply through the cabin's stillness. The whine of the starter backed off and was replaced with the sounds of power, cylinders filled with fire, the roar of the wind--the sweet smell of exhaust smoke.

The tachometer's needle jumped off its peg and the oil pressure needle slowly started moving into position. I leaned back against the cool seat and relaxed. The engine temperature slowly inched up. All instruments were telling me that the Piper was indeed alive and ready for flight.

Yet, there was something beyond the flickering instruments and the sound of that old Lycoming. What was it? How could it be put into words? Was it possible for a man to feel a bond, an attraction to aircraft--mere fabric, steel tubing, wood and steel? How could anyone in his right mind say, "Yes"? Yet, while sitting there, I wondered.

I moved the throttle forward and the engine raced to a new level of excitement. Torque tightened the rope on the right wing and the aircraft shook while tugging at its leash, begging to be turned loose. I sat in silence while trying to ignore my own desire to take the Piper up.

A quiet muffled pop, almost an explosion without sound--the snow that had covered the windshield was gone. Lifted by the hurricane forces from the propeller, it was carried off in the slipstream. The brightness of the morning sun was unbelievable. Driven by the wind from the propeller, little droplets of water, sparking like diamonds, danced and scurried back and forth across the plexiglas.

I thought about of the memorable times I'd had around the airplanes and the people who were part of Utah Central. It was a known and an exciting past. What lay ahead? At that point, I wasn't even sure which direction the roads were going--military, school, marriage, family? The trouble in Cuba and Russia, who knew where all that was headed. Everything was up in the air. I cleared my mind, relaxed and listened to the sounds of the present and a little of the past. There in the Cruiser, everything was right. The future? There would be time for it later.

I could have stayed in the Piper longer, much longer, but it wasn't my place. Reluctantly, I reached over to the mag switch and turned it to the "Off" position.

The engine instantly obeyed and the unwinding propeller blades flickered across the sun as the rpm's bled off. The engine hit a compression point and stopped. Then, except for the faint popping and ticking sounds of the cooling engine, there was silence. Like the genie of old, the Piper's spirit of flight was back in its lamp, satisfied to wait for another time, for another individual who could set it free.

I sat for a moment or two, thinking, looking, and trying to collect images that I could look back on. Reaching off to my right, I turned the door handle and the door popped open. I slid out of the seat, stepped down to the ground, paused and looked back into the cabin. During the time I had been in there it had grown warm. And like a bed on a cold morning, I didn't want to leave.

I closed the door, the bolt clicked into place. With that sound, aviation as I knew and loved came to an end.

10

Looking Back on Time

Many Roads Traveled

Chad Jenkins stayed on at Utah Central for a time after I left, but he too finally gave up. He found greener pastures in Nevada working for the Nevada State Highway Department. However, his love for airplanes, cars and engines continued and heaven only knows how many of each he tore down and rebuilt. Over the years, he's owned several aircraft. If he wasn't flying, he was tearing them down or rebuilding them. Engines and aircraft have always and would always be a big part of his life.

Mel Rozema left the airport shortly before Earl took over. For about a year, circumstances prevented him from doing any flying at all, but it was never far from his mind. He got things turned around, built up some flying time and got his Commercial License. With that, he was able to hire on with a fixed base operator up in Idaho Falls. The company had a contract with the Idaho State Fish and Game Department. He later told me that it turned out to be one of the more interesting jobs of his career.

Like most professional pilots, Mel was always working towards a job with the airlines. After he had accumulated some solid flight time, he was able to hire on with Western Air Lines.

His first assignment was a Flight Engineer on the four engine Douglas DC–7 aircraft. Then with a vacancy, he moved up to the co-pilot's seat.

And with that front seat assignment, there was a Check Out Flight. At that time, Western Airlines had an old DC–4 set aside for just that purpose. On the appointed day, Mel followed his instructor out to the old Douglas, took his place in the left seat, the instructor in the right, and they went flying.

"Ron, once you get used to the height and develop a knack for keeping the wings level, the DC–4 is not that hard to fly," he told me with more than a little excitement. He added that today he would have missed the fun of that type of check-out, because the company does everything in aircraft simulators. He flew the propeller aircraft from both the right and then the left seats before moving up into Boeing passenger jets.

His youthful looks followed him to the airlines, where occasionally a few eye-brows would be raised, especially among some of his older, more conservative passengers. Some must have thought his uniform a bit extravagant for someone who was obviously there to fluff pillows, right? Then they watched him sit down in the Captain's seat and proceed with the checklist. He flew with Western (later Delta) until he retired.

After his retirement, he bought a hangar over at the Bountiful, Woods Cross Airport and filled it with a very nice-looking Cessna 180.

Richard Thomason left shortly before I did. He got a job with an airline in Michigan, flying four-engine Lockheed Electra Turboprops. Later, he hired on with Western Airlines. I lost track of him shortly before he retired.

When I hired on at Utah Central, Mel Reeves was in the process of getting his Commercial License. Once he got his Commercial, he got a job working out of Sky Haven, also called the Bountiful Woods Cross Airport as a flight instructor and charter pilot. About two years later, he was on assignment as a pilot for the Atomic Energy Commission.

On the first day of August 1957, he took off from the Logan Cache Airport at 4:00 A.M. and headed for Billings, Montana where he picked up a co-worker, a geologist. They were on an aerial survey assignment not far from Billings. At some unknown hour, their PA–18 hit a ridge at the 8,000-foot level of the Pryor Mountains. Both Mel and his co-worker were killed. The accident site was in a remote section of Montana, located 43 air miles from Billings and 8 miles from the Big Horn River.

We all tried to put a reason for an accident that made absolutely no sense. Somehow he must have broken his own rules trying to please his boss, or the pressure of his work made him more aggressive than he normally would have been. For most, "wind sheer" was the only possible answer. I guess no one will ever know for sure. He was just a few days short of his twenty-second birthday.

After Max Green left Utah Central, he found steady employment in the charter flight business. On November 16, 1988 he was returning to Salt Lake City from St. George, Utah in a Cessna 421 Golden Eagle. It was a particularly bad day and he was flying in and out of IFR (Instrument Flight Rules) weather conditions. Shortly after 1:00 A.M., just east, southeast of Tooele, Utah, his aircraft hit the 10,589 foot Lowe Peak at the 9,700 foot level. Both Max and his passenger were killed.

A few months after the accident, I was talking to an old friend who was also an FAA employee. Curious about his accident, I asked him if the investigators had turned up any reason for the crash. His expression saddened. He shook his head and told me that they were never able to pinpoint the exact cause. Apparently, Max had lost the vacuum that had powered some of his flying instruments. Under IFR conditions, with no instruments and in mountainous terrain, he didn't have much of a chance. Max was 65.

Other than my pre-license Check Ride, I didn't spend a lot of time in the air with "Smitty" Dent, but we had many conversations on flying and who knows how many other subjects.

Like many pilots at Utah Central, he had his sights set on the airlines. Occasionally, I would see him come into the office shaking his head after an interview with one of the carriers in the area. I guess the airline industry didn't need many new pilots at the time, and their requirements were all rather high. One lazy afternoon we sat down at the lunch counter and jokingly put together a hypothetical list of airline requirements for the hiring of new pilots. I include it here as some of the humor of the day:

> The applying pilot must be 18 years of age or younger, be in perfect health, possess a masters degree in Engineering from MIT, hold a current A & E license, with a minimum of ten years hands-on experience. He must also have several logbooks filled with a minimum of 20,000 hours of Pilot-in-Command flight time, 90 percent of which must be in heavy multi-engine aircraft. The applicant must also posses every flight ticket ever offered by the FAA, and a bunch of test-pilot experience in experimental jet and rocket airplanes would be helpful! One more thing, he must posses a doctorate degree in psychology to help him better understand the mind and behavior of the typical passenger. We debated tooth fillings and warts, but decided that a few airlines might overlook these "rather serious health defects."

Yes, we did exaggerate some, and we laughed a lot. It was fun!

I'm not sure when he left Utah Central, but many years later we crossed paths and had a nice long talk. He was then flying Boeing 727s for Delta Airlines. He called the 727s "Three Holers" in reference to the three jet engines mounted on the tail. (The "Three Holer" name made me smile. I can remember when they called three-seated outhouses "Three-Holers." My, how times have changed.)

Later I heard that Smitty had moved up to the left seat of the Lockheed L–1011. He spent most of his working career at, and retired from Western/ Delta airlines. In February of 1998, he passed away after a courageous battle with cancer.

Happ Darnell was a fairly aggressive person. More than once, he had locked horns with management over one point or another. He was employed at Utah Central for several months, and then one day he was gone. We later heard he was flying out of Hobbs, New Mexico. Then like so many others, he was one remembered.

Kay Andersen started his Valley Airmotive career with Roy up north, at the Logan Cache Airport. Later, he transferred to Utah Central. After a few months, Roy pulled him back to Logan. He ended up working wherever he was needed. He played the game for a few months, but he wanted something a little more stable. He applied for and got a position with Kemp and Kelsey, one of the old fixed-base operators located at the Salt Lake Municipal Airport.

Just before leaving for his new employment, he told me he was headed for a "real job." Sometimes however "real jobs" don't work out. I ran into him later and he told me he was tired of "working ten hours and getting paid for eight."

Finally, the long underpaid hours finally got the best of him. He submitted a bill for his accumulated but unpaid overtime. Kay told me his boss hit the ceiling and was about ready to fire him when he quit. They later came to an understanding, and Kay returned to Kemp and Kelsey flying the "Power Line Patrol" under contract with the Utah Power and Light Company. His job was statewide, flying along high voltage transmission lines, visually inspecting them for damage.

On November 15, 1957, five miles southwest of Payson, Utah, his Piper PA–18 hit some kind of "non standard guy wire" running from the top of a transmission tower diagonally to the ground. His plane spun in and he died on impact. The aviation community in the valley was tight-knit. I don't think it was two hours after the accident that we at Utah Central got word. Kay was 35 years old.

Glen Dellinger stayed on in management and continued with his spraying duties. His flying career was terminated at the completion of a very normal spray run.

Just north of Utah Central Airport, there was a small canal called the Brighton Canal. It crossed 2100 South east of the airport and continued west by northwest, towards the Great Salt Lake. Glen had the canal on his list to be sprayed. It being so close to the airport, he had scheduled it for the last run of the day. After its completion, he would just swing around, enter the pattern and be home.

When the time came, he set up his run from the west and made a descending turn for alignment. Leveling out, just feet above the canal, he pulled the release and the insecticide mist erupted from his boom nozzles. In a few more moments, he'd be home.

Unknown to Glen, Doris his wife happened to be out scanning the sky to the north. Occasionally, if her timing was right, she would be able to watch Glen flying in towards the airport and home.

On that day she was in luck. A couple miles northwest of the airport, she caught sight of Glen's airplane. She stood in silence, hands shading the sun's glare from her eyes while watching her husband's little spray plane grow in size. Thinking he was headed for the pattern, she was a little surprised when he rolled over into a descending turn.

The Piper continued down and soon disappeared behind the raised highway. Not knowing what was going on, she stood there frozen with fear, visualizing the worst. Time passed, she waited for Glen's aircraft to reappear, but it didn't happen. There was no doubt in her mind that her husband had gone down.

Glen, having completed his run, flew up to pattern altitude, far to the right of his wife's field of view. He entered the airport's pattern and landed, all unnoticed by his wife.

When Doris finally saw Glen's airplane, her fears had completely run their course. She was almost hysterical, and expressed herself in tears and some very persuasive language. She had lived with a spray pilot much too long. Sam's accident was never more than a thought away. She told him that if he continued spraying, she was history. Glen argued and debated, but he could see that his words would not stand up against what she had been through, real or imagined. Next day, he was out looking for a new line of work.

He got a job as a salesman in the lumber industry, and was thus employed the rest of his career. He occasionally did a little charter work, sometimes to help a friend and sometimes because he just wanted to fly. His wife was not totally against flying, but Glen knew her limits.

Glen and I would run into each other from time to time, mostly at air shows and shopping centers. A few weeks before his death, I invited him over and we had a memorable evening talking about the old days and setting a few items straight for this writing.

He passed away in February 2001, at the age of 79. He had been in aviation continually since his youth while protecting aircraft from hungry cattle on the old Hunt Field up in Wyoming.

Ray Daynes was one of our flight instructors. He was employed for a short time at Utah Central. One day he was there and then he was gone.

Pat--I never saw her after Sam's funeral. I hope she found someone to help to her through what must have been a very difficult time.

Wally Wahlquist worked part time at Utah Central for most of the time I was there. When he wasn't doping fabric or adjusting little carburetors or magnetos at Utah Central, he was working on the big stuff at Western/Delta Airlines. And to our benefit, while he was working with us, Western Airlines began phasing out all its old piston-engine aircraft and replacing them with jets. Wally was right in the middle of the transition.

Ever so often, Wally would get Chad and I in some corner and tell us something of interest about the new jet engines. To us Piper Cub people, working on little Continental four-bangers—well, the stories held us spellbound. Jet engines were relatively new, probably more so for me than Chad.

Moreover, I'll admit that I didn't fully understand how you could blow air in one end, add a little kerosene, a little spark and have lots of powerful fire come rushing and pushing out the other end. I think what impressed Wally most was the simplicity and dependability of the new engines.

"Except for the accessories, there was almost never a problem," he proudly boasted on one occasion. He couldn't praise them enough.

He worked with Western/Delta Airlines until he retired. I used to see him occasionally but it's been a while now.

Bruce Holtby gave me the beginning of the story. I will always be grateful that he was there, willing to let me play with his airplane. Our paths never crossed after Utah Central. Many years later, I heard that he had died in 1987. He was in his 70s.

Lou Pangman was another one that was there one day and then he too was gone. We did hear that he was still buying, flying and having fun. His personality and airplanes will always be a part of what Utah Central was. I'm glad our paths crossed when they did.

So many others! Norma, the teen-age girl in pigtails throwing newspapers at houses from her buzzing Cessna.

Bob Miller was a full-time mechanic at Hill Field. During his off hours, he spent a few months working with us. While we were slapping dope, he used to talk about his job at Hill Field and some of the military aircraft that he saw up there. He spent most of his time working on the big twin jet engine Northrop Scorpions. He was always telling us something interesting about those big, high-tailed aircraft.

Then there were the Airport Bums, all those wonderful people with their very special smiles and the never-to-be-forgotten twinkle in their eyes. They all kind of melted away, but I suspect that somewhere they're telling their wild yarns to even bigger crowds.

There were others, fellow pilots, flight instructors and mechanics. Some were there only long enough to leave a name, some maybe a little longer. Many only wanting to be even a small part of the field they loved, or expand their résumé as proof that they had a right to stay in aviation. Most faces I can picture, most names have drifted from memory. But somehow I could never say they are forgotten.

And me. I never lost my love for airplanes and flying. I occasionally flew and still look up at about everything that flies over. Sadly, it's been a long time since I've seen a little yellow airplane putting away up in the sky. I somehow ended up as a mechanical designer. It's interesting work, but for me, there was never anything that duplicated the excitement and interest that I enjoyed at Utah Central.

I'll be forever grateful that I was able to spend a few years at that little dirt field.

Sad Reunion, Sad Departure

A year or two after leaving Utah Central, I was walking down the flight line at the Salt Lake Municipal Airport. Off to my right were rows of business, executive aircraft, some of the most modern, expensive and beautiful aircraft every built. Just looking at their sleek lines and trying to imagine the technology that went into their development was overwhelming.

Then glancing back to the back row, I caught a glimpse of the wing of a little white aircraft. It looked odd, even out of place. A little curious, I moved to a position where I could see more clearly what type of aircraft it was. It was an old tail dragger, a J–3, a Piper Cub sandwiched in between all the modern executive aircraft. Man, did it look out of place!

The multi million-dollar business aircraft were put out of my mind and I headed for the Cub.

Unlike all the highly polished business aircraft around it, the Cub was covered with a thick layer of dust. One tire was low on air, allowing the aircraft to lean rather heavily to one side. It was obvious that the Cub had not received any attention for quite some time.

I walked around the little Piper trying to compare it to our old Piper Cubs. But to be honest, it was difficult. Our Cubs, although not always top-of-the-line in appearance were well used and stood tall on the line, looking ready and able. This poor Cub appeared to be anything but.

When I got to the tail, the serial number stood out like some huge neon light, N38308. I couldn't believe it! It was one of the Cubs from Utah Central--the tan one. I hadn't seen any of our old airplanes since I had left the airport. It was like seeing an old lost friend. I could almost hear it say, "Hi Old Buddy."

My body was filled with strange feelings, even excitement. Boy, wouldn't it be something to take it out for a spin, to feel the wind and to hear the pounding of that little Continental engine again.

I cupped my hands against the dirty plexiglas and peered into the cabin. Dusty images, covered with shadows were all that came through. Somewhat saddened, I backed away.

I walked, stood, and wandered around the little Piper. Then pausing, I stood for a time just looking. It was so dirty, so sad. I bet it hadn't seen its owner in weeks, maybe months. Why didn't the owner come and clean her up?

Once, a long time ago, it had been my job to keep it clean, fueled, oiled and protected. I've got to admit that I would have enjoyed cleaning up the old Cub again. However, it belonged to someone else, and as sad as it looked I had no right to touch it. Times had changed. I had changed. We had all moved on. At that moment, probably for the first time, I fully realized that except for memories, yesterday and everything connected with Utah Central were gone--forever.

Time and Trends

Like Ford's Model A, Piper J–3 Cub's replacement parts are being fabricated and are available from a variety of sources. However, duplicating some of the old J–3 parts are rather expensive, and because of the higher cost, some things on the Cub have changed. Those big balloon tires, to me the hallmark of the Cub, are not that common anymore. Also, the old standard Piper "Diaphragm" wheel brakes have also taken a step back behind their more modern counterparts. I'm not sure if they are too expensive to manufacture or if modern owners want something a little more advanced than the original "squishy" system.

The often troublesome left side window that slides up and down is often replaced with something that requires a little less effort. Most are simply swing windows that are hinged along the top or bottom. And I guess one of the more obvious signs of the times--most of the simple Off-On Magneto switches have been replaced with or backed up with semi-theft-proof ignition switches with built-in lock and key.

Sadly, you just don't see J–3's sitting around airport ramps like you used to. They are, for the most part, locked up behind heavy steel doors, safe from the elements or maybe more correctly, safe from those who want to take them home as their very own.

Many Cubs have been restored to a state where they are almost more art than aircraft. You can't look at some of the people who restored these Cubs as hobbyists or even aircraft mechanics. They are artist by about any definition. I've got to admit that many of today's restored Cubs would almost be out of place at Utah Central. Would anyone dare turn a green student loose in some of today's beautiful Cubs on one of our old dirt runways? Probably not!

I can't help but wonder what C.G. Taylor and William Piper's feelings would be if they could see how the modern world views their little Cub that they created. I bet you could find a tear or two in their eyes. I'm glad the Cubs have found favor in the eyes of collectors. I hope there're around a thousands years from now.

I was at an air show in the late 90's looking over a beautifully restored J–3 that was part of the display. The propeller was in the horizontal position and hanging from it was a hand written sign stating that it was indeed a real Piper J–3 Cub. A young man standing nearby was explaining some of the attributes of the Cub to his very young son. Part of the conversation included a boastful statement that he had once been up in one. The middle-aged owner who was standing nearby took note of the conversation and wandered over to the pair.

Soon, the owner and the father were engaged in a friendly discussion--the Piper Cub being the main topic. It was interesting, that we were all view-ing the Cub from such different perspectives. The father was feeling rather privileged because he had once been up in one. The owner was proud of the fact that he was the owner of such an historical aircraft. The young boy, look-ing up in his youth, with sparkling eyes darting back and fourth was excited about being there and hearing about such a special airplane.

And me, not participating in the dialog, stood tall on a self-made pedestal as some kind of relic whose fondness for Cubs extended back to the days when Cubs were just a trainer--a school ship with oil, bugs, mud and dust as part of its décor. A day when it was a common sight to see a J–3 sitting out on the grass waiting patiently for one of its fifty or so students to take it up. Out of the four of us in that circle, did I feel the privileged one of the group? As a matter of fact, I did.

Above the Experience

Below is a poem that keeps popping up around airports, in books, in maga-zines and even on TV. It would be near impossible to be in the field of avia-tion and not having run across it somewhere.

A young Spitfire pilot by the name of John Gillespie Magee wrote it during World War II. The words first appeared on the back of a letter he wrote to his parents. That letter simply stated, "I am enclosing a verse I wrote the other day. It started at 30,000 feet, and was finished soon after I landed." A short time later, John was killed in a mid air collision. Somewhere along the way, his parents happened to show the lines to someone, and the rest is history.

Volumes have been written trying to express the profound but elusive feelings that are involved with the sensations of flight, with varying degrees of success. John Magee, through some God-given gift has bridged that gap, and to my knowledge he has never been challenged. Fighter Pilots, Private Pilots, Astronauts, even Line Boys, and so many dreamers who fall in between have experienced the world of flight, felt the spirit and have quietly added "Amen" to John's simple words.

Below are the words of one individual that have expressed the feelings of so many.

HIGH FLIGHT

Oh! I have slipped the surly bonds of Earth
And danced the skies on laughter-silvered wings;
Sunward I've climbed, and joined the tumbling mirth
Of sun-split clouds, -- and done a hundred things
You have not dreamed of -- wheeled and soared and swung
High in the sunlit silence. Hov'ring there,
I've chased the shouting wind along, and flung
My eager craft through footless halls of air....

Up, up the long, delirious, burning blue
I've topped the wind-swept heights with easy grace
Where never lark, or even eagle flew --
And, while with silent, lifting mind I've trod
The high untrespassed sanctity of space,
Put out my hand, and touched the face of God.

-Pilot Officer John Gillespie Magee, Jr., RCAF

Today, I am a little older, a little slower and not an active pilot. Yet I still follow aviation and love to listen to the old "flying stories." Occasionally, I feel a little boastful and quietly slip in one of my old Piper Cub yarns. And sometimes my limited experiences bring out a few smiles and occasionally provoke a humorous statement that runs along the lines of "Yah, Yah, That happened to you did it? And did I ever tell you that I once flew from one airport to another, without refueling!"

I started in Cubs and finished in Cubs--you know the little yellow ones that don't go very fast, or far, nor high. With that experience, I could never claim to have flown aircraft whose size astonished even its builders, nor could I ever state boldly that my aircraft created the thunder heard by populations, but seen by no man. However, once in a while, I can look up into a sky filled with beautiful clouds, soft and colored, and thinking of John Magee's words, I say to myself, with more than just a little pride, "Been there, done that!"

P.S. If any of you are lucky enough to be up in some lonely part of the sky, alone in the back seat of a little yellow Piper J–3 Cub, open up the door on your right and drop the window on your left, roll the stick around and kick the pedals. Grab the wind; let it drift across your face; feel the adventure in the seat of your pants; listen to the music from the heavens, and enjoy freedom as no one else can. And if you hear sounds out beyond the wind and the roar of your Continental, or feel the presence of another individual, it's probably me cheering you on!

In the Introdunction of this book I refer to an old calendar picture and one unknown individual in that photo. Thanks to the Smithsonian Institution, I now have some information on that photograph. "It was taken at San Diego, where the *Spirit of St. Louis* was built, prior to its journey to the East Coast via St. Louis for its epic transatlantic flight." The following information describing the photo is from the Smithsonian Institution:

Ryan Aeronautical Company personnel posing with Charles A. Lindbergh and the Ryan NYP "*Spirit of St. Louis*", at San Diego, California, before its takeoff for St. Louis.

H. J. van der Linde is on top of the NYP, fueling it through a funnel. On the ground, left to right are O. R. McNeel, welding foreman; and George Hammond, student mechanic pilot (holding ends of banner NEW YORK-PARIS FLIGHT); Lindbergh; Donald Hall, Chief Engineer; and A. J. Edwards, sales manager of Ryan Airlines, Inc.

National Air and Space Museum, Smithsonian Institution (SI 94-8819)
The individual standing in the shadows does have a name, George Hammond, student mechanic pilot. George, if we ever meet, I would sure like to buy you dinner. I have a million questions.

19439172R00216

Made in the USA
Charleston, SC
23 May 2013